# First World War
and Army of Occupation
# War Diary
France, Belgium and Germany

15 DIVISION
44 Infantry Brigade
Black Watch (Royal Highlanders)
4/5th (Angus and Dundee) Battalion (Territorial)
and Black Watch (Royal Highlanders)
9th (Service) Battalion
3 July 1915 - 31 March 1919

WO95/1937

The Naval & Military Press Ltd
www.nmarchive.com
Published in association with The National Archives

Published by

## The Naval & Military Press Ltd

Unit 10 Ridgewood Industrial Park,

Uckfield, East Sussex,

TN22 5QE England

Tel: +44 (0) 1825 749494

www.naval-military-press.com

www.nmarchive.com

*This diary has been reprinted in facsimile from the original. Any imperfections are inevitably reproduced and the quality may fall short of modern type and cartographic standards.*

© **Crown Copyright**
**Images reproduced by permission of The National Archives, London, England, 2015.**

# Contents

| Document type | Place/Title | Date From | Date To |
|---|---|---|---|
| Heading | 15. 9th Black Watch Vol 9 | | |
| Heading | 15th Division 9th Black Watch Vol I From 3 Jly To 3 Aug. 15 | | |
| War Diary | Parkhouse Camp. | 03/07/1915 | 08/07/1915 |
| War Diary | Folkestone | 08/07/1915 | 08/07/1915 |
| War Diary | Boulogne | 08/07/1915 | 09/07/1915 |
| War Diary | Moulle | 10/07/1915 | 13/07/1915 |
| War Diary | Hazebrook | 14/07/1915 | 14/07/1915 |
| War Diary | Basrieux | 15/07/1915 | 16/07/1915 |
| War Diary | Houchin | 17/07/1915 | 01/08/1915 |
| War Diary | N. Maroc | 02/08/1915 | 03/08/1915 |
| Heading | 15th Division 9th Black Watch Vol II From 4-31.8.15 | | |
| War Diary | N. Maroc | 04/08/1915 | 10/11/1915 |
| War Diary | Noeux. Les. Mines | 11/08/1915 | 17/08/1915 |
| War Diary | Mazingarbe | 17/08/1915 | 25/08/1915 |
| War Diary | Quality. St. | 26/08/1915 | 29/08/1915 |
| War Diary | Mazingarbe | 30/08/1915 | 31/08/1915 |
| Miscellaneous | | | |
| Heading | 9th Battn. The Black Watch (Royal Highlanders). September 1915 44th Inf. Bde. 15th Div. | | |
| Heading | Report On Operations 25th September. | | |
| Miscellaneous | Head Quarters 44th Brigade. | 25/09/1915 | 25/09/1915 |
| Heading | War Diary. | | |
| War Diary | Mazingarbe | 01/09/1915 | 24/09/1915 |
| War Diary | Mazingarbe And Trenches In XI Sector | 24/09/1915 | 25/09/1915 |
| War Diary | In Action | 25/09/1915 | 25/09/1915 |
| War Diary | Philosophe Vermelle line and XI Trenches also former German trenches | 26/09/1915 | 26/09/1915 |
| War Diary | Mazingarbe | 27/09/1915 | 28/09/1915 |
| War Diary | Houchin | 29/09/1915 | 30/09/1915 |
| Miscellaneous | G.O.C., 1st Army. | 11/09/1915 | 11/09/1915 |
| Heading | 15th Division 9th Black Watch Vol 4 Oct 15 | | |
| War Diary | Houchin | 01/10/1915 | 02/10/1915 |
| War Diary | Lillers | 03/10/1915 | 12/10/1915 |
| War Diary | Noeux Les. Mines | 13/10/1915 | 21/10/1915 |
| War Diary | Noyelles | 22/10/1915 | 25/10/1915 |
| War Diary | Trenches in C1 area. ref Trench Maps 1/10000 | 26/10/1915 | 31/10/1915 |
| Heading | 15th Division Nov 15 9th Black Watch November 1915 | | |
| War Diary | Trenches CI. | 01/11/1915 | 07/11/1915 |
| War Diary | Noeux Les. Mines. | 08/11/1915 | 13/11/1915 |
| War Diary | Trenches G5d.13. to G.12c.5.4 Ref-trench Map 1/10000 | 13/11/1915 | 14/11/1915 |
| War Diary | Trenches | 15/11/1915 | 15/11/1915 |
| War Diary | Trenches & Vermelles | 16/11/1915 | 16/11/1915 |
| War Diary | Vermelles | 17/11/1915 | 17/11/1915 |
| War Diary | Trenches | 18/11/1915 | 22/11/1915 |
| War Diary | Noyelles | 23/11/1915 | 23/11/1915 |
| War Diary | Noyelles to Vaudricourt | 24/11/1915 | 24/11/1915 |
| War Diary | Vaudricourt | 25/11/1915 | 30/11/1915 |
| Heading | 15th Div 9th Black Watch December 1915 | | |
| War Diary | Vaudricourt To Noyelles | 01/12/1915 | 01/12/1915 |

| Type | Description | Start | End |
|---|---|---|---|
| War Diary | Noyelles | 02/12/1915 | 03/12/1915 |
| War Diary | Noyelles to Trenches | 04/12/1915 | 04/12/1915 |
| War Diary | Trenches | 05/12/1915 | 05/12/1915 |
| Map | Sketch Of Hairpin | | |
| Map | | | |
| War Diary | Trenches | 06/12/1915 | 13/12/1915 |
| War Diary | Trenches To Lozinghem | 14/12/1915 | 14/12/1915 |
| War Diary | Lozinghem | 15/12/1915 | 31/12/1915 |
| Heading | 9th Black Watch Vol 7 Jan 16 | | |
| War Diary | Lozinghem | 01/01/1916 | 05/01/1916 |
| War Diary | Lozinghem to Ligny | 05/01/1916 | 05/01/1916 |
| War Diary | Ligny | 06/01/1916 | 06/01/1916 |
| War Diary | Ligny to Lozinghem | 07/01/1916 | 07/01/1916 |
| War Diary | Lozinghem | 08/01/1916 | 14/01/1916 |
| War Diary | Trenches | 15/01/1916 | 26/01/1916 |
| Map | H 19 | | |
| War Diary | Trenches | 26/01/1916 | 26/01/1916 |
| War Diary | Noeux Les Mines | 27/01/1916 | 31/01/1916 |
| War Diary | Philosophe | 01/02/1916 | 04/02/1916 |
| War Diary | Trenches | 02/02/1916 | 11/02/1916 |
| Miscellaneous | Supplementary Report On Enemy Mire Blown On The Enemy Of 11-2-16 In Right Subsection Of Hulluch Section | 12/02/1916 | 12/02/1916 |
| Diagram etc | Graphic Of Relief Right of 19/20 Feb. to 2/3 March Puits 14 Bis Section. | | |
| War Diary | Trenches | 11/02/1916 | 13/02/1916 |
| War Diary | Mazingarbe | 14/02/1916 | 19/02/1916 |
| War Diary | Trenches | 20/02/1916 | 29/02/1916 |
| Miscellaneous | Graphic Showing Prepared to Relief of 8/9th March-20th. 21st March Hulluch Section. | | |
| Miscellaneous | Instructions in Case of A Gas Attack When The Battalion Is In Billets in Mazingarbe. | 15/02/1916 | 15/02/1916 |
| Miscellaneous | Battalion Orders By Lieutenant Colonel J. Stewart. Commanding 9th (S) Battalion. The Black Watch. In The Field, 15-2-1916 | 15/02/1916 | 15/02/1916 |
| Heading | D.A.G. 3rd Echelon. | | |
| Miscellaneous | 44th Infantry Bde Graphic of Reliefs Might Of 1/2nd Feb To Might Of 15th 14th Feb 1916 | | |
| Miscellaneous | Provisional Defence Scheme. Right Sub-section. Hulluch Section. | 13/03/1916 | 13/03/1916 |
| War Diary | Trenches | 01/03/1916 | 02/03/1916 |
| War Diary | Noeux Les Mines | 03/03/1916 | 08/03/1916 |
| War Diary | Trenches | 09/03/1916 | 17/03/1916 |
| War Diary | Philosophe | 18/03/1916 | 25/03/1916 |
| War Diary | Burbure | 26/03/1916 | 31/03/1916 |
| Miscellaneous | List of Casualties During Last Tour of Duty in The Trenches. | | |
| Miscellaneous | 9th (S) Battalion, The Black Watch. | 26/03/1916 | 26/03/1916 |
| Miscellaneous | Casualties, etc., during March, 1916 | | |
| Miscellaneous | Duties of Orderly Officer. | 26/03/1916 | 26/03/1916 |
| Miscellaneous | Duties of Men in Charge of Recreation Room. | | |
| Miscellaneous | 9th (S) Battalion, The Black Watch. | 26/03/1916 | 26/03/1916 |
| Miscellaneous | 9th (S) Battalion, The Black Watch. | 07/04/1916 | 07/04/1916 |
| Miscellaneous | Suggestions regarding the formation of a Divisional Sniper's Company. | | |

| | | | |
|---|---|---|---|
| Heading | 15th Division 44th Infy Bde 9th Bn Roy. Hdrs (Blk Watch) Jly 1915-1918 May (15th) To 16 Div 47 Bde | | |
| Diagram etc | Herr Franz Von Laager shifter's Spring Dream. | | |
| War Diary | Burbure | 01/04/1916 | 08/04/1916 |
| War Diary | Cuhem | 08/04/1916 | 09/04/1916 |
| War Diary | Burbure | 10/04/1916 | 24/04/1916 |
| War Diary | Sailly Labourse | 25/04/1916 | 25/04/1916 |
| War Diary | Trenches | 26/04/1916 | 30/04/1916 |
| Miscellaneous | 9th (S) Battalion, The Black Watch. | 15/04/1916 | 15/04/1916 |
| Miscellaneous | 9th (S) Battalion, The Black Watch. | | |
| Miscellaneous | Casualties during last tour of duty in the trenches. 26/4/16-11/5/16 | 26/04/1916 | 26/04/1916 |
| Miscellaneous | List of Casualties During Last Tour in The Trenches. | 29/04/1916 | 29/04/1916 |
| Miscellaneous | 9th (S) Battalion, The Black Watch. Programme Of work for period 17-4-16 to 22-6-16 | 17/04/1916 | 17/04/1916 |
| Miscellaneous | 9th (S) Battalion, The Black Watch. | 01/04/1916 | 01/04/1916 |
| Miscellaneous | Confidential Information Obtained From a raid on a German trench near Richebourg L'Avoue on the 12th April. 1916 | 12/04/1916 | 12/04/1916 |
| Heading | To D.A.G. 3rd Echelon Vol II from O.C. 9th (S) Bn Black Watch Herewith Original copy of War Diary For the month of May. 1916 | | |
| Miscellaneous | 44th (Highland) Brigade, Graphic Showing Reliefs Night Of 26/27 April to night of 11/12 May. | | |
| Map | Right Battalion Grenade Stores. | | |
| War Diary | Trenches | 01/05/1916 | 08/05/1916 |
| War Diary | Noyelles | 09/05/1916 | 14/05/1916 |
| War Diary | Sailly La Bourse | 15/05/1916 | 20/05/1916 |
| War Diary | Right Sub-Section Of Hohenzollern Section | 21/05/1916 | 31/05/1916 |
| Miscellaneous | Instructions in Case of Gas Attack When The Battalion is in Billets in Noyelles, Sailly Labourse & Labourse. | 10/05/1916 | 10/05/1916 |
| Miscellaneous | 44th Infantry Brigade Provisional Defence Scheme. | 09/05/1916 | 09/05/1916 |
| Miscellaneous | Headquarters, 44th Brigade. | 09/05/1916 | 09/05/1916 |
| Heading | D.A.G. 8th Echelon Rouen Herewith War Diary for February. | | |
| Miscellaneous | Defence Scheme | 19/05/1916 | 19/05/1916 |
| Operation(al) Order(s) | Operation Order No. 44 By Lieut. Col. J. Stewart. Commanding 9th (S) Battalion, The Black Watch. | 18/05/1916 | 18/05/1916 |
| Miscellaneous | To accompany O.O.45. O.C. Company | 25/05/1916 | 25/05/1916 |
| Miscellaneous | Casualties, etc., during month of May, 1916 | | |
| Operation(al) Order(s) | Operation Order No. 46 By Major A.D. Carmichael Commanding 9th (S) Bn. The Black Watch. | 29/05/1916 | 29/05/1916 |
| Miscellaneous | Defence Scheme for Battn. in Brigade Support Hohenzollern Section. Appendix 2 | 18/05/1916 | 18/05/1916 |
| War Diary | Centre Subsection of Hohenzullern Section. | 01/06/1916 | 04/06/1916 |
| War Diary | Sailly-La-Bourse | 05/06/1916 | 11/06/1916 |
| War Diary | Centre Sub-Section & Hulluch Section. | 12/06/1916 | 28/06/1916 |
| War Diary | Bethune | 28/06/1916 | 06/07/1916 |
| Miscellaneous | Casualties during june, 1916 | | |
| War Diary | Bethune | 01/07/1916 | 01/07/1916 |
| War Diary | Hohenzollern Section R. Subsector | 06/07/1916 | 13/07/1916 |
| War Diary | Brigade Support Cannon St. | 14/07/1916 | 14/07/1916 |
| War Diary | Hohenzollern Section Centre Subsection | 18/07/1916 | 21/07/1916 |
| War Diary | Houchin | 22/07/1916 | 22/07/1916 |
| War Diary | Lathieuloye | 23/07/1916 | 23/07/1916 |
| War Diary | Magnicourt Sur Canche | 26/07/1916 | 26/07/1916 |

| | | | |
|---|---|---|---|
| War Diary | Occoches | 27/07/1916 | 27/07/1916 |
| War Diary | Longuevillette | 28/07/1916 | 29/07/1916 |
| War Diary | Naours | 31/07/1916 | 31/07/1916 |
| Miscellaneous | Headquarters. 15th Division | 01/08/1916 | 01/08/1916 |
| Heading | Confidential War Diary of 9th (S) Bn The Black Watch. From 1st July 1916. To 31st July 1916 (Volume) | | |
| Miscellaneous | | 27/02/1916 | 27/02/1916 |
| Miscellaneous | Notes for O.C. Companies, Officer i/c Transport Machine Gun, & Headquarters Details. | | |
| Miscellaneous | Defence Orders. Left Subsection. Puits 14B15 Section. | 26/02/1916 | 26/02/1916 |
| Miscellaneous | Ref Map 1/10,000 36 C, N.W. 3 Edition 6 | | |
| Operation(al) Order(s) | Operation Order No. 45 By Major A.D. Carmichael Commanding 9th (S) Battn. The Black Watch. | 26/05/1916 | 26/05/1916 |
| Operation(al) Order(s) | Operation Order No. 42 By Lieut. J. Stewart. Commanding 9th (S) Battalion, The Black Watch. | 10/05/1916 | 10/05/1916 |
| Heading | 44th Brigade. 15th Division. 1/9th Battalion Black Watch August 1916 Attached:- Report On Operations 17/18th | | |
| Miscellaneous | Confidential. 44th Infantry Brigade. | 03/09/1916 | 03/09/1916 |
| War Diary | Naours | 01/08/1916 | 02/08/1916 |
| War Diary | Mirvaux | 04/08/1916 | 04/08/1916 |
| War Diary | Lahoussoye | 05/08/1916 | 06/08/1916 |
| War Diary | Albert | 08/08/1916 | 08/08/1916 |
| War Diary | O.B.I. (X 26 a cent) Albert map | 12/08/1916 | 12/08/1916 |
| War Diary | Becourt | 13/08/1916 | 13/08/1916 |
| War Diary | Contalmaison | 14/08/1916 | 14/08/1916 |
| War Diary | Firing Line | 16/08/1916 | 17/08/1916 |
| War Diary | Firing Line 1m. N. of Contalmaison | 17/08/1916 | 17/08/1916 |
| War Diary | Contalmaison | 18/08/1916 | 18/08/1916 |
| War Diary | Scots Redoubt | 19/08/1916 | 19/08/1916 |
| War Diary | Peake Wood | 20/08/1916 | 21/08/1916 |
| War Diary | Contalmaison | 22/08/1916 | 23/08/1916 |
| War Diary | Firing Line | 24/08/1916 | 25/08/1916 |
| War Diary | Scots Redoubt | 26/08/1916 | 27/08/1916 |
| War Diary | Peake Wood | 28/08/1916 | 28/08/1916 |
| War Diary | Albert | 30/08/1916 | 31/08/1916 |
| Miscellaneous | 44th I.B. Appendix H4 | 18/08/1916 | 18/08/1916 |
| Miscellaneous | 44th I.B. Situation Report | 18/08/1916 | 18/08/1916 |
| Miscellaneous Map | | 18/08/1916 | 18/08/1916 |
| Heading | Confidential War Diary Of 9th (S) Bn. The Black Watch. From 1 Sept 16 To 30 Sept 16 (Volume XV) | | |
| War Diary | Albert | 01/09/1916 | 02/09/1916 |
| War Diary | Shelter Wood | 04/09/1916 | 04/09/1916 |
| War Diary | Firing Line | 06/09/1916 | 09/09/1916 |
| War Diary | Albert | 10/09/1916 | 10/09/1916 |
| War Diary | Shelter Wood | 11/09/1916 | 11/09/1916 |
| War Diary | Albert | 13/09/1916 | 13/09/1916 |
| War Diary | Albert Scots Redoubt | 14/09/1916 | 14/09/1916 |
| War Diary | Martin Puich | 17/09/1916 | 18/09/1916 |
| War Diary | Becourt | 19/09/1916 | 19/09/1916 |
| War Diary | Lavieville | 19/09/1916 | 19/09/1916 |
| War Diary | Franvilliers | 20/09/1916 | 29/09/1916 |
| Heading | War Diary 9th Black Watch 1/10/16 31/10/16 Volume 16 | | |
| War Diary | Franvillers | 01/10/1916 | 04/10/1916 |

| | | | |
|---|---|---|---|
| War Diary | Becourt | 06/10/1916 | 06/10/1916 |
| War Diary | Le Sars | 08/10/1916 | 10/10/1916 |
| War Diary | Martin Trench | 11/10/1916 | 13/10/1916 |
| War Diary | Scots Redoubt | 14/10/1916 | 14/10/1916 |
| War Diary | Martin Trench | 18/10/1916 | 18/10/1916 |
| War Diary | Crescent Alley | 19/10/1916 | 22/10/1916 |
| War Diary | Le Sars | 23/10/1916 | 24/10/1916 |
| War Diary | Scots Redoubt | 25/10/1916 | 28/10/1916 |
| War Diary | Crescent Alley | 31/10/1916 | 31/10/1916 |
| Heading | 9th. (S) Bn. The Black Watch. War Diary November 1916 Vol 17 | | |
| War Diary | Crescent Alley | 01/11/1916 | 01/11/1916 |
| War Diary | Becourt | 02/11/1916 | 02/11/1916 |
| War Diary | Bresle | 05/11/1916 | 30/11/1916 |
| Heading | 9th (S) Battn The Black Watch War Diary December 1916 Vol. XVII | | |
| War Diary | Albert | 01/12/1916 | 13/12/1916 |
| War Diary | Shelter Wood | 16/12/1916 | 17/12/1916 |
| War Diary | Contalmaison | 19/12/1916 | 27/12/1916 |
| War Diary | 26th Avenue | 23/12/1916 | 27/12/1916 |
| War Diary | Scots Redoubt North | 27/12/1916 | 30/12/1916 |
| War Diary | Pioneer Camp | 31/12/1916 | 31/12/1916 |
| Heading | 44/15 9th. (S) Battn., The Black Watch. January, 1917 | | |
| Heading | Confidential 9th (S) Bn. The Black Watch War Diary January 1917 Vol 19 | | |
| War Diary | Pioneer Camp | 01/01/1917 | 01/01/1917 |
| War Diary | Seven Elms | 02/01/1917 | 03/01/1917 |
| War Diary | Flers Switch | 04/01/1917 | 08/01/1917 |
| War Diary | Shelter Wood South | 08/01/1917 | 11/01/1917 |
| War Diary | Twenty Sixth Avenue | 12/01/1917 | 15/01/1917 |
| War Diary | Acid Drop Camp | 16/01/1917 | 18/01/1917 |
| War Diary | Villa Camp | 19/01/1917 | 20/01/1917 |
| War Diary | Shelter Wood South | 21/01/1917 | 23/01/1917 |
| War Diary | Flers Switch | 24/01/1917 | 27/01/1917 |
| War Diary | Pioneer Camp | 28/01/1917 | 30/01/1917 |
| War Diary | Sevenelms | 31/01/1917 | 31/01/1917 |
| Miscellaneous | | 16/12/1917 | 16/12/1917 |
| Miscellaneous | | | |
| Operation(al) Order(s) | Operation Order 62 By Capt. K.V. Bowell M.C. Cmdg. 44th Machine Gun Coy. | | |
| Operation(al) Order(s) | Operation Order No. 61 By Capt. K.V. Barrett M.C. Cmdg No 44 M.G. Coy | 01/12/1917 | 01/12/1917 |
| Heading | 9th (S.) Battn, The Black Watch February, 1917 | | |
| Heading | 9th (S) Bn The Black Watch War Diary for month ending 28th February 1917 Vol 2 | | |
| War Diary | Seven Elms | 01/02/1917 | 01/02/1917 |
| War Diary | Becourt Camp | 01/09/1917 | 02/09/1917 |
| War Diary | Bresle | 04/02/1917 | 11/02/1917 |
| War Diary | Vadencourt | 13/02/1917 | 13/02/1917 |
| War Diary | Beauval | 14/02/1917 | 14/02/1917 |
| War Diary | Outrebois | 15/02/1917 | 15/02/1917 |
| War Diary | Ligny | 16/02/1917 | 16/02/1917 |
| War Diary | Croisette | 17/02/1917 | 17/02/1917 |
| War Diary | Buneville | 18/02/1917 | 23/02/1917 |
| War Diary | Ambrines | 23/02/1917 | 28/02/1917 |
| Heading | 15th Div War Diary March 1917 9th Black Watch | | |

| | | | |
|---|---|---|---|
| War Diary | Ambrines | 01/03/1917 | 08/03/1917 |
| War Diary | Arras | 10/03/1917 | 22/03/1917 |
| War Diary | Duisans | 26/03/1917 | 31/03/1917 |
| Heading | Confidential War Diary April 1917 9th Bn. The Black Watch | | |
| War Diary | Duisans | 01/04/1917 | 01/04/1917 |
| War Diary | Front Line | 03/04/1917 | 09/04/1917 |
| War Diary | Hermes Trench | 09/04/1917 | 10/04/1917 |
| War Diary | Feuchy | 11/04/1917 | 11/04/1917 |
| War Diary | Arras | 12/04/1917 | 18/04/1917 |
| War Diary | Wancourt Feuchy Line | 19/04/1917 | 22/04/1917 |
| War Diary | Marliere | 23/04/1917 | 23/04/1917 |
| War Diary | N 15 A | 24/04/1917 | 24/04/1917 |
| War Diary | Brown Line | 25/04/1917 | 25/04/1917 |
| War Diary | Between Marliere & Guemappe | 25/04/1917 | 27/04/1917 |
| War Diary | Arras | 28/04/1917 | 28/04/1917 |
| War Diary | Simencourt | 29/04/1917 | 30/04/1917 |
| Miscellaneous | Headquarters, 44th Infantry Brigade. | 30/04/1917 | 30/04/1917 |
| Miscellaneous | Report On Raid Carried Out On 8th April 1917 at 10 Am | | |
| Operation(al) Order(s) | Operation Order No. 151 By Lieut. Col S.A. Innes. D.S.O. Commanding 9th (S) Battalions, The Black Watch. | 22/04/1917 | 22/04/1917 |
| Miscellaneous | O.O. No. 154 By Lieutenant Colonel S.A. Innes, D.S.O., Commanding 9th. (S) Battalion The Black Watch. | 26/04/1917 | 26/04/1917 |
| Heading | 9th Royal Highlanders May 1917 | | |
| Miscellaneous | DAG 3rd Echelon. | | |
| War Diary | Simencourt | 01/05/1917 | 07/05/1917 |
| War Diary | Grand Rullecourt. | 08/05/1917 | 15/05/1917 |
| War Diary | Ligny Sur Canche | 21/05/1917 | 21/05/1917 |
| War Diary | Vieil Hesdin | 22/05/1917 | 31/05/1917 |
| War Diary | 15 9th Black Watch Vol. 8 | | |
| Heading | 9th S. Battn The Black Watch War Diary June 1917 | | |
| War Diary | Vieil Hesdin | 01/06/1917 | 18/06/1917 |
| War Diary | Hernicourt | 21/06/1917 | 21/06/1917 |
| War Diary | Pernes | 22/06/1917 | 22/06/1917 |
| War Diary | St Hilaire | 23/06/1917 | 23/06/1917 |
| War Diary | Steenbecque | 25/06/1917 | 25/06/1917 |
| War Diary | Caestre | 26/06/1917 | 26/06/1917 |
| War Diary | Toronto Camp | 27/06/1917 | 27/06/1917 |
| War Diary | 2nd S.W. Of Ypres Menin Road | 29/06/1917 | 29/06/1917 |
| War Diary | 1/2m S.E. Ypres | 30/06/1917 | 30/06/1917 |
| Heading | 9th Royal Highlanders July 1917 | | |
| Heading | War Diary 9th (S) Battn. The Black Watch July 1917 | | |
| War Diary | Ypres Menin Road. | 01/07/1917 | 01/07/1917 |
| War Diary | Ypres | 02/07/1917 | 02/07/1917 |
| War Diary | Dragoon Fm | 02/07/1917 | 05/07/1917 |
| War Diary | Menin Road | 06/07/1917 | 07/07/1917 |
| War Diary | Menin Rd Ypres | 08/07/1917 | 08/07/1917 |
| War Diary | Toronto Camp Ruerouck | 09/07/1917 | 15/07/1917 |
| War Diary | 1m. N. of Winniezeele | 21/07/1917 | 21/07/1917 |
| War Diary | 2m S.E. of Watou | 22/07/1917 | 22/07/1917 |
| War Diary | Toronto Camp | 23/07/1917 | 24/07/1917 |
| War Diary | 1m. W Of Ypres | 25/07/1917 | 26/07/1917 |
| War Diary | Cambridge Trench | 30/07/1917 | 31/07/1917 |

| | | | |
|---|---|---|---|
| War Diary | Frezenberg | 31/07/1917 | 31/07/1917 |
| War Diary | O.G.3 | 31/07/1917 | 31/07/1917 |
| Operation(al) Order(s) | Operation Order No. 178 By Lt. Col. S.A. Innes, D.S.O., Commanding 9th (Service) Battalion The Black Watch. | 28/07/1917 | 28/07/1917 |
| Heading | 9th (S) Bn. The Black Watch War Diary August 1917 | | |
| War Diary | O.G. Verlorenhoek | 01/08/1917 | 03/08/1917 |
| War Diary | LMS. W. of Ypres | 03/08/1917 | 03/08/1917 |
| War Diary | Winnezeele | 04/08/1917 | 16/08/1917 |
| War Diary | Poperinghe | 17/08/1917 | 17/08/1917 |
| War Diary | Toronto Camp | 19/08/1917 | 20/08/1917 |
| War Diary | 1m. W. Ypres O.G. Line | 21/08/1917 | 22/08/1917 |
| War Diary | Pommern Redoubt | 23/08/1917 | 26/08/1917 |
| War Diary | In W Ypres | 27/08/1917 | 27/08/1917 |
| War Diary | Toronto Camp | 27/08/1917 | 29/08/1917 |
| War Diary | No. 2 Area Watou | 30/08/1917 | 31/08/1917 |
| Heading | 9th (S) Battn The Black Watch War Diary September 1917 | | |
| War Diary | Watou No 2 Area | 01/09/1917 | 01/09/1917 |
| War Diary | Caestre | 02/09/1917 | 02/09/1917 |
| War Diary | Arras | 02/09/1917 | 02/09/1917 |
| War Diary | Montenescourt | 03/09/1917 | 03/09/1917 |
| War Diary | Blangy Barossa Camp | 07/09/1917 | 07/09/1917 |
| War Diary | Barossa Camp | 07/09/1917 | 10/09/1917 |
| War Diary | Stirling Camp H.13.d.8.8 (France 51B) | 14/09/1917 | 02/10/1917 |
| Heading | 9th, (S) Bn. The Black Watch. War Diary October 1917 | | |
| War Diary | Rifle | 03/10/1917 | 03/10/1917 |
| War Diary | Camp. G.24.6.8.5 | 04/10/1917 | 08/10/1917 |
| War Diary | Wilderness Camp | 09/10/1917 | 13/10/1917 |
| War Diary | 1m. N.W. Monchy Le Preux | 17/10/1917 | 25/10/1917 |
| War Diary | Arras | 25/10/1917 | 31/10/1917 |
| Heading | 9th Royal Highlanders November 1917 | | |
| Heading | War Diary 9th. (S) Bn. The Black Watch. November 1917 | | |
| War Diary | Arras | 01/11/1917 | 01/11/1917 |
| War Diary | Rifle Camp | 02/11/1917 | 02/11/1917 |
| War Diary | Fampoux | 06/11/1917 | 06/11/1917 |
| War Diary | Roeux | 10/11/1917 | 18/11/1917 |
| War Diary | Arras | 18/11/1917 | 24/11/1917 |
| War Diary | 1m N.W. Of Monchy-Le-Preux | 26/11/1917 | 28/11/1917 |
| War Diary | Arras | 28/11/1917 | 30/11/1917 |
| Heading | 9th Royal Highlanders December 1917 | | |
| Heading | 9th Battn The Black Watch War Diary December 1917 | | |
| War Diary | Arras | 01/12/1917 | 01/12/1917 |
| War Diary | 1m.N. Of Roeux | 01/12/1917 | 05/12/1917 |
| War Diary | Northumberland Lane | 05/12/1917 | 07/12/1917 |
| War Diary | 1m N. Of Roeux | 09/12/1917 | 17/12/1917 |
| War Diary | Arras | 17/12/1917 | 17/12/1917 |
| War Diary | Roeux | 23/12/1917 | 27/12/1917 |
| War Diary | Fampoux Cutting | 27/12/1917 | 31/12/1917 |
| War Diary | Fampoux Cutting | 01/02/1918 | 01/02/1918 |
| War Diary | Arras | 02/02/1918 | 15/02/1918 |
| Miscellaneous | Headquarters. 15th Division | 10/02/1918 | 10/02/1918 |
| War Diary | Arras | 15/01/1918 | 31/01/1918 |
| Heading | War Diary 9th. (S) Bn. The Black Watch. February 1918 | | |

| | | | |
|---|---|---|---|
| War Diary | S. Bank Of River. Scarpe | 09/02/1918 | 13/02/1918 |
| War Diary | Arras | 01/02/1918 | 05/02/1918 |
| War Diary | Bois Des Boeufs | 06/02/1918 | 06/02/1918 |
| War Diary | Monchy Sector | 07/02/1918 | 08/02/1918 |
| War Diary | Arras | 14/02/1918 | 19/02/1918 |
| War Diary | S. of Scarpe | 20/02/1918 | 28/02/1918 |
| War Diary | Welford Reserve | 28/02/1918 | 28/02/1918 |
| Heading | 46th Brigade. 15th Division. 9th Battalion The Black Watch March 1918 | | |
| Heading | 9th (S) Battalion The Black Watch. War Diary For March 1918 Volume XXXIII | | |
| War Diary | Arras | 03/03/1918 | 03/03/1918 |
| War Diary | Wellford Reserve | 10/03/1918 | 16/03/1918 |
| War Diary | Johnson Avenue | 11/03/1918 | 31/03/1918 |
| Miscellaneous | 9th (S) Bde The Black Watch H.Q. 46th Inf Bde R Port On Operations From. | 29/03/1918 | 29/03/1918 |
| Heading | 15th Division, 46th Infantry Brigade 9th Battalion The Royal Highlanders. April 1918 | | |
| Heading | War Diary Of 9th Bn. The Royal Highlanders. From 1-4-18 To 30-4-18 Vol 34 | | |
| War Diary | Imperial Caves Arras | 01/04/1918 | 04/04/1918 |
| War Diary | Front Line E Of Arras | 05/04/1918 | 14/04/1918 |
| War Diary | Blangy System. | 15/04/1918 | 15/04/1918 |
| War Diary | Y Huts Etrun | 16/04/1918 | 20/04/1918 |
| War Diary | Blangy System | 21/04/1918 | 22/04/1918 |
| War Diary | Y Huts Etrun | 23/04/1918 | 23/04/1918 |
| War Diary | Burbure | 24/04/1918 | 30/04/1918 |
| Heading | War Diary 9th. Bn The Black Watch 1st To 15th May 1918 | | |
| War Diary | Burbure | 01/05/1918 | 03/05/1918 |
| War Diary | Arras | 04/05/1918 | 04/05/1918 |
| War Diary | Fampoux Sector | 05/05/1918 | 10/05/1918 |
| War Diary | Wakefield Camp | 11/05/1918 | 15/05/1918 |
| Heading | 15th Division 44th Infy Bde 4-5th Bn. Roy HDRS (Blk Watch) May 1918-Apl 1919 From 39 Div 118 Bde | | |
| Heading | M Dudes Jan 1918 | | |
| Heading | War Diary 4/5th. Bn. Black Watch 16th 31st May. 1918 | | |
| Miscellaneous | Proposal For Raid To be carried out by 4/5th Bn The Black Watch | 26/05/1918 | 26/05/1918 |
| Operation(al) Order(s) | 4/5th Black Watch Operation Order No. 2 | 29/05/1918 | 29/05/1918 |
| Miscellaneous | 46th Inf Bde. | 26/05/1918 | 26/05/1918 |
| War Diary | Trenches | 02/01/1918 | 02/01/1918 |
| War Diary | Arras | 04/01/1918 | 31/01/1918 |
| War Diary | War Diary Of 4/5th Battalion The Black Watch (R.H) From 1/6/18 To 30/6/18 Vol | | |
| War Diary | War Diary Of 4/5th Battalion The Black Watch For May 1918 Volume V | | |
| War Diary | | 01/05/1918 | 17/05/1918 |
| War Diary | Wakefield Camp | 16/05/1918 | 16/05/1918 |
| War Diary | Fampoux Sector | 17/05/1918 | 31/05/1918 |
| War Diary | Brigade Support | 01/06/1918 | 01/06/1918 |
| War Diary | Wakefield Camp | 02/06/1918 | 06/06/1918 |
| War Diary | Fampoux Sector Front Line Left Sub Sector | 07/06/1918 | 12/06/1918 |
| War Diary | Brigade Support Railway Cutting | 13/06/1918 | 18/06/1918 |
| War Diary | Portsmouth Camp | 19/06/1918 | 25/06/1918 |
| War Diary | Right Section | 25/06/1918 | 30/06/1918 |

| | | | |
|---|---|---|---|
| War Diary | In The Field | 01/07/1918 | 01/07/1918 |
| War Diary | War Diary Of 4/5th Battalion The Black Watch (R.H) From 1st July, 1918 To 31st July 1918. Vol. 34 | | |
| War Diary | Front Line Fampoux Sector (North) | 01/07/1918 | 05/07/1918 |
| War Diary | Support Battalion Stirling Camp. | 06/07/1918 | 13/07/1918 |
| War Diary | Arras | 14/07/1918 | 14/07/1918 |
| War Diary | Billets In Berles. | 15/07/1918 | 16/07/1918 |
| War Diary | Billets in Monchy St. Eloi. | 17/10/1918 | 19/10/1918 |
| War Diary | Billets In Cuise La Motte | 20/07/1918 | 21/07/1918 |
| War Diary | St. Pierre Aigle | 22/07/1918 | 22/07/1918 |
| War Diary | Divisional Reserve Near Chaudon Village | 23/07/1918 | 25/07/1918 |
| War Diary | Front Line Near La Foulerie | 26/07/1918 | 26/07/1918 |
| War Diary | Brigade Support Valley East of La Foulerie | 27/07/1918 | 27/07/1918 |
| War Diary | B. Gerard East Of Buzancy. | 28/07/1918 | 28/07/1918 |
| War Diary | Brigade Support. B. Gerard East Of Buzancy. | 28/07/1918 | 29/07/1918 |
| War Diary | Divisional Reserve Chazelle Valley. | 30/07/1918 | 31/07/1918 |
| War Diary | | | |
| War Diary | 4/5th Battn. The Black Watch. War Diary. From 1/8/18 To 31/8/18 Vol | | |
| War Diary | Support Line Near La Raperie | 01/08/1918 | 01/08/1918 |
| War Diary | Front Line Near La Raperie. | 02/08/1918 | 02/08/1918 |
| War Diary | La Raperie | 03/08/1918 | 03/08/1918 |
| War Diary | Dommiers Village | 04/08/1918 | 04/08/1918 |
| War Diary | Mogneville Village. | 05/08/1918 | 06/08/1918 |
| War Diary | Penin Village. | 07/08/1918 | 15/08/1918 |
| War Diary | Front Line Neuville Vitasse Sector. | 16/08/1918 | 21/08/1918 |
| War Diary | Reserve Line | 22/08/1918 | 22/08/1918 |
| War Diary | Dainville | 23/08/1918 | 23/08/1918 |
| War Diary | Bois Du Froissart Camp. | 24/08/1918 | 24/08/1918 |
| War Diary | Support Line. Hulluch Sector | 25/08/1918 | 28/08/1918 |
| War Diary | Front Line Hulluch Sector. | 29/08/1918 | 31/08/1918 |
| War Diary | | | |
| War Diary | War Diary. 4/5th Battn. The Black Watch From 1/9/18 To 30/9/18 Vol | | |
| War Diary | Hulluch Sector Front Line. | 01/09/1918 | 07/09/1918 |
| War Diary | Mazingarbe | 08/09/1918 | 12/09/1918 |
| War Diary | Hulluch Sector The Quarries | 13/09/1918 | 22/09/1918 |
| War Diary | Mazingarbe | 23/09/1918 | 27/09/1918 |
| War Diary | Hulluch Sector Front Line | 28/09/1918 | 30/09/1918 |
| War Diary | | | |
| War Diary | War Diary. 4/5th Bn. The Black Watch. From 1/10/18 To 31/10/18 | | |
| War Diary | Hulluch Sector Front Line | 01/10/1918 | 09/10/1918 |
| War Diary | Hulluch Sector Support Line | 10/10/1918 | 15/10/1918 |
| War Diary | Wingles Support Line. | 16/10/1918 | 16/10/1918 |
| War Diary | Meurchin | 17/10/1918 | 17/10/1918 |
| War Diary | Carvin | 18/10/1918 | 18/10/1918 |
| War Diary | Bois D' Epinoy | 19/10/1918 | 19/10/1918 |
| War Diary | La Rosiere | 20/10/1918 | 20/10/1918 |
| War Diary | Hucquinville | 21/10/1918 | 21/10/1918 |
| War Diary | L'Ecuille | 22/10/1918 | 29/10/1918 |
| War Diary | Antoing Sector Front Line. | 30/10/1918 | 31/10/1918 |
| War Diary | | | |
| Heading | Hd. Qrs., 44th Infy. Bde. | 05/12/1918 | 05/12/1918 |
| Miscellaneous | A.A.G. 3rd Echelon. | 06/12/1918 | 06/12/1918 |
| Miscellaneous | A Form Messages And Signals. | | |

| | | | |
|---|---|---|---|
| War Diary | War Diary 4/5th Battn. The Black Watch. From 1/11/18 To 30/11/18 Vol. 40 | | |
| War Diary | Bruyelles-Jollain-Merlin Sector Front Line | 01/11/1918 | 04/11/1918 |
| War Diary | Guignies Support Line | 05/11/1918 | 10/11/1918 |
| War Diary | Blicquy | 11/11/1918 | 11/11/1918 |
| War Diary | Huissignies | 12/11/1918 | 26/11/1918 |
| War Diary | Chievres | 27/11/1918 | 30/11/1918 |
| War Diary | | | |
| War Diary | 4/5th Bn. The Black Watch War Diary in December 1918 Volume No. 421 | | |
| War Diary | Chievres. | 01/12/1918 | 17/12/1918 |
| War Diary | Soignies. | 18/12/1918 | 18/12/1918 |
| War Diary | Ronquieres. | 19/12/1918 | 22/12/1918 |
| War Diary | Nivelles | 23/12/1918 | 31/12/1918 |
| War Diary | 4/5th Bn. The Black Watch. War Diary For Period ending 31-1-19 Vol 42 | | |
| War Diary | Nivelles Belgium | 01/01/1919 | 31/01/1919 |
| War Diary | 4/5th Bn. The Black Watch War Diary For February 1919 Vol 43 | | |
| War Diary | Nivelles | 01/02/1919 | 24/02/1919 |
| War Diary | Braine Le Comte | 25/02/1919 | 28/02/1919 |
| War Diary | | | |
| War Diary | 4/5th Bn The Black Watch War Diary For March 1919 Serial No. Vol. 44 | | |
| War Diary | Braine Le Comte | 01/03/1919 | 30/03/1919 |
| War Diary | 4/5th Bn. The Black Watch War Diary For April 1919 Serial No. Vol 45 | | |
| War Diary | | | |
| War Diary | Braine Le Comte Belgium. | 01/03/1919 | 31/03/1919 |
| War Diary | | | |

15.   44.

9ᵗʰ Black
Watch
Vol 9

B1.

121/6607

9th Black Watch
July 1915.

15th Division

9th Black Watch
Vol: I
from 3 July to 3 Aug. 15

4/15

Dec 1917

Army Form C. 2118.

No 1.

# WAR DIARY
## or
## INTELLIGENCE SUMMARY.
(Erase heading not required.)

Instructions regarding War Diaries and Intelligence Summaries are contained in F. S. Regs., Part II. and the Staff Manual respectively. Title pages will be prepared in manuscript.

| Place | Date | Hour | Summary of Events and Information | Remarks and references to Appendices |
|---|---|---|---|---|
| PARKHOUSE CAMP. | 3/7/15 | 10 am. | Telegram received from 15 Div'n. "Embarkation for France starts Wednesday." | |
| " | 7/7/15 | 8 am. | Senior Major (Major J. STEWART), No1 Machine gun Section, and Transport left TIDWORTH STATION for HAVRE via SOUTHAMPTON. Day showery. | |
| " | 8/7/15 | 1.30 pm. | C.O (Lt. Col. T.O. LLOYD), Adjt (Capt R.E. HARVEY). Q.Mr (Lieut + Q.Mr W. CLARK), M.O (Lieut. F.A. BEARN. R.A.M.C) and A + C Coys left TIDWORTH STATION for BOULOGNE via FOLKESTONE. Day fine. | |
| " | " | 2.10 pm. | B + D Coys, under Major M.W. HENDERSON followed, bound for BOULOGNE. | |
| FOLKESTONE | " | 7.40 pm. | A + C Coys arrived at FOLKESTONE QUAY. | |
| " | " | 8.20 pm. | B + D Coys arrived at FOLKESTONE QUAY. Embarkation started at once. | |
| " | " | 9.0 pm. | Boat left, with 9th B.W. & 8th SEAFORTH HIGHLANDERS, for BOULOGNE. (S.E. Steam S.S. "Invicta") Passage very smooth. Two Destroyers were given as an escort. All lights were put out. Soon after leaving harbour we passed a large neutral liner ablaze with light. | |
| BOULOGNE | " | 10.30 pm. | 9th B.W disembarked at BOULOGNE. C.O and Q.M motored to OSTROHOVE CAMP to Conference with CAMP COMMANDANT, 9th B.W following under MAJOR HENDERSON. | |
| " | 9/7/15 | | The Batt. stayed overnight and the forenoon of 9/7/15 at this camp, on the site of NAPOLEON's camp of 1805, under canvas. Weather fine + warm | |

1577 Wt. W10791/1773 500,000 1/15 D. D. & L. A.D.S.S./Forms/C. 2118.

Army Form C. 2118.

No. 2

# WAR DIARY
## or
## INTELLIGENCE SUMMARY.
(Erase heading not required.)

Instructions regarding War Diaries and Intelligence Summaries are contained in F. S. Regs., Part II. and the Staff Manual respectively. Title pages will be prepared in manuscript.

| Place | Date | Hour | Summary of Events and Information | Remarks and references to Appendices |
|---|---|---|---|---|
| BOULOGNE | 9/7/15 | 6.00 pm | At Orders received to entrain at PONT DE BRIQUES STATION at 6 p.m. The Batt. marched down & Soon Train steamed in with MAJOR STEWART, Machine Gun Section & Transport in the rear end. The Batt. entrained in 5 minutes and at about 6.15 pm the train pulled out bound where we did not know. However at the first halt we were informed we were bound for WATTEN, where we arrived soon after Dark. At BOULOGNE we had been joined by our Interpreter SERGT ANDRE BONSARGENT of the French Corps de liaison, and under his guidance we went our way from WATTEN to MOULLE, a small place a few miles off and about 5 miles from ST OMER, where G.H.Q. was stationed. | |
| MOULLE | 10/7/15 | 12.30 am | Arrived at MOULLE about 12.30 am., and endeavoured to get men into billets. This with Some time &/, the Major being on leave, we were left to the tender mercies of M. LE SECRETAIRE a garrulous individual, and it was not until 1.30 am that we stripped him of his billeting dockets and the Corps could begin getting into billets. Day had dawned, fortunately fine, before the last Coy was billeted, our area being very much dispersed and one of the Coys. being two miles from Battn H.Q. Here the People were very friendly, and we were comfortable enough for a few days. | |

Army Form C. 2118.

No. 3.

# WAR DIARY
## or
## INTELLIGENCE SUMMARY.
(Erase heading not required.)

Instructions regarding War Diaries and Intelligence Summaries are contained in F. S. Regs., Part II and the Staff Manual respectively. Title pages will be prepared in manuscript.

| Place | Date | Hour | Summary of Events and Information | Remarks and references to Appendices |
|---|---|---|---|---|
| MOULLE | 12/10-14 1915 | | The Batt<sup>n</sup> kept fit by daily routemarches, which were very necessary as for the last few months training had been specialized and bayonet fighting & bombing instruction had been the order of the day. The Commander in Chief visited Battalion on 12<sup>th</sup>. The rest of K<sup>s</sup> & 44<sup>th</sup> Bde were in billets close by, 7<sup>th</sup> CAMERON HIGHLANDERS in HOULLE, 8<sup>th</sup> SEAFORTH H<sup>rs</sup> at GANSPETTE, and 10<sup>th</sup> GORDON H<sup>rs</sup> at EPERLECQUES. Bde H.Q were at HOULLE. Weather constantly very bad. | |
| " | " 13<sup>th</sup> | | All general & commanding officers of Division attended the active service lecture at WISQUES. | |
| HAZEBROUCK | 14<sup>th</sup> | 6.55 a.m. | The Battalion marched to HAZEBROUCK and went into Billets there, march about 20 miles, the whole Division marched as a unit. Hot day trying march for the men. | |
| BAS RIEUX | 15<sup>th</sup> | 8.30 a.m. | The Brigade marched today as a unit rest of Division by other routes. Battalion led and went into Billets at BAS RIEUX - about 12 miles, arrived after a 1 hour halt at ST VENANT. at about 3 p.m. | |
| | 16<sup>th</sup> | 7.50 p.m. | Brigade marched at eight Candlestrand 9.30 p.m. at CHOQUES arrived about 1 a.m. 17<sup>th</sup> at HOUCHIN where went into Billets. | |
| HOUCHIN | 17<sup>th</sup> | | Owing to congestion of billeting area permission granted by G.O.C. Jr A/B Coys to bivouac. | |

# WAR DIARY or INTELLIGENCE SUMMARY

Army Form C. 2118.
No 4.

| Place | Date | Hour | Summary of Events and Information | Remarks and references to Appendices |
|---|---|---|---|---|
| HOUCHIN | 1915 July 18-23 | | Time employed in Route marching. Physical exercises, etc. Nothing of interest occuring. G.O.C. 1st Army visits Battalion on 23rd. Khaki round Bonnets issued to Bn on 28th. | |
| " | 24th | | Following attachments for instruction in Trench warfare commenced from this date 2nd in Command, acting Gen officer 2 by S.M. 2 by Q.M.S. 1 M.G. N.C.O. to 21st London Regt. (T). | |
| " | 24-26 | | " " " " " " " 2nd Sussex Regt. | |
| " | 27-28 | | C.O. adjutant. 2 by S.M. 2 by Q.M.S. 1 M.G. N.C.O. " 2"B" K.R. Rifles. | |
| " | 28-30 | | " " " " " " " 22nd London Regt. (T). | |
| " | 31-1 | | " " " " " " " ( " " " ) | |
| " | 28-30 | | A & B. Companies by platoons. (A. to 22nd London B. to 23rd & 24th London Regt.) | |
| " | 30-1 | | C & D " " " " ( C " " " D " " " ) | |
| " | Aug 1. | | Instructions received that Brigade would take up a sector (W). on 2nd Aug, C & D intend to Remain in Trenches and not to return to H.Q. | |
| N. MAROC | 2nd | 8 p.m. | A & B Cos. marched from HOUCHIN to N.MAROC. H.Q. of W.3 Section of W Sector. C Coy. taking over from W.2 to W.3 where D were already undergoing attachment. Batts. taking over from 23rd London Regt & 24th Lon Regt. | |
| " | 3rd | 1.20 a.m. | Relief completed at 1.20. am. Very quietly carried out. Corp. distributed as follows. C Right Sub Section of W.3 Fire trench. D Left ditto. B in Support. A Batt. Reserve at MAROC | |

B 2

121/6607

9ᵗʰ Black Watch

August 1915.

15ᵗʰ Division

9ᵗʰ Black Watch
Vol: II
From 4 - 31. 8. 15

4/15

# WAR DIARY
## or
## INTELLIGENCE SUMMARY.

Army Form C. 2118.

No. 8.

(Erase heading not required.)

| Place | Date | Hour | Summary of Events and Information | Remarks and references to Appendices |
|---|---|---|---|---|
| QUALITY St. | 1915 Aug. 29. | | Capt. J. Gilchrist (2nd Capt. of D. Coy) when out in front of the wire, mortally wounded. Sergeants Mitchell, McCann went out and very gallantly brought him in. It took them about 20 minutes to get their through the wire as it's lay had to cut. They were exposed all the time to the hostile fire of the Sniper who was in the front at Capt Gilchrist was at where he was hit and – after they got him being the wire left Hunte also went out to help. This was in daylight 6am. Capt Gilchrist was Carried as soon as possible but died in Hospital at Chocque about 12 noon. | |
| " | 30th | | Battalion relieved in X1 & 7" B" R.S.F. relief carried out in daylight commencing at 2 pm. Baln moving back to Billets in Divisional Reserve at MAZINGARBE. | |
| , MAZINGARBE. | | | it is a different Billeting area to that previously occupied. | |
| " | 31st | | Battalion employed in cleaning up & the arms & of Trenches at night 6 officers & 300 men employed under 73rd Coy R.E. in digging trenches in Sector X. | |

at MAZINGARBE.
31.8.15.

J. O. Aluri Lt. Colonel
Comdg 9th Batln
The Black Watch.

## CLOTHING.

| | | | NECESSARIES. | |
|---|---|---|---|---|
| Aprons, kilt. | 1. | | Brushes, shaving. | 1. |
| Boots, ankle. | 1. | |        tooth. | 1. |
| Capes, waterproof. | 1. | | Cap comforter. | 1. |
| Caps, Balmoral. | 1. | | Comb. | 1. |
| Cardigan. | 1. | | Fork. | 1. |
| Coats, great. | 1. | | Holdall. | 1. |
| Coats, under, dg. | 1. | | Knives - clasp. | 1. |
| Covers, cap, waterproof. | 1. | |        table. | 1. |
| Drawers, short. | 2 prs. | | Razor. | 1. |
| Garters, Highland. | 1pr. | | Spoon. | 1. |
| Hosetops. | 2prs. | | Towels. | 2. |
| Iron ration. | 1. | | | |
| Jackets S.D. | 1. | | | |
| Kilt. | 1. | | | |
| Mufflers, short. | 2prs. | | | |
| Shirts. | | | | |
| Socks. | 3prs. | | | |
| Vests, woollen. | 2. | | | |

## ARMS & ACCOUTREMENTS.

| | | | | |
|---|---|---|---|---|
| Bayonets. | 1. | | Hook. | 1. |
| Belt. | 1. | | Pouches. | 2. |
| Bottles, oil, brass. | 1. | | Pull through. | 1. |
| Box, 1/OPt Fin. | 1. | | Rifle. | 1. |
| Braces. | 2. | | Satchels. | 1. |
| Covers, belt. | 1. | | Scabbard. | 1. |
|     rifle, long. | 1. | | Sling. | 1. |
|     Entrenching Tool Head. | 1. | | Smoke Helmet. | 1. |
|     do    carrier. | 1. | |    do   P.H. | 1. |
|     do    helve. | 1. | | Straps supporting. | |
|     do    carrier. | 1. | |       pack. | 2. |
| Frog. | 1. | | Waterbottle. | 1. |
| Field Dressing. | 1. | |    carrier. | 1. |
| Goggles, antigas. | 1pr. | | Waterproof sheet. | 1. |
| Haversack. | 1. | | | |
| Holding magazine. | 1. | | | |
| Identity disc & cord. | 1. | | | |
| Mess tin & cover. | 1. | | | |

44th Inf.Bde.
15th Div.

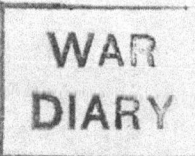

9th BATTN. THE BLACK WATCH (ROYAL HIGHLANDERS).

S E P T E M B E R

1 9 1 5

Attached:

Report on Operations
25th September.

REPORT ON OPERATIONS 25TH SEPTEMBER.
-----------------------------------------

C

Head Quarters
44 Brigade.

Reference order to furnish a short
Report on operations of 25-9-15.

1. The Battalion was drawn up in the
various trenches in X.1. at the hour
named. viz. 11. p.m. 24.9.15.
2. At 5.5. a.m. on 25.9.15. orders received
that Zero hour would be 5.50. a.m.
3. At 5.50 a.m enemy commenced
a very heavy bombardment of our
trenches which was continued up to the
time our Brigade cleared their trenches.
4. At the hour (6.30. a.m.) ordered for
the Infantry advance. The Battalion
crossed our trenches in the order named
previously — A, B, C, and D Cos capturing in
succession the enemy 1st & 2nd line
trenches — the village of LOOS and Hill 70
5. Heavy casualties occurred in our ranks
from the moment we crossed our
Trenches. Between this point and
the enemy 1st trench (few lose)
all Company officers and machine
gun officer fell.
6. The advance across the intervening

2. ground between 1st & 2nd German lines - and the capture of the village of LOOS was comparatively easy work -

7. Had reinforcements followed close on our tracks the capture and consolidation of Hill 70 would have been an easy matter.

8. At 12 noon I sent a message to G.O.C. asking for reinforcements and received at 1.25 p.m. information from him that our guns were in new positions and that reinforcements would arrive shortly - No reinforcements arrived at the section held by us till we were relieved about 2 am on 26.9.15.

9. The position on Hill 70 was consolidated early in the day. It was owing to heavy casualties that occurred on the Hill but lightly held.

10. On receiving orders for relief I withdrew what men were left abt 150 - and reached PHILOSOPHE at 3 am. 26.9.15

11. The 9th Black Watch more than maintained the traditions of its parent Battalion this day. J. Q. Wat. M.W.
Com. 9. B.W.

29.9.15 HOOCHIN -

WAR DIARY.

# INTELLIGENCE SUMMARY.

(Erase heading not required.)

Instructions regarding War Diaries and Intelligence Summaries are contained in F.S. Regs., Part II. and the Staff Manual respectively. Title pages will be prepared in manuscript.

| Place | Date | Hour | Summary of Events and Information | Remarks and references to Appendices |
|---|---|---|---|---|
| HAZINGRADE | 1915 Sept: 1st | | Nothing Special to record. Large working party under R.E. working in X Sector | |
| " | 2nd | | " " " " | |
| " | 3rd | | Pte McIntosh 13 Coy severely wounded & McPherson C Coy slightly wounded both accidentally while teaching Sgts McGor coms on twirling a class. Working Parties as usual. First day of rain we have had for a long time— | |
| " | 4th | | During night 3-4. Following casualties to working party in rear house leach in X1. Pte Q. Mackay killed (buried in QUALITY Street Burial Ground) B Coy Pte McIntyre & Meikle all of B Coy. Rifle Grenade fell into trench. G.O.C. held interview with C.O. | |
| " | 5th | | C.O. and Company Commanders visited Trenches in X1. Such a view to becoming of rear Trenches under care Baths. Crews out of Trenches bad. | |
| " | 6th | | Conference at Brigade H.Q. at NOEUX-les-MINES - Battalion H.Q. changed to another House to make room for H.Q. 3rd Brigade - Billets further closed up to make room for "Seaforth Highrs" up Brigade went but with Brigade Reserve "Camerons Highrs" Taking over relieve of Sector X. | |
| " | 7th | | Further Closing Seaforths took NOEUX. 9 "B.W." remain in Billets - 10 Bordero party in our Billets (2 Coys) remainders in Trenches GRENAY. VERMELLES. Line. | |
| " | 8th | | Working Parties of 300 to 400 men nightly. Began training by day & rest in vicinity of Billets. | |

# WAR DIARY
## or
## INTELLIGENCE SUMMARY.
(Erase heading not required.)

Instructions regarding War Diaries and Intelligence Summaries are contained in F. S. Regs., Part II. and the Staff Manual respectively. Title pages will be prepared in manuscript.

| Place | Date | Hour | Summary of Events and Information | Remarks and references to Appendices |
|---|---|---|---|---|
| MAZINGARBE | 1915 Sept. 9th | | Working special & report, continued reading reports. Instructions in Bombing etc. | |
| " | 10 | | Instructed that a blanket per man is to be issued. | |
| " | 11th | | Conference of G.O.C. with Battalion Commanders. | |
| " | 12th | | Working Party of X.1. was shelled but all ten casualties. Completed wiring of Red Heck L6 to Battn | |
| " | 13th | | C.O. visited Trenches with G.O.C. | |
| " | 14th | | Dug outs for whole Battalion completed today. | |
| " | 15th | | Usual working parties at night wiring, checks & upot. | |
| " | 16th | | " " " " " " " | |
| " | 17th | | Brigadier saw all Platoon Commanders at B.H.Q. | |
| " | 18th | | Conference at D.H.Q. re: Antillery Co-operation, Enf: of. O.C. Battn at B.H.Q. Special duty. | |
| " | 19th | | Working Parties on Special duty again employed level 2 wires on weeks 2 w Coyd | |
| " | 20th | | No working Parties detailed. C.O. & 2nd in Comd & W in Cu observation Post at MAROC | |
| " | 21st | | This date will be noted in certain connections which cannot yet be chronicled | |
| " | 22nd | | Working Hours to "lay down" ordinary working parties suspended too been employed to & Coyd | |
| " | 23rd | | Conference at Brig. H.Q. C.O. authorized to issue all details of impending operations. | |
| " | 24th | | Battalion moving up Companies took up positions in X.1. Sector of our line of A frontage going from C.T. 6 inclusive A.Cy. to Fire Trench B.Cy. in Support from C.T. Trenches 27 and T.D. in C.T. 21. The D also shows up parts of C.T. 12 two dugout | |

aux Trenches in X1 Sector

# WAR DIARY
## or
## INTELLIGENCE SUMMARY.

| Place | Date | Hour | Summary of Events and Information | Remarks and references to Appendices |
|---|---|---|---|---|
|  | 1915 Sept 25 | am 5.5 am | Orders received that at 5.50 gas cylinders that had been previously placed in our Trenches would be discharged as follows: 12 minutes gas followed by 5 minutes smoke candles and 30 m. [?] 40 minutes — at the hour named the enemy commenced a very heavy bombardment of our Trenches. The men not being of sufficient strength a portion of the gas blew back into our Trenches. At the hour named for attack H.Q. 6 S.W. and the Battalion gallantly charged out of our Trenches and captured the enemy's main trenches — The portion of enemy's line allotted to the Battalion and known as the "Fecnd Work" was looking strong. The 8th Seaforths had been allotted the task of assaulting on our left. 1 "Cameron Hypds" on support on right 13 W. + Seaforths were to follow Hypds in Reserve. I think the advance some little time before the Seaforths left than the Hynds. If this is so, it would be to some extent for the fact that our casualties were very heavy chiefly other Battalions of the Brigade. Between our own trenches and the German front lines at the Jerus WOEI 6 Officers were killed and seriously wounded and about 100 other Ranks Killed. The officers being — Valter Major W.M. Anderson — Capt. J. McBean — Lieut J Crighton Lieut J [?] Macleod as Hamilton — 2nd Lieut J. McLellan — Alf P.M. Graham — deily wounded Col. A. [illegible] R.G. Haney |  |

# WAR DIARY
or
## INTELLIGENCE SUMMARY.
(Erase heading not required.)

Instructions regarding War Diaries and Intelligence Summaries are contained in F. S. Regs., Part II. and the Staff Manual respectively. Title pages will be prepared in manuscript.

| Place | Date | Hour | Summary of Events and Information | Remarks and references to Appendices |
|---|---|---|---|---|
| In action. | 1915 Sept. 25 | abt 7.25 a.m. | The orders prior to assault were that the 44th Brigade was to take (1st) the German 1st line (Front line). 2nd The German 2nd line also two isolated post East of Village of LOOS. (3rd) The Village of LOOS. (4th) Hill 70.— The 9th Black Watch & 8th Seaforths had taken the 2nd German line and were pushing their way through the village of LOOS. | |
| | | 8.30 a.m. | Officer Commanding 9th B.W. also two wire in LOOS received information that the Battalion was already established on Hill 70. From this hour up to the time the Brigade was relieved on Hill 70 at about 1 a.m. on 26th Sept: of the 8.2nd Brigade — The situation was as follows — On the Hill being captured the several units of the Brigade were of necessity much mixed up and several of the remaining portion of the Battalion were scattered along the front, C.O. and 2nd in Comd 9.B.W. remained at the foot of the Hill abt. 250 yards from firing line. On the crest of the Hill being reached a general continued advance ST AUGUSTE and DINAMENTIERE (the latter to the right front) were objects.) was made. But owing to heavy enfilading fire from both flanks the remnant of the Brigade was forced to entrench on the eastern side. | |

# WAR DIARY
## or
## INTELLIGENCE SUMMARY.
*(Erase heading not required.)*

Instructions regarding War Diaries and Intelligence Summaries are contained in F.S. Regs., Part II. and the Staff Manual respectively. Title pages will be prepared in manuscript.

| Place | Date | Hour | Summary of Events and Information | Remarks and references to Appendices |
|---|---|---|---|---|
| In action | 1915 Sept. 26th | | of Capt. McGill. Throughout the day & night the X.Y. and Coy threatened to attack the position, were well executed. The right flank was a source of worry to the C.O. Throughout this day as it was not possible to determine what was going on beyond the CRASSIER (in which our right rested). At about 2 Vizs C.O. received from Bryoll H.Q. to continue to assist for reinforcements — intimation their reinforcements were very lost up and that there were turnout of the enemy before the 45th Byrole — He demand of Battalion was relieved about 1 am and were ordered to rejoin the new Bryoll H.Q. to billets at | |
| P.H.1080 P.H.E | 3rd | | P.H.1080 P.H.E. to bie 2 (C.O. & 2nd in Com) were either killed or wounded. In addition to the 7 officers ronned all 20 being taken within the 18 hours of the action (i.e. to following the few hours). 2nd Lt. A. Sharp was killed at the 2nd German line. A German officer had come up to surrender when Lt. Sharp ordered his own men not to fire at him, when a German behind the officer treacherously killed him. Lt. Colonel J.H. Creadore was severely wounded & Lt. A. C. Dennistoun d/d S.R. Wilson — The following Officers were wounded. |
| VERMELLES line | | | Capt. A.K. Tedcroo — Lt.Col. R. Creadoos — d.a.j.a.o. Dennistoun — d/d S.R. Wilson — | |
| XI. Wescher also former GERMAN trenches | | | 2nd Lt. D. J. Gleeney — 2nd Lt. J. Campbell — 2nd R. Sterling — 2nd Lt. J. Scott Pearse — 2nd Lt. W. Clarke | |

# WAR DIARY
## or
## INTELLIGENCE SUMMARY

Army Form C. 2118.

| Place | Date | Hour | Summary of Events and Information | Remarks and references to Appendices |
|---|---|---|---|---|
| | 1915 Sept 26 | | 2nd Lt. F. R. Wilson. also Capt. F. A. Bearne R.A.M.C.] wounded. — In the other Ranks there were 680 Casualties it has not been possible so far to ascertain the numbers actually killed. Total 78 Killed — 1 died of wounds 1 missing believed killed — 71 wounded. After a few hours out at PHILOSOPHE, the remnant of Battalion was ordered to hold 8. RENAY-VERMELLES line before proceeding two hours up there & ordered to proceed to hold our original "this" Trenches to A.1. So. of LENS Road — during the evening of 26.", a further order came to occupy old 1st German line and take trench of old German Support heads. | |
| MAZINGARBE | 27" | | At 2 am. orders received to return to Billets at MAZINGARBE arrived there 5 am. Remained in billets at MAZINGARBE. | |
| " | 28" | | | |
| HOUCHIN | 29" | 9.30 am | Marched to Maisles & HOUCHIN and occupied our former billets there. Received a draft of 28 men from 3rd & 11th Battalions. | |
| " | 30" | | Received a draft of 43 N.C.O.'s & men from 3rd & 11th Battalions — Sent out Burial Parties to Battlefield of 25th. estimated that between our trenches and German 1st line about 100 other ranks were killed. | |

SECRET.

**HEADQUARTERS.**
**11 SEP. 1915**
No. S. 34
**44th INFANTRY BRIGADE**

I.

G.O.C., 1st Army.

It has come to the notice of the French and British military authorities that cases have occurred where cartridges have been found on enemy prisoners of which the bullets have been tampered with, i.e., the nose cut off or blunted, or the envelope slit; also cartridges have been discovered with the point inwards. It will be made known to officers in command of units that whenever enemy prisoners are found in actual possession of such cartridges three officers will be at once assembled to verify the facts and to record the prisoner's name, regiment, etc. If there is no doubt that the man is in possession of such ammunition, which is a contravention of Appendix 2 of the Hague declaration dated 29th July, 1899, he will be shot at once, the record signed by the officers and the cartridges found on the man being despatched to A.G.G.H.Q.

Care will be taken to discriminate between bullets as above mentioned and those which, although not in conformity with the Hague Declaration, have evidently been issued to the men and have not been tampered with by them. In such cases the blame is with the authority issuing and not with the individual soldier.

Please acknowledge.

G.H.Q. 22.3.15.    Sd/ C.F.N. MACREADY, Lt.Gen., Adjt.Gen.


II.    44th Brigade S.G.

O.C. 9th Black Watch.
    8th Seaforths.
    10th Gordons.
    7th Camerons.


For information and necessary action.

Acknowledge.

                                Captain,
                      for Brigade Major,
111.9.15.             44th Infantry Brigade.

**HEADQUARTERS.**
**12 SEP. 1915**
No. S/34
**44th INFANTRY BRIGADE**

9th Black Watch

October 1915.

15th Division.

9th Black Watch
Vol 4

Oct 15

# WAR DIARY or INTELLIGENCE SUMMARY

Army Form C. 2118.

| Place | Date | Hour | Summary of Events and Information | Remarks and references to Appendices |
|---|---|---|---|---|
| HOUCHIN | 1915 Oct. 1. | | Brigade addressed by Sir H. Rawlinson commanding 4th Corps. who congratulated them on their splendid doing. the action fought on Sept. 25th. | |
| | 2. | | Burial party again sent up — went had the unpleasant duty to bury shelling — Lieut. Pitcairn from 3rd Batt. joined. Battalion addressed (as were other officers & ng) Several times attacked since 15th Division — who congratulated Battalion on their work on 25th Sept. | |
| LILLERS | 3. | | Orders received about 10 a.m. to be ready to march to LILLERS. — Brigade marched off at 12 noon. arrived about 4.15 p.m. went into billets. Orders received that Training of Battalion is to be resumed. and | |
| " | 4. | | programme of work submitted as usual training at home. | |
| " | 5. | | Following officers from 11th Batt. reported themselves 2nd Lt. R. H. Robertson – H. S. Reynold R. W. Reid – R. C. H. Scott – L. B. A. Morrison – O. L. Bearne – L. Murray Stewart Total 7. Leave to U.K. opened. Officer Lts. J. Flewind & Miss Rawls. proceeded home. | |
| " | 6. | | Following officers joined from 11th Batt & 2nd Lts. Lt. W. the Begg – J. de Denson – J. Searle J. B. Robertson – R. Campbell. Total 5. Leave of absence to 1 officer. 2nd Lieut G. Leys to U.K. and 7 other ranks. Gourlee to U.K. | |

# WAR DIARY
## or
## INTELLIGENCE SUMMARY.

(Erase heading not required.)

Army Form C. 2118.

| Place | Date | Hour | Summary of Events and Information | Remarks and references to Appendices |
|---|---|---|---|---|
| LILLERS | 1915 Oct 7 | | Following officers joined from 11"Bn. 2"Lt. A.J. Howard, T.J. Loades = 2 | |
| " | 8 | | Training continued daily — Drafts receiving first addresses of J.O.C. 15" Division | |
| " | 9 | | Draft of 70 other Ranks and 2 officers 2"Lt J.d. Mcphee & a Wethenfer = 2 | |
| " | 10th | | Training as usual — Nothing special to chronicle = 2 Lt. | |
| " | 12.4th | | Orders received to move up to NOEUX-LES-MINES — Brigade moved by Train arriving (V'Pam) abt 6 pm. 2"Lt T.C. Tweedie joined from 11"Bn. making a total of 18 2"Lieutenants joined since action of 25" Sept. | |
| NOEUX LES MINES. | 13th | | Billets in Billets — Training continued — New drafts of Pioneers, Stretcher Bearers etc. from our Base training commenced. | |
| " | 14th | | | |
| " | 15th | | Draft of 120 other Ranks arrived — less L.C.O. 9 canulles for 7 days. Lieut 6.0.h. Liesch Q.M. W. Clarke & 1 other Ranks. | |
| " | 16th | | Training as usual — Nothing Special to Chronicle — Lieut Col Rivatt & 2 other Ranks | |
| " | 17-20 | | Batt'n moved to billets at NOYELLE — 2 coys of Brigade remaining at NOEUX. | |
| NOYELLES | 22 | | Training as usual. | |
| " | 23 | | | |
| " | 24 | | Draft of 190 other Ranks arrived from 11" Batt'n C.O. M'Lean Tees etc. others joining us all told 9 men from 25th May & 26th | |

# WAR DIARY or INTELLIGENCE SUMMARY

Army Form C. 2118.

| Place | Date 1915 | Hour | Summary of Events and Information | Remarks and references to Appendices |
|---|---|---|---|---|
| NOYELLE | Oct 25 | | Brigade ordered to take over a new line of Trenches from 10" Gordons & 7" Cameronians in front line. 9" B.W. & 8" Seaforths in support. Reserve Brigade Reserve Bivouac at 9 a.m. | |
| TRENCHES in C.1. Area Ref Trench Map 1/10000 | 26 | | Batts took over portion in Section C.1. immediately South of Hulloch. Moved from 7th R.S & 6th Fusiliers. O. enemy old British Support Trench in Brigade Reserve. 3 men killed by an enemy shell as the men taking over line — 4/7. London Bttn on our immediate right. | |
| | 27 | | 4/6 Yo. Fus. (L. on Bttn on our left) | |
| | 28 | | Very wet weather. Lot of men sent heavies over 12" deep in water, large working parties employed in improving trenches etc. | |
| | 29 | | Relieved 10" Gordons in front line, they being over pieces to Bry. Reserve. Relief carried out & keen. Enemy shelled our trenches heavily but parties was much damaged | |
| | 30 | | Enemy shelled our trenches heavily but parties was much damaged. 1 man wounded | |
| | 31 | | E shells 8th Front. Support & Reserve lines also | |

9th Bn. Black Watch
Vol. 5

Miss Brown (2)

B 4

121/7693  9th Black Watch.

November 1915.

Jan. 15

15th Division

4/15

K

nil
Eny

Army Form C. 2118.

# WAR DIARY
## or
## INTELLIGENCE SUMMARY.
(Erase heading not required.)

| Place | Date | Hour | Summary of Events and Information | Remarks and references to Appendices |
|---|---|---|---|---|
| Trenches G.1. | 1915 Nov. 1. | | Changed horses again with 10" Gordons. Gen Babb did not get back to old British support trenches till 2.30 am. owing to General being near the shell burst deep in land — | |
| | 2 | | Means of [?] of these hee shelter pees is only to [?] within day & night to repair same | |
| | 3 | | Same as 2 w. | |
| | 4 | | Charged ten as again with 10" Gordons. Enemy are eds of earth to 3 feet. let them in the relief took 10 hours to complete | |
| | 5 | | Shelling as part of every battalion — 2nd D. at. Dieppe L.2 other scouts killed. 2 wounded | |
| | 6 | | Noting the end to report Battalion as above strikes | |
| | 7 | | Rel. of Myself by 4/6" Rif. Commenced at 11 am | |
| NOEOX. LES. MINES. | 8. | | Battn. reached Philosto at abt. 9 p.m. | |
| | 9. | | Batt. occupied in clearing up — ch. they then had a hot Bath. | |
| | 10. | | Draft of 49. other Ranks joined. Lecture on one link theory of trench feet. | |

Army Form C. 2118.

# WAR DIARY
## or
## INTELLIGENCE SUMMARY.
*(Erase heading not required.)*

Instructions regarding War Diaries and Intelligence Summaries are contained in F. S. Regs., Part II. and the Staff Manual respectively. Title pages will be prepared in manuscript.

| Place | Date | Hour | Summary of Events and Information | Remarks and references to Appendices |
|---|---|---|---|---|
| | 11/15 | | | |
| NOEUX-LES-MINES | Nov. 11 12 | | The weather continued bad — Coys were engaged on cleaning up & lecture. Batt. made preparations for another tour of duty in the trenches, 250 pairs of gum boots were issued, also each man received a pair of woollen drawers, cut down for wear with the kilt. | |
| TRENCHES Gsd13.G.18.a.5½ | 13 | 8 AM | Batt. paraded & marched, platoons at 3 min. intervals, via MAZINGARBE & PHILOSOPHE to VERMELLES & thence to the trench, sector D2 — the 5th Seaforths being on right & the 39th Brigade on the left. The Battn relieved the 9th R.S.F. The trenches, which were not only very unpleasant with mud, in some places up to the knees, but in the firing line (particularly in that part held by the centre Coy, called the NAIRP(N) the parapet was found to be in a very bad state & not bullet proof, D Coy had one man hit in the head through a sandbag shortly after the relief also died within an hour. | Note: v. Instruction No 3 & 4 for improving the parapet & draining the mud. |
| App - Trench Map 1/10,000 | 14 | | 16 men poected to Bolye Bombing School till 17/11/15. Coys were hard at work improving the parapet & draining the mud. At 3.30 p.m. Lt T.D.G. MILLER, O.C. D Coy, was hit in the head by a sniper & died about midnight. 2nd Lt F.W. CRONNE joined from 6th Black Watch on first appointment to a commission. | |
| | | | Enemy snipers were very active round the NAIRP(N) & our line were shelled heavily in the morning. | Shelon Lyon T.O.L |

| Place | Date | Hour | Summary of Events and Information | Remarks and references to Appendices |
|---|---|---|---|---|
| Trenches | 1915 Nov 15. | | Weather improved – a lot of work was done in clearing the trenches – one man was accidentally wounded – our lines were shelled throughout the afternoon, chiefly in reply to our own "frightfulness" by artillery – little damage – two casualties. The Battn was relieved by the 10th Gordons during the afternoon – just before the relief the right Coy was heavily shelled, Sgt Robertson (acting C.S.M.) & Cpl Gibson being killed & 4 men wounded, Battn H.Q. moved down to the large dug out at VERMELLES. The companies being billeted in the village – one Coy "B" remained in the old British front line, under command of O.E. Cameron temporarily – Battn in Local Reserve. | |
| VERMELLES | 16 | | Coy engaged in cleaning up & foot inspection – several men's feet were found to be in a bad state on account of standing water in the trenches in many cases, in spite of extreme care in the use of antifrost bite grease. Working parties of 1 off & 50 men in the morning & 2 officers & 100 men at night were employed under R.E. digging new communication trench. Also permanent parties (for the three days in reserve) of 1 sgt & 19 men were engaged all day in clearing mud from C.T.s & repairing some where damaged. | S.W. for T.W. |
| VERMELLES | 17 | | | |

**Army Form C. 2118.**

# WAR DIARY
## or
## INTELLIGENCE SUMMARY.
(Erase heading not required.)

| Place | Date 1915 | Hour | Summary of Events and Information | Remarks and references to Appendices |
|---|---|---|---|---|
| Trenches | Nov. 18 | | 1st & 2nd Lt. F.R. CLOW joined from R.E. on first appointment to a Commission. | |
| | | | 1st & 2nd Lt. F.R. CLOW joined from the Brigade (44th). The C.O. Lt. Col. T.D. LLOYD had for some time been suffering from Sciatica & Lumbago, but refused to go sick, however he was eventually ordered to go sick by the medical authorities. Major W.W. MacGREGOR D.S.O. 9th Gordon Highlanders (Pioneer) assumed temporary Command. The Battalion moved into the 1st line Trenches, relieving the 10th Gordon Highlanders & occupying the line from G 5 & 13 to G 12 & 54 (Trench Map -36 c N.W.3) The day was very frost-starry & cutting on both sides seemed to be having a rest. The relief worked very smoothly, both battalions knew the line, having been in it before. The communication trenches has been newly boarded & so the walking was easy. The 1st Company 9th Black Watch entered communication trenches at 10.30 am & the relief was reported complete at 1.30 pm. No. S/4254 Pte. S. GIRVAN "C" Coy. was wounded in the head, the bullet probably came through a sand bag. The weather was fine, but the trenches had have not been boarded and very muddy, the work clearing them up & repairing parapets & revetting. | WW |

**Army Form C. 2118.**

# WAR DIARY
## or
## INTELLIGENCE SUMMARY.
*(Erase heading not required.)*

Instructions regarding War Diaries and Intelligence Summaries are contained in F. S. Regs., Part II. and the Staff Manual respectively. Title pages will be prepared in manuscript.

| Place | Date | Hour | Summary of Events and Information | Remarks and references to Appendices |
|---|---|---|---|---|
| Trenches | 1915 Nov. 20 | 7 a.m. | General Wilkinson, comdg. 44th Brigade paid the Battalion a visit in the morning — he urged the necessity of an active campaign against enemy snipers, who had become most aggressive. Also the need for clearing mud out of the trenches, and suggested initially that the order forbidding men to hang up waterproof sheets on the sandbags of the parapets should be obeyed. The sniping campaign was carried out with marked success, resulting in much greater peace. Progress was made with cleaning the trenches. Men were warned about destroying the fire parapets. The difficulty is that the line is a new one & there are strict & absolutely no cover from rain, so to remedy this they hang a waterproof sheet on the sandbags of the parapet; by means of this if stirring & licks the result is, the small holes made in the parapet — unseen, until the parapet falls down when it has to be built up again. A very troublesome day — our artillery any action which always brings about enemy retaliation. There were 3 frightful influences by our own guns, which means many available field guns in the Division firing in hand in tray can go for about 3 minutes — then rounds cannot be observed or many burst short. | W |

# Army Form C. 2118.

# WAR DIARY
## or
## INTELLIGENCE SUMMARY.
*(Erase heading not required.)*

| Place | Date 1915 | Hour | Summary of Events and Information | Remarks and references to Appendices |
|---|---|---|---|---|
| Trenches | Nov. 20 (cont.) | | as the height was the German front line, which at one part was only 30 yards — ten of our men were wounded. One of our shells also exploded a German magazine, not 30 yards from our line & cartridge cases strewn were blown into our trench — two men injured by the beams, one of which was 5 foot long × 6 inches diameter. Many coloured lights also went up inside the explosion. Two men were accidentally wounded, their rifles went off inadvertently, one man while he was cleaning his rifle, the other man caught his trigger in something as he was getting on to the parapet. Weather fine but cold. To-day, casualties 6 men wounded. | |
| | 21 | 7. am | Our Spurs had a "frightfulness" shells were again bursting short — a rifle & bayonet were damaged. A much quieter night than usual — the company against enemy snipers having good effect. A quiet day — cold & fine. Casualties — 2 men wounded. | lll |

# WAR DIARY
## or
## INTELLIGENCE SUMMARY.

Army Form C. 2118.

| Place | Date 1915 | Hour | Summary of Events and Information | Remarks and references to Appendices |
|---|---|---|---|---|
| Trenches | Nov 22 | | A very quiet night - our guns fired 6 shells, but there was no reply. A very misty morning, men were walking about outside the trenches, burying some dead & collecting souvenirs - unfortunately the mist lifted rather suddenly & two men were wounded, but they managed to hurry them in. A German was found inside his feet tied together, he had been dead some time - he was buried. Battalion was relieved by 1st to 5th Gordon Highlanders went into Brigade (44th) Reserve in billets in NOYELLES. The relief, as before, worked very smoothly & was completed at 5p.m. The trenches were dry & in very good order. The day fine, with a very thick mist which only eventually lifted for ½ an hour. Billets in NOYELLES consist of the supplyhouses, a good deal knocked about by shell fire, has most of the windows are gone, they are very cold. Casualties 2 men wounded. The total casualties of the town in the trenches were - 1 Officer killed other ranks 1 killed 15 wounded 3 accidentally wounded. | hh |

Army Form C. 2118.

# WAR DIARY
## or
## INTELLIGENCE SUMMARY.
(Erase heading not required.)

| Place | Date 1915 | Hour | Summary of Events and Information | Remarks and references to Appendices |
|---|---|---|---|---|
| | Nov. 22 | | The following working parties were formed permanently while in the trenches working under the R.E. {working under Tunnelling Coy. R.E.} {working billets or Ration Pleury.}  1 Officer  1 N.C.O  50 other ranks  25 other ranks  19 other ranks.  Total 2 officers 95 other ranks.  This reduced the strength of the Battalion in the trenches to 16 Officers + 60 other Ranks. Among the Officers there was one Captain & Companies were commanded as under:— A. 2nd Lt. R.H. ROBERTSON  B. Capt. G.A. RUSK  C. Lt. W. STOR[BY] WILSON  D. 2nd Lt. J. SMALL  (N.B. Capt. A.D. CARMICHAEL on leave.) | Uhl |

# WAR DIARY
## or
## INTELLIGENCE SUMMARY.

Army Form C. 2118.

| Place | Date 1915 | Hour | Summary of Events and Information | Remarks and references to Appendices |
|---|---|---|---|---|
| NOYELLES | Nov. 23 | | Went to Battalion to have a day & rest - cleaning up equipment & rifles, but - found the surroundings & the billets so intolerably filthy, that a Battalion fatigue was necessary. A fatigue party of 3 Officers & 150 other ranks was found at night for work on STAFFORD LANE. also 1 Officer & 50 other ranks for work by day under R.E. Fine day. — 2Lt. A.M. DRUMMOND joined from 11th Bn. Black Watch. | |
| NOYELLES to VAUDRICOURT | 24 | | 44th Brigade relieved by 46th Brigade — 44th moved into Divisional Reserve. Battalion left NOYELLES at 8.0 a.m. moved into billets at VAUDRICOURT, marching via SAILLY LABOURSE & arriving about 10.15 a.m. Nothing new to billets from the 7th K.O.S.B. 2 men were sent to a Trench Mortar Course " 1 " " " " Machine gun " " 1 " " " " " " Fine day. | |
| VAUDRICOURT | 25 | | Cleaning up equipment, clothing & rifles. LIEUT. W.B. BINNIE joined from 11th Bn. Black Watch | WM |

| Place | Date | Hour | Summary of Events and Information | Remarks and references to Appendices |
|---|---|---|---|---|
| VAUDRICOURT | 1915 Nov 26 | | The whole Battalion went into NOEUX-LES-MINES & had a bath at the divisional bath house. Working party 2 officers & 100 other ranks found for work under the Pioneer Battalion 9th Gordon Highlanders. They were taken to PHILOSOPHE in buses & on the return journey the buses dropped them at NOEUX-LES-MINES so that they could have a bath. They were working in GORDON ALLEY in the open soon after they had finished a large shell landed close to where they had been working. General WILKINSON commdg. 44th Renegade paid the Battalion billets a short visit. | |
| — do — | 27 | | The weather after three showers were mixed with brilliant sunshine. The O.C. 9th Black Watch inspected all men of the Battalion — on the whole they were very clean, though the equipment, clothing showed signs of the work in the trenches. General indulgency of his inactive. The transport horses were particularly good, considering the difficulties of life continually in the open. Weather colder & frost set in. | WM |

# WAR DIARY
## or
## INTELLIGENCE SUMMARY.
(Erase heading not required.)

Army Form C. 2118.

| Place | Date 1915 | Hour | Summary of Events and Information | Remarks and references to Appendices |
|---|---|---|---|---|
| VAUDRICOURT | Nov. 26 | | Hard frost many colds. - 2 Lt. O.L. BEARN went to hospital with a dislocated knee. Church Service under Company arrangements - transmitted to the Rev. CRAWFORD C.F. gave real company about ½ hour service. 4 Officers & 40 other ranks were sent for instruction under the R.E. in tunnelling. I walked mine entanglements. | CRAWFORD C.F. |
| - do - | 29 | | Weather changed - train set in & snow all day. Waterproof covers for Balmoral bonnets were issued. 2nd Lt. E.N.L. RAYMOND joined the Battalion was posted to "D" Coy. Two officers from the Cavalry were attached to the Battalion. 2 Lt. A.T. POWLETT Royal House Guards & Lt. G.P.R. ALLSOPP 3rd Dragoon Guards. A draft of 22 other ranks joined the Battalion, all except one previously served with the Battalion. | |
| - do - | 30 | | 2 Lt. L. MURRAY STEWART & Lt. R. CARSWELL were admitted to hospital with chilled feet. 1 Officer & 6 other ranks were sent for instruction to the Brigade Bombing School. | |

# WAR DIARY
## or
## INTELLIGENCE SUMMARY.
(Erase heading not required.)

Army Form C. 2118.

Instructions regarding War Diaries and Intelligence Summaries are contained in F. S. Regs., Part II. and the Staff Manual respectively. Title pages will be prepared in manuscript.

| Place | Date 1915 | Hour | Summary of Events and Information | Remarks and references to Appendices |
|---|---|---|---|---|
| | Nov. | | | |
| VAUDRICOURT | 30 | | A billeting party was sent to take over the billets of the 6th Cameron Highlanders at NOYELLES. Preparatory to moving to the Battalion moving tomorrow. The strength of the Battalion was – 31 Officers, 139 N.C.O's, 2 Pipers, 674 Privates. 846 (total) | |
| | | | During the month 100 men evacuated sick & 9 returned. Casualties during the month – Officers killed 1, 2nd Lt. M. MACKENZIE – died of wounds 1, Lieut. J.D.C. MILLER. Other ranks – Killed 8, Wounded 23, Accidentally wounded 10. | |
| | | | W.M. Machrque Major Commander 9th Black Watch | |

9th Bl: Watch
Vol: 6

121/7935

9th Black Watch

December 1915.

**Army Form C. 2118.**

# WAR DIARY
## or
## INTELLIGENCE SUMMARY.
*(Erase heading not required.)*

Instructions regarding War Diaries and Intelligence Summaries are contained in F. S. Regs., Part II. and the Staff Manual respectively. Title pages will be prepared in manuscript.

| Place | Date | Hour | Summary of Events and Information | Remarks and references to Appendices |
|---|---|---|---|---|
| VAUDRICOURT to NOYELLES | 1915 Dec 1 | | The 44th Brigade relieves the 45th Brigade. The Battalion left VAUDRICOURT at 9.0 a.m. marched to billets at NOYELLES where they were in Brigade Reserve to the 44th Brigade. The march took a long time — the roads were full of traffic — a few shells came near the road during the march, but no damage was done. Two officers 1/4th Black Watch were attached to the Battalion hist. W.S. ROBERTSON attached to "D" Co., 2 Mr. E.C. OSBORNE — "A" - Heavy rain early, which cleared off into a lovely day, so that the men did not suffer during the march. The Battalion again has to find a permanent working of 1 officer 25 men, working under the R.E. Three guards of 1 N.C.O & 3 men each are found by the Battalion, while in Brigade Reserve — these guards are on keeps close to NOYELLES. Germans shelled mine about ½ mile W. of NOYELLES. | |

Army Form C. 2118.

# WAR DIARY
## or
## INTELLIGENCE SUMMARY.
(Erase heading not required.)

Instructions regarding War Diaries and Intelligence Summaries are contained in F. S. Regs., Part II. and the Staff Manual respectively. Title pages will be prepared in manuscript.

| Place | Date | Hour | Summary of Events and Information | Remarks and references to Appendices |
|---|---|---|---|---|
| NOYELLES | 1915 Dec 2 | | Another guard 1 N.C.O. 3 men found on 44th Brigade Headquarters. | |
| | 3 | | A working party of 1 Officer 200 men for work after dark under the R.E. | |

**Army Form C. 2118.**

# WAR DIARY
## or
## INTELLIGENCE SUMMARY.
*(Erase heading not required.)*

Instructions regarding War Diaries and Intelligence Summaries are contained in F. S. Regs., Part II. and the Staff Manual respectively. Title pages will be prepared in manuscript.

| Place | Date | Hour | Summary of Events and Information | Remarks and references to Appendices |
|---|---|---|---|---|
| NOVIELLES to TRENCHES | 1915 Dec 4 | | Relieved 10th Gordon Highlanders in the trenches. Thing was the line from G & 5 & 14 to G.11.b.99. There had been very heavy rain early in the evening, the men got soaked to the skin on the way to the trenches. The leading company left billets at 7 a.m. the relief was reported complete at 11.45 a.m. The trenches were very muddy, & would being in their filthy state which makes every step an effort. ST. ELIE AVENUE was 2 feet deep in water — it has been pumped out continually, but the water runs in again. The day was quiet till the evening when at 9 pm & 9.45 pm the Germans opened on matters of artillery fire in this - frightfulness - but so far as we were concerned no damage was done and our guns replied with great vigor - instant & sensible delay. | |

1577 Wt.W10791/1773 500,000 1/15 D. D. & L. A.D.S.S./Forms/C. 2118.

**WAR DIARY**
or
**INTELLIGENCE SUMMARY.**
(Erase heading not required.)

Army Form C. 2118.

| Place | Date | Hour | Summary of Events and Information | Remarks and references to Appendices |
|---|---|---|---|---|
| TRENCHES | 1915 Dec 5 | | A day of great artillery activity. It has been decided that enemy workings in THE QUARRIES must be knocked about; and to this effect our men to be withdrawn from the HAIRPIN, as it was so close to the QUARRIES. The operation was apparently a great success — the HAIRPIN was evacuated & reoccupied, his meantime the QUARRIES were heavily bombarded by the field guns (18 pr.) of the 15th Division, the 70th, 71st, 72nd, 73rd Brigades R.F.A., the 2nd Siege Battery R.G.A. 6". Two batteries 4.7" 1 Battery 8". The following report of the bombardment of the QUARRIES was sent to the 44th Brigade. The general idea was that the HAIRPIN should be evacuated during the bombardment not more momentous than it came to an end. The withdrawal of the infantry commenced at 7.45 p.m. the ESSEX (Lionel) & N.E. Sap being first evacuated — the field guns started firing at 1.50 p.m. to cover the withdrawal. The infantry were then off the HAIRPIN at 8 p.m. when the bombardment commenced. To accommodate the men evacuating the HAIRPIN the 1st/4th Black Watch (2 Platoons) went into dug-outs in the line hitherto having 7/time line was reoccupied by | |

# WAR DIARY
## or
## INTELLIGENCE SUMMARY.

Army Form C. 2118.

| Place | Date | Hour | Summary of Events and Information | Remarks and references to Appendices |
|---|---|---|---|---|
| | 1915 Aug 5 | | 2 platoons from the HAIRPIN. 2 platoons of "A" Coy. holding the lines of the HAIRPIN leading to the support line running N.W. from ST ELIE AVENUE. This place was taken by two storming platoons from the HAIRPIN. Bombing parties were ready at the end of each leg of the HAIRPIN to advance to recently taken german positions. These bombers advanced at 2.20 p.m. followed by the rest of the Company. These operations were carried out perfectly successfully the HAIRPIN was occupied without a trouble at all. The bombardment seems to have been very successful. Much damage was done to the QUARRIES - some timber was blown into the air as a german was seen to be blown over the parapet. No damage was done to our trenches in the HAIRPIN at all. Enemy retaliation was directed at our Support trenches, but there was no direct hit, the shells going over. The OLD GERMAN LINE and O.B.1 & GOEBEN ALLEY were shelled. | |

| Place | Date | Hour | Summary of Events and Information | Remarks and references to Appendices |
|---|---|---|---|---|
| Trenches | 1915 Dec 5 | | 40 shells were fired by the Germans at O.B.B. 4 & 5 but these were no direct hits all fell between the trenches in his front. (as the soldiers call it) Our casualties were 2 men very slightly wounded, by they think, by some bullet, before the bombardment began & as he Company were entrenching from the HAIRPIN. The German artillery though very active today has failed to touch either own men or own trenches. During the bombardment one of our prisoners was broken by a German sniper. — Reports — It is only hoped that our artillery did more damage than the Germans. The two Cavalry officers attached went back to join their regiments. 2nd Lt. G.B. BROWNE joined from the 3rd Batt. Black Watch. | |

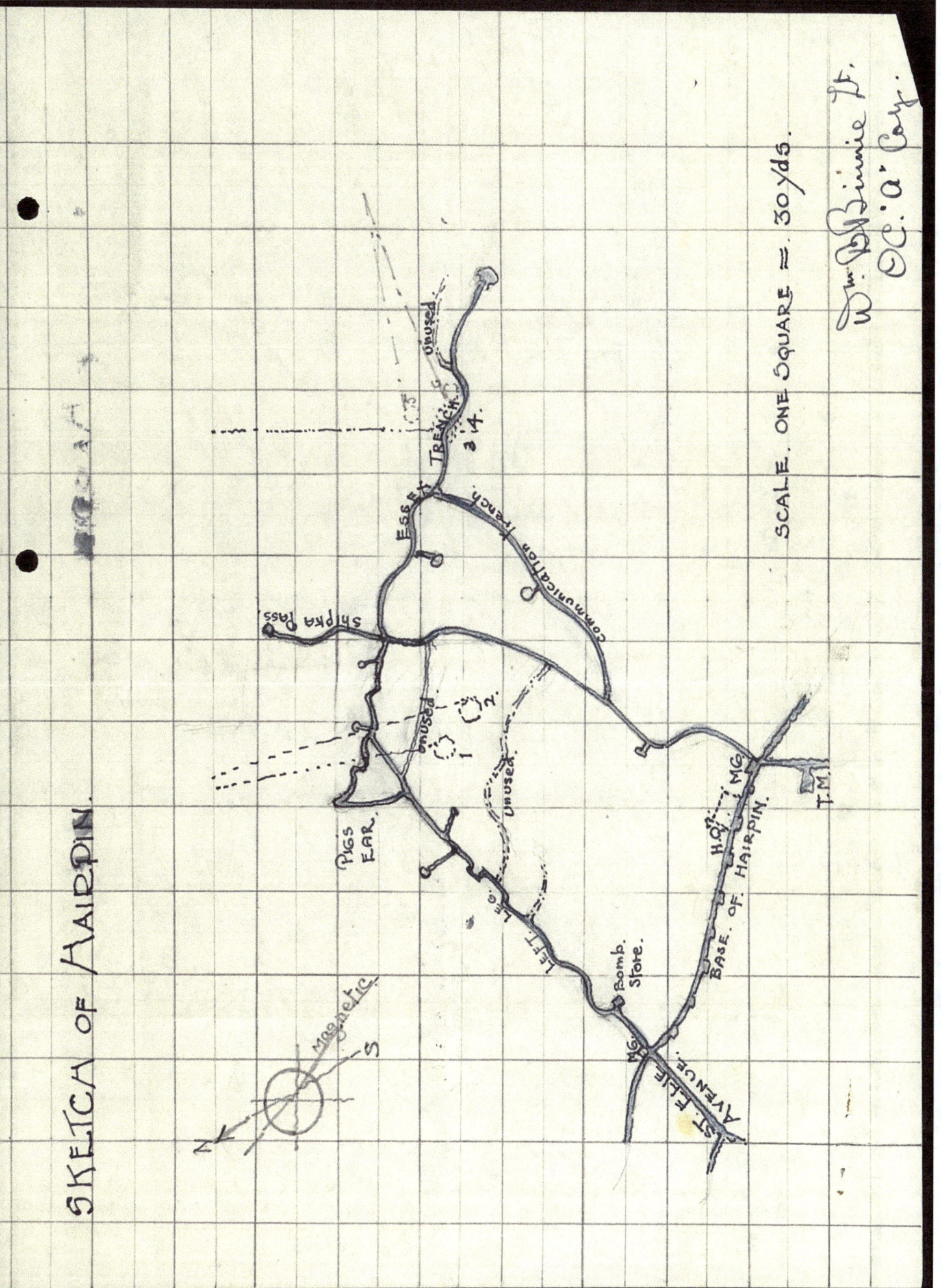

# WAR DIARY
## or
## INTELLIGENCE SUMMARY.
(Erase heading not required.)

Army Form C. 2118.

Tracing from Aeroplane photograph showing Trenches occupied by 9th BLACK WATCH and disposition of Companies "D" Coy. in Reserve 4th to 7th Dec. 1915

NORTH

GERMAN TRENCHES

QUARRIES
GERMAN LINES

SHIPKA PASS
PIG'S TAIL
ESSEX
"C" Coy
HAIRPIN
1 Plat "B" Coy
2 Plats "C" Coy
2 Plats "A" Coy
1 Plat 2 Plats "A" Coy
1/4 Black W.
GOEBEN ALLEY
ELIE AV.
ST.
OLD GERMAN LINE
FOSSE WAY
STAFFORD LANE
HULLUCH ALLEY
QUENNIS LANE
STANSFELD ROAD

# WAR DIARY
## or
## INTELLIGENCE SUMMARY.
*(Erase heading not required.)*

Army Form C. 2118.

| Place | Date | Hour | Summary of Events and Information | Remarks and references to Appendices |
|---|---|---|---|---|
| TRENCHES | 1915 Dec. 6 | | A quiet night - though enemy in spite of bombardment were had working in the QUARRIES. It was reported that enemy were trying to mine the ESSEX T. trench between further investigation it does not seem probable. Our Artillery had a "frightfulness" which lasted ½ an hour from 2.15pm to 2.45pm on the German trenches on either side of the QUARRIES, but there was little retaliation. Two other Cavalry officers were attached for instructional purposes - Captain T.S. KINGHAM and 2nd Lt M.H. DULSON both of 3rd Dragoon Guards. All available pumps were started working on ST. ELIE AVENUE in the hopes of having clear if not dry trench for the relief tomorrow. A german sniper was observed to leave the German line during our artillery frightfulness. At 5.30 pm. Some new crumps were coming from the direction of Headquarters dug out shouting "You coming everyone turned out, but on inquiry from the firing line it was found that it was a joke, started some think by a working party. Enemy are reported to be running under the SHIPKA SAP von officers. | |

Army Form C. 2118.

# WAR DIARY
## or
## INTELLIGENCE SUMMARY.
(Erase heading not required.)

| Place | Date | Hour | Summary of Events and Information | Remarks and references to Appendices |
|---|---|---|---|---|
| TRENCHES | 1915 Dec. 6 | | 9 to 170th Tunnelling Coy. is continually listening. The 70th Brigade R.F.A. did some pretty shooting this afternoon. The shells passing over the HAIRPIN thundering not 10 yards away to the German lines — but this is too close to be safe I think. Very careful observation. General Wilkinson visited the trenches today. Many other staff officers were about — but no one that has not actually lived in the trenches realises the difficulties that have to be contended with. Heavy rain fills up the trenches with mud & water. The sides begin to fall in with hard work you clear up things dug, & then no sooner have you got a little ship shape, than more rain comes. | |
| — do — | 7 | 9.30 to 10 pm. | There was a machine gun fusillyphers — 8 guns firing 1000 rounds each. Casualties — 1 man killed, 3 wounded, not badly. Were relieved by 4 to 10th Gordon this afternoon in the morning. The relieving battalion started into the trenches at 8.0 a.m. The relief was reported complete by 11.0 a.m. The weather was fine early, but heavy rain in the afternoon & evening. | |

# WAR DIARY
## or
## INTELLIGENCE SUMMARY.
*(Erase heading not required.)*

Army Form C. 2118.

| Place | Date | Hour | Summary of Events and Information | Remarks and references to Appendices |
|---|---|---|---|---|
| | 7 | | The Battalion is now in Local Reserve – distributed as follows – 3 companies in billets in PHILOSOPHE, 1 company in Reserve trenches, Battalion H'Qrs. in a large dug-out, half way between the two. Casualties. 1 man died of wounds, 1 man slightly wounded. 3 large shells landed close to Batt. H'Q., soon afterwards was occupied the billets in PHILOSOPHE were shelled, but no damage was done. Working parties were found by the Battalion as follows – 2 Officers & 100 men working under R.E. (permanent with 73rd C. R.E.) 1 " 50 " " " (permanent-while in Local Reserve.) 1 " 24 " water party & permanent. 1 " 25 " with 170th Tunnelling Coy. (permanent-) 1 N.C.O. 29 " working on trench railway (permanent-) Two parties of 25 men each for keeping communication trenches in repair. | |

**Army Form C. 2118.**

# WAR DIARY
## or
## INTELLIGENCE SUMMARY.
*(Erase heading not required.)*

Instructions regarding War Diaries and Intelligence Summaries are contained in F. S. Regs., Part II. and the Staff Manual respectively. Title pages will be prepared in manuscript.

| Place | Date | Hour | Summary of Events and Information | Remarks and references to Appendices |
|---|---|---|---|---|
| | 1915 Dec | | | |
| | 8 | | Working party 2 officers 100 men have found for work under the R.E. in boarding trenches. | |
| | 9 | | Working party 2 officers 100 men for work under R.E. | |
| | 10 | | Working party 2 officers 100 men for work under R.E. The Battalion being in local Reserve. The above working parties went in addition to the permanent working parties found by the Battalion – has been very hard on the men, who never really get a chance to get their feet dry. No working if the Headquarter day but nearly fell in the damage trenches to be serious – but the orderly Room staff knotted it up, & worked on it until a working party of the 9 - Gordons the arrived. | |

**Army Form C. 2118.**

# WAR DIARY
## or
## INTELLIGENCE SUMMARY.
*(Erase heading not required.)*

| Place | Date | Hour | Summary of Events and Information | Remarks and references to Appendices |
|---|---|---|---|---|
| TRENCHES | 1915 Dec. 11 | | The Battalion went into the trenches, in the same place as before, relieving the 10th Gordon Highlanders. Heavy rain on the return, but - trenches luckily were full of water - ST. ELIE AVENUE 2 feet deep in places. The relief was effected very well, starting at 8 a.m. being completed by 11.45 p.m. The day was spent, with the usual amount of artillery firing on both sides. At night the enemy got a trench mortar battery going against the HAIRPIN & fired over 14 bombs at intervals — two of them landed in the ESSEX TRENCH & completely destroyed it — cutting off the end of this sap from all communication, but luckily it was a very dark night - this damage was mostly repaired in the evening — the bombs caused no casualties — as the ESSEX TRENCH is only lightly held by bombers. Enemy snipers active as usual. Casualties 1 left wounded by two bullets one in head one in arm. 2 Lt. T.H. BELL joined from 3rd Black Watch, bringing a draft of 40 men from the 11th Black Watch. | |

# WAR DIARY or INTELLIGENCE SUMMARY

Army Form C. 2118.

| Place | Date | Hour | Summary of Events and Information | Remarks and references to Appendices |
|---|---|---|---|---|
| TRENCHES | 1915 Dec 12 | | The weather still continued fine throughout. Clearing up & repairing damage went on. A redoubt (Artillery "STRAFE" on the DUMP, drew further no retaliation, on the line held by the Batt. In the afternoon the Germans started shelling our Reserve line, but improvements in retaliation by our own Artillery soon silenced them. At 4.35pm. the trench mortars broke out again at the ESSEX trench and although they caused no casualties they did great material damage completely wrecking the bannocade at the end of it. This necessitated a new bannocade of sandbags being made & this was finished by daylight. In retaliation our guns fired 20 rounds shrapnel at the German support trenches. The usual work went on of clearing up throughout and the trenches, breastwork & dug outs. | the Batt. |
| - do - | 13 | | Nothing very special happened – there was the usual artillery duel – in the evening the Germans had another attempt to destroy the ESSEX trench with a trench mortar bomb, but it fell short – its a trench-dropper into their own self loads. Weather mild. | |

# WAR DIARY
## or
## INTELLIGENCE SUMMARY.
(Erase heading not required.)

Army Form C. 2118.

| Place | Date 1915 Dec | Hour | Summary of Events and Information | Remarks and references to Appendices |
|---|---|---|---|---|
| TRENCHES to LOZINGHEM | 14 | | Battalion was relieved by the 18th City of London Regiment, 47th Division and moved into billets at LOZINGHEM — having trains from NOEUX-LES-MINES to LILLERS. | |
| | | | The relief took place in the morning, the Battalion arrived at PHILOSOPHE where the men had a meal, which was prepared in canteen, borrowed from the 11th Bn. Argyll & Sutherland Highlanders and had to & run were very acceptable. The Battalion then marched to NOEUX-LES-MINES where they entrained at 5 p.m. & arrived at LILLERS about 6 p.m. & marched 4 miles to billets at LOZINGHEM. By having motor lorries sent to help men who were foot — no stragglers were left behind. Weather fine. | |
| LOZINGHEM | 15 | | Battalion rested routing much happened — Lt. ROBERTSON went to an officers training course. | |
| — do — | 16 | | A working party 1 Officer 50 men found for work under 91st Coy. R.E. | |
| — do — | 17 | | Battalion resting & cleaning up. — 2Lt. DRUMMOND & 4 men to a Machine gun course | |
| — do — | 17 | | 2Lt. MORRISON, 1 N.C.O. & 3 men to a Supplying course. 3 men to a Brigade Signalling course | |

**Army Form C. 2118.**

# WAR DIARY
## or
## INTELLIGENCE SUMMARY.
*(Erase heading not required.)*

Instructions regarding War Diaries and Intelligence Summaries are contained in F. S. Regs., Part II. and the Staff Manual respectively. Title pages will be prepared in manuscript.

| Place | Date | Hour | Summary of Events and Information | Remarks and references to Appendices |
|---|---|---|---|---|
| | 1915 Dec | | | |
| LOZINGHEM | 18 | | A draft of 13 men arrived — all except one being men returning from Hospital in France. A scheme of training commenced today, which was to continue while the Battalion was resting — the time is to be divided as under. 18ᵗʰ to 22ⁿᵈ December Platoon Training 23/12/15 to 5/1/16 Company 6/12/15 to 12/1/16 Battalion  The training was very necessary as so many men in the Battalion have very short service training in trenches building, extended order drill, bayonet fighting &c. Hours were 8.45 am to 12.30 pm. Lectures in the evening — the afternoons were to be devoted to football. The Machine Gunners were also to be specially trained & the R.E. men to give demonstrations in mine enlargements, revetting &c. A working party of 1 Officer & 150 men was found for work on the Bombing School. | |

Army Form C. 2118.

# WAR DIARY
## or
## INTELLIGENCE SUMMARY.
(Erase heading not required.)

Instructions regarding War Diaries and Intelligence Summaries are contained in F. S. Regs., Part II. and the Staff Manual respectively. Title pages will be prepared in manuscript.

| Place | Date | Hour | Summary of Events and Information | Remarks and references to Appendices |
|---|---|---|---|---|
| | 1915 Nov | | | |
| LOZINGHEN | 19 | | A working party of 1 Officer & 50 men was found for work on the bowling ground. Church parade — Presbyterians — voluntarily in the School House. 10.30 – 11.30 am. Church of England in the School House 10 am. Roman Catholics in the Church at 9.0 am. | |
| – do – | 20 | | A working party of 1 Officer & 50 men was found for work on the bowling ground. 2/Lt. BELL & other ranks went to a Bombing course. | |
| – do – | 21 | | A working party of 1 Officer & 50 men was found for work on the bowling ground. 1 N.C.O & 4 men were attached to 170th Tunnelling Coy. 2/Lt. J.B. ROBERTSON & 2 men went to a Trench mortar course. 2/Lt. J. SMALL went to Divisional Officers Training School. | |
| – do – | 22 | | 1 Officer & 50 men working party on bowling ground. A Company football league was started — B Coy beat A Coy. 2 – 0. | |
| | 21 | | A very successful concert was held by A Coy. – items were contributed by 8 – Scotsmen, 7 – Cameron | |

# WAR DIARY
## or
## INTELLIGENCE SUMMARY.

Army Form C. 2118.

| Place | Date | Hour | Summary of Events and Information | Remarks and references to Appendices |
|---|---|---|---|---|
| LOZINGHEM | 1915 Dec 23 | | Company training commenced today. 1/2 Officers & N.C.O's were sent for instruction by 74th Field Coy. R.E. in simple engineering work, to help them in keeping trenches in repair; resulting proving A 30 yards rifle range was also at the disposal of the Battalion, on which the snipers of the per. Company have received. A company concert was organised by "B" Company. | |
| - do - | 24 | | 1/2 Officers & N.C.O's were sent for instruction by 74th Coy. R.E. | |
| - do - | 25 | | Xmas Day - was observed as a holiday - the officers dined together at night. Church Parades - Services 7.0 am 10.0 am Church of England 7.30 am 8.15 am 10.0 am Roman Catholic | |
| - do - | 26 | | Sunday - Church parades - Presbyterian (voluntary) 10.15 am 11.30 am. Church of England 7.30 am. Roman Catholic 9.0 am. | 1. Off. & 1 D.R. went to a machine gun course |
| - do - | 27 | | Xmas messages received from H.M. the King. Instruction to 1/2 Officers & N.C.O's by 74th Coy. R.E. 2 men went to a recruit musketry course. — Baths at MARLES-LES-MINES have allotted to the Battalion. | |

# WAR DIARY
## or
## INTELLIGENCE SUMMARY.
(Erase heading not required.)

Army Form C. 2118.

| Place | Date | Hour | Summary of Events and Information | Remarks and references to Appendices |
|---|---|---|---|---|
| | 1915 Dec | | | |
| LOZINGHEM | 28 | | 4 Officers & NCO's went for instruction by 74th Coy. R.E. — whales at MARLES-LES-MINES were allotted to the Battalion. A draft of 46 other ranks arrived. | |
| — do — | 29 | | The following Xmas presents were received by the Battalion from Colonel Lloyd £12.10.0 to divide his health on New Years Day. ,, ,, Mrs Lloyd — 252 lbs. Plum pudding, 84 Rums, 8 boxes Nuts, 19 tins Shortbread, 150 pipes, 80 lbs tobacco, 8000 cigarettes — also hire lotto, shirts, socks, scarves, helmets, body belts. ,, ,, Mr. Rusk — 8 cases apples 8 cases oranges. ,, ,, Daily News Army Pudding Fund — ½ lb. per man. | |
| — do — | 30 | | A 30 yards Rifle range was allotted to the Battalion. The officers dined together at night to see the New Year in — but did not whole the Battalion slept in it. | |
| — do — | 31 | | A Company football league had been played during the last fortnight — the winners was B & D Companies tied & a dividing match has to be played — the ground is a very good one. | |

**Army Form C. 2118.**

# WAR DIARY
## or
## INTELLIGENCE SUMMARY.
*(Erase heading not required.)*

| Place | Date 1915 | Hour | Summary of Events and Information | Remarks and references to Appendices |
|---|---|---|---|---|
| LOZINGHEM | Dec 31 | | The Battalion strength was 28 Officers, 944 other ranks. Casualties during the month: 2 men killed, 6 wounded. Numbers evacuated sick to Hospital 17. Returned from " 8. 8 Officers & 34 men were sent on leave to England during the month. | |

WCohryson Lt. Colonel.
Comdg. 9th Black Watch

31/12/15

B 6.

9th Black Watch
Vol: 7
Jan? 16

15

Army Form C. 2118.

# WAR DIARY
## or
## INTELLIGENCE SUMMARY.
(Erase heading not required.)

Instructions regarding War Diaries and Intelligence Summaries are contained in F. S. Regs., Part II. and the Staff Manual respectively. Title pages will be prepared in manuscript.

| Place | Date 1916 | Hour | Summary of Events and Information | Remarks and references to Appendices |
|---|---|---|---|---|
| LOZINGHEM | Jan. 1 | | New Year's Day was observed as a holiday. R.C. mass was held at 8.30 am. Involuntary service 7.0 am. Football B Coy. v. A.S.C. his A.S.C. running 3.0. Some of the companies had dinners to which the C.O. paid a visit. General WILKINSON comdg. 44 Renegade visited his Battalion wished them a Happy New Year. Colonel Wanwell who formerly commanded the Battalion visited and from home, wishing them a Happy New Year. | x |
| - do - | 2 | | 2/Lt WALDIE rtn Arnmanes Sergeant went to a Machine Gun course Sunday. Church parades - Quietly levees 9.15 am. 4-11.30 am. Church of England 10 am. Roman Catholic 10.0 am in parish church. | |
| - do - | 3 | | A very wet & rainy day. Nothing to record | |
| - do - | 4 | | - do - | |
| - do - | 5 | | 1 Corporal & 3 men went to a Signalling school. 1 Offr. & 16 other ranks went to a Bombing course 2 " " " " Trench Mortar course | |

**Army Form C. 2118.**

# WAR DIARY
## or
## INTELLIGENCE SUMMARY.
*(Erase heading not required.)*

| Place | Date 1916 | Hour | Summary of Events and Information | Remarks and references to Appendices |
|---|---|---|---|---|
| LOZINGHEM | Jan. 5 | | The following is an extract from the London Gazette dated 1/1/16. Mention in despatches. Major (Temp. Lt. Col.) T. D. Lloyd Captain (Temp. Major) J. Stewart Temp. Captain C. S. Tuke " " lieut. E. R. Wilson Captain F. A. Brown R.A.M.C. S/6323 Sgt. J. Henderson S/7977 Pte. G. Book S/4295 L/Cpl. A. Brown S/4294 L/Cpl. R. Dallie | |
| | 16 | | Divisional Exercise began today, & the whole Division was on the move. The Battalion paraded at 9.0 a.m. marched into billets at LIGNY-LEZ-AIRE about 10 miles W. of LOZINGHEM, when they arrived about 2.45 p.m. & baggage & rations soon followed. The Battalion found a man guard of one company. At 10.30 p.m. orders were received that the Battalion was | |

# WAR DIARY
## or
## INTELLIGENCE SUMMARY.
(Erase heading not required.)

Army Form C. 2118.

| Place | Date 1915 | Hour | Summary of Events and Information | Remarks and references to Appendices |
|---|---|---|---|---|
| LOZINGHEM to LIGNY | Jan 5 | | Formed part of the Advanced Guard, composed as under:— 1/4 Platoon Cyclists, 4 sections 74th Field Coy. R.E., B. Battery 70th Punjabis R.F.A. & 9th Bhopal Watch under command of Lt-Col. W.W. MACGREGOR. | |
| LIGNY | 6 | | The Battalion paraded at 7.0 am. and marched to COYECQUES about 8 miles when orders were received that the Advanced Guard was to take up a covering position holding the main body. This was completed about 1 pm. when orders were received to retire on the previous night's billets. The Battalion to find a small rear guard. The retirement commenced about 3 pm. after a billets were reached about 5.30 pm. The men were very tired having marched about 22 miles they having continually on the move for 10 hours. | |
| LIGNY to LOZINGHEM | 7 | | The Division returned to their original billets. The Battalion formed part of the main body & paraded at 9.15 am. arrived at LOZINGHEM at 1 pm. A draft of 59 arrived. | |
| LOZINGHEM | 8 | | Posted to the bn at MARLES-LES-MINES have been disposed 2 men went to 2 Trench Mortar Course — 1 Off & 5 men to M.G. Course. | |

**Army Form C. 2118.**

# WAR DIARY
## or
## INTELLIGENCE SUMMARY.
*(Erase heading not required.)*

Instructions regarding War Diaries and Intelligence Summaries are contained in F. S. Regs., Part II. and the Staff Manual respectively. Title pages will be prepared in manuscript.

| Place | Date 1916 | Hour | Summary of Events and Information | Remarks and references to Appendices |
|---|---|---|---|---|
| LOZINGHEM | Jan 9 | 9.0 am | Sunday - Church parades held by the R.C.s. | |
| | | 11.30 am | A gas demonstration was held by the Roman Catholics & Church of England & Presbyterian Voluntary (Communion) | |
| | | | 1 Officer & 6 other ranks went to a Bombing class. The following orders were received from the Divisional Commander:- "The Divisional Commander desires me to inform you that he considers the work performed during the trench tour reflects credit on all concerned. The Division received and will & should have "trenches have met" important to efficiency. Incidents were however made which might have been avoided, and the Divisional Commander feels sure that Commanders will spare no effort to rectify faults. He wished to notice & so raise still higher the fighting value of the Division." | |
| - do - | 10 | | Major J. STEWART arrived from England. | |

Whitehyper Lt Colonel
9th Black Watch

# WAR DIARY or INTELLIGENCE SUMMARY.

Army Form C. 2118.

| Place | Date | Hour | Summary of Events and Information | Remarks and references to Appendices |
|---|---|---|---|---|
| LOZINGHEM | Jan. 11, 12, 13 | | Bn. at LOZINGHEM. Companies at disposal of O/C. Companies. " " " " | |
| -do.- | 14 | | Bn. left LOZINGHEM at 7A.M. and marched to BULLERS enroute it entrained for NOEUX LES MINES about 10A.M. After resting there till 4 P.M. The Bn. left for the trenches where it took up position as Reserve Bn. to 44th Bde. three Companies, A, B, and C. occupying the old German front line trenches from (Ref. French Ref. 36 C NW 3. 1/10,000.) 17 D 2.5. to 23 A 7.6. with one Company in the front-line trenches from H 19 A 2.5. to H 19 A 0.6. A Coy. also found guards for NORTHERN SAP REDOUBT, 65 METRE REDOUBT and LENS ROAD REDOUBT. (formerly known to us as "The Jews Nose") with Bn. H.Q. off PONT STREET at G 23 B 7.7. | |
| TRENCHES | 15th | | Nothing to report except slight shelling of front-line by enemy. Our artillery was not active. In the evening "D" Company was relieved by a Company of 10th Gordon Highrs and rejoined the Bn. in the Reserve Trenches in "TENTH AVENUE." | |
| -do.- | 16th | | Enemy shelled Reserve Trenches from 10A.M. to 11:30A.M. Our artillery replied. Bn. engaged on deepening and cleaning out trenches, lifting the boards and making a few old dug outs in TENTH AVENUE habitable. | |

# WAR DIARY
## or
## INTELLIGENCE SUMMARY.
*(Erase heading not required.)*

Army Form C. 2118.

| Place | Date | Hour | Summary of Events and Information | Remarks and references to Appendices |
|---|---|---|---|---|
| TRENCHES | Jan. 17" | | B" in Reserve Trenches. Work carried on in improving trenches and thoroughly cleaning out and deepening PONT STREET which was in a very bad condition. Enemy were very quiet during the day and night. The B". relieved 10" Gordon High". in the front line from H.19.C.8.2. & H.19.A.0.8. | |
| —do— | 18" | | Enemy Coy B". was distributed in the trenches as follows:— RIGHT Section from H.19.C.8.2. to H.19.C.5.8. was occupied by A Coy. LEFT Section from H.19.C.5.8. to VENDIN ALLEY, H.19.A.0.8. was occupied by B Coy. C Coy. was in Support in trenches in vicinity of H.19.C.23 and D Coy. was in Reserve in Reserve Trench running from G.24.D.2. to G.24.D.24. B". H.Q. was on GUN TRENCH? ALLEY at G.24.D.0.4. | |
| —do— | 18" | | Enemy snipers were rather active during the relief but were silenced by a few bursts of rapid fire. Early in the morning No. 9693 Pte Gibb of B. Coy. was shot by a sniper. A patrol we sent out to certain some fresh enemy saps in their line opposite our sector of the line. The enemy wire is very strong and our own is weak. Owing to the brightness of moonlight it will not be possible to do anything to it for a few days. Our support line trench, with the exception of a few bays near VENDIN ALLEY is nothing more or less than a fence and wherever first treated it should be newly dealt with. It consists of a perfectly straight and shallow trench about 3 feet deep and is enfiladed from the enemys position on HILL 70. | |

# WAR DIARY
## or
## INTELLIGENCE SUMMARY.
*(Erase heading not required.)*

Army Form C. 2118.

| Place | Date | Hour | Summary of Events and Information | Remarks and references to Appendices |
|---|---|---|---|---|
| TRENCHES | 19th | | Enemy shelled all of HUGO LANE, apparently ranging on this trench, this shelling came from the direction of WINGLES. Enemy were heard working on their wire and stakes in H19A during the night 17-18th. Latter were dispersed by our M.G. fire. They did not resume work. Our working parties were employed on constructing Support Trench, deepening POSEN ALLEY and C.Ts, wiring front of Support line and strengthening wire in front of ally which is very weak. Bright moonlight interfered with the work. | |
| —do— | 20th | | Enemy shelled our front trenches with 6"-Squeaks from 11 AM to 11:15 AM, at one minute intervals but did no damage. B.H.Q. at junction of GUN ALLEY and POSEN ALLEY, were shelled intermittently all day, one casualty, slightly wounded. On the whole the night 19-20th was quiet, very little enemy sniping. A strong enemy patrol was driven back by one of our patrols about H19C8.8. One of the enemy patrol was killed and is lying just outside their wire. We lost one severely wounded ~~sergeant~~ No.8228 Cpl. J. WELSH, A Coy. Our artillery shelled the front line enemy trenches intermittently throughout the day. Our working parties continued work on Support Trenches C.Ts, wiring and strengthening front wire. | |
| —do— | 21st | | Enemy were very quiet during night 20-21st. It is thought that a relief was carried out. Our R.E. and rapid fire shows in two small enemy patrols. Enemy shelled our lines more or less all day, as our own | |

# WAR DIARY or INTELLIGENCE SUMMARY

Army Form C. 2118.

| Place | Date | Hour | Summary of Events and Information | Remarks and references to Appendices |
|---|---|---|---|---|
| TRENCHES | Jan 21st contd | | guns replied occasionally. We had one casualty, No.11153 Pte J. Taylor, C Coy shot by a sniper and one wounded, No.7153 Pte W. McINTYRE wounded. Our work consisted of repairing front line parapet where it had been damaged by shell fire, continued work on support line, wiring same and strengthening front wire. About 5.15 P.M. on 20th the enemy sent up three white rockets simultaneously, followed by one red rocket. | |
| do | 22nd | | Enemy heavily shelled Reserve line trenches in RESERVE TRENCH and Bn. H.Q. in GUN ALLEY but no damage was done. During the evening of 21st, about 5 P.M. & 6 P.M. enemy tunnelling operations were heard at H.19.A.2½.5., the work is apparently stopped at night. Our snipers were very active during night of 21–22nd. Our work was continuation of previous night's work. | |
| do | 23rd | | Enemy M.G. and sniping fairly active during night 22-23rd. One of our patrols reported enemy working on new saps in H.19.C. It was noted that the enemy were in good spirits as the working parties were whistling and singing. The mining operations heard on the 22nd were continued, its galleries seem to be running under, and parallel to our front trench. | |
| do | 24th | | Enemy very quiet throughout the night. Our support and reserve trenches were fairly heavily shelled between 2.30 and 3.45 P.M. One of our snipers actually silenced an enemy M.G. opposite POSEN ALLEY. Our own artillery fired during the night but did no damage to enemy trenches | |

# WAR DIARY
## or
## INTELLIGENCE SUMMARY.
(Erase heading not required.)

Army Form C. 2118.

| Place | Date | Hour | Summary of Events and Information | Remarks and references to Appendices |
|---|---|---|---|---|
| TRENCHES | Jan 24th contd | | opposite as they all fell just about 5 yards in front of our own wire. A patrol under 2/Lt Howard investigates state of enemy front wire opposite our sector. It is apparently everything but has been cut in four places, each gap being about 10 ft. wide, evidently to allow free passage for patrols. (The hot wires have just been cut in these gaps.) Our fatigues were employed on the same work as previously, i.e. support trenches, wiring and repairing trenches. | |
| -do.- | 25th | | During the night 24-25th one of our snipers shot one of the enemy's snipers in H.19.A. Another man was shot at H.19.C.68. He had left the enemy's line to carry back the body of the man we shot on the night of 19th-20th. He was seen and killed just as he began to carry the body away. Our M.G.s were very active throughout the night on the enemy's wire and daps, from H.19.D.14 to H.19.C.9.8 (by Divisional orders) (bursts of Rapid Fire were also thought to bear on the enemy's line too). Activities of these succeeded in stopping enemy's work on his trenches and dugs. It had been arranged to send out a bombing expedition against this part of his line, but this had to be put off owing to Divisional orders being received to open M.G. fire. Enemy transport was very clearly heard opposite our sector about 1.30 A.M. It was moving from RIGHT to LEFT. Our work on support line, wiring, etc was continued. | |
| TRENCHES | 26th | | During the night of 25th H.Q. and Reserve Trench were heavily and consistently shelled but no | |

| Place | Date | Hour | Summary of Events and Information | Remarks and references to Appendices |
|---|---|---|---|---|
| TRENCHES | Jan 26th cont. | | damage was done. A Bombing expedition, organized by Capt. W. STOREY WILSON was carried out very successfully against the enemy's saps in H.19.C. It was exceedingly well arranged and was carried out as follows — thirdly it was dark the wire in front of our trenches was cut in two places and reconnoitring patrols consisting of three from the trenches who were to carry out the attack, went out and noted three saps in which the enemy were then working. About 10 P.M. three parties went out, one under 2nd Lt. BROWN, one under 2/Lt. R. W. Phipps and the third under 2/Lt Brown. A certain time was given them - half an hour - in which to reach the saps; At the end of that time one of our M. Guns opened fire on the enemy's front line trench and we threw out a "Very Light" whereupon the parties threw their bombs, 6 into each sap. 2nd Lt Brown's sap was occupied and his bombs must have done a considerable amount of damage; 2/Lt B.W. Phipps's party also got all their bombs into their sap but could not say whether it was occupied or not. The third party got hung up in wire and had to return without throwing their bombs. The enemy did not reply at all and all three parties returned without enterference; some time later two trench mortar bombs were thrown into our trenches but did no damage. As usual work on support and communicating trenches was continued. The enemy shelled Reserve | |

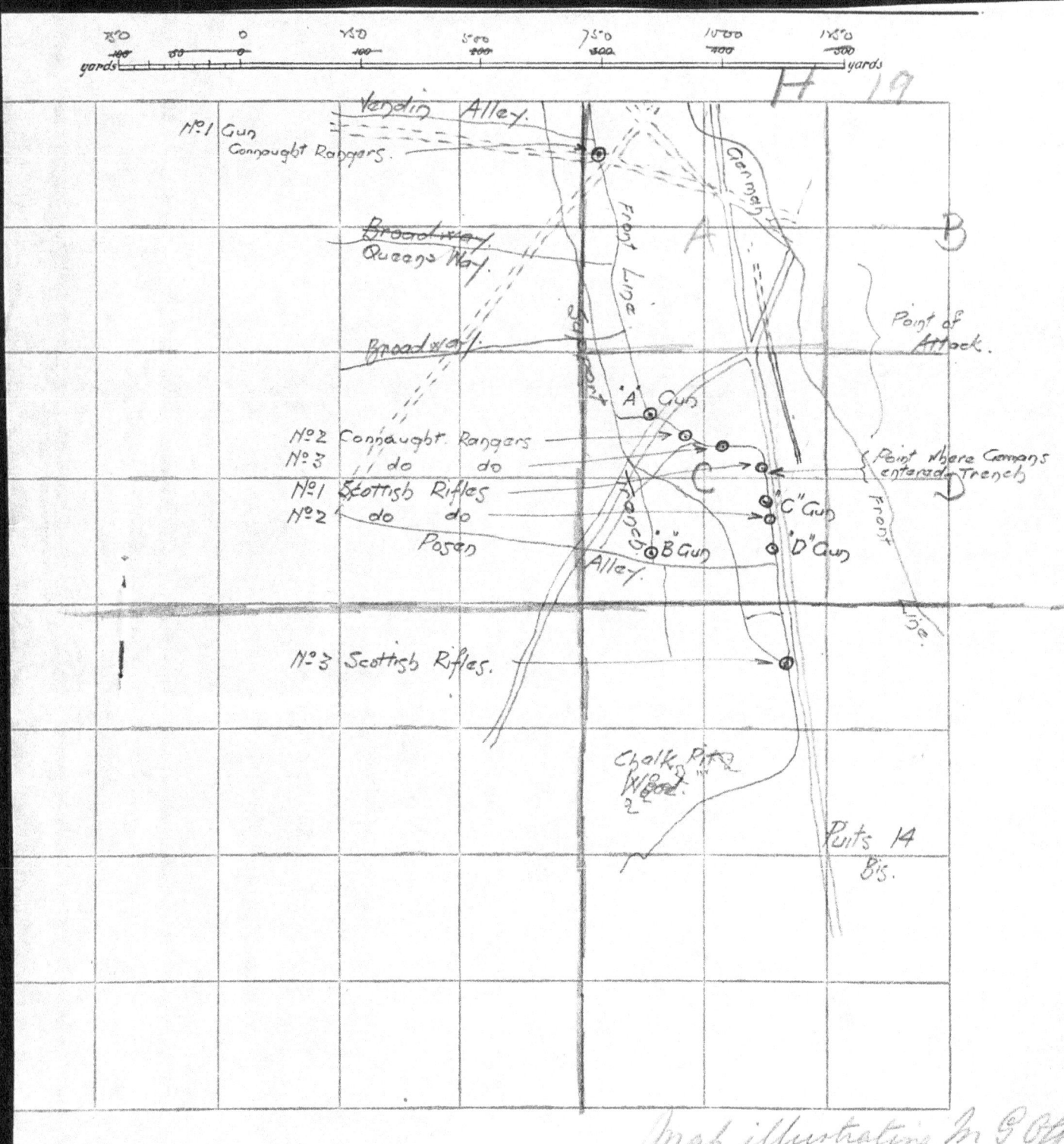

# WAR DIARY
## or
## INTELLIGENCE SUMMARY.

*(Erase heading not required.)*

Army Form C. 2118.

| Place | Date | Hour | Summary of Events and Information | Remarks and references to Appendices |
|---|---|---|---|---|
| TRENCHES | Jan 26th contd |  | trenches and B⁸. A pretty heavy strafe throughout the day, they were banging on its different areas. In the evening of 26th the B⁸. was relieved in its trenches by the 10th Scottish Rifles. A good deal of delay was caused by some of them, overburdened with packs etc. taking its way up and then blocking the trenches but the relief was eventually completed by 10 P.M. Very unfortunately the enemy shelled POSEN ALLEY at the junction of GUN TRENCH just as the last Platoon of the B⁸. — No 16. — was going out and we lost one man killed — No 9112 Pte H. JOHNSTON killed and two wounded. The whole of the B⁸. reached NOEUX LES MINES by 4.30 A.M. where it went into billets. During the morning of 26th there seemed to be signs of the enemy attempting an attack so the C.O. regretted and obtained permission to retain the 4 M.G⁸ of the B⁸. in the trenches. They together with the M.G⁸ of the other 3 B⁸. were to have been relieved before the B⁸. went out. These guns were distributed along the front of the Company holding the RIGHT part of the B⁸. Sector, from H19 D.1 & 6. H.19 C.9.8. and as events proved it was very lucky that they were left in the line. As the B⁸. had had a hard night's work on account of the relief, nothing but the usual routine work was done. At 5.30 P.M. the C.O. attended a conference of | ? |
| NOEUX LES MINES |  |  |  |  |

# WAR DIARY or INTELLIGENCE SUMMARY

Army Form C. 2118.

| Place | Date | Hour | Summary of Events and Information | Remarks and references to Appendices |
|---|---|---|---|---|
| NOEUX LES MINES | 27th contd | | Commanding Officers at "D"44B" to "H.Q. during which, at about 6.10 P.M. a message was brought in to say that the 46 B" was being attacked heavily on H.19.C and D —just at the spot where the 4 B.W. Machine Guns had been left. The B" to "food %" and orders were issued for a move towards MAZINGARBE, but these were cancelled about 7.30 P.M. when another message came in to the effect that the enemy attack had been repulsed with severe enemy losses. | |
| -do- | 28th | | About 11 A.M. the following message was received by C.O. 9/B. re. wounded through H.Q. 44 B" from G.O.C. 46. I.B. to G.O.C. 44. I.B. "Black Watch Machine Guns" did splendid work during attack yesterday AAA. Had one gun knocked completely AAA. Remaining guns intact AAA had about half a dozen casualties AAA. Local numbers not yet obtained AAA. Have ordered them back into 10th Avenue and will return them to MAZINGARBE tonight AAA. Will you arrange for limbers at Victoria Station". The B" "Stood %" in billets all day as the enemy were reported to be attacking our front in the neighbourhood of the HOHENZOLLERN REDOUBT. About 9 P.M. we received orders that all was quiet and that the men could turn in. | |
| do. | 29th | | The G.O.C. 44 B" saw 2nd Lt. Howard, 2nd Lt. Brown and L/C. R. Artzie at 11 A.M. and | |

# WAR DIARY
## or
## INTELLIGENCE SUMMARY.

*(Erase heading not required.)*

Army Form C. 2118.

| Place | Date | Hour | Summary of Events and Information | Remarks and references to Appendices |
|---|---|---|---|---|
| NOEUX LES MINES | Jan. 29 | | expressed his approval of their work as regards recruiting and the booking expedition carried out during the last tour. Nothing to report regarding the work for the day. The G.O.C. saw the Machine Gun Section at 12 noon and expressed his approval of their work. The following is a copy of the report of 2nd Lieut. G.S. Waldie on what happened during the German attack on Jan. 27.<sup>th</sup>:- | |
| | | | "From 2<sup>nd</sup> Lt. G.S. Waldie, M.G.O. 9<sup>th</sup> B.W. To. The Officer Commanding 9<sup>th</sup> Black Watch (Roy<sup>l</sup> Regt.) 10,000 Sir, I have the honour to report as follows with reference to the German attack on our line about Front H.19.C. on 27<sup>th</sup> inst. When the Brigade Machine Guns were relieved on the night of 25<sup>th</sup>. I was ordered to take my guns into the Support line. This was done, and on a further order from my Commanding Officer I moved three guns into the firing line at 4 A.M. on the 26<sup>th</sup>. The fourth gun was left under O.C. Support Coy. The positions were as shown in enclosed map. | |
| -do- | | 3.0 P.M | The 9<sup>th</sup> Black Watch was relieved by the 10<sup>th</sup> Seaforth Rifles on the night of the 26<sup>th</sup>. The enemy had shelled our Supports and Reserves for three days to 2.30 P.M. on 24<sup>th</sup>, when they suddenly stopped. At 3.45 P.M. the shelling re-commenced on the front line. This bombardment was extremely intense and played havoc with our trenches. The trees were knocked from the road into the trenches and in many places the trenches themselves were levelled. | |

# WAR DIARY or INTELLIGENCE SUMMARY.

Army Form C. 2118.

| Place | Date | Hour | Summary of Events and Information | Remarks and references to Appendices |
|---|---|---|---|---|
| NOEUX LES MINES | Jan 30th | | At the commencement of the bombardment I went round my guns and found that "D" gun had been blown into the trench and buried. With the help of Sgt. Bayne this was dug out and taken to the next traverse. L/C. Thomson was slightly wounded in the head but rallied his men over and kept a thorough control of "C" gun's action. On going to the LEFT I found the trench from H.19.C.7.8. to H.19.C.3.8. had practically disappeared. "A" gun and all its equipment except some magazines had been blown up by a shell and was absolutely useless. Privates Cooper and Shannon rendered great assistance in digging out these magazines, which were carried to the Connaught Rangers No.2 gun. The men also attached themselves to this gun. As the N.C.O. of the Connaught Rangers was at this point I returned to the two guns that were left in the salient.<br>The artillery fire, accompanied by all sorts of Trench Mortars, Rifle Grenades, etc. continued till about 5 P.M. when the artillery lifted and fires, throwing up large quantities of smoke, were observed burning in front of our line. I ordered "Stand To" up and down the line, and shortly afterwards the enemy were observed advancing through the smoke on our LEFT. "C" Gun got them in enfilade and simply wiped them out. A few that were missed tried to run back, but I doubt if they got to their trenches. No 3 gun of the Rangers | |

# WAR DIARY
## or
## INTELLIGENCE SUMMARY.
(Erase heading not required.)

Army Form C. 2118.

| Place | Date | Hour | Summary of Events and Information | Remarks and references to Appendices |
|---|---|---|---|---|
| NOEUX LES MINES | Jan 30th | | saw a few crossing the road and emptied their one magazine into them; several went down, but by this time their line was broken and the largest had disappeared. In case of a ruse on the Germans part I continued for some time to search the ground over which the attack had been made. During the attack the artillery lifted somewhat, but the French Mortar, Grenade, etc continued over the front line. Rapid fire also came from the line opposite my two guns. By this time the 10th S.R. had opened rapid fire from about point H.19.C.8.3 to H.19.C.7.7. (The French from H.19.C.7.7 to H.19.C.3.9 was unoccupied except for the two Connaught Ranger guns) Our rifle fire was certainly very rapid but in my opinion the noise was the only effective part of it. After the attack the artillery fire wore off until about 6 P.M. when all was fairly quiet. All telephone wires were mended at the beginning of the bombardment and we could get no communication through. I saw two red lights go up from our supports, Although I was keeping a good look out I saw no one leaving the line enemy line SOUTH of the front shown on the sketch. The actual number of men seen leaving the enemy trenches was perhaps that of a platoon, but I rather think they extended a good long way beyond our range of sight. | |

| Place | Date | Hour | Summary of Events and Information | Remarks and references to Appendices |
|---|---|---|---|---|
| NOEUX LES MINES | Jan 30. | | which was fairly small, owing to the natural darkness and smoky atmosphere. One of my men states that he saw the Germans in our trench at H.19.c.7.8. I never saw them, but, from the grabs details I do not doubt it. He describes one as being dark and looking rather like a Turk. German hand grenades were found at their point afterwards.<br><br>Before closing my report, Sir, I would like to add a few notes about the men of my section. Every man played a splendid part and it is difficult to pick all their names out. Sgt. Bayne, L/C. Thomson, Pte Cooper & Thomson, I specially wish to bring to your notice for the coolness they showed and the work they performed before and during the attack. These men looked after their guns and killed the men and otherwise showed real spirit that they deserve this special mention.<br><br>I have the honour to be, Sir, Your obedient servant, (Sgd) J.S. Waldie 2/Lt. 9th Black Watch | |
| do | 31. | | Nothing to report. Bn. moves tomorrow, Feb. 1st to PH1 & OSO PH2 where it will be in Bn. Reserve.<br><br>Bn. Strength 29 Officers 981 Other Ranks (1010) Casualties Killed 5. Wounded 16 Missing 1. Evacuated sick 31. In Hospital 9. (62) Returned from Hospital 3.<br>Lewis Officers 6th Others 100.<br><br>R Stewart Lt. Col<br>Cmdg 9/Black Watch | |

# WAR DIARY or INTELLIGENCE SUMMARY

Army Form C. 2118

| Place | Date | Hour | Summary of Events and Information | Remarks and references to Appendices |
|---|---|---|---|---|
| PHILOSOPHE | Feb. 1st | | The 8th left NOEUX LES MINES at 9 A.M. and proceeded via MAZINGARBE to PHILOSOPHE where it took over billets from the 1st R. Scots Fusiliers, and took over the duties of 83rd Reserve Bn. The remaining Bns of the 94th Bde relieved the remaining Bns of the 45th Bde on the night of 1st/2nd. The new line held by K.O.S.B. being the "HULLUCH" Sector from YENDIN ALLEY exclusive to DEVON LANE inclusive. This is subdivided into RIGHT Sector — V. ALLEY to R'way exclusive to 6th AVENUE inclusive, and LEFT Sector from 6th AVENUE exclusive to DEVON LANE inclusive, with Support Bn. on 10th AVENUE. The relief was completed by 10.30 A.M. In the afternoon Brigade A.H.Q. → DENNISTOUN, 3rd Bn. the Black Watch reported for an instructional tour with the Bn. | Mise Foster |
| —do— | 2nd | | The Bn. occupied billets in PHILOSOPHE being in 83rd Reserve. They were working parties for carrying R.E. stores etc. were furnished. New French maps were issued to the Bn. on Feb. 4. | Ref reference Armaments to 6 TRENCH MAP 36CNW3 Edition 6 scale 1/10,000 and FRANCE Sheet 36C Edition 6 scale 1/40,000 |
| " | 3rd | | On the night of Feb. 4th/5th the Bn. relieved 8th Bn. Seaforth Highlanders in RIGHT sub section HULLUCH Sector of line — from H.19.A.3.4. to H.13.A.0.2. Relief completed by | |
| " | 4th | 9.30 P.M. | It was later than was expected owing to some of the guides going the wrong way. Patrols were sent out during the night and reported much noise of traffic on HULLUCH. Enemy had strong patrols out as they were working on their wire. Copy of | |

# WAR DIARY or INTELLIGENCE SUMMARY

Army Form C. 2118

| Place | Date | Hour | Summary of Events and Information | Remarks and references to Appendices |
|---|---|---|---|---|
| TRENCHES | Feb 4th Contd | | Defence orders for front Sub Section attached. A Coy occupied RIGHT half of line, D Coy LEFT half, B Coy support trenches and C Coy in Bn Reserve in 18th AVENUE. | |
| — do — | Feb 5th | | On night of 4/5th enemy were heard sawing down trees on their front, on the HULLUCH Road. Our men were engaged in strengthening parapet all along line, and 150 were employed in wiring support trench. Enemy were quiet during the day. 2nd Lt. Raymond slightly wounded. Hostile Artillery was inactive but as an Officers patrol was fired on about 10 PM. on night of 5/6th, our artillery were asked to fire on enemy's saps and front line trenches, this was done. Two Batteries each fired two salvoes at 11.45 PM. and two more about 7 minutes later, the enemy did not reply. Result of fire not known. Work carried out similar to that on 5th. | |
| — do — | „ 7th | | On night of 6/7th Enemy snipers very active. Enemy also busy all afternoon of 7th with rifle grenades. 2nd Lt. G. B. BROWNE (D Coy) was shot dead by a sniper at 1.15 PM whilst observing the two retaliatory fire of our rifle grenades. His body was brought down and he was buried early in the morning of Feb. 8th at VERMELLES. | |
| — do — | „ 8th 6th | | During night of 7/8th the Bn was relieved by 6th Seaforth Highrs and took up its position, the Bn HQ in Bn Support. A, B and C Companies being in 10th Avenue and D Company in Old Bristol 2nd Line immediately SOUTH OF LERUTOIRE ALLEY. At 9.50AM, the front line trenches from ESSEX LANE to a point 400 yds NORTH were heavily shelled by the enemy, about 50 shells bursting; our artillery retaliated | |

# WAR DIARY
## or
## INTELLIGENCE SUMMARY
*(Erase heading not required.)*

Army Form C. 2118

Instructions regarding War Diaries and Intelligence Summaries are contained in F.S. Regs., Part II. and the Staff Manual respectively. Title Pages will be prepared in manuscript.

| Place | Date | Hour | Summary of Events and Information | Remarks and references to Appendices |
|---|---|---|---|---|
| TRENCHES | Feb. 8th contd. | | A considerable number of our shells bursting on a wide front of enemy trenches. A distinct smell of gas was noticeable about 5 P.M. The wind was SOUTH at this time and probably came from the French area when an attack was in progress. | |
| –do– | 9th | | Between 9.30 & 10 P.M. on the 8th the enemy exploded a mine in the vicinity of B10 WILLIE. The B/n was employed in carrying material for RE (30 men) and the party of 143 men and 4 Officers digging new support trench at G'12 D 5,6, and 100 men carrying bombs from Dump to new B'de store. 2nd/Lt. T.H. BELL was killed and two men wounded. They were part of the 1st Relief digging the new support trench. 2nd/Lt. BELL'S body was brought down and he was buried at VERMELLES early in the morning of the 9th. During night of 9th – 10th. Enemy were very quiet, their front line trench is reported to be badly knocked about by our artillery fire. At 7.30 A.M. enemy shelled our front line pretty heavily for about ½ hour, took cover. 163 men digging new reserve trench (referred to in yesterdays diary (G.O.C. 44th Bde expressed great satisfaction at work done) 70 men carried bombs. 30 men under R.E. carried material. 80 men carried sandbags (from mine at G'12 D. Weather fine, a good deal of rain, a few degrees of frost at night. | |
| –do– | 10th | | | |
| –do– | 11th | | On night of 10th/11th 9th B.W. Officers relieved the 8th Seaforth Highlanders in RIGHT sub section; the relief was completed by 6.40 P.M. The work that night consisted mainly of repairing parapets of firing line and supports where damaged by shell fire. The | |

Supplementary Report on Enemy
Mine Blown on the evening of 11-2-16
in Right Subsection of HULLUCH SECTION

A. Three men of the Bn. are missing. One,
L/Cpl. Watt D. Coy., was at the top of
SOUTHERN SAP when the mine was blown.
There was a great deal of blood there and
the man's rifle was found there this
morning, but no trace of the man himself.
The other two were in the fire trench
with the remainder of the coy and enquiries
are being made at the two dressing
stations as it is thought they may have
gone to one of them on their own
account after being wounded. The result
of the enquiries will be notified later.

B. From reliable reports it can be
reckoned that 4 enemy dead were seen
on the lip of the crater after the attack,
but they were taken in by the enemy
during the night. These probably formed
part of the bombing party who ran
over towards our lines from the
Craters to the north of SOUTHERN SAP.
The enemy evidently intended, in the event
of finding our line thinly held or
unprepared, to press home a serious

attack as they were seen to line their parapet and prepare to come out, but found the fire too hot & retired.

C. With this report I send a German wire cutter, which was found this morning close to the head of SOUTHERN SAP.
   Note: In the event of this not being required by the Division, I would be much obliged if it could be returned to me.

D. The mine craters to N & S of SOUTHERN SAP are within bombing distance of that SAP.

E. I would like to call attention to the following few points noticed during the affair
   (a) When retaliation was asked for, it was very promptly given but unfortunately was poor, as 90% of the shells fired failed to explode.
   (b) German Artillery ~~frage~~ seems yesterday to have been overestimated by about 1 1/2 yds. This possibly was due to the atmospheric conditions and while it is worth noting that the

fire on our front. Support & Reserve
trenches fire 15/20 yds behind them
(c) OC Coys do not consider 200
rounds SAA per coy in the firing line
are sufficient. During the attack
D Coy alone expended more than
120 rounds per man.
(D) As regards the enemy's bombing
parties it would appear that
either the mine went up a little
before its time or else the arrangements for the attack were not so
skillfully prepared as they should
have been. My reason for
saying this is that a number of
enemy hand grenades were thrown
into our trenches without the string
having first been pulled, and it
would seem therefore that the whole
affair had either been badly
organised or the mine had
been blown a few minutes too
soon.

H. ~~Henry~~ Lt Col
Comdg 9th Black Watch

17/4/16

# 44th Bde.

## Graphic of Reliefs night of 19/20 Feb. to 2/3 March
### PUITS 14 BIS SECTION.

| | Feb 19th | 20th | 21st | 22nd | 23rd | 24th | 25th | 26th | 27th | 28th | 29th | 1st | 2nd | 3rd |
|---|---|---|---|---|---|---|---|---|---|---|---|---|---|---|
| 9th Black Watch | | | | | | | | | | | | | | |
| 8th Seaforth Hrs | | | | | | | | | | | | | | |
| 10th Gordon Hrs | | | | | | | | | | | | | | |
| 7th Cameron Hrs | | | | | | | | | | | | | | |

Denotes in occupation of RIGHT Subsection
" " " " CENTRE "
" " " " LEFT "
" " " Brigade Support

# WAR DIARY or INTELLIGENCE SUMMARY

Army Form C. 2118

(Erase heading not required.)

Instructions regarding War Diaries and Intelligence Summaries are contained in F.S. Regs., Part II. and the Staff Manual respectively. Title Pages will be prepared in manuscript.

| Place | Date | Hour | Summary of Events and Information | Remarks and references to Appendices |
|---|---|---|---|---|
| TRENCHES | Feb 5th 11th contd. | | weather changed during the night and the morning of the 11th was wet, the wind slightly round to the EAST. Our part of the line was intermittently bombarded all day, the shelling getting worse as the afternoon wore on till about 3:30 P.M. when the enemy exploded a mine 40 yards to the SOUTH of SOUTHERN SAP (H.13.C.2.6.) and attacked with bombs; a full report, copy of which was sent in to G.O.C. 94 B[de] is attached. All was quiet by 6 P.M. Our losses were 4 O.R. killed and 3 wounded. The G.O.C. 94 Bde telephoned to the Commanding Officer as follows :— "Your message received. Regret casualties but much appreciate steadiness of your men." The night was quiet, a good deal of repair work had to be carried out and a large party was employed under R.E. on Support Trench. | |
| —do— | 12th | | It rained slightly all night and early morning but the wind, changing to the WEST, cleared the air and the sun came out. Enemy shelled our front and support lines from 2 P.M. to 5 P.M. a few trays in the front line were blown in but no other damage was done. We were again shelled between 9 and 9.30 P.M. Our artillery replied and silenced the enemy fire. The reply to a bombardment of our front trenches with rifle grenades about 6 P.M. we replied with rifle grenades, rifle fire and Trench Mortars, the latter silencing the enemy. Enemy were quiet remainder of the night evidently from the sound repairing his front trenches. Our work (?) was repairing our trenches. | |
| —do— | 13th | | Clear and frosty morning with WEST wind. Enemy shelled front trenches heavily about 4.45 P.M. for about half an hour. The B'n was relieved by the 10th Scottish Rifles and two Companies of the 4th 5th B'n Suffolk Regt. relief completed by 7.10 P.M. The B'n | |

# WAR DIARY or INTELLIGENCE SUMMARY

Army Form C. 2118

| Place | Date | Hour | Summary of Events and Information | Remarks and references to Appendices |
|---|---|---|---|---|
| TRENCHES | Feb 13th | | to MAZINGARBE where it was reported as all quiet in billets at 10.45 P.M. During the period the Bn. was in the trenches - from 1-2-16 to 13-2-16 its casualties were 2 Officers killed, 1 Officer wounded, 7 other ranks killed, 29 wounded, 2 other ranks missing. (Last attack.) | |
| MAZINGARBE | Feb 14th | | On the morning of the 14th the Assistant Provost-Marshal notified the C.O. that sentence of death had been passed and had been confirmed in the case of No.9672 PTE. J. DOCHERTY of D Coy. for a desertion, and that the sentence was to be executed between 7A.M. and 8A.M. on the 15th. All arrangements were made and Pte. Docherty was informed at 6.45 P.M. (more than 12 clear hours before execution.) Postings. The following officers joined for duty during the tour in the HULLUCH sector on the dates named and were posted to the Coys as under. 2nd Lt. R.J.K. SCOTT joined 4-2-16. Posted to "A" Coy.; 2nd Lt. J.S. STRANG joined 7-2-16. Posted to D Coy. | |
| -do- | 15th | | The sentence on Pte. J. DOCHERTY was duly carried out at 7.12 A.M. at the abbatoir MAZINGARBE and he was buried in the civilian cemetery at that place. | |
| -do- | 17th 18th 19th | | The Bn. occupied billets in MAZINGARBE. Beyond the usual routine work there was nothing worthy of mention to report. The 1st Bn. came into MAZINGARBE and occupied billets alongside us on Feb.17th. Lt. Col. HAMILTON was in command. | |

Army Form C. 2118

# WAR DIARY
## or
## INTELLIGENCE SUMMARY
*(Erase heading not required.)*

| Place | Date | Hour | Summary of Events and Information | Remarks and references to Appendices |
|---|---|---|---|---|
| TRENCHES | Feb. 20. | | The first Coy. (A) leaving MAZINGARBE at 5 P.M. on the 19th, the Bn proceeded to the trenches via PHILOSOPHE and LOOS, and took over the CENTRE sub-section of the PUITS 14 BIS section of the trenches from ENGLISH ALLEY inclusive to ROSEN ALLEY exclusive. D Company held the RIGHT half of the front line and A Company the LEFT, with B Company in support and C Company in Reserve (in Reserve Trench) H.Q. Coy. in LOOS in cellars at 6.36 A.3.5. The relief was completed by 9 P.M. The relieved 10th-13th R. Scots. Men working out the trenches are not good, and a very great deal of work is required. From H.25 - D.28.9 to H.25 B.2.5. There is only one coil of French wire in front. The night was quiet; no aircraft. Two or more aircraft were heard above our own lines between 10.30 and midnight. They dropped coloured lights behind the enemy lines and were shelled by them. At 6.30 A.M. a German was seen standing on the enemy parapet. He was shot at by one of our snipers and fell into his trench. The Companies were employed lifting trench boards, repairing parapet in places. In the afternoon a message was received by the C.O. to the effect that No.S/3982 L/Cpl BAYNE and No.S/16660 L/C THOMSON of the Machine Gun Section had been awarded the Distinguished Conduct Medal for conspicuously gallant conduct on Jan 27th. | |
| do- | Feb. 21. | | The enemy were fairly quiet all day, only sending a few shells into LOOS. The Bn was equally quiet. Messages were sent out by 15th Division at 9 A.M. The usual precautions were taken. Between 9 and 10 P.M. heavy artillery firing was heard to the SOUTH and shortly afterwards a message was received from 44.I.B. that the enemy had attacked the | |

Army Form C. 2118

# WAR DIARY
## or
## INTELLIGENCE SUMMARY
(Erase heading not required.)

| Place | Date | Hour | Summary of Events and Information | Remarks and references to Appendices |
|---|---|---|---|---|
| TRENCHES | Feb 20th | | Trench at GIVENCHY with gas. — The actual GIVENCHY was not shelled. | |
| " | 21st | | The Bn. was employed during the night 20/21st deepening his trench, making and improving fire steps and repairing parapet. A working party from 9th Gordons (Pioneers) should have come up to work on front wire but did not turn up. Enemy were very quiet all night, no patrols reported they were working on their front trenches, their parties were dispersed on three occasions by our M.G. fire. Our snipers were active during the night and one claimed a hit as a loud yell was heard after he shot. Our artillery opened fire on enemy front line about midnight but half the shells were short and the others landed very close to our own wire, no damage was done to the enemy. In the afternoon the enemy sent over 8 Rifle grenades which unfortunately killed one man and wounded three others, all of the M.G. Section. A large party of 9th Gordons (Highrs.) — Pioneers — were engaged during the night wiring our front line, very good work done. Our own snipers were employed in sniping trench boards, repairing parapets and making new fire steps. Enemy very quiet during the night. | |
| " | 22nd | | Early in the morning of 22nd the wind changed to N.W. and then to W. and at 10. A.M. a message was received from 15th Div. cancelling the "Gas Alert." It began to snow about 9 A.M. and continued more or less all day. The enemy were very quiet. only shelling LOOS slightly during the afternoon. The Bn. was relieved by 10th Gordons on night 22-23rd starting at 6.30 P.M. Relief was completed by 8.11 P.M. and the Bn. took up position in Bn. support, "B" Coy occupying GUN TRENCH, "C" Coy garrisoning NORTHERN SAP REDOUBT and 65 METRE POINT REDOUBT, "A" & "D" Coys being in 10th AVENUE | |

Army Form C. 2118

# WAR DIARY
## or
## INTELLIGENCE SUMMARY
(Erase heading not required.)

Instructions regarding War Diaries and Intelligence Summaries are contained in F. S. Regs., Part II. and the Staff Manual respectively. Title Pages will be prepared in manuscript.

| Place | Date | Hour | Summary of Events and Information | Remarks and references to Appendices |
|---|---|---|---|---|
| TRENCHES | Feb. 22nd contd | | with H.Q. in PONT STREET. | |
| -do- | 23" | | Owing to relief no work was done during the night all night though fell intermittently all day. The enemy was remarkably quiet but with that exception all was quiet on our front. Working parties were furnished for trench maintenance by and for improving RIGHT mb. section. B line. | |
| -do- | 24" | | Enemy very quiet all day, scarcely any shelling at all, weather fine. Gen Alert ordered came out during night 23/24". | |
| -do- | 25" | | During the night 24/25" working parties of 200 men were sent to work under R.E. and in RIGHT sub-section. Enemy very quiet all night. Slight thaw. "Gas Alert" was cancelled at 4.30 A.M. Defence orders for sector attached. Relieved by F. Camerons in LEFT sub. sector. | |
| -do- | 26" | | Night of 25-26". exceedingly quiet, it would appear that enemy has withdrawn guns and men from this front in order to assist his attack in the neighbourhood of VERDUN. Word changed round to S.E. in early morning and "Gas Alert" was ordered. In the afternoon enemy bombarded part of our front line with rifle grenades and trench mortars, artillery were asked to retaliate, reports report attached. Weather milder, slight thaw all day. | |
| -do- | 27" | | Night of 26 F. 27". very quiet. Companies at work on repair of their trenches which were in a very bad condition owing to the thaw. Some too had been blown in by shell fire and French mortar fire. During the afternoon the enemy bombarded part of our front line with rifle grenades and French mortar bombs about 3.15 P.M. Our artillery promptly replied and silenced him; No damage done except to the trenches. Gas Alert was cancelled | |

# WAR DIARY or INTELLIGENCE SUMMARY

Army Form C. 2118

| Place | Date | Hour | Summary of Events and Information | Remarks and references to Appendices |
|---|---|---|---|---|
| TRENCHES | Feb 27th contd | | at 3.15 P.M. About 4 P.M. a telephone message was received saying that 2nd Lt. A. W. MACGREGOR, 9th (Black Watch) – Reserve Machine Gun Officer – had been killed by a shell in MAZINGARBE. Afternoon and evening quiet, weather mild. Wind South. | |
| – do – | 28th | | Twice during the night the enemy attempted to work on his front-line trenches but on each occasion our artillery opened fire on him, as third attempt was made. Work done by days on night 27th/28th was repair of trenches as before. Enemy very quiet all night, only a few influential. Enemy sent-over a few shells in neighbourhood of GUN TRENCH and RESERVE TRENCH about 12 noon. In the afternoon our front line trenches and support at H.3 central from 4.12 – 5.27 P.M. our artillery vigorously replied but then fire did not appear to have much effect in stopping this enemy fire although considerable damage was done to front-line trenches no casualties on our side. A good deal of damage was done to our trenches and that combined with damage done to them by frost & thaw will take some time to repair. Every available man was turned on to repair trenches and lift floor-boards during the day. About 4 P.M. enemy shelled centre of sub-section. Our artillery vigorously and accurately replied. The shooting of 70 F.B.de R.F.A. has been exceptionally good throughout, the accuracy of the fire has been little short of marvellous. A good deal of damage has been done to enemy's trenches and in some places his front wire has been totally destroyed. Weather fine but turned to wet about 6 P.M. | |
| – do – | 29th | | Enemy very quiet during night 28/29 & apparently occupied in repairing trenches, on artillery fired at intervals during night and notified the work. During the day enemy were very quiet. Our men were occupied repairing trenches destroyed by enemy T.M. fire, and by thaw. Weather fine. About 2 P.M. an enemy observation balloon got adrift and came over our lines, blown very high up and drifted in a Northerly direction. | B.H. Strength 27 Officers 882 Other Ranks. Total 909 Casualties Killed 3 Officers 9 O.R. Wounded 1 Officer 32 O.R. Total 33 Prisoners 2 Evacuated Field 71 Leave Officers Other Ranks Hospital 23 Returned from Hospital 8 Steward Lt. Col. |

## 44th I. Bde.

### Graphic showing proposed Reliefs of 8/9th March — 20th 21st March
### HULLUCH SECTION

| March 8th | 9th | 10th | 11th | 12th | 13th | 14th | 15th | 16th | 17th | 18th | 19th | 20th | 21st |
|---|---|---|---|---|---|---|---|---|---|---|---|---|---|
| 9. Black Watch | | | | | | | | | | Reserve in PHILOSOPHE | | | |
| 8. Seaforth Hd | | | | | | | | | | | | | |
| 10. Gordon Hd | | | | | | | | | | | | | |
| 7. Cameron Hd | | | | | | | | | | | | | |

— Denotes in occupation of RIGHT Sub Section.
— " " " " CENTRE "
— " " " " LEFT "
— " " " Brigade Support.

## INSTRUCTIONS IN CASE OF A GAS ATTACK WHEN THE BATTALION IS IN BILLETS IN MAZINGARBE.

-------------------------------

1. Immediately on receipt of the Alarm over the wire one of the two signallers on duty will at once proceed to the Battalion Quarter Guard and warn the Guard.
   A runner from the Battalion will be stationed at the Headquarters of the Brigade at the Chateau, MAZINGARBE between dusk and 7 A.M. each day to act as an additional means of communication during the night. On receipt of the Alarm, he will at once notify the Quarter Guard as above.

2. The Quarter Guard will be immediately notified by signaller or runner and all men of the guard will put on their smoke helmets and except the sentry, who will remain on duty, will proceed to Company guards, Headquarters Staff, Machine Gun Unit and Quartermaster's St and give the warning.
   These instructions are to be handed over each day the Guard is relieved and the Sergeant of the Guard must draw the attention of th relieving Sergeant to them, notifying him of the position of Company guards and billets to be warned.

3. Company Guards, on being warned by the Quarter Guard, will proce in a similar manner to warn all company billets. All officers and men on receiving the warning, will immediately put on smoke helmets and companies will stand to arms at their company Alarm Posts. Company Rolls will be called at once and any absentees will be searched for.

4. On receipt of the Alarm, all Buglers will immediately sound the Alarm ( several G's. ) On hearing this call, wherever they may be, all men will at once put on their smoke helmets and return to their companies.

5. On receipt of the Alarm all food should be put into dixies, the lids being put on and firmly secured.

6. Weather Cocks will be erected in suitable places by O.C. Coys., who will notify the Adjutant immediately the vane is showing any East in the wind.

7. The Transport Officer at NOEUX-LES-MINES will take every necessary precaution for the protection of the men and animals under his charge.

8. In the event of a Gas Attack the new "P.H." Helmet will be used. first. In the event of a Practice Gas Alarm the old pattern "P" helmet will be used with Goggles.

                                                    Lieut. Colonel,

15-2-16.               Commanding 9th (S) Battalion, The Black Watch.

Battalion Orders contd. Page 2.   15-2-16.

**209. Evacuations.** The following N.C.Os. and men having been evacuated sick are struck off the strength from dates stated.

A. Coy.
| | |
|---|---|
| S/7941. Pte. J. Porter, | 10-2-16. |
| S/4002. Pte. G. Leggate, | do. |
| S/4723. L/C. W. Dunn, | 9-2-16. |
| S/4180. Pte. R. Muir, | do. |
| S/6735. L/Sgt. J. Higgins, | do. |
| S/8878. Pte. H. Henderson, | do. |
| S/9737. L/C. A. Robertson, | 7-2-16. |
| S/11264. Pte. J. Darling. | 4-2-16. |
| 3/3377. C.S.M. W. Taylor, | 4-2-16. |
| S/8788. Pte. G. Couldry, | 14-2-16. |
| S/10446. Pte. J. Smith. | 12-2-16. |
| S/5478. Pte. P. Danskin, | do. |

B. Coy.
| | |
|---|---|
| S/9339. Pte. J. Williamson, | 7-2-16. |
| S/8249. Pte. J. Somerville, | 11-2-16. |
| 819. Pte. A. Whyte, | 12-2-16. |

C. Coy.
| | |
|---|---|
| S/11398. Pte. J. Holley, | 10-2-16. |
| S/4436. Pte. A. Gibson. | 6-2-16. |
| 3/2579. Pte. J. Dixon, | 12-2-16. |
| S/3996. Pte. N. White, | 9-2-16. |
| 1871. S/Sgt. S. Sprintall, | 7-2-16. |
| S/4365. Pte. R. Leggate, | 7-2-16. |
| S/7317. Pte. W. Simpson, | 7-2-16. |

D. Coy.
| | |
|---|---|
| S/6781. Pte. W. Bentham, | 4-2-16. |
| 1561. Sgt. J. Winn, | 4-2-16. |
| S/9113. Pte. T. Kirkwood, | 4-2-16. |
| S/4669. L/Sgt. W. Reidie, | do. |
| S/9279. Pte. J. Shephard, | 3-2-16. |
| S/8774. Pte. F. Beckson, | do. |
| S/9471. Pte. T. Keith, | 5-2-16. |
| S/6037. Pte. D. Stewart, | 9-2-16. |
| S/11230. Pte. S. Dean, | 9-2-16. |
| S/4314. Pte. T. Reid, | 2-2-16. |

**210. Leave.** Leave of absence has been granted as under :-
Capt. A.D.Carmichael, from 18-2-16 to 25-2-16.

**211. Furlough.** Furlough has been granted as under :-
| | | | |
|---|---|---|---|
| S/3972. L/C. J. Murray, | A. Coy. | From 16-2-16 to 25-2-16. | |
| S/3985. Pte. W. Smith | do. | do. | |
| S/4333. Pte. J. Everest, | do. | From 16-2-16 to 24-2-16. | |
| S/4721. Pte. D. Thomson, | do. | From 16-2-16 to 25-2-16. | |
| S/7336. Pte. R. Finlayson, | B. Coy. | do. | |
| S/5328. Pte. C. Hamilton, | do. | do. | |
| S/4116. Pte. J. Gibb, | do. | do. | |
| S/7808. Pte. J. Donaldson, | do. | do. | |
| S/4821. Pte. R. Patterson, | do. | do. | |
| S/4371. Pte. J. Craig, | C. Coy. | do. | |
| S/5344. Pte. E. McNeil, | do. | do. | |
| S/4327. Pte. W. Ogilvie, | do. | do. | |
| S/7818. Pte. J. Smith, | do. | do. | |
| S/4322. Pte. J. Nicholson, | D. Coy. | do. | |
| S/4476. Pte. R. Kirk, | do. | do. | |
| S/6433. Pte. J. McKenzie, | do. | do. | |
| S/5163. Pte. A. Young, | do. | do. | |

**212. Orderly Room.** Orderly Room tomorrow will be at 9.30 A.M.

(Sgd) S. Norie Miller, Capt. & Adjt.

P A R T   II.

N I L.

(Sgd) S. Norie Miller, Capt & Adjt.

BATTALION ORDERS BY LIEUTENANT COLONEL J. STEWART.
COMMANDING 9th (S) BATTALION. THE BLACK WATCH.
In the Field, 15-2-1916.

---

**205. Posting.**

The undermentioned Officers having reported for duty with the Battalion are taken on the strength and posted to Companies as under :-
2nd Lieut. R.J.L.Scott, Posted to "A" Coy., from 4-2-16.
2nd Lieut. J.S.Strang, Posted to "D" Coy., from 7-2-16.

**206. Dogs.**

The following extract from G.R.O. dated 9-2-16 is published for information :-
1393. Dogs. The importation of Dogs into France from Great Britain by officers and other ranks is forbidden.

**207. Reversion.**

S/9422 L/Cpl., A. Brown, "A" Coy., is permitted to revert to Private at his own request.

**208. Court Martial.**

Lieut. Colonel J. Stewart is detailed as a Waiting Member of a General Court Martial ordered to assemble at the Office of the A.P.M., 15th Division, NOEUX-LES-MINES, at 10 A.M. on Thursday, 17-2-1916.

**209. Casualties.**

The following are the Casualties during the last tour of duty :-

| | | | |
|---|---|---|---|
| 2nd Lieut. G.B.Brown, | | Killed. | 7-2-16. |
| 2nd Lieut. T.H.Bell. | | Killed. | 9-2-16. |
| 2nd Lieut. E.N.L.Raymond. | | Wounded. | 5-2-16. |
| S/4511. Pte. J. McBride, | A. Coy. | Killed. | do. |
| S/8962. Pte. W. Meech, | A. " | do. | do. |
| S/9453. Pte. D. Sim, | D. " | do. | 11-2-16. |
| S/6635. Pte. A. Simmie, | D. " | do. | do. |
| S/9480. Pte. F. Millar, | D. " | do. | do. |
| S/6529. Pte. A. Livingstone. | D. " | Died of ) | 6-2-16. |
| S/9413. Pte. A. Davidson. | D. " | Wounds. ) | do. |
| S/9527. Pte. J. Shannon, | D. " | Wounded. | 6-2-16. |
| S/9219. Pte. R. Ferguson, | D. " | do. | do. |
| S/11365.Pte. J. Linton, | D. " | do. | 11-2-16. |
| 630. Pte. D. Syme, | D. " | do. | do. |
| S/9786. Pte. R. Clunie, | D. " | do. | do. |
| S/8224. Pte. H. Hynd, | D. " | do. | do. |
| S/9842. Pte. A. Cassidy, | D. " | do. | do. |
| 2029. L/C. J. Connel, | D. " | do. | do. |
| S/6525. Pte. W. Kerr, | D. " | do. | do. |
| S/9702. Pte. A. McGuire, | D. " | do. | do. |
| S/9634. Pte. A. McLaren, | D. " | do. | do. |
| 3217. Pte. D. Darkers, | D. " | do. | do. |
| S/6669. Pte. J. Donaldson, | D. " | do. | do. |
| S/9483. Pte. A. McGonigal, | D. " | do. | do. |
| S/4409. Pte. R. Scobbie, | B. " | do. | 9-2-16. |
| S/9446. Pte. A. Patterson, | B. " | do. | do. |
| S/5403. Pte. E. Dougall, | B. " | do. | 6-2-16. |
| S/11551.Pte. J. Forsyth, | B. " | do. | do. |
| S/4533. C.Q.M.S. W. Allan, | A. " | do. | 5-2-16. |
| S/11461.Pte. A. Miller, | A. " | do. | 12-2-16. |
| S/9209. Pte. W. Michie, | A. " | do. | do. |
| S/4098. Pte. A. Kerr, | C. " | do. | 9-2-16. |
| S/6631. Pte. R. Thomson, | C. " | do. | do. |
| S/9241. Pte. J. Mason, | C. " | do. | 12-2-16. |
| S/9765. Pte. H. McKay, | C. " | do. | do. |
| S/9526. Pte. W. Shannon, | D. " | do. | 6-2-16. |
| S/11193.Pte. J. Clark, | A. " | do.) | 11-2-16. |
| S/9375. Pte. J. McGuire, | D. " | do.) | 10-2-16. |
| S/11123.Pte. J. McNay, | D. " | do.) | 11-2-16. |
| At duty. Not struck off strength. | | | |
| S/9988. L/C. J. Watt, | D. Coy. | Missing. | 11-2-16. |
| S/11043.Pte. G. Agnew. | D. " | do. | do. |

D.A.G. 3rd Echelon.

Herewith War Diary for the month of March 1916

J. Stewart, Lt Col
Commd 9th (S) Bn.
1-4-16.     The Black Watch

## 44th Infantry Bde.

### Graphic of Reliefs night of 1/2nd Feb. to night of 13th/14th Feb. 1916

| Feb 1st | 2nd | 3rd | 4th | 5th | 6th | 7th | 8th | 9th | 10th | 11th | 12th | 13th | 14th |
|---|---|---|---|---|---|---|---|---|---|---|---|---|---|
| 9th B.W. | | | | | | | | | | | | | |
| 8th Sea. Hrs | | | | | | | | | | | | | |
| 7th Cam. Hrs | | | | | | | | | | | | | |
| 10th Gor. Hrs | | | | | | | | | | | | | |

Denotes in occupation of RIGHT Sub section
" " " " LEFT " "
" " " " Brigade Support.
" " " " Reserve.

Copy No. 3

## PROVISIONAL DEFENCE SCHEME.

### Right Sub-section.    HULLUCH Section.

**Boundaries.**    POSEN ALLEY (exclusive) to VENDIN ALLEY (inclusive).

**Disposition.**    Two Companies in Firing Line.
One Company POSEN ALLEY (exclusive) to BROADWAY (inclusive).
One Company BROADWAY (exclusive) to VENDIN ALLEY (inclusive).

One Company in Support Trench as follows :-
Two Platoons North of POSEN ALLEY.
Two Platoons South of VENDIN ALLEY.

One Company in Reserve Trench.

Battalion Headquarters - G.23.B.6.9.

**Machine Guns.**    Firing Line.    5.
Support Line.    1.
Reserve Line.    2.

**Trench Mortor.**    A/44.    L.M.

**Defence.**    The front line will be held at all costs.
Directly an enemy attack is evident, O.C. Support and Reserve Companies will send two runners to front line and support line Company Hd. qrs. respectively. Battalion Hd. qrs. will do the same to the Reserve Company.
These runners will supplement the existing runners in case of telephonic breakdown.

Should any portion of our section, or the section to the right or left be driven in, defensive flanks will at once be formed and bombing parties launched against the lost portion of trench. The support Company will be prepared to re-inforce the firing line, when and where required.

The Reserve Company is under the orders of the C.O. and will be prepared to organize a flank defence should the units on the RIGHT or LEFT be driven back. For this purpose POSEN ALLEY on the RIGHT and VENDIN ALLEY on the LEFT will be utilized.

**Reference previous information.**    O.C. Coys. will ensure that all their officers are thoroughly acquainted with the action necessary in case of enemy mine explosion, gas attack and S.O.S. signals, as per instructions already issued.

**Preparation & Organization.**    Prompt action is necessary and O.C. Coys. will also prepare by reconnaisance and previous organization all steps they may have to take as regards ammunition supply, supply of bombs, etc.
O.C. Support and Reserve Coys. will thoroughly reconnoitre the ground over which it may be necessary for them to pass, if called upon to re-inforce a counter attack.
It must be borne in mind that in all probability the existing C.Ts. will be so knocked about by hostile pre--paratory fire as to render them useless, and any advance made will have to be carried out over the open, hence the necessity of thorough knowledge of the ground over which any advance may have to be made.

/over.

Provisional Defence Scheme.  Contd. page 2.

Reports.   By wire and runners as fully and as frequently as the situation permits to Battalion Headquarters.

                                      G. Stewart.  Lieut. Colonel,
13-3-16.  Commanding 9th (S) Battalion, The Black Watch.


        Copy No. 1. to O.C. A. Coy.
             2.         B.
             3.         C.
             4.         D.
             5. Commanding Officer.
             6. 2nd in Command.
             7. Adjutant.
             8. Sergeant Major.
             9. 44th Brigade.
            10. File.
            11.
            12.

## After Order.

Ref S.O.S.

5 Green Rockets will be sent up irrespective of whether telephone communication exists or not.

14/3/16                      G. Stewart.  Lt. Col.
                      Comdg 9th (S) Bn The Black Watch

**Army Form C. 2118**

9th Block [?]

# WAR DIARY
## or
## INTELLIGENCE SUMMARY
*(Erase heading not required.)*

Instructions regarding War Diaries and Intelligence Summaries are contained in F.S. Regs., Part II. and the Staff Manual respectively. Title Pages will be prepared in manuscript.

| Place | Date | Hour | Summary of Events and Information | Remarks and references to Appendices |
|---|---|---|---|---|
| TRENCHES | March 1st 1916 | | Night of 2/6/29th March 1st very quiet. Our guns shelled enemy working parties at intervals during the night causing them to cease work. Enemy did not shell front or support trenches during the day but 13th H.Q. at the junction of GUN TRENCH and POSEN ALLEY was shelled at 1.30 P.M. and 6.15 P.M. No damage done except that part of the trench was knocked in. Gas Alert was cancelled at 11.20 A.M. Companies engaged on repair of trenches. Weather fine and warm, sunny all day. | |
| to NOEUX LES MINES | 2nd 3rd 4th 5th 6th 7th 8th | | Companies relieved by 10 R.S.F. on night 2/3rd. Relief completed 11 P.M. Battalion marched to NOEUX LES MINES billets in NOEUX LES MINES. Nothing of note happening during the period. The 13th attacked a demonstration of forming gas and smoke ("P" and "M" bombs) a day, also in which were placed a cylinders emitting fumes the strength of the gas & smoke and a bar that would be seen over by the enemy. The R.H. [?] Merrill [?] was on [?] all efforts from enemy gas attack and [?] Aird it [?] sounds to [?] in a good order and are put on at once. 2/Lt. W. S. MCINTYRE reported sick (from hospital) on March 4th and 2/Lt. E.M.L. RAYMOND on March 6th. 2/Lt. W.S. MCINTYRE was again sent to hospital on March 7th. The weather during the "rest" period was bad, Snow fell every day but nearly always melted as it fell. | |

Army Form C. 2118

# WAR DIARY
## or
## INTELLIGENCE SUMMARY
*(Erase heading not required.)*

| Place | Date | Hour | Summary of Events and Information | Remarks and references to Appendices |
|---|---|---|---|---|
| TRENCHES | March 9" | | On the afternoon and evening of 9th the B"." relieved 11th E. & S. Highlrs (No 1 B) in 10th Avenue on the 44" Cº relieving 45"; and became B"." in Brigade Support. The B"." left NOEUX LES MINES at 2:30 P.M. and proceeded via MAZINGARBE and VERMELLES. Relief completed at 6.45 P.M. The night was quiet the Company put on all available men to clean up the trenches as far as possible; they were in a very bad condition owing to snow and frost. 2 parties of 20 men and 1 Officer started work under 2/3rd Coy R.E. (Tunnelling) at midnight 8/9" working in 6 hour shifts all day 9" the remainder of B"." was engaged on cleaning up trenches and on the night of 9/10" 2 Officers & 80 men were engaged carrying trench gratings up to firing line, and 50 men worked under 7th Cameron Highl"." clearing mud in DEVON LANE. CPL. HARLAND of B Coy. was hit on the head by a fragment of a rifle grenade and died of the wound a few hours later. He was employed with the Tunnelling Company at the time. The G.O.C. 1st F Division visited the Support trenches occupied by the B"." between 6 & 7 A.M. and expressed himself as satisfied with the state they were in. |  |
| —do— | 10" | | A very quiet night, working parties on mine shafts were continued; other parties were engaged in cleaning DEVON LANE and Support trench. About 9.25 P.M. on the night of 10" a mine was "blown" by us in the neighbourhood of HOHENZOLLERN REDOUBT. The shock was very distinctly felt in the H.Q. dug-out. The enemy opened a very feeble rifle fire for about 10 minutes but did not otherwise reply; a barrage was received from 441.B. to say that our troops had occupied the far lip of the crater without opposition. Nothing to report all day, enemy very quiet. Se several working parties were out and also parties to clean up communication trenches. |  |
| —do— | 11" | | A very quiet day and nothing of interest to report. |  |
| —do— | 12" | | Clearing evening 12", the B"." was relieved by 8th B"." Seaforth Highlrs. Less 2 Coys and 2 Coys R. Inniskilling Fusrs and took over RIGHT Subsection of HULLUCH Sector (POSEN ALLEY exclusive to |  |

Army Form C. 2118

# WAR DIARY
## or
## INTELLIGENCE SUMMARY
*(Erase heading not required.)*

Instructions regarding War Diaries and Intelligence Summaries are contained in F.S. Regs., Part II. and the Staff Manual respectively. Title Pages will be prepared in manuscript.

| Place | Date | Hour | Summary of Events and Information | Remarks and references to Appendices |
|---|---|---|---|---|
| TRENCHES | March 12th cont'd | | VENDIN ALLEY (inclusive) salient being completed by 6.49 P.M. and during the night a good deal of work was done in clearing up the trenches. | |
| -do- | 13th | | During the night 12/13th a party of 50 men from 8th Seaforth High'rs worked on Support trench. An officers patrol under 2nd Lt. HOWARD went out at 4 A.M. returning at 4.45 A.M. and reported very little work going on in enemy lines. The day was very quiet, practically no shelling in front of enemy. The usual work of repairing parapets, cleaning trenches etc. was carried out. | |
| -do- | 14th | | An officers patrol went out at 11 P.M. on the night of 13/14th returning at 12.40 A.M. reported that a large enemy working party was out on their 2nd line wire at about H19D1.8. and was scattered over a front of about 100 yds. with a covering party in front. The enemy machine gun at the end of VENDIN ALLEY thereupon opened fire in the spot and loud ecstasied yells were heard, the party did not resume work. When dawn broke it was very misty and nothing could be seen but when the sun got up about 12 dead Germans were counted where their working party had been seen. The day was clear, bright and sunny. Work was continued on the Support line. The usual work was done on the trenches. Enemy quiet throughout the day. The Bn H.Q. was shifted from 105 AVENUE to the old German dug-out in PONT STREET at Point G24C½.10. 2nd Lt. A.H. MEARNS reported for duty and was posted to "C" Coy. | |
| -do- | 14th | | A considerable amount of work was done in clearing, deepening, and boarding Support Trench and C.Ts at BROADWAY and QUEENSWAY. a party of 100 R. Innisskilling Fusiliers assisting. Another party of the same strength should have worked on PONT STREET but only 27 turned up and practically no work was done. Weather warm and sunny all day. Enemy shelled 105 AVENUE | |

1875  Wt. W593/826  1,000,000  4/15  J.B.C. & A.  A.D.S.S./Forms/C. 2118.

# WAR DIARY or INTELLIGENCE SUMMARY

(Erase heading not required.)

Army Form C. 2118

| Place | Date | Hour | Summary of Events and Information | Remarks and references to Appendices |
|---|---|---|---|---|
| TRENCHES | March 14th cont'd | | pretty heavily during the morning otherwise very quiet. | |
| –do– | 15th | | Quiet during the night. A party of 100 R. Inniskilling Fusiliers worked on support trench and did excellent work. Enemy shelled our front line between 11 A.M. and 1 P.M. with 4·2 H.E. The first form shells landing and exploding in their own front-line. Between 4 & 5 P.M. our trenches were again shelled with pit aggrets. The enemy were very noisy during the night 14–15th, whistling and singing "Die Wacht am Rhein", the Coys Commander, G.O.C. 15th Divn and G.O.C. 44th B. visited the trenches in the morning. Day was bright and sunny. At 9 P.M. a small enemy mine was blown in the vicinity of NORTHERN SAP, destroying an enemy mine. On the explosion taking place rapid and M.G. fire was opened on enemy trenches for about 10–15 minutes after which things became quiet. | |
| –do– | 16th | | A quiet day; there was little work going on in enemy front line. Sap x's appear to have some new earth on them – had, but have not advanced more than a yard or two. Work was also heard on Sap 4. Work was continued in our trenches on – mainly the clearing of support trench, two fire-stairs and 75½ bench gratings laid. C.T.s QUEENSWAY, BROADWAY and C.T. 80 North of POSEN ALLEY were completed. | |
| –do– | 17th | | About 8.15 am the enemy shelled our front and support line for ½ hr. There were 6 casualties (all wounded); at 11.15 they shelled again (including the trench tunnel) for about ½ hr.; there were three more casualties – my orderlies, 2nd Lieut. Howard & 2nd Lieut. Chase were killed and 2.O.R. all told there were about 20 casualties. The Batt: was relieved by the 9th R. Innis: Fusrs. The relief was completed at 8.15 pm from the Bath: proceeded to PHILOSOPHE and were all sett: in billets by 10.15 pm. | |

# WAR DIARY or INTELLIGENCE SUMMARY

Army Form C. 2118

| Place | Date | Hour | Summary of Events and Information | Remarks and references to Appendices |
|---|---|---|---|---|
| PHILOSOPH. | 18th | | Battn. rested during the day and men engaged in cleaning up after the trenches. H.M. Drummond and 2nd Lieut. H.M. Drummond reported for duty. | |
| do | 19th | | PHILOSOPHE was heavily shelled @ 11 a.m. and again from 5.30 p.m. to 7 p.m. gas from each. Shells were distinctly noticed. Deficiencies made up in town by Capt. PHILOSOPHE was heavily shelled from 5.30 p.m. to Working parties told out as follows. 1 Off. 75 O.R. [B. Coy. 8th Seaforths attached to 9th Black Watch] to work on RUTOIRE ALLEY. 1 Off. 75 O.R. on buff or track South of BROADWAY. 1 Off. 25 O.R. cleaning TONT STREET. 2 Off. 108 O.R. to carry files boards up to Support trench. 2 Off. 40 O.R. to carry S.A.A. + bombs from HULLUCH ROAD DUMP to BRIG. H.Q. STORE. | |
| do | 20th | | Coys. engaged as per yesterday. Inspection of billets by C.O. Working parties — 1 Off. 40 O.R. 30 O.R. under 74th Coy R.E. for loading at FOSSE 3. 2nd Lieut. Hunter reported for duty at 2 p.m. He brought a draft of 50 O.R. | |
| do | 21st | | Fatigue parties as per previous day. Coys. engaged refitting. | |
| do | 22nd | | — do — also 1 Off. 9 + 25 O.R. on RUTOIRE ALLEY. | |
| do | 23rd | | Fatigue parties as per previous day. Coys. engaged filling billets, jackets, etc. | |
| do | 24th | | Heavy fall of snow. An inspection by G.O.C. 1st Army which was ordered for 10.30 a.m. was cancelled. | |
| do | 25th | | The 44th Brig. went back to rest billets at ALLOUAGNE, except the 9th Black Watch who went to BURBURE, going by train from NOEUX-LES-MINES, and arriving in BURBURE and were reported in billets by 1.15 p.m. | |
| BURBURE. | 26th | | Inspection by G.O.C. 1st Army ordered for 9.30 a.m. at ALLOUAGNE was cancelled owing to the rain: the Battn. marched to ALLOUAGNE and returned on receiving cancel order to their billets. | |

# WAR DIARY
## or
## INTELLIGENCE SUMMARY
*(Erase heading not required.)*

Army Form C. 2118

Instructions regarding War Diaries and Intelligence Summaries are contained in F. S. Regs., Part II. and the Staff Manual respectively. Title Pages will be prepared in manuscript.

| Place | Date | Hour | Summary of Events and Information | Remarks and references to Appendices |
|---|---|---|---|---|
| BURBURE | 27th | | The Batt. 543 strong marched in to LILLERS arriving there @ 10 a.m., formed up in mass on the square. Lt. Col. Sandilands and a staff capt. 15th Div. was present to see if the Brigade could be inspected on the square. By reducing the strength of Batts. to 100 men per Coy it was considered the Battn. then proceeded home again. (Lieut. McMurray returned from leave. Inspection by B. O. C. 1st Army at LILLERS at 3 p.m. K. Brigade being formed up on 3 sides of the square. [2nd Lieut Scott returned from leave) | |
| — do — | 28th | | | |
| — do — | 29th | | Platoon training in progress. Armourer S/t examining rifles to Coys. [Draft of 31 O.R. arrived. 27 belonged to the 4th Battalion do— | |
| — do — | 30th | | As per programme of work. 2 Coys. fired practice at the HAUT RIEUX road range. Wiring made instruction by I.N.C.O. and 1.O.R. 9th Gordons. A lecture on sniping was attended, at GOSNAY, by 6 officers of the Battn. | |
| — do — | 31st | | Platoon training as per programme of work. 2nd Lieut. F. J. Fell, and Lieut. J. McIntyre, 2nd Lieut. E. M. Reid reported for duty with the Batt. | |
| — do — | April 1st | | Batt. enjoyed bathing and on the rifle range. | |
| — do — | 2nd | | The Batt. was inoculated by the M.O. | |

Signed Howard Lt. Col.
for O.C. 9 / Black Watch

LIST OF CASUALTIES DURING LAST TOUR OF DUTY IN THE TRENCHES.

## KILLED.

2nd. Lieutenant R.T.P. Howard.     17-3-16.
2nd. Lieutenant    G.R. Clow.      17-3-16.
3/3242. Cpl. Mitchelson R. "D" Coy. 11-3-16.
S/7853. Sgt? Horsburgh. W. "A" Coy. 17-3-16.
S/9740. Pte. Clegg J.        do.   17-3-16.

## DIED OF WOUNDS.

S/4802. Cpl. Harland H.  "B" Coy.  9-3-16.
S/4205. Pte. Stanley J.  "C" Coy. 15-3-16.
S/9384. Pte. Brown W.        do.  18-3-16.

## WOUNDED.

S/7826.  L/C. Donnelly J.   "B" Coy. 10-3-16.
S/11220. Pte. Malcolm J.    "A" Coy. 12-3-16.
S/4496.  Pte. Allan J.          do.  12-3-16.
S/6323.  Sgt. Henderson J.  "B" Coy. 12-3-16.
S/9541.  Cpl. Keely W.      "A" Coy. 14-3-16.
S/11459. L/C. Cottan J.         do.  15-3-16.
S/4176.  Cpl. Swanson M.    "B" Coy. 15-3-16.
S/9384.  Pte. Brown W.      "C" Coy. 15-3-16.
S/5016.  Pte. Taylor W.     "D" Coy. 15-3-16.
S/6731.  Sgt. Higgins J.    "A" Coy. 17-3-16.
S/9078.  Pte. Law W.            do.  17-3-16.
S/9443.  Pte. Clark H.          do.  17-3-16.
S/7941.  Pte. Porter J.         do.  17-3-16.
S/9548.  Pte. Watson J.     "D" Coy. 17-3-16.
S/4476.  Pte. Kirk R.           do.  17-3-16.
S/11355. Pte. McInstrey R.      do.  17-3-16.
S/9526.  Pte. Shannon J.        do.  17-3-16.
S/6438.  Pte. Stitt J.          do.  17-3-16.
S/4999.  Pte. Hurlock R.        do.  17-3-16.
S/4461.  Pte. Campbell R.       do.  17-3-16.
S/4392.  Pte. Roddick G.        do.  17-3-16.
S/4488.  Pte. Thornton R.       do.  17-3-16.
S/9388.  Pte. Brand J.      "B" Coy. 17-3-16.
S/9882.  Pte. Buchannan G.      do.  17-3-16.
S/11467. Pte. Aldridge T.   "C" Coy. 17-3-16.
S/3996.  Pte. White N.          do.  11-3-16.  S.I.

---

Evacuated Sick.     52.

Returned.            8.

---

9th (S) Battalion, The Black Watch.

## Programme of Work.

26-3-16 31-3-16.

| Date. | 7 A.M. to 7.45 A.M. | 9 A.M. to 12.45 P.M. | 5.30 P.M. |
|---|---|---|---|
| 26-3-16. Sunday. | | Church Parades, at hours to be detailed later. | |
| 27-3-16. Monday. | Running & Physical Exercises. | Platoon Drill - Arm Drill - Fire Control Guard Duties and Saluting Drill Bayonet Exercises. | Lectures with reference to training in hand and following items. Discipline, Smartness, Self-respect, Trench Work & Warfare, Gas & Flame Attacks, System of Supply of S.A.A. & Bombs, Attack formation & Re-organization, Care of Arms, Outposts, Advance, Flank & Rear Guards, Wood & Village Fighting. |
| 28-3-16. Tuesday. | do. | Platoon Drill - Arm Drill - Fire Control - Bayonet Exercises - Gas Helmet Practice - Throwing Dummy Grenades. | |
| 29-3-16. Wednesday. | do. | Platoon Drill - Arm Drill - Guard Duties and Saluting Drill - Gas Helmet Practice - Bayonet Fighting. | |
| 30-3-16. Thursday. | do. | Platoon Drill - Arm Drill - Fire Control - Bayonet Fighting - Gas Helmet Practice - Throwing Dummy Grenades - Extended Order from Artillery Formations. | |
| 31-3-16. Friday. | do. | Platoon Drill - Arm Drill - Fire Control - Bayonet Fighting - Gas Helmet Practice - Extended Order from Artillery Formations. | |

Wiring under instruction of 9th Gordon Highlanders.

Musketry on the Range.

Afternoons to be devoted to Football, Runs and Training for various Sports Events. Days to be allotted for different for different items by Sports Committee.

---

21-3-16.   *[signature]* Major for, Lieut. Colonel,
Commanding 9th (S) Battalion, The Black Watch.

Casualties, etc., during March, 1916.

|                 | Officers | Other Ranks |
|-----------------|----------|-------------|
| KILLED.         | 3.       | 5.          |
| DIED OF WOUNDS. | Nil.     | 7.          |
| WOUNDED.        | Nil.     | 29. 1 S.I.  |
| EVACUATED.      | 1.       | 111.        |
| RETURNED.       | 1.       | 58.         |
| HOSPITAL.       | 1.       | 26.         |
| FURLOUGH.       | 8.       | 62.         |

7 Officers joined for duty.

Two Drafts = 82 Other Ranks Joined.

========================

## DUTIES OF ORDERLY OFFICER.

1. He will be on duty from Reveille to Reveille.

2. He will turn out <u>all</u> Guards, once by day and once by night.

   He will inspect Guards, Guard-rooms and Prisoners.

3. He will inspect with the Battalion Orderly Sergeant,

   (a) The Regimental Work-shops, Company Cookers and Latrines.

   (b) Recreation Rooms during the hours they are open.

   (c) The Regimental Estaminets, once during the hours they are open.

4. He will remain in the Battalion Billeting Area during his tour of duty.

5. He will collect the Tattoo reports and verbal reports of "Lights Out".

   He will report to the Adjutant at Orderly Room at 9 A.M. after completion of his tour of duty.

   signed. S. NORIE MILLER.
   Capt. & Adj.
   9th (S) Battalion, The Black Watch.

26/3/16.

## DUTIES OF MEN IN CHARGE OF RECREATION ROOM.

1. On Sundays the room is open from 10 A.M. to 8-30 P.M. On week days from 5 P.M. to 8-30 P.M. During the whole time the room is open, one man will be on duty to attend to the fire, keep the room tidy, etc., roster of duties is attached.

2. A quarter of an hour before the room opens each day, the man for duty will get fuel from the Qr.Mr. Store and light the fire. He will then get the papers and stationary from the Orderly Room and set them out on the benches.

3. At 8-30 P.M. all men will be warned to leave, papers, etc., will be collected and taken to Orderly Room – the stove cleaned and ashes removed, and the room made tidy, ready for the school next morning.

4. Any complaints are to be reported to Major Carmichael.

5. The men on duty will see that no damage is done and will check, and report any irregularities.

6. The men on duty will be excused early morning parade and evening lecture.

9th (S) Battalion, The Black Watch.

## Duties of Guards and Sentries.

1. Guards will always be alert and ready to turn out at a moment's notice.

2. Guards will turn out at Reveille, Retreat and Tattoo, in case of fire, or anyother unusual occurrence.

    They will turn out and present arms to all General Officers, to the Brigadier 44th Brigade once by day; to the commanding officer once by day.

    To a Battalion of Infantry.

    To a Regiment of Cavalry.

    To a Half Battalion of Engineers.

    To a Battery of Artillery with its Guns.

    They will turn out to the Orderly Officer when called upon.

3. Sentries must patrol their posts in a smart soldier-like manner and when standing at ease, must stand at ease properly.

4. Sentries will turn out the Guard to all General Officers every time they pass.

    To the Brigadier once by day.

    To the Commanding Officer once by day, and as mentioned in para. 2.

5. When the Guard is turned out, the Sentry will present arms, &c. with the Guard on the Commander's word.

6. Sentries will present arms to all armed parties passing his post, (parties with side arms are armed parties.) They will pay proper compliments to all Officers according to rank. Presenting arms to all Field Officers and saluting all others by turning to their front and bringing the right hand smartly across the small of the butt.

Captain and Adjutant,
9th (S) battalion, The Black Watch.

26/3/1916.

9th (S) Battalion, The Black Watch.

## Programme of Work.
### Period 1-4-16 to 7-4-16.

| Date. | 7 A.M. to 7.45 A.M. | 9 A.M. to 12.45 P.M. | 5.30 P.M. |
|---|---|---|---|
| 1-4-16. Saturday. | Running & Physical Exercise. | Company Drill - Arm Drill - March Discipline - with Artillery formation and extended order where opportunity offers when on the march. | Lectures with reference to training in hand and following items. Discipline. Smartness. Self-respect. Trench Work & Warfare. Gas & Flame attacks. System of Supply S.A.A. & Bombs. Attack formation & Reorganization. Care of Arms. Outposts. Advance, Flank & Rear Guards. Wood & Village Fighting. |
| 2-4-16. Sunday. | — | Church Parades at hours to be detailed later. | |
| 3-4-16. Monday. | do. | Company Drill - Arm Drill - Guard Mounting & Sentries - Rifle Exercises - Bayonet Fighting - Throwing of Dummy Grenades - Gas Helmet Practice. | |
| 4-4-16. Tuesday. | do. | Company Drill - Arm Drill - March Discipline - Company in Attack with attention to supply of S.A.A. & Grenades - The duties and first elements of Outposts. | |
| 5-4-16. Wednesday. | do. | Company Drill - Arm Drill - Fire Control - Gas Helmet Practice - Throwing Dummy Grenades. | |
| 6-4-16. Thursday. | do. | Company Drill - Arm Drill - Guard Mounting & Saluting Drill - Bayonet Fighting - Fire Control - Gas Helmet Practice. | |
| 7-4-16. Friday. | do. | Divisional March, under orders of I Corps. | |

Simple tactical exercises for Company Commanders under instruction of C.O.
Musketry courses will be fired on the HAUTLIEU Road Range on 1st, 4th and 6th inst.
Training of Wiring Parties by systematic organised drill to go on as continuously as possible.
Afternoons to be devoted to Football, Runs and Training for various Sports Events. Days to be allotted for different items by sports committee.

A.D. Carmichael Major, for Lieut. Colonel,
31-3-16. Commanding 9th (S) Battalion, The Black Watch.

## Suggestions regarding the formation of a
## Divisional Sniper's Company.
- - - - - - - - - - - - - - - -

Composed of four men and one N.C.O. from each Battalion in the Division. Commanded by a Captain and 2 Subalterns. Total 3 Officers and 60 O.R.

All Sniping arrangements during the time the Division is in the line to be under the control of this officer and to be carried out by the men of the company. They will be responsible for the construction and care of all snipers posts in the sector occupied by the Division and these posts should never be used, under any consideration whatever, by units occupying the line.

I would suggest that this Sniper's Company be in really good dug-outs in the Reserve portion of the line, e.g., TENTH AVENUE- for the whole time the Division is up. Half of the snipers would be on duty and half resting. All would have their nights in the dug-outs, as I don't think much good would result from sniping at night, except on very rare occasions. Of course, if such occasions do arise the snipers would be out.

As regards the whole of the Company actually being in the line for the whole period, this, I know, is open to argument. But I think it would be preferable to keep them all up than to split them, say half in PHILOSOPHE and half in the line. The reason for this being that, although they would all have every night resting, they would have to be in position upwards of one hour before daylight, and the long walk first from PHILOSOPHE would be detrimental to their work.

The area occupied by the Division would be divided up into sectors, each sector having its own particular body of snipers allotted to it, who would keep that part during the whole period.

Rations for the Snipers Company would be brought up by another Corps to some point not far from the Company Headquarters, whence they would be fetched by men of the Company itself.

The reason I suggest this Sniper's Company is in order to obtain continuity of work, which I think does not exist at the present. Units occupying the line appear to have different ideas not only as to the siting of Snipers Posts, but as to the actual

/over

Continued page 2.

use of the Snipers themselves. No unit is long enough up in the line at present to thoroughly master the situation as regards the particular part of the line it holds, and the result is that, just as the Battalion is getting accustomed to the particular portion of the line and has probably half-constructed several Sniper's posts ( having discarded the Sniper's posts constructed by the unit it relieved ) then it is moved out to another sector, leaving the work unfinished and having got no value from its snipers.

Both Officers and men for this Company would have to be very carefully selected and it would be as well if each unit had a few men it could furnish as a reserve. I think, however, that, out of the whole Division it would be quite easy to select the number required, and if it was known that a Sniper's Company, a kind of "Corps D'Elite" was being formed, we would have at hand a force of Snipers equal, if not superior, to anything the enemy can at present produce.

The Officer Commanding the Company would have to have a very free hand given him as regards the controlling of the company.

These are the main points of the scheme, the details of which it would not be difficult to work out.

*These suggestions were sent in about Feb 3rd 1916*

*J Stewart Lt.*
*O.C. 9th K.O.W.*

15TH DIVISION
44TH INFY BDE

9TH BN ROY.HDRS (BLK WATCH)
JLY 1915 - 1918 MAY (15th)

To 16 DIV 47 BDE

## Herr Franz Von Laagershifter's Spring Dream
(Spring in France commences at 10.47 p.m. on March 20th).

Drawn by special request for the 1st Corps with Captain Bairnsfather's compliments.

Army Form C. 2118

9 Black Watch vol 10

139

# WAR DIARY or INTELLIGENCE SUMMARY

(Erase heading not required.)

| Place | Date 1916 | Hour | Summary of Events and Information | Remarks and references to Appendices |
|---|---|---|---|---|
| BURBURE | April 1. | | Batt. engaged bathing at AUCHEL and also on the HAUT RIAUX Road rifle range. Notification contained in Gazette of 29-2-16 2nd Lt F.N.L. RAYMOND appointed 2nd Lt. 2nd Dragoons | |
| – do – | 2 | | The Batt. was inoculated by the M.O. | |
| – do – | 3 | | The Batt. off duty suffering from the effects of inoculation | |
| – do – | 4 | | The Batt. Training (as per programme – some men still suffering from effects of inoculation). At 2:30 p.m. there was a tactical scheme for O.C. Batt. without troops. The G.O.C. 15th Div. was present. | |
| – do – | 5 | | The Batt. training as per programme and wiring the HAUT RIAUX rural range. | |
| – do – | 6 | | — do —    2nd Lt. D.D. BROWN reported for duty and posted to "D" Coy | |
| – do – | 7 | | 2nd Lts J. MACGREGOR and A. BAILLIE reported for duty and posted to "A" and "B" Coys respectively. A draft of other ranks joined from the Base. The Bn. paraded at 8.20 A.M. and proceeded by march route to CUHEM, for Divisional Exercise, & joined the 44th I.B. at BELLERY, and formed Advance Guard for 15th Bde. On arrival at CUHEM the two Coys. (A & D) took up an outpost position N.W. of the village. Several mistakes were made and the exercise was most instructive for all ranks. The outposts were withdrawn after dusk. Weather dull and cold. Road discipline was very good. | |
| CUHEM. | 8. | | Bn. paraded at 8.35 A.M. and marched with 44 I.B. to training area. In the morning a practice attack was carried out under the supervision of the G.O.C. Bde. and in the afternoon | |

# WAR DIARY
## or
## INTELLIGENCE SUMMARY

Army Form C. 2118

| Place | Date | Hour | Summary of Events and Information | Remarks and references to Appendices |
|---|---|---|---|---|
| CUHEM. | April 8th contd. | | The same attack was practised as a B⁸. The exercise was finished by 3.30.P.M. and the B⁹s reached its billets about 4.30 P.M.; B and C Coys mentioned the same outpost position and errors were pointed out and corrected on the ground, the line was withdrawn when the night dispositions had been made. Weather dull and cold, a little hoarfrost at night. | |
| -do- | 9th | | The B⁹ paraded at 8.45 A.M. and gained the 441.B. at the cross roads at from whence it returned via BELLERY to its former billets at BURBURE which was reached about 2 P.M. The march discipline on this exercise was very good but a good many other things required and received attention on the whole valuable work was done and much experience was gained by all ranks; it was a pity that it was not any longer duration. Weather fine and warm, sunshine most of the morning. | |
| BURBURE | 10th | | A smoke demonstration was held under 1ˢᵗ. Div. arrangements at the trenches used by the Bombing School 1 mile E of BURBURE. "C" Coy under Capt. Stong Wilson furnished 100 men to act as attacking force. The scheme was to show how an attack or a portion of enemy trenches might successfully be carried out under cover of smoke bombs which would allow the attackers to enter cut the enemy wire, enter their trenches, do as much damage as possible in a short time, and return to their own trenches under cover of the smoke. The demonstration was very successful, French mortar bombs containing H.E. were used to cut the enemy wire (unfortunately the shooting was not very accurate and not much wire was cut) after which smoke bombs were thrown and our men with wire cutters went forward and cut the enemy wire; bomb throwers advanced, threw dummy bombs and hand smoke grenades down the C.T's and the whole party then retired to their trenches under cover of the smoke. The remainder of the 44 I.B. watched the demonstration | |

# WAR DIARY
## or
## INTELLIGENCE SUMMARY
*(Erase heading not required.)*

Army Form C. 2118

| Place | Date | Hour | Summary of Events and Information | Remarks and references to Appendices |
|---|---|---|---|---|
| BURBURE | April 10th cont'd | 11E | from the top of a neighbouring slag heap. | |
| -do- | 11E | | 2 Coys. used the range in the morning, the other two (C & D) carrying out an outpost scheme. Rain interfered with the programme. | |
| -do- | 12E | | Work carried out according to the programme. | |
| -do- | 13E | | All four Companies and Lewis Gun Det. used the range. Coys. inspected by C.O. | |
| -do- | 14E | | Training continued as per programme. | |
| -do- | 15E | | Coys. bathed at AUCHEL. Training continued. The C.O. visited the training camp at Etaples. | |
| -do- | 16E | | Etaples. ETAPLES. All drafts for the front are sent direct to one or other of the several institutions of this kind in France. Said division has a separate area allotted to it and that area is under the command of a Colonel, assisted by an Adjt., Q.M., Sgt. Major, and a certain number of officer instructors. On the arrival of a draft it is inspected at once by the O.C. Div. Camp and on the morning of the following day it is sent off to the training area where it goes through a number of tests in drill, intrenching, bombing, etc. in order to ascertain its fitness, or otherwise, for the front. Should the draft pass these tests it is then as is mostly the case — it then is sent to the miniature range where it is tested in musketry, each man firing 15 rounds (5 deliberate & 10 rapid) out of which 6 shots have to be on the target. If this is satisfactory the next two days are spent in lectures in trench discipline, sanitation etc. after which it is pronounced fit for service and awaits orders, containing its training until such orders arrive. Should the majority of the draft fail to pass the above mentioned tests it is "put back" for 5 or 7 days for further instruction at the end of which time it is again examined and, if necessary, again put back, but each course is seldom necessary. The training is very thorough and is of | |

**Army Form C. 2118**

# WAR DIARY
## or
## INTELLIGENCE SUMMARY
*(Erase heading not required.)*

Instructions regarding War Diaries and Intelligence Summaries are contained in F. S. Regs., Part II. and the Staff Manual respectively. Title Pages will be prepared in manuscript.

| Place | Date | Hour | Summary of Events and Information | Remarks and references to Appendices |
|---|---|---|---|---|
| BURBURE | April 15" cont" | | very great value. The camp itself is extremely well run; the men are accommodated in huts but they have dining halls, bath houses, sleeping rooms and a very good Y.M.C.A. hut and canteen. The camp and arrangements are both better than anything I have seen in England erected since the outbreak of war. Great care is taken to see that each man is fully equipped in every way before he leaves the camp to join his unit. | |
| -do- | 16" | | The usual Church Parades were held and the officers, together with the S.O.C. and B.H. Major | |
| -do- | 17" | | 44" (Highland) B"" were photographed in the afternoon. | |

1875  Wt. W593/826  1,000,000  4/15  J.B.C. & A.  A.D.S.S./Forms/C. 2118.

# WAR DIARY or INTELLIGENCE SUMMARY

Army Form C. 2118

(Erase heading not required.)

Instructions regarding War Diaries and Intelligence Summaries are contained in F.S. Regs., Part II. and the Staff Manual respectively. Title Pages will be prepared in manuscript.

| Place | Date | Hour | Summary of Events and Information | Remarks and references to Appendices |
|---|---|---|---|---|
| BURBURE | April 16. | | Church Parades and cleaning equipment; weather cold and wet. | |
| – do – | 17. | | Bad weather interfered with training. | |
| – do – | 18. | | The C.O. inspected Companies in full marching order; many deficiencies and irregularities had to be pointed out. The webbing equipment in most cases is very much worn and requires replacement. | |
| – do – | 19. | | Reg[t]. paraded as strong as possible to be inspected for the last time by Brigadier Gen. R.J. Kentish C.B., D.S.O. who vacates command of the 184th. (W. Ryland) Bde. The 18th was much turned out. Brigadier General Marshall took over command of the 184th. | |
| – do – | 20. | | A Guard of Honour was provided at B⁴ H.Q. at ALLOUAGNE on the occasion of the departure of Brigadier General R.J. Kentish. Companies and H.S. Section used the rifle range and continued instruction in Bayonet fighting. | |
| – do – | 21. | | The Bⁿ was inspected by the G.O.C. 18th Division in the morning. B and A Coys were inspected in Drill orders and Drill "C" Coy was inspected in Trenching, Roller, and carried out Junction in the Range, whilst D Coy was inspected in Billing and Bombing. Both exercises of the inspection. The G.O.C. told the Commanding Officer that he was very much pleased with the way the Bⁿ had turned out. | |
| – do – | 22. | | A very wet and cold day. A large working party of 15 & 20 O.R., a large working party also worked ... | |
| – do – | 23. | | Regt. paraded 26 O.R. and 11 Officers under Major Gamidel (Easter Sunday) Church Parade. A draft of 80 Other Ranks joined the Bⁿ. | |
| – do – | 24. | | The Commanding Officer, Signalling Officer, Lewis Gun Officer and the Company Commanders proceeded by motor bus from ALLOUAGNE to PHILOSOPHE and reconnoitred the RIGHT Section of the Q.V.R.V. Sector of the trenches. The Sunday Transport arrived in a suitable state owing to rain. The party marched BURBURE on return about 7 P.M. at 1.P. Coy Hill was slightly wounded in the head whilst in the front trenches by some fragments of a rifle grenade. | |

# WAR DIARY or INTELLIGENCE SUMMARY

Army Form C. 2118

| Place | Date | Hour | Summary of Events and Information | Remarks and references to Appendices |
|---|---|---|---|---|
| SAILLY LABOURSE | April 25th | | The Bn. left BURBURE and proceeded by march to SAILLY LABOURSE. 1½ Companies went Bn. on G.S. wagons detrained at BETHUNE and 2½ at H.Q. detrained at NOEUX LES MINES. The latter party arrived and entrained over ordinary road to Bn. billets at about 3.30 P.M. The lorry party arriving about noon later. | |
| | 26 | | The 8th Bn. SAILLY LABOURSE at 12.30 A.M. and proceeded to VERMELLES, was to take its turn after this in the RIGHT Section of the QUARRY Sector (The STONE STREET subsection) S BROOKWOOD TRENCH and SWINBURN loop were the relief was completed by 3.45 A.M. the 9th Bn. Welch Regt (58th Bde) being relieved. The trenches were in a very bad state indeed, particularly owing to the number and depth of shell and minnenwerfer bomb craters. There is little or no wire in front and communication trenches are few and failing. From 2 o'clock 1 A.C.O. & 300 men were also employing themselves from morning & out from | |
| | 27 | | During the night of 26th-27th. All available men worked in forward support and communication trenches. At 11 P.M. and 2 A.M. 27.5 A.M. in the morning the enemy opened a heavy fire with trench mortar shells. French border and 2 A.M. Artillery, but the Battery Kelley appeared to be directed against the R.E. & R.Q. Division on the RIGHT of our sector and immediately SOUTH of the HOLLUCH Read, who at times fairly heavy on our own front and extended as far NORTH as the HAIRPIN. Retaliation by us was asked for, and given by the gunners at 5.15 A.M. but did not check the enemy's fire effectively. At 5.15 A.M. O.C. "C" Coy. reported that gas was coming over in front lines. He had already been detailed at Bn. H.Q. at O.C.I. and 8th to have been warned. The gas P.G. were located and all hands donned their smoke helmets. The gas came from the RIGHT and had been ejected opposite that part of the line held by the 18th Division. As far as the Battalion was concerned very little harm was done as the wind up to this time was quickly and gas soon about. We closed only though the fringe of it (8 front line but the full face of the gas was felt by the Platoon on the support line and the 2nd R.Q. staff and reserve generally faintly heavily till | |

# WAR DIARY or INTELLIGENCE SUMMARY

Army Form C. 2118

| Place | Date | Hour | Summary of Events and Information | Remarks and references to Appendices |
|---|---|---|---|---|
| TRENCHES | [date] | | About 1.25 A.M. when it lightened, at 6.15 A.M. (?) received a signal from O.C. "D" Coy that a mine had been blown in the vicinity of the HAIRPIN at 5.15 A.M. at 6.40 A.M. communication with "B" and "D" Coys was broken and returns were sent re Bombardment began to increase and made it the highest about 6.45 A.M. when a message from O.C. "B" Coy that a party of eight or nine Germans had entered the trenches near the old BRECON SAP. This party of Germans was on patrol and subjected to heavy bombardment. We however bombed out and in three minutes they (Germans) were all Killed. 2/Lt. R.W. REID and 2 men were wounded. The enemy continued the bombardment and shelled support trench and GREENWOOD TERRACE fairly heavily till 9.15 A.M. when it lessened and returned from becane normal about 9.30 A.M. Our casualties were 4 O.R. Killed, 2/Lt. R.W. REID and 14 O.R. wounded and 2 O.R. buried. Very considerable damage was done to our trenches and no trace of them could be found. T.M. in GUN SUPPORT TRENCH being practically levelled between PILGRIMS PROGRESS and H.L.I. TRENCH. as regards the actual effects of the the enemy's artillery and fire our men suffered inconvenience while they had Our the damage done was practically Nil. A few men suffered inconvenience while they had not put on their smoke helmets quickly, but otherwise no one suffered. The gas was experienced in R.O.6.1. that one could not see more than 50 to 60 ft. It was impossible to tell the Gas was bad in BETHUNE and was distinctly smelt as far back as LILLERS. In fact trench hands had had any thing original except moppers little work could be done owing to day It when the trenches |  |
| do | 28 | | During the night 27 - 28 a great deal of work was done in repairing the trenches damaged by shell fire although still remain to be done. H.E. shells and trench mortar Knocked in a trench and some of the mortars in the B.T. sector were practically Buried. A good many men were employed carrying ammunition up to front line during the day. On the whole the day was quiet with considerable shelling. |  |

# WAR DIARY
## or
## INTELLIGENCE SUMMARY

Army Form C. 2118

| Place | Date | Hour | Summary of Events and Information | Remarks and references to Appendices |
|---|---|---|---|---|
| TRENCHES | 28th/29th | | During night of 28th-29th. Work was continued in clearing damaged trenches, repairing parapets and strengthening defences, look outposts or craters. At 3.50 A.M. one green and one red lights went up from the enemy lines and immediately they began an intense bombardment of our lines. Every form of shell was used. About 4.12 A.M. gas was observed. It was a thick green cloud. It was very strong, and was accompanied by a few lachrymatory shells which fell in the vicinity of PUTTY TRENCH. The gas cloud appeared to pass over BRECON SAP southwards, and was not felt very much in the Reserve at O.C. 1 Coy. in the Battalion line, very little was encountered in NEWPORT SAP and none by "C" Company who held the LEFT of the sector. The Company Commander experienced the opinion that the enemy succeeded in putting in and that the gas was sent for his own machine, thro' it would appear to be possible as the enemy did not apply to our right and flanks gun fire though he could have well seen the front of the morning. About 4.45 A.M. the gas got thinner and appeared to be moving the bombardment practically ceased at 5 A.M. but from sounds heard to the RIGHT it appeared that an enemy attack in some force was being made to the SOUTH on the 165 Division front. At 5 A.M. O.C. "A" Coy reported that a bombing attack had been made on LOOKOUT CRATER but the enemy had not been able to enter, our Lewis Gun crews and that he had lost some men, one of whom was dragged into our trench wounded by left. He proved to be a private of the 17th 2 Bital 2nd Bavarian Regt. but died before any information could be obtained from him. At 5.10 A.M. all was reported as normal on Battalion front. Every outlet to the enemy was at once made to get their helmets on in time, no more trouble (from information since gathered by the E.O.) because the men were told to take their helmets off too soon. The casualties were heavy. Our line is not quite complete but thoroughly tenable. 1.40 all (Rank & incluing 2nd Lt. H.M. DRUMMOND returned by J.SMALL Killed (gas) and 2nd Lts. J. MACINTYRE and J.M. DEWAR gassed & like of Wounds & shell ounce shock shown by an enemy of LOOKOUT CRATER. No actual cross was found. Our action was occupied then position up till the explosion and accounted for four German | |
| R.R. | 30. | | Bn was relieved by 8/ Seaforth Highlanders (relief complete 12.45 P.M.) and proceeded to billets at position as B. in Bde Support occupying dugouts in the OLD BRITISH LINE between DEVON LANE and HULLUCH ALLEY. | |

## 9th (S) Battalion, The Black Watch.

Programme of Work for period 10-4-16 to 15-4-16.

| Date. | Nature of Training. | Lectures. |
|---|---|---|
| Monday. 10-4-16. | Company Drill, Gas Helmet Practice. Saluting Drill. | Officers by C.O. in the recent Div. march. N.C.O.s by Bn. Sgt. Major on Discipline. |
| Tuesday. 11-4-16. | Outposts and Protection. | Outposts and March discipline. |
| Wednesday. 12-4-16. | Route March. | By C.O. to Officers on Supply of S.A.A. in the Field. N.C.O.s by Bn. Sgt. Major on Guards & Duties. |
| Thursday. 13-4-16. | Company and Battalion Drill. | Attack format-ions by Coy. Commanders. |
| Friday. 14-4-16. | Attack formations and Open Order Drill. | By O.C. Coy's. on Marches and March discipline. |
| Saturday. 15-4-16. | Route March. | |

Notes :—
(1) Running and Physical Exercises daily at 7 A.M.
(2) Rapid loading and musketry every day.
(3) Instruction continue in bayonet fighting and wiring.
(4) Training of Lewis Gun Teams, Signallers, and Stretcher Bearers.
(5) Inoculation of all ranks who have not yet been done.

*Stewart*

Lieut. Colonel.
Commanding 9th (S) Battalion, The Black Watch.

9-4-16.

9th (S) Battalion, The Black Watch.

Casualties during April, 1916.

|                  | Officers. | Other Ranks. |
|------------------|-----------|--------------|
| KILLED.          | 1.        | 33.          |
| DIED OF WOUNDS.  | ---       | 5.           |
| WOUNDED.         | 4.        | 101.         |
| MISSING.         | ---       | 4.           |
| Evacuated Sick.  | ---       | 25.          |
| In Hospital.     | 3.        | 15.          |
| Returned.        | ---       | 8.           |
| Furlough.        | 4.        | 28.          |

Casualties during last tour of duty in the trenches. 26/4/16 - 11/5/16

------------------------

|  | Officers. | Other Ranks. |
|---|---|---|
| KILLED. | 1. | 33. |
| DIED OF WOUNDS. | --- | 8. |
| WOUNDED. | 4. | 117. |
| MISSING. | --- | 4. |

--------------

| | | |
|---|---|---|
| Evacuated Sick. | xxx 1. | 13. |
| In Hospital. | 2. | 9. |
| Returned from Hospital. | --- | 3. |

====================

LIST OF CASUALTIES DURING LAST TOUR IN THE TRENCHES.
-------------------------------

KILLED.

LIEUTENANT J. SMALL.          29-4-16.

S/4399.  Pte. Louden W.      "A" Coy.     27-4-16.
S/11371. Pte. Munns T.       "B" Coy.     do.
S/12181. Pte. Gibbon A.       do.         do.
S/5358.  L/C. Gray R.        "D" Coy.     do.
S/11262. Pte. Sim J.         "B" Coy.     29-4-16.
S/8893.  Pte. Campbell J.     do.         do.
S/4501.  Cpl. Mason J.       "A" Coy.     do.
S/8788.  Pte. Couldrey G.     do.         do.
S/3982.  Sgt. Bayne A.        do.         do.
S/9387.  Pte. McGregor H.    "B" Coy.     do.
S/4753.  Pte. Taggert W.      do.         do.
S/6626.  Pte. O'Neil H.       do.         do.
S/9060.  Pte. Mullins T.      do.         do.
S/11185. L/C. Dow J.          do.         do.
S/11217. Pte. Brown J.        do.         do.
S/9964.  Pte. Cascani J.      do.         do.
S/9727.  Pte. Dunn R.         do.         do.
S/6563.  Cpl. Black A.        do.         do.
S/12256. Pte. Christian F.    do.         do.
S/9352.  Pte. Ferguson J.     do.         do.
S/9052.  Pte. Patterson J.    do.         do.
S/4540.  Cpl. Hefferman R.    do.         do.
S/9435.  Pte. Bain A.         do.         do.
S/8385.  Pte. Erskine T.      do.         do.
S/9371.  Pte. Ewing J.        do.         do.
S/9313.  Pte. Whyte J.        do.         do.
S/4408.  Pte. McLaren D.      do.         do.
S/11255. Pte. McLennan M.     do.         do.
S/4420.  Sgt. McPherson J.    do.         do.
S/6856.  Cpl. Dymock T.       do.         do.
S/8909.  Sgt. McIvor T.       do.         do.
3/7484.  Cpl. McIntyre J.    "D" Coy.     30-4-16.
~~S/11952.~~

DIED OF WOUNDS.

S/11952. Pte. Grant J.       "D" Coy.     29-4-16.
S/9842.  Pte. Jess J.        "B" Coy.     do.
S/4160.  L/C. Couper A.       do.         30-4-16.
3/3521.  Pte. McKim W.        do.         do.
S/9234.  Pte. Graham A.       do.         do.
S/9292.  Pte. Fisher A.       do.         1-5-16.
S/9332.  Pte. Chandler W.     do.         do.
S/9238.  Pte. ~~Campbell~~ Marshall J. "B" Coy. 1-5-16.

WOUNDED.

S/8812.  Pte. Brady W.       "A" Coy.     27-4-16.
S/5321.  Pte. Hastie J.       do.         do.
S/4747.  Pte. Glen A.         do.         do.
S/9161.  Pte. Stark W.        do.         26-4-16.
S/9522.  Pte. McKenzie A.    "C" Coy.     27-4-16.
S/12179. Pte. Sharkey J.     "D" Coy.     do.    (Accidently)
3/3013.  Sgt. Neil D.        "A" Coy.     do.
S/11216. Pte. McAlear D.      do.         do.
S/6439.  Pte. Irving K.      "D" Coy.     do.
S/11302. Pte. Mitchell G.     do.         do.
S/6438.  Pte. Stitt J.        do.         do.
S/4855.  Pte. Green I.        do.         do.
S/11956. Pte. Cunningham R.   do.         do.
S/9150.  Pte. Quinn W.       "B" Coy.     do.
S/9022.  Pte. Glenn J.        do.         do.
S/3943.  Pte. Mair J.        "C" Coy.     do.        over.

## WOUNDED. Contd.

| | | | |
|---|---|---|---|
| S/4797. Pte. Couper W. | "E" Coy. | 27-4-16. |
| 2nd. Lieutenant H.M. Drummond. | | 28-4-16. |
| S/11585.Pte. Smith W. | "A" Coy. | do. |
| S/8930. Pte. Herkes G. | do. | do. |
| S/11461.Pte. Miller A. | do. | do. |
| S/9851. Pte. Lockett A. | "D" Coy. | 29-4-16. |
| S/11254.Pte. Scott P. | do. | do. |
| S/4929. Pte. Owen R. | do. | do. |
| S/12232.Pte. McKerron G. | do. | do. |
| S/4939. Pte. Walker J. | do. | do. |
| S/7742. Pte. Watson D. | do. | do. |
| 3/3266. Pte. Gorman R. | do. | do. |
| S/6433. Pte. McKenzie J. | do. | do. |
| S/5351. Pte. Dick W. | do. | do. |
| S/7797. Pte. Sturgeon W. | do. | do. |
| S/11936.Pte. Richard J. | do. | do. |
| S/5355. Pte. Devine J. | do. | do. |
| S/9699. Pte. Symington J. | do. | do. |
| S/4930. Pte. Lloyd E. | do. | do. |
| S/4100. Cpl. Arthur G. | "A" Coy. | do. |
| S/12227.Pte. Hawkesworth J. | do. | do. |
| S/3959. Pte. Geddes J. | do. | do. |
| S/10087.Pte. Higginbottom R. | do. | do. |
| S/5173. Pte. Duncan G. | do. | do. |
| S/3972. Cpl. Murray T. | do. | do. |
| S/12142.Pte. Bryson J. | do. | do. |
| S/4529. Pte. Jones J. | do. | do. |
| S/5728. Pte. McFadyen M. | do. | do. |
| S/9459. Pte. Lawerence G. | "C" Coy. | do. |
| S/4040. Cpl. Penman J. | "B" Coy. | do. |
| S/6838. C.S.M. Wilson J. | do. | do. |
| S/9858. Pte. Howat J. | do. | do. |
| 3/3201. Pte. Clark F. | do. | do. |
| S/11328.Pte. Bird H. | do. | do. |
| S/8231. Pte. Moore J. | do. | do. |
| S/11521.Pte. Stratton P. | do. | do. |
| S/9822. Pte. Willette F. | do. | do. |
| S/3785. Pte. Miller T. | do. | do. |
| S/4417. Pte. Todd A. | do. | do. |
| S/4419. Pte. Wilson A. | do. | do. |
| S/9297. Pte. Stewart R. | do. | do. |
| S/11258.Pte. Clark P. | do. | do. |
| S/4801. Pte. Houston W. | do. | do. |
| S/7336. Pte. Finlayson R. | do. | do. |
| S/4116. Pte. Gibb J. | do. | do. |
| S/11712.Pte. Collins W. | do. | do. |
| S/11568.Pte. Walton W. | do. | do. |
| S/6516. Pte. Lawrie C. | do. | do. |
| S/9897. Pte. Greene A. | do. | do. |
| S/11354.Pte. Brough W. | do. | do. |
| S/12111.Pte. Bell J. | do. | do. |
| S/11217.Pte. Searle F. | do. | do. |
| S/9059. Pte. Logan T. | do. | do. |
| 3/2902. Pte. Cameron C. | do. | do. |
| S/4150. Pte. McDonald J. | do. | do. |
| 3/2764. Pte. Fairbairn J. | do. | do. |
| S/12422.Pte. Duncan D. | do. | do. |
| S/11423.Pte. Abercromby J. | do. | do. |
| S/9412. Pte. Corcoran E. | do. | do. |
| S/6834. Pte. McNab D. | do. | do. |
| 3/3474. Pte. McRosty M. | do. | do. |
| S/9617. Sgt. Simpson T. | do. | do. |
| S/9937. L/Sgt. Cody C. | do. | do. |
| S/6764. Cpl. Anderson W. | do. | do. |
| S/9497. Sgt. Risk A. | do. | do. |
| S/9371. L/C. Bowie J. | do. | do. |
| S/6330. L/C. Keddie A. | do. | do. |
| S/11358.L/C. Louden G. | do. | do. |

## WOUNDED. Contd.

```
S/9200.  Pte. McKay R.        "B" Coy.    29-4-16.
S/4141.  Pte. Robertson W.      do.        do.
S/4142.  Pte. Donald W.         do.        do.
S/11384. Pte. Riley J.          do.        do.
S/5054.  Pte. Jenkins D.        do.        do.
S/11505. Pte. Havlin J.         do.        do.
S/9803.  Pte. Waters R.         do.        do.
S/12221. Pte. McLoed G.         do.        do.
S/9772.  Pte. Whyte J.          do.        do.
S/9251.  Pte. Waddell A.        do.        do.
S/11257. Pte. Costain A.        do.        do.
S/12259. Pte. Dewar T.          do.        do.
S/12341. Pte. Butchart J.       do.        do.
S/9393.  Pte. Coats D.          do.        do.
S/12333. Pte. Calvert W.        do.        do.
S/11917. Pte. Homer C.          do.        do.
2nd. Lieut. J.M. Dewar.                    do.
2nd. Lieut. J. McIntyre.                   do.
S/11849. Pte. Harrison S.    "A" Coy.    5-5-16.
S/7172.  Pte. Anderson G.       do.        do.
S/11833. Pte. Miller J=      "D" Coy.      do.
S/9525.  Pte. Shannon H.        do.        do.
S/9707.  Cpl. Sellars G.     "B" Coy.      do.
S/4509.  Pte. Thomson J.     "A" Coy.    6-5-16.
S/9860.  Pte. Thomson J.        do.        do.
S/8985.  Pte. Rodgers A.        do.        do.
S/3545.  Pte. Wallace J.        do.        do.
S/4499.  Pte. Wallace W.        do.        do.
S/9678.  Pte. Smith J.       "D" Coy.      do.
S/4722.  L/C. McLean D.      "A" Coy.      do.
S/8601.  Pte. McPherson C.      do.        do.
S/12363. Pte. Turner W.      "D" Coy.    7-5-16.
S/9370.  Pte. Smith S.       "B" Coy.      do.
```

## MISSING.

```
S/9548.  Pte. Watson J.      "D" Coy.    27-4-16.
S/4158.  Pte. Kinnear J.     "B" Coy.      do.
S/6638.  Pte. McDonald J.    "C" Coy.    11-5-16.
S/10412. Pte. Brown W.       "B" Coy.      do.
```

9th (S) Battalion, The Black Watch.

Programme of Work for period 17-4-16 to 22-4-16.

| Date. | Nature of Training. | Lectures. |
|---|---|---|
| Monday. 17-4-16. | Brigade Gymkhana. | On subjects suitable to work in hand by C.O. and Coy. Officers. |
| Tuesday. 18-4-16. | Route March with Artillery and extended order formations where suitable ground offers and rapid appreciation of Outpost Position as final objective of march. | do. |
| Wednesday. 19-4-16. | Tactical Schemes for O.C. Coys. under C. O. without troops. Coys. under Company Officers, wiring, throwing dummy grenades and Gas Helmet Practice. | do. |
| Thursday. 20-4-16. | Tactical Schemes for a proportion of Company Officers under the O.C. Coy. Coys. under remaining Officers at Company Drill, Wiring, Grenade Throwing, Gas Helmet Practice and Fire Control. | do. |
| Friday. 21-4-16. | Inspection of Companies by G.O.C. 15th Division. | do. |
| Saturday 22-4-16. | Route March with Artillery and extended order formations where suitable ground offers and rapid appreciation of Outpost Position as final objective of march. | do. |

Running and Physical Exercise daily at 7 A.M.
Rapid Loading and Musketry every day.
Instruction continued in bayonet fighting and wiring.
Training of Lewis Gun Teams, Signallers and Stretcher Bearers.

*A D Carmichael* Major, for Lieut. Colonel,

15-4-16. Commanding 9th (S) Battalion, The Black Watch.

9th (S) Battalion, The Black Watch.

## Programme of Work.
### Period 1-4-16 to 7-4-16.

| Date. | 7.A.M. to 7.45 A.M. | 9 A.M. to 12.45 P.M. | 5.30 P.M. |
|---|---|---|---|
| 1-4-16. Saturday. | Running & Physical Exercise. | Company Drill - Arm Drill - March Discipline - with Artillery formation and extended order where opportunity offers when on the march. | Lectures with reference to training in hand and following items. Discipline. Smartness. Self-respect. Trench Work & Warfare. Gas & Flame attacks. System of Supply S.A.A. & Bombs. Attack formation & Reorganization Care of Arms. Outposts. Advance, Flank & Rear Guards. Wood & Village Fighting. |
| 2-4-16. Sunday. | | Church Parades at hours to be detailed later. | |
| 3-4-16. Monday. | do. | Company Drill - Arm Drill - Guard Mounting & Sentries - Rifle Exercises - Bayonet Fighting - Throwing of Dummy Grenades - Gas Helmet Practice. | |
| 4-4-16. Tuesday. | do. | Company Drill - Arm Drill - March Discipline - Company in Attack with attention to supply of S.A.A. & Grenades - The duties and first elements of Outposts. | |
| 5-4-16. Wednesday. | do. | Company Drill - Arm Drill - Fire Control - Gas Helmet Practice - Throwing Dummy Grenades. | |
| 6-4-16. Thursday. | do. | Company Drill - Arm Drill - Guard Mounting & Saluting Drill - Bayonet Fighting - Fire Control - Gas Helmet Practice. | |
| 7-4-16. Friday. | do. | Divisional March, under orders of I Corps. | |

Simple tactical exercises for Company Commanders under instruction of C.O.
Musketry courses will be fired on the HAUTRIEUX Road Range on 1st, 4th and 6th inst.
Training of Wiring Parties by systematic organised drill to go on as continuously as possible.
Afternoons to be devoted to Football, Runs and Training for various Sports Events. Days to be allotted for different items by sports committee.

A W Carmichael    Major, for    Lieut. Colonel,
31-3-16.    Commanding 9th (S) Battalion, The Black Watch.

CONFIDENTIAL.

Information obtained from a raid on a German trench
near RICHEBOURG L'AVOUE on the 18th April, 1916.

WIRE. There was about 15 yards of wire on downward stakes 4 feet
high; wire very loose and broken up. Inside this, 10 yards from the
parapet, chevaux-de-frise, not very strong.

LISTENING POST. There was a listening post just inside the wire. It
was a small hole with a good deal of sand lining it, and was empty.

TRENCH. The borrow pit was practically non-existent. Fire trench
8 feet deep. Firestep narrow 3 sandbags. Sides of trench boarded all
round and the bottom of trench floored everywhere, floor being washed
clean, no mud whatever and no sandbags. Trench was regularly traversed
with square corners. There was a bomb store in the side of one traverse
holding about 12 boxes ready for use.

Dug-outs held about 4 men and had double bunks, one above
another. There were no signals visible and candles were burning as if
there was hurried departure.

SENTRIES. Sentries were double and were about 20 yards apart. On getting
halfway through wire, an alarm like the cry of a pee-wit was given and
passed along by sentries, and firing ceased for the moment.

All bombs thrown at our men came from behind the German line.
They got out before counter-attack up the trench could be begun. Shouts
of command were heard from the German support line as they were leaving.
No fixed rifles and no machine guns were found, though two night
emplacements for the latter were seen.

Rapid fire was opened from the flanks, but no machine gun fire
was evident at all, a most remarkable thing noted by everyone.

German trenches were not strongly held, and immediately alarm
was given men rushed to a flank.

Very lights were sent up from their support line.

-o-o-o-o-o-o-o-o-o-

MISCELLANEOUS.

Our raiding party reported as follows :-

Knob-kerries were found to be the best weapons. Rifles should
not be taken, as they are apt to cause clatter in "No Man's Land".
Flashlamps are most useful.

All bombers should know the working of the Ordinary German
bombs the raiding party found a store and used them to cover their
withdrawal. Our machine guns fired intermittently from each flank,
drowning all noise, and deluded the enemy completely. A diversion
with Very lights on one flank during the withdrawal drew a good deal
of their fire.

19-4-16.
No.771 (I.M.)

Major,
General Staff, First Army.

To D.A.G. 3rd ECHELON  Vol II
from O.C. 9th Bn. the Black Watch

Herewith original copy of WAR
DIARY for the month of
MAY. 1916.

8.6.16.  A D Carmichael major.
       commd. 9th Black Watch.

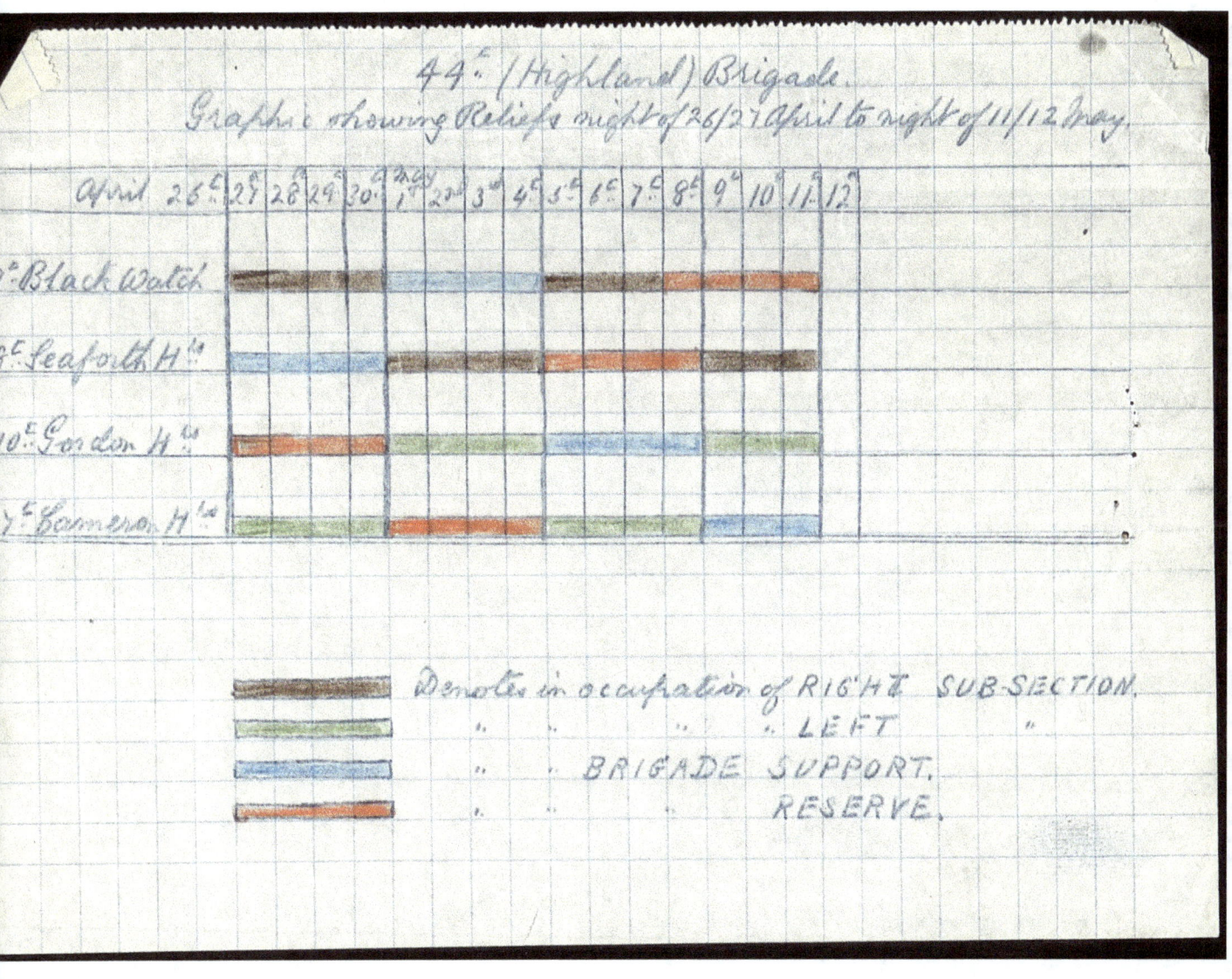

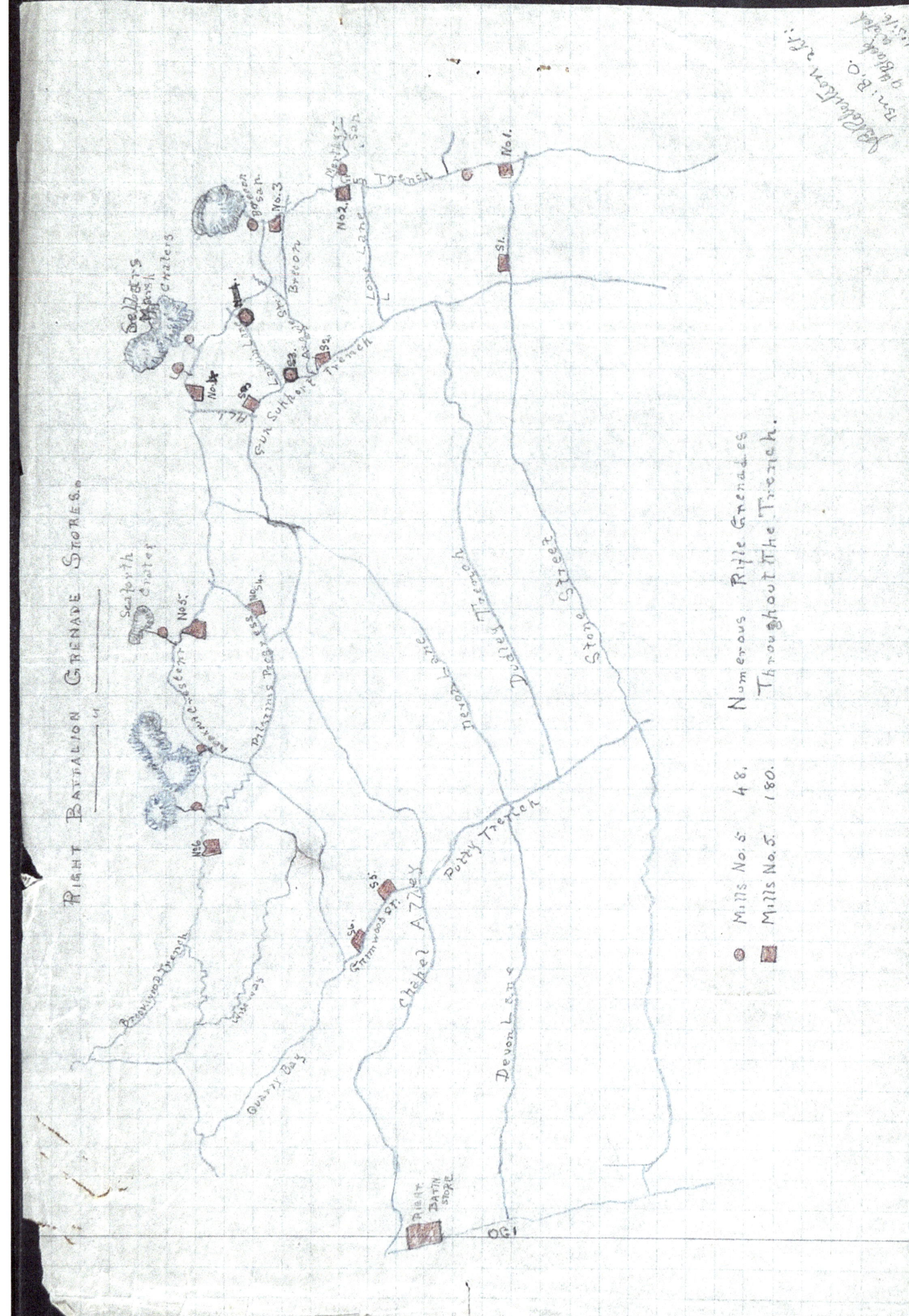

**Army Form C. 2118**

# WAR DIARY
## or
## INTELLIGENCE SUMMARY
*(Erase heading not required.)*

Instructions regarding War Diaries and Intelligence Summaries are contained in F.S. Regs., Part II. and the Staff Manual respectively. Title Pages will be prepared in manuscript.

B 10

| Place | Date | Hour | Summary of Events and Information | Remarks and references to Appendices |
|---|---|---|---|---|
| TRENCHES | May 1st to 3rd | | The Bn. being in Bde Support was employed on Bde fatigues, carrying out S.A.A., Trench Mortar ammunition, Bombs etc. Working parties were found for carrying away the spoil of various mine galleries on the Bde front. Although in support we were not free from false alarms, e.g. one night the alarm came from the 16th Div. (Brit.) on our RIGHT, and on another occasion steam from 8th FB Seaforth Highlrs hit on both occasions nothing happened. The usual number of mines, both our own and those of the enemy were blown (about 2 per day) with a certain amount of enemy artillery bombardment. As usual too, our own guns very seldom replied and even when they did the bulk of the fire came from 18 phrs and very little indeed from anything larger. From an ordinary infantryman's point of view the enemy have very decidedly gained the upper hand as regards artillery retaliation. WHY cannot we have sufficient ammunition. | Miss Brown (?) |
| — do — | 4. | | We relieved 8th F.B. Seaforth Highlrs in the RIGHT Subsection, which being completed by 11.25 A.M. C Coy occupied the RIGHT of the line, D held the centre and A the LEFT, with B Coy in Seaforth and Reserve. At 7 P.M. ——— we blew three large mines at the HAIR PIN, apparently with great success as a huge column of earth and flames shot into the air. Shortly after the explosion the enemy shelled enemy ammunition or bomb store also went up. Directly after the explosion the enemy shelled heavily our part of the line very heavily, showing especially that part of O.C.I. & DEVON LANE in the vicinity of Bn. H.Q. and the Commanding Officers dug-out. A good deal of damage was also done to the front and support line trenches in the vicinity of QUARRY BAY and LOOK OUT CRATERS. We sent over 39 Heavy Trench Mortar shells and enemy activity ceased about 8.30 P.M. | |
| — do — | 5. | | During the night 4—5 the whole Bn was employed in repairing damaged trenches and in deepening sap to SEAFORT CRATER; a certain amount of work was also done to the E of this crater but the party had to stop owing to hostile machine gun fire. A | |

1875  Wt. W593/826  1,000,000  4/15  J.B.C. & A.  A.D.S.S./Forms/C. 2118.

# WAR DIARY or INTELLIGENCE SUMMARY

Army Form C. 2118

| Place | Date | Hour | Summary of Events and Information | Remarks and references to Appendices |
|---|---|---|---|---|
| TRENCHES | May 6th (cont) | | Patrol went out and managed to get right behind SEAFORTH CRATER. A large number of Germans dead lie behind this crater. At 1.30 A.M. the enemy appeared at MARSH CRATER but a shower of 20 bombs drove them back. The day was very quiet (for this sector) but at 6. P.M. the enemy shelled O.G.1. with H.E. No damage done. The enemy sent up many coloured lights during the evening but made no attempt to attack. Owing to the quietness of the enemy it is supposed that a relief took place. | |
| - do - | 7th | | QUARRY BAY was again blown in by heavy T.M's and just as it had been relaid after working practically all night, it was again levelled between 8 and 10 A.M. It is a tiresome spot, mending out trenches that one knows for a certainty will be levelled again in a few hours, but it is absolutely necessary. About 7.30 A.M. a report was received that one of the mine shafts near LOOK OUT CRATER was on fire. It was at once blocked with sandbags. The cause was a lighted candle left by one of the sappers. The smoke and fire were too dense to allow a party being sent down. We observed enemy working parties during the evening with Machine Gun fire. But otherwise located a new enemy battery in vicinity of B.26.c.6.8.5. Map.1/20,000 36 C.N.W. 2nd Lt. STIRLING reported for duty. | |
| - do - | 8th | | During night (6th/7th) enemy were very active with Trench Mortars and small aerial torpedoes, about 30 of the latter falling in vicinity of STONE ST. & the morning enemy shelled Reserve Trench (O.G.1) from 9. to 9.30 A.M. (no damage) Day relatively quiet.
QUARRY BAY and adjoining trenches were heavily shelled during night 7/8th and levelled. Good work that night consisted in repairing own trenches. An officer patrol went out opposite | |

# WAR DIARY
## or
## INTELLIGENCE SUMMARY

*(Erase heading not required.)*

Army Form C. 2118

| Place | Date | Hour | Summary of Events and Information | Remarks and references to Appendices |
|---|---|---|---|---|
| TRENCHES | Oct 8 Cont. | | DEVON LANE and reported enemy working on their mine which opened deep and there The fire in the mine shaft was put out by the R.E. but its damage will take some week or 10 days to repair. The B⁰ⁿ was relieved by 8ᵗʰ Seaforth Highlrs in the afternoon (relief completed by 5.15 P.M.) and proceeded into B⁰ⁿ Reserve, 2 Coys under Major O.C. CARMICHAEL to VERMELLES and H.Q. and remainder to billets in NOYELLES all in billets by 7 P.M.. | |
| NOYELLES | 9ᵗʰ | | Shared working parties as detailed by B⁰ⁿ were furnished, also control posts etc. | do |
| - do - | 10ᵗʰ | | do | |
| - do - | 11ᵗʰ | | The B⁰ⁿ was relieved by 12ᵗʰ H.L.I. and proceeded to SAILLY LABOURSE on the 4/6ᵗʰ B⁰ⁿ going into Divisional Reserve. All were in billets by 2.15 P.M. At 4.30 P.M. The B⁰ⁿ received orders to "Stand To" as our trenches in vicinity of HOHENZOLLERN REDOUBT and THE KINK were being very heavily bombarded. At 8.29 P.M. orders were received to find two Coys (A & B) under Capt. BINNIE were sent) and 2 Lewis guns to LANCASHIRE TRENCH and to report to H.Q. 4/5ᵗʰ B⁰ⁿ at Point G.9.A.3.2. This was completed by 10.45 P.M. Meanwhile H.Q. and remainder of B⁰ⁿ moved up to NOYELLES and took over the billets they had left that morning, H.L.I. having moved on to VERMELLES. | |
| - do - | 12ᵗʰ | | Enemy shelling continued. It appears that they attacked THE KINK and now hold it in spite of our counter attacks. It is on the whole a good thing that but has gone, as it is no use to us and cannot be used by the enemy; it is a regular trap and is better abandoned. | |

# WAR DIARY
## or
## INTELLIGENCE SUMMARY

Army Form C. 2118

| Place | Date | Hour | Summary of Events and Information | Remarks and references to Appendices |
|---|---|---|---|---|
| NOYELLES | Aug 13th | | Working parties furnished from Coy in LANCASHIRE TRENCH to carry out wire defence de[illegible] for Pioneer Bt. Enemy shelling lighter. Only news from prisoners that R.S.F. and Scottish Rifles had lost heavily and that enemy was in possession THE KINK, HUSSAR HORN, ANCHOR TRENCH and part of RIFLEMANS ALLEY and | |
| NOYELLES | 14th | | CROWN TRENCH, all of which are no news to him as to us. Bt. moved back to SAILLY LABOURSE, move completed by 11.30 AM. & the afternoon orders were received to send two Coys up again (A & B under Capt Bennie) to NOYELLES and remainder of Bt. to be ready to move at ½ hours notice. Move was completed by 8.30 PM. | |
| SAILLY-LA-BOURSE | 15th 16th 17th 18th | | Battalion was engaged in finding working parties as per details received. Batt. [illegible] on 1 hour notice. | |

# WAR DIARY or INTELLIGENCE SUMMARY

Army Form C. 2118

| Place | Date | Hour | Summary of Events and Information | Remarks and references to Appendices |
|---|---|---|---|---|
| SAILLY-LA-BOURSE | May 19 | | The Bn. relieved the 6th Cameron Hrs. in the right sub-section of the HOHENZOLLERN Section. The relief was complete at 12.20 p.m. // During the night repeated efforts were made to put up heavy wire in front of the alteration of the enemy prevented anything being done. // 2 men killed with a working party engaged fixing up BOYAU 897. // Work was carried on during whom on the trenches which again // | |
| | 20th | | a deplorable state. // The enemy was dropping high explosive shells & aerial torpedoes into the trenches all night, 3 men were dangerously wounded by M.G. fire, quite apart from M.G. fire, quite a few rifle grenades returned the bombs shelled our H.L.S. in front also from CAMPBELL'S CUT and LYNCE LANE Safe and in the morning shelled with coup attachment + T.M. turned on to enemy posts on the HAIRPIN CRATERS in retaliation. // We fired 100 trench mortars. | |
| RIGHT SUB-SECTION of HOHENZOLLERN SECTION | 21st | | Enemy M.G. active all through the night, especially from Trench 99 — and they were using a great number of very light // Enemy a trench in the trenches. // We arranged a put up certain amount of wire in N.y FARMERS HOLE, good difficult — we interred in the work in front of trench 98 & our fatal quite impossible to work in MAUMETZ trenches for any left - In front of trench 98 & our fatal quite impossible to work in MAUMETZ trenches for any left - HAIRPIN Sap, also repair work throughout. | |
| —do— | 22nd | | A great duty of enemy shells were noticed throughout the day, with H.E. + T.M.S. The battalion suffered some damage to the trenches. We fired some T.M.S. and grenades in retaliation. // Enemy also very busy in his trenches especially in ANCHOR TRENCH & BOYAU 99. // Work continued & some effort was made to put our // Our Snipers claimed 1 off y 3 ens who appeared a good chance to him in new sap. | |
| —do— | 23rd | | Wiring continued, but it is not a an fair prospects, also every consolidating the trenches, some fresh firing in CROWN TRENCH an bayonet report; also HULLUCH ALLEY. | |
| —do— | 24th | | Enemy showed usual activity with heavy T.M. doing considerable damage to trenches // He retaliated effectively with heavy + medium T.M. on HAIRPIN Craters // Enemy busy on ANCHOR TRENCH and on wiring opposite G.11.3. HULLUCH ALLEY deepened HULLUCH SAP lengthened with sand bags. Ammunition Reserve hade at emplacement G.11.6.2.½ + G.11.6.1.8, & new emplacement started | |

# WAR DIARY or INTELLIGENCE SUMMARY

Army Form C. 2118

| Place | Date | Hour | Summary of Events and Information | Remarks and references to Appendices |
|---|---|---|---|---|
| RIGHT SUB-SECTION of HOHENZOLLERN SECTION | MAY 24th | | in CROWN trench for 4 pdrs. | |
| | 25th | | HAIRPIN Saptheads bombed during the day. Our Saptheads & support line heavily bombarded. 11 2 mines were blown at 9 pm. followed by artillery fire for about one hour. After the blots our trenches at once occupied the Old Saphead & started throwing bombs. Considerable damage was done to enemy's trenches by our T.M.'s. One Sap being completely demolished. Trenches in vicinity of HAIRPIN were damaged by T.M. fire. These were repaired thus reducing the number of mining parties. Enemy here quiet at night. Apparently doing very little work. HULLUCH ALLEY fire trench deepened, & HULLUCH Sap deepened & revetted | |
| —do— | 26th | | HAIRPIN CRATERS bombed throughout the day. Our Snipers in FARMER'S SAP fired on party of 3 men seen on top of the left HAIRPIN crater; one was seen to fall. Artillery fired 2 salvos on enemy working party in ANCHOR trench at 3.15 am, 2 hour ceased. Mining continued along most of our front trench, and HULLUCH ALLEY fire trench deepened | |
| —do— | 27th | | Our front & support trenches on right blocked by H.E. Shell-fire at 7 am. Quiet on rest of line. Our T.M.'s retaliated effectively. We also bombed enemy SAPHEADS in HAIRPIN craters. Mining continued in front of HULLUCH ALLEY fire trench. ALEXANDRA trench, HAIRPIN craters, trench 98, and for 40 yds from BORDER REDOUBT southwards. Batt. relieved (Scots 1 Plat) by 4th Cameronians & relief completed at 11 am. The Bat. proceeded into Brigade Support, + supplied working parties as per detail. | |

Army Form C. 2118

# WAR DIARY
## or
## INTELLIGENCE SUMMARY
*(Erase heading not required.)*

| Place | Date | Hour | Summary of Events and Information | Remarks and references to Appendices |
|---|---|---|---|---|
| RIGHT SUB-SECTION of HOHENZOLLERN SECTION | MAY 28th | | Working parties as per Surface detail. R/Co work has proceeded to 1 hour. Order was received to return to Batt. H.Q. on account of activity in rear of enemy's lines, pointing to a possible attack. Lieut. MacKillaw was killed while at work on mens C.T. | |
| -do- | 29th | | Working parties engaged on detonating bombs, carrying up S.A.A., fixing up collars and carrying to R.E. | |
| -do- | 30th | | Batt. engaged in carrying parties, fatigues etc | |
| -do- | 31st | | Batt. relieved the 5/10 "Gordon Hrs. in ? L.S. of Central Sub section of the HOHENZOLLERN SECTION. | |

## INSTRUCTIONS IN CASE OF GAS ATTACK WHEN THE BATTALION IS IN BILLETS IN NOYELLES, SAILLY LABOURSE & LABOURSE.

1. Immediately on receipt of the Alarm over the wire one of the two Signallers on duty will at once proceed to the Battalion Quarter Guard and warn the Guard.

2. On being notified by signaller, all men of the Guard will put on their smoke helmets and, except the sentry, who will remain on duty will proceed to Company Guards, Headquarters Staff, Machine Gun and Trench Mortar Detachments and Quartermaster's Store and give the warning.
   These instructions are to be handed over each day the Guard is relieved and the Sergeant of the Guard must draw the attention of the relieving Sergeant to them, notifying him of the position of Company Guards and billets to be warned.

3. Company Guards, on being warned by the Quarter Guard, will proceed in a similar manner to warn all company billets. All Officers and men, on receiving the warning, will immediately put on smoke helmets and companies will stand to arms at their company Alarm Posts. Company rolls will be called and any absentees will be searched for.

4. On receipt of the Alarm, all Buglers will immediately sound the Alarm (Several G's.) On hearing this call, wherever they may be, all men will at once put on their smoke helmets and return to their companies.

5. On receipt of the Alarm all food should be put into dixies, the lids being put on and firmly secured.

6. Weather Cocks will be erected in suitable places by O.C. Coys= who will report to the Adjutant immediately the vane is showing any East in the Wind.

7. The Transport Officer will take every precaution for the protection of the men and animals under his charge.

8. All Officers and men will be practiced daily in the rapid adjustment of Gas Helmets and in firing and moving about in them. All ranks are to be trained to adjust the helmet with the great-coat on and when in marching order.

9. At all inspections of Helmets, Officer's Helmets will be inspected as well as the mens.

                                                    Lieut. Colonel,
10-5-16.        Commanding 9th (S) Battalion, The Black Watch.

S E C R E T.

## 44th INFANTRY BRIGADE.
## PROVISIONAL DEFENCE SCHEME.

DIVISIONAL RESERVE.    LEFT DIVISIONAL AREA.

Tuesday, 9th May, 1916.

1. **LINES OF DEFENCE.**

    (a) VILLAGE LINE runs through CHAPEL KEEP along CROSS WAY - JUNCTION KEEP - GORDON ALLEY - BART'S ALLEY - LANCASHIRE TRENCH.
    (b) The GRENAY - VERMELLES LINE includes MARSDEN and MILL'S KEEPS, VERMELLES, WATER TOWER, INGLES, CLARKE'S and FOUNTAIN KEEPS, and joins the GRENAY - NOYELLES LINE just south of the Railway.
    (c) The GRENAY - NOYELLES LINE includes NOYELLES CENTRAL, NOYELLES NORTH and BULLY KEEPS.
    (d) The SAILLY-LABOURSE LINE includes SAILLY, CHATEAU DES PRIS CENTRAL and CHATEAU DES PRIS NORTH KEEPS.
    For boundaries of the above Lines see Appendix "A".

2.  (a) Should the enemy attack the IV Corps, the Brigade will stand fast ready to move at one hours' notice, without packs.
    (b) Should the enemy attack the XI Corps, the Right or Centre Divisions 1st Corps, the Brigade will on receipt of orders, concentrate via the BETHUNE - NOEUX-LES-MINES road in the area SAILLY- LABOURSE - LABOURSE - VERQUIGNEUL.
    (c) Should the enemy attack the front held by the 15th Division, the Brigade will concentrate as in (b) and will be prepared to occupy - preliminary to counter-attack - the GRENAY - VERMELLES and GRENAY - NOYELLES Lines on receipt of orders, the Battalion billeted at SAILLY LABOURSE and the 44th Machine Gun Company sending forward at once garrisons to KEEPS as per the following table :-

| POST. | Map Reference. | Garrison required. Men | M.G. | REMARKS. |
|---|---|---|---|---|
| WATER TOWER KEEP | G.9.c.0.5. | 1 Platoon | 2 | Guns from 44th M.G.Coy. |
| INGLIS KEEP. | G.8.b.2.0. | 1 Platoon | 2 | Guns from 44th M.G.Coy. |
| CLARKE'S KEEP. | G.8.a.7.3. | 1 Company | 2 | Guns from Battalion in SAILLY LABOURSE. |
| FOUNTAIN KEEP. | G.2.c.7.0. | 1 Platoon | 2 | Guns from 44th M.G.Coy. |

The movement of the Brigade to these lines from billets will be practised as a Staff exercise on a date to be notified later.
    (d) In certain eventualities the Brigade may be required to move as Corps Reserve from the area SAILLY LABOURSE - LABOURSE - VERQUIGNEUL South Towards the line PETIT SAINS - SAINS EN GOHELLER or North towards BEUVRY.

3. The following Machine Guns are placed at disposal of the Brigade occupying QUARRIES SECTION to occupy emplacements in the VILLAGE LINE.
    (a) For Nos. 1 and 2 emplacements, 2 guns 11th Motor Machine Gun Batty.
    (b) For Nos. 3, 4, 4a and 5 emplacements, 4 guns of 44th Machine Gun Coy.
    O.C. 44th Machine Gun Coy, will reconnoitre the positions allotted to guns of his Company and be prepared to move guns there on receipt of orders.
    The Officer Commanding the Battalion at SAILLY LABOURSE will arrange to reconnoitre for the movement of his Battalion into the    over.

3. Contd.  VILLAGE LINE should such a move be ordered.

(Sgd) E.A. Beck, Major,
Brigade Major,
Issued through Signals.    44th Infantry Brigade.


## APPENDIX "A".

JUNCTION BETWEEN DIVISIONS ON LINES OF DEFENCE.
6

Reference Sheet - 36 B. 1/40,000.

| Line of Defence. | Junction between Centre Division I Corps and Left Division I Corps. | Junction between Left Division I Corps and XI Corps. |
|---|---|---|
| VILLAGE LINE. | Junction with LE RUTOIRE ALLEY inclusive to CENTRE Division. | Junction with Railway inclusive to XI Corps. |
| GRENAY - VERMELLES LINE. | G.14.b.5.0. MILLS, MARSDEN and NOYELLES CENTRAL KEEPS inclusive to Left LEFT DIVISION. | Junction with Railway inclusive to XI Corps. |
| GRENAY - NOYELLES LINE. | Junction with LENS ROAD inclusive to CENTRE Division. | Junction with Railway inclusive to XI Corps BRAY KEEP to XI Corps. |
| SAILLY LABOURSE LINE. | L.9.d.4.9. | Road Crossing at F.27.b.4.4. CHATEAU DES PRIS NORTH KEEP to LEFT Division. |

Headquarters,
    44th Brigade.

        Reference Map, 1/20,000, 36 C. N.W., for the information of the G.O.C.

        For some time I have been observing the enemy work in the neighbourhood of the HOHENZOLLERN REDOUBT from point G.11.d.5.2. and from G.11.b.10.9. and yesterday morning an Artillery Officer assisted me from the latter spot. He took the range far from this point of the work in question; also various angles to it, and we both came to the conclusion that a good many of the back trenches; that is, those on the North East side of the Redoubt could be seen very well from this point. As far as we could gather, the range, by the Barr and Stroud Range Finder, was 16/1700 yards, taken to a large stump which could be clearly made out on the Southern side of the work. I should imagine somewhere in the neighbourhood of the craters in G.5.c.2.5.

        The enemy were apparently quite unconscious that they were being watched or could be seen from any part of our lines, as they worked in full view, several showing themselves, head and shoulders, above the parapet. They worked all day and are evidently improving an already strong redoubt.

        There is an enemy M.G. emplacement on the South side of the work and not very far from the stump already mentioned. I saw it fire three shots the day before yesterday. It was apparently firing in the direction of the MINE.

        Although I have carefully watched this spot for some time I have not seen a single British shell fired anywhere near these trenches and I very much doubt if it has been seen from any of our ordinary Artillery observation posts. Owing to the height of the redoubt above the nearest part of the British line, the work in progress cannot, I think, be seen from anywhere there. It would not take very much work to construct

/over

Contd. page 2.

a good Observation Post in the dis-used communication trench off STORK STREET, but care would have to be taken that it was not visible from the EIFFEL Towers or the HOHENZOLLERN REDOUBT during its construction.

                                                            Lieut. Colonel,

9-8-16.       Commanding 9th (S) Battalion, The Black Watch.

B.E.F
6-3-16

D.A.G.
3rd Echelon
Rouen.

Herewith War Diary for February.

Hewett Lt. Col.
Comdg 9th Black Watch

SECRET                                    Coy No. _____

## DEFENCE SCHEME.

Right Subsection-HOHENZOLLERN Section.
Ref Trench Map 36c 1/20000                              19-5-16.

1.  The Subsection extends from BOYAU 9. (9.11.B.c.5.) to junction
    of HULLUCH ALLEY and SACKVILLE ST. and is held as follows:-
    One Coy. from BOYAU 94 to
    One Coy. from BOYAU 94 to S.W. end of BOYAU.
    These Coys. find their own supports.
    One Coy.- one platoon in HULLUCH ALLEY from S.W. end of BOYAU
    98 (inclusive) to junction of HULLUCH ALLEY AND SACKVILLE ST.
    (exclusive) and 3 platoons in O.B.I. between FOSSEWAY AND
    HULLUCH ALLEY.
    One Coy.- one platoon in CROSS TRENCH between BOYAU 94 and
    ST.ELIE AV. 3 platoons in O.B.4 and 5.

2.  Communication Trenches are:-
    "UP"- HULLUCH ALLEY and O.B.S.4 - FOSSEWAY.
    "DOWN"- STANSFIELD RD. - HULLUCH ALLEY -.
    O.C. Coys concerned will post controls on their
    communication trenches in O.B.5 and O.B.1 with written orders
    to prevent any use of these trenches against the traffic except
    by:-
    (a) Staff Officers,(b) Signallers,(c) Officers in possession of
    pass signed by Brigade Major.

3.  Battalion Headquarters are in O.B.I pt. 9.11.c.4.7. and Brigade
    Headquarters on RAILWAY at 9.9.d.4.4.

4.  GENERAL PRINCIPLES OF DEFENCE.
    (1) The front line is to be held at all costs and it is the
    duty of every commander on the spot to counter-attack should
    the line be broken.
    (2) The support line is never to be left vacant.
    (3) Troops will not fall back from any one line to another,but
    all points will be defended whether their flanks are turned or
    not.
    (4) Should the enemy succeed in penetrating our defence,keeps
    and supporting points previously garrisoned together with
    communication trenches prepared to fire both ways,will hold him
    in a pocket in which his flanks will be exposed to our fire,
    to attacks by grenades and to counter attacks.
    (5) All subordinate commanders must realise that no ground
    capable of being held should be given up and that a counter
    attack must be made as soon as possible, with object in view,
    directly the attack is threatened reinforcements will be sent up
    so as to move sufficient troops to hand for local counter
    attacks, the success of which depends upon rapidity and good
    organisation; Coy. Commanders on flanks of the trench captured
    will immediately institute bombing attacks inwards without
    awaiting orders. Coy. Commanders must always have in mind the
    probability of having to make a counter attack. Counter
    attacks to be successful
        (1) must be delivered as soon as possible
        (2) must be well organized
    These requirements can only be fulfilled if commanders have
    carefully considered all possible eventualities. Counter attack
    plans will be recorded in writing and handed over on relief. They
    should be rehearsed by the personnel who would actually carry them
    out.
    (6) In the event of the front of the Brigade on our right being
    penetrated the O.C. Right Subsection in the front line will
    arrange for formation of a defensive flank along CUTTLEBONE CUT -
    GOEBEN ALLEY and bombing squads will proceed along _____ TRENCH
    & LANCER TRENCH. O.C.Coys in reserve will arrange to reconnoitre

the ground on this flank.

NOTE. Commanders of Coys. will act on the principle that above all the front line should never be turned back for a greater distance than is absolute necessary.

(7) In all bombing counter attacks Coy. Commanders must bear in mind that to be successful a constant supply of bombs must be kept going. If the supply stops the counter attack is doomed to failure. They will therefore arrange an organization that will immediately line up and pass bombs from the bomb store to that part of the line where the enemy have gained a footing. Further orders will be issued re the supply of Bombs from Battalion Store to stores in the front system.

5. Action in Case of Attack.

(1) Artillery support will be called for by S.O.S. signal on the telephone or by firing green rockets in quick succession from Coy. or Battalion Headquarters, when communication by telephone has failed. At least 12 of these rockets, with apparatus for firing them, will be kept by all Coy. and Battalion Headquarters in the trenches. These signals are only to be used when, in the opinion of the officer on the spot, the immediate establishment of an Artillery barrage is necessary and an Infantry attack is advancing.

(2) Commanders of platoons in Support Line will at once communicate with the Commander in front of them and keep themselves posted as to situation.

(3) O.C.Coys in Reserve must hold their men in readiness to move forward for counter attack at once and communicate with the C.O. by 'phone and runner.

(4) Working parties in the trenches occupied by the Battalion will report to the nearest Commander concerned in the front line to O.C.Coys. who will use them in the defence of the line.

(5) Personnel of Tunnelling Coys. and Infantry with them will come out of the mine shafts at once and report to the nearest platoon Commander who will use them in the defence of the line.

(6) The situation will be reported to C.O. at frequent intervals by 'phone and runner.

6. Special Instructions.

(a) Gas The Code signal to denote attack by gas is "S.O.S. GAS" followed by Battalion reporting. Troops will at once put on their gas helmets and be kept as still as possible. No movement must be allowed except that necessary to man the parapet. A Strombus horn or bugle will be sounded at Battalion Headquarters directly a Gas message is received. As soon as the cloud has passed O.C.Coys. will report at once to Battalion Headquarters the condition of the men, stating to what extent they have been affected by the gas. This is most important. All ranks must be warned not to take off helmets until ordered from Battalion Headquarters.

In the event of a Gas attack it is of utmost importance that messages should be passed from Front to rear. O.C.Coys. will arrange for this to be done.

(b) Flammenwerfer. In the event of an attack by Flammenwerfer all troops in the front line trenches will remain there; they will be at the bottom of the trench. Troops in the support line will man the parapet and open rapid fire and machine gun fire in the direction of the attack. All ranks will be warned that Flammenwerfer cannot harm men lying in the trench close to the parapet.

(c) In an enemy mine is exploded as a general rule the near lip of the crater will be occupied by digging a trench around it with a communication trench to the main line from either flank. The procedure will be as follows:-

A bombing squad will at once occupy the near lip of the crater pushing out a bombing post on each flank. The remainder of the squad will dig themselves in, in the centre of the near lip; this action is to be taken before commencing to sap out to the crater. The sap from fire trench to crater will be commenced as soon as we are in possession of the near lip.

Four shovels per bombing squad will be kept where they will

3.

be available to be taken forward at once.

All Craters within about 40 yards of our line must be dealth with in this manner. The Commander on the spot is responsible for taking the necessary action. A report will be rendered to Battalion Headquarters stating the action taken and further report when the new trench has been completed and occupied.

(d) Bombardment. If during a bombardment the men have to be withdrawn from the front line to dugouts, lookouts under an officer must be maintained in the front line. Officers previously detailed must watch for the lift of the Artillery and at once occupy the front line. M.Gs and especially L.Gs and their teams will when shell proof cover exists take their guns under cover during a bombardment. They must keep in touch with the lookout men and be prepared to man their gun at the shortest notice. This does not apply to guns in permanent emplacements.

7. Medical Arrangements

(a) Wounded will be evacuated from the front system by "DOWN" trenches.
(b) Battalion Aid Post is at junction of O.B.1 and STANSFIELD RD.
(c) Advanced Bearers Station F.A. is at junction of HULLUCH and GORDON Alleys.
(d) Advanced Dressing Station F.A. BARTS ALLEY (at junction with AUCHY ALLEY-VERMELLES RD.) at BREWERY, VERMELLES.

(Sgd) S.Hotie Miller, Capt. and Adjt.
9th Black Watch.

After Addition to B attn. Defence Scheme.
Right Section-HOHENZOLLERN SECTION.
Extracts from Appendix "B" (Ref.para.5 Battn.Defence Scheme)
Arrangements for disposal of Tunnellers and Infantry parties working with them in the event of enemy attack or an attack being imminent.

| Unit. | Position for Tunnellers. | Position for Fatigue Parties |
|---|---|---|
| 180th Tunnelling Coy. Parties Working in Mine Shafts between saps 94-96. | Proceed to Battn. bomb at G.11.b.3½.1. and assist platoon told off for bomb carrying.Ref.App."B" Bde. Defence Scheme-para. 5 (1) One platoon is detailed from the Support Battn.to carry from Bde.advanced store at junction O.B.2 and FOSSEWAY to Right Battn. Grenade store in O.G. 2 between GOEBEN ALLEY & FOSSEWAY. | Man parapet near their Mine Shafts. |
| 180th Tunnelling Coy. Personnel in 3 Listening posts N.of SAP 95. | Proceed to Bomb Store at junction of ST.ELIE AV. AND CROWN TRENCH | Man parapet by their post. |

Ref.para.5 (5) of Battn. Defence Scheme.
A definite place will be allotted Tunnellers and Infantry working with them by O.C.Coys concerned.
Men untrained in firearms must be used as bomb carriers.
They must be given the strictest orders to at once come out of the mine shaft and occupy the places allotted to them.

(Sgd) L.G.Morrison,2nd Lieut.and A/Adjt.
9th Black Watch.

24-5-16.

S E C R E T.                                        Copy No.........

Operation Order No. 44 by Lieut. Col. J. Stewart.
Commanding 9th (S) Battalion, The Black Watch.
Ref. Map. 36b.   1/20,000.            Thursday, 18-5-16.
               ooooo--------------

1. The 44th I.B. will relieve the 45th I.B., in the HOHENZOLLERN Section on 19-5-16.

2. The 9th B.W. will relieve the 6th Camerons in Right Sub-section between BOYAU 94 (exclusive) to junction of ~~Sackvill~~ SACKVILLE STREET and HULLUCH ALLEY, as under :-
   C. Coy. will relieve B. Coy. 6th Camerons on Right.
   D. Coy.      do.    D.        do       Left.
   A. Coy.      do.    A.        do.   One platoon in HULLUCH ALLEY
           Three platoons in O.B.I.
   B. Coy. will relieve C. Coy. 6th Camerons in O.B.4.

3. Companies will move in above order, platoons at 200 paces interval via Cross Roads in L.6.C. The leading platoon passing the Cross Roads SAILLY at 8.15 A.M. Guides will meet platoons at CLARKE'S KEEP VERMELLES at 9.15 A.M.

4. Lewis Gun Detachment will move up with the Battalion, one Gun going with each Coy.     A. Coys Gun will go with the leading platoon to the front line.

5. Transport will move under Brigade arrangements at SAILLY LABOURSE where O.C. Transport will take over the lines of the 6th Camerons  Qr. Mr. advance store will be at SAILLY LABOURSE.

6. Packs and blankets, as usual, will be handed in at Q. M. Store at 6.30 A.M.

7. Men in possession of Steel Helmets will not take their bonnets into the Trenches, but leave them in their packs.

8. Rations for the Battalion will be loaded at MANSION HOUSE Stn. at 9.45 P.M. and will be met at the Dump at RESERVE TRENCH at 10.15 P.M.

B. Coy. will provide Ration parties for C. & D. Coys. Water will be drawn from GORDON ALLEY, between O.B.I and RESERVE TRENCH.

9. R.E. Dump is at the junction of BART'S ALLEY and RESERVE TRENCH.

10. Receipts for Trench Stores to be handed into the Adjutant immediately on completion of relief.

11. Reveille tomorrow will be at 5 A.M.   Breakfast at 7 A.M.

                    (Sgd)     S. Norie Miller, Capt. & Adjt.
                                    9th Black Watch.

To accompany O.O.45.

O.C.     COMPANY.

## GUIDES.

A.C. & D.Coys will have guides at Battalion Headquarters at 2 P.M. 26-5-16 to Guide O.C. Coys. of 7th Camerons.  B. Coy. and Headquarters will have a guide at junction of the Railway and HULLUCH ALLEY at 1.30 P.M. tomorrow 26-5-16.    B. Coy. guide will guide O.C. Coy. relieving B. Coy. to B. Coys. Headquarters direct.    Headquarters guide will guide remaining Company Commanders to Battalion Headquarters.    B.S.M. and C.S.M's will be met by guides at the junction of Railway and STANSFIELD ROAD at 2 P.M. tomorrow to reconnoitre Coy. dispositions in LANCASHIRE TRENCH - RAILWAY RESERVE TRENCH - CENTRAL KEEP AND JUNCTION KEEP.

B. Coy. RAILWAY RESERVE TRENCH and CENTRAL KEEP ( 1 platoon)
A. Coy. LANCASHIRE TRENCH/and JUNCTION KEEP ( 1 platoon )
C. Coy.         do.         (on the left)
D. Coy.         do.         (in the centre)

B.S.M. and C.S.M's will take over Trench Stores when reconnoitring the platoons in the position tomorrow.

(Sgd) L.G.Morrison, 2nd Lieut. and A/Adjt.
     ;th Black Watch.

25-5-16.

Casualties, etc., during month of MAY, 1916.

|  | Officers. | Other Ranks. |
|---|---|---|
| KILLED. | 1. | 8. |
| DIED OF WOUNDS. | 2. | 6. |
| WOUNDED. | 1. | 56. |
| MISSING. | Nil. | 2. |
| EVACUATED. | 1. | 69. |
| RETURNED. | Nil. | 17. |
| IN HOSPITAL. 31-5-16. | 3. | 23. |
| LEAVE. | 6. | 58. |

S E C R E T.                                           Copy No. .........

Operation Order No.46 by Major A.D.Carmichael
Commanding 9th (S.) Bn. The Black Watch.
Ref. Map 36b,1/20,000. Monday 29-5-16.
-------------------

1. The 9th Black Watch will releive the 8/10th Gordons in the Centre
   Sub-Section HOHENZOLLERN SECTION on the 31st May 1916.
   B. Coy. 9th Black Watch will releive A. Coy. 8/10th Gordons in Firing
                                                                Line Right.
   C. Coy.  "    "    "    "    "    "    B. Coy.  "    "    "    " Left.
   A. Coy.  "    "    "    "    "    "    C. Coy.  "    " Support O.G.I.
                                                    and GORDON ALLEY.
   D. Coy.  "    "    "    "    "    "    D. Coy. in Reserve in VILLAGE
                                                                LINE.
   The Companies in firing line will find their own support.

2. The Coys. will releive in the following order:-
   C. Coy. via HULLUCH ALLEY - GORDON ALLEY - POKER STREET & VIGO STREET Junct.
   B. Coy. via HULLUCH ALLEY - SACKVILLE STREET.
   A. Coy. via HULLUCH ALLEY - GORDON ALLEY to O.B.I.
   D. Coy. via HULLUCH ALLEY - VILLAGE LINE.
   H.Q. via HULLUCH ALLEY and GORDON ALLEY.
   L.Guns will move in front of the Battalion.

3. Guides ( 4 per Company and 1 for Headquarters) from 8/10th Gordons
   will be at JUNCTION KEEP at 8.30 A.M.
      Guides for the Lewis Guns at the same place at 7.30 A.M.

4. O.C. Companies will each send 1 officer and 1 N.C.O. and Headquarters
   the B.S.M. to take over Trench Stores.  Guides from 8/10th Gordons
   will be at JUNCTION KEEP at 7.30 A.M. on the 31-5-16  Receipts for
   Trench Stores will be rendered to Battalion Headquarters by 6 P.M.
   31-5-16, at G.10.B.I.5.

5. Companies will be releived as follows:-
   B. Coy. 8/10th Gordons will releive B.Coy. 9th Black Watch.
   D. Coy.    "      "      "      "    A.Coy.      "
   A. Coy.    "      "      "      "    D.Coy.      "
   C. Coy.    "      "      "      "    C.Coy.      "

      O.C. Coys will send 4 guides per company to conduct releiving
   Coys and Headquarters one guide as follows:-
      B.Coy. 4 Guides to junction of BARTS ALLEY and RESERVE TRENCH.
      D.A. & C. Coys. guides to JUNCTION KEEP.
      H.Qrs. 1 guide to JUNCTION KEEP.

6. Completion of relief will be reported to Battalion Headquarters as
   soon as after the releif is completed.

7. O.C. Companies will ensure that all trenches are left in a thoroughly
   clean and sanitary condition.

                           (Sgd) L.G.Morrison, 2nd Lieut. and A/Adjt.
                                 9th Black Watch.

Copy No.1.  O.C. A Coy.      Copy. 6.  Qr. Mr.
     2.        B.                  7.  B.S.M.
     3.        C.                  8.
     4.        D.                  9.
     5.       M.G.O.              10.  File.

S E C R E T.                                                                    Copy No.........

Defence Scheme for Battn. in Brigade Support
HOHENZOLLERN SECTION.
Appendix 2 Defence Scheme 44th I.B. d/18-5-16.
P A P E R  X.
----------------

In the event of an enemy bombardment and threatened attack against our front line between HAIRPIN Saps the following movements will take place with a view to counter attack.

1. C. Coy will proceed to O.B.s between FOSSEWAY & HULLUCH ALLEY.
2. A. Coy less 2 platoons will proceed to VILLAGE LINE.
3. B. Coy in RAILWAY RESERVE TRENCH and its platoon in CENTRAL KEEP, also 1 platoon of A.Coy in JUNCTION KEEP will stand fast and await separate orders.

D.Coy plus the remaining platoon of A.Coy in LANCASHIRE TRENCH will be employed as follows, carrying grenades :-

(1) 1 platoon A.Coy to carry grenades from Brigade Advance Store at Junction of O.B.2 and FOSSEWAY to RIGHT Bn. Grenade Store in O.G.2 between GOEBEN ALLEY & FOSSEWAY.

(2) ½ platoon of D.Coy to carry grenades from Bde. Advanced Store at Junction of GORDON ALLEY & CLIFFORDS to CENTRE Bn. Grenade Store at Junction of GORDON ALLEY & O.B.1.

(3) ½ platoon of D.Coy to carry grenades from Bde. advanced store in CANON ST. off QUARRY ALLEY pt. G.13.B.3.0. to LEFT Bn. grenade store at the QUARRY.

(4) 3 platoons D.Coy to carry grenades from Reserve store in CLARKS KEEP to Bde. advanced stores as under :-
1 platoon (1) Junction of O.B.2. and FOSSEWAY.
1 do      (2)     do     GORDON ALLEY AND CLIFFORD STREET.
1 do      (3) in CANON STREET off QUARRY- pt.G.5.B.3.0.

All these platoons and ½ platoons must contain 30 and 15 men respectively. If that is impossible then parties must be strong as possible.

O.C.Coys will take the very earliest opportunity of reconnoitring the route to the positions allotted and will ensure that all officers, C.S.M.s, and N.C.O.s, acting as platoon commanders are conversant with the routes to forward positions of Company and to all their grenade stores by parties that are detailed for supply of bombs.

In the event of an attack, the order to move being received, Coys will immediately act in accordance with above scheme on receipt of the order.

Move in accordance with PAPER X, and will report by telephone and runner to Bn. H.Q. when they have moved off.

                              (Sgd) A.D. Carmichael, Major,
26-5-16.             Commanding 9th (S) Bn. The Black Watch.

          After Order in Addition to Defence Scheme
          for Battalion in Brigade SUPPORT.
          -----------------

Should an attack develope while working parties from the Battn. are away from the Battalion.
Action to be taken :-

(i) In the case of men detailed to carry grenades to and from the various grenade stores the men will be marched to their respective stores.

(ii) Men who are not detailed to carry grenades will be organized by the officer or officers in charge of parties as per instructions received by the officer or officers in charge prior to leaving; the officer or officers will receive instructions as to the necessary action, from Battn. H.Q. where they will report to receive same.

                              (Sgd) A.D. Carmichael, Major,
26-5-16.             Commanding 9th (S) Bn. The Black Watch.

Army Form C. 2118

9 Black Watch

Vol 12

B 11

# WAR DIARY or INTELLIGENCE SUMMARY
(Erase heading not required.)

| Place | Date | Hour | Summary of Events and Information | Remarks and references to Appendices |
|---|---|---|---|---|
| CENTRE SUB-SECTION of HOHENZOLLERN SECTION | June 1st | | Own and enemy snipers and M. & L. guns active during the night, also a fair exchange of bombs at night and T.M.s during the day. Enemy were observed working on what may roughly be taken as our T.M. rifle grenade & when this was completed Minnie Martin in front of KAISERIN TRENCH and another in front of DRUMMOND trench. A lot of revetting work with sand bags is being done on DRUMMOND TRENCH, VIGO STREET, KAISERIN TRENCH and SACKVILLE STREET. They all require a lot of revetting. | |
| -do- | 2nd | | Enemy shell F.D.S. a little, but their heavy T.M. carries all the bombs in blown in trenches our T.M. to fire two or three were all & silence (permanently) to produce is not get accurately placed. If 2 minnie Martins were out some in previous nights; accordingly fire steps and debris clearing etc.) DRUMMOND trench carried on work in the trenches which seems rather unsure work each night. Trench in BORDEN ALLEY has been put in fine order. 2nd Lieut. J.F.N. McCrae reported for duty with the Batt. | |
| -do- | 3rd | | Enemy T.M. blew in a considerable part of KAISERIN trench 10 heavy T.M.s opened in & about the trench; our T.M. fired in retaliation. A lively exchange of trench trench mortars took place during the night. Our snipers must have knocked out some enemy snipers as 2 enemy loopholes which are damaged a third enemy have done very little work in these trenches the past 3 nights. Working party in the detailed job carried on good work from 2 pm till stand to with 1/2 hr interval for tea. | |
| -do- | 4th | | The night passed & without any machine gun fire & few T.M. and some casual bomb throwing. Our artillery had made a respected T.M. emplacement. A little work was going on in enemy front line. We get through a good night-work wiring, also on DRUMMOND TRENCH and the general repair of the front line and VIGO STREET. A party of the 9/10 Gordons | |

**Army Form C. 2118**

# WAR DIARY
## or
## INTELLIGENCE SUMMARY
*(Erase heading not required.)*

Instructions regarding War Diaries and Intelligence Summaries are contained in F. S. Regs., Part II. and the Staff Manual respectively. Title Pages will be prepared in manuscript.

| Place | Date | Hour | Summary of Events and Information | Remarks and references to Appendices |
|---|---|---|---|---|
| CENTRE SUB SECTION HOHENZOLLERN SECTION | 4th (cont) |  | Worked upon SAVILLE Street deepening it. The Batt. was relieved by the 12th H.L.I. relief was complete at 11.30 a.m. The Batt. proceeded to SAILLY-LA-BOURSE and were all in billets by 1 p.m. |  |
| SAILLY-LA-BOURSE | 5th |  | Batt. engaged cleaning clothing equipment &c. Inspection of same. |  |
| —do— | 6th |  | Working parties were supplied by the Batt. at certain detailed hours. The Batt. at LABOURSE him and by all available. Programme of training carried on by Coys. as far as men were then available. 2nd Lieut. G.B. Ireland and 2nd Lieut. G.N. Humble reported for duty from the 11th Batt. Black Watch. |  |
| —do— | 7th |  | } While in Bde. Reserve working parties were furnished as per detailed instructions received – the men of the Batt. who were not employed on working parties were trained in their Coys. in accordance with the programme of training issued to each coy. |  |
| —do— | 8th |  |  |  |
| —do— | 9th |  |  |  |
| —do— | 10th |  |  |  |
| —do— | 11th |  |  |  |

# WAR DIARY or INTELLIGENCE SUMMARY

Army Form C. 2118

| Place | Date | Hour | Summary of Events and Information | Remarks and references to Appendices |
|---|---|---|---|---|
| CENTRE SUB-SECTION HULLUCH SECTION | June 12th | | The 9th Black Watch left SAILLY-LA-BOURSE at 10.15 am and relieved the 11th A & S. Hrs. in the centre subsection of the HULLUCH SECTION; relief was completed at 3.2 pm. Owing to the condition of the trenches after the recent rains all coys. were engaged clearing out the trenches and lifting trench boards; no other work was attempted. The enemy were very quiet all night; a M.G. occasionally traversed the parapet and a few rifle bullets also a few rifle grenades at 2 am on junction of WING1 WAY and front line which did no damage. 2nd Lieut. A.F. Walton – H.S. Muir – S. Allan – N. Bartmann reported for duty. 1 Coy of the 11th K.O.Y. Lancs. by night. | was attached to the Bn. for instruction. It joined the Bn. at SAILLY-LA-BOURSE where it was inclined up 1 Plat. gas to each Black Watch Coy. |
| — do — | 13th | | Morning bright and as it had been through the night. |  |
| — do — | 14th | | Quiet 24 hours. Weather conditions very unfavourable and trenches in a bad state with mud and water. Gun to thin adverse conditions the work had been organised was a great deal held up due to the movement of clearing up required. Wiring of H.L.I. trench and about 50 yds of front line from DEVON LANE executed part of 1.9 pm – 5.0 pm work done respectively. The second important item of work, the repairs of front line support line due to lack of men and the frightful state of the trenches has not got on any well but much practicable work to strew for a great many hours. Kent worked 2 Relief from 7.30 or each at 4 pm o 10 am worked under R.E. men Bomb trap – 1 off – 70 O.R. worked under R.E. on all jobs. |  |
| — do | 15th | | A small parts of 8 enemy probably a mining party came out of their trenches at midnight off sap – NEWPORT SAP, active during the night with M.G. rifle and after grenades and 3 trench mortar bombs carried in each. The enemy were heard working in his own attack at 6.12.21 he had a working party out at the time and intended to withdraw 1/2 an hour later he had to put his on them but he withdrew and first on our Wire of DEVON LANE southward continued; also in front of posts BO.C.T. Work continued in advance of front and support trench also DEVON LANE, DUDLEY trench and WING1 WAY. A patrol went out from MERTHYR SAP and worked northwards. The enemy wore works on their own at the time and telling as some places the wire was thin but generally 5 ft. in wire which about this parts of their front line. |  |

1875  Wt: W593/826  1,000,000  4/15  J.B.C. & A.  A.D.S.S./Forms/C. 2118.

| Place | Date | Hour | Summary of Events and Information | Remarks and references to Appendices |
|---|---|---|---|---|
| CENTRE SUB-SECTION of HULLUCH SECTION | 16th | | A small party of the enemy came out & threw 4 bombs at our mining party at the junction of Boyau 86 & the fire trench about 3 P.M. enemy fired Lorbus 20 aerial darts at junction of STONE STREET & FIRING LINE and in retaliated with about 36 rifle grenades. Enemy snipers & machine guns were active during the night. Our Lewis guns dispersed an enemy working party. A new Boyau was dug from Boy No 9, in Support trench to a point 80 yds South of where Boyau "4" cuts the front line and about 40% of the work was done at NEWPORT SAP commenced last night and the Support was then his mine was strengthened between LARKIN LANE & STONE STREET. Working parties were supplied to the R.E. & our trenches were cleared. A patrol went out from a point almost midway between Boyaux 83 & 84. It patrolled the enemy wire & found it to be strong there. The enemy was working on his parapet.  // MAJ. S.A. INNES reported for duty with the Batt ½ the Coy of the 11th K.O.R. LANCS. Reg. was attached and left the trenches at 7pm // the 13th E. SORREY Reg. came in at 11A.M. and were distributed (1 Mn Coy.) 1 Plat. to each Coy of the Black Watch — to scrutinize. | |
| -do- | 17th | | Enemy was moderately active with his [?] artillery. They have been for some days [?] the [?] Round there was slight shelled on the HULLOCH rd. fully tramp heavily with H.E. and N.E. shrapnel; also a few aerial darts, mainly aimed on STONE Street and Em [?] stone line some night grenades, the [?] latter were placed to go between 3 to 7. During the night they rather were more active, due probably to them not having a working party and our patrols had first difficulty in getting out in [?] to them and having [?] to the them successful in laying any work. Intended trench repair were carried on. Sap on our patrol - and the new Boy A.4,7.6.A, 75% complete, the machine change in which arriving in built and an spoil removed and during walk a [?] from the N.E. / Wing was continued on Support - arriving front. | |

# War Diary / Intelligence Summary

**Army Form C. 2118**

| Place | Date | Hour | Summary of Events and Information | Remarks and references to Appendices |
|---|---|---|---|---|
| CENTRE SECTION HULLUCH SECTION. | JUNE 18th | | Enemy fired a few aerial darts about 5 am. on the right of STONE STREET in front of SUPPORT line, no damage was done. He shelled the Reserve line about noon 17th with H.E. no serious damage was done. The Support and Reserve line was shelled during the afternoon with Pencil H.E. During the morning of 19th eng sent over an occasional rifle grenade to which we replied effectively. About 1.30 am eng sent over our a bomb party to NEWPORT SAP which was driven off by an bomber. One of our patrols observed a line of 7 eny trenches smelling of SULLARS cradle – eng who had a then patrol and EAST of BRECON SAP which was surrounded another of our patrols. We could obtain no information as to the meaning of this, for work and carrying details out of the trenches, not enough men were available. BOYAU 76-A was finished – BOYAU 77A was taped out ready for depth. BOYAV 76-78 | |
| —do— | 19th | | At 7.30 am enemy fired 40-50 rounds of rifle grenades into our T.L.S. between BOYAU 76-78-80. He retaliated by firing grenades in batteries and silenced him at 8.30 am. The SUPPORT line was shelled with H.E. during afternoon of 19th and DEVON LANE slightly with H.E., about 8.15 pm. A good many aerial darts were fired into front line and BOYAV 79-80 during the afternoon. Our sniper claim 4 hits – Jerro 2 carts and 3 small periscope. Eny men seen doing a little work in their front line opposite G.118.A. saving wounded and weeth. No wire was done on our front. It is good, and to presume was given to the New BOYAU 77A, this was worked and about 25% work was done, ???? of available men were employed during number; the various carrying and work parties that came to be provided did not leave many men available for work. 2 N.Cos reported for duty, but owing to the number of officers in trenches his District is 2-3, this new officer was sent to | |

# WAR DIARY or INTELLIGENCE SUMMARY

Army Form C. 2118

| Place | Date | Hour | Summary of Events and Information | Remarks and references to Appendices |
|---|---|---|---|---|
| CENTRE SUB-SECTION HOHULLUCH SECTION. | JUNE 20 | | 13th East Surrey Regt. left the trenches at 9 am. after the tour of 4 days, relieved by the K.O.R. Lanc. Regt. came in on a company for company basis, and took up position 1 Platn. in fire line, 1 Platn. in support, and 1 Platoon in reserve line — and a column in Support. Quiet day except for slight trench mortars with H.E. & RESERVE LINE. M.G. played on working parties who were seen digging new BOYAU 77A. Afficial works that were left and carrying parties took away a large amount of all available that were left. Men employed in trench repair work, work on claim front line & main road between BOYAU 79 & 80 — on DEVON LANE and Y.L.S. & Reserve line. | |
| | JUNE 21 | | There was an intermittent bombardment of our front line throughout the day, though light aerial darts and rifle grenades to which we replied with rifle grenades. Our trenches were successful against trophies opposite BRECON SAP. An enemy working party was dispersed by our M. Fire. Men employed on construction of BOYAU 76A & 77A, spoil dumps, and repair of communication trench tracks. | |
| | JUNE 22 | | About 11.0am F.L.S. between BOYAUX 80—84 shelled with H/pneumatic aerial darts and front support lines during afternoon — no damage — Replied with rifle grenades at front support line. 9.15am 1 of our VICKERS aeroplanes brought down one Fokker. Enemy men available. Employed St ELIE & HULLUCH. After front by day and night. | |
| | JUNE 23 | | On reporting duties front by day and night. Intermittent rifle grenade & aerial darts firing by day & M.G. by night — very quiet all day. Enemy M.G. yesterday obtained some hit among men who rushed up to look at our damaged aeroplane. Heavy working Wired. The enemy replied with rifle grenades brought together retaliated with rifle trench mortars in our support. | |
| | JUNE 24 | | 2/Lt J. ALLAN slightly wounded left eye, to hospital. Quiet save for bombardment by aerial darts & grenades, to which we retaliated the same construction in trench clearing afternoon. (OC 13th E. SURREYS arrived yesterday to be attached for instruction. At 12 noon batt'n was relieved by 8/10 Gordon Hrs. and moved to Pt Support. | |

1875  Wt. W593/826  1,000,000  4/15  J.B.C. & A.  A.D.S.S./Forms/C. 2118.

# WAR DIARY or INTELLIGENCE SUMMARY

Army Form C. 2118

| Place | Date | Hour | Summary of Events and Information | Remarks and references to Appendices |
|---|---|---|---|---|
| CENTRE SUB-SECTION HULLUCH SECTION | JUNE 25 | | In Ramparts – Support. Very quiet. | |
| | June 26 | | "D" Co. 13 EAST SURREYS, on conclusion of some of intensive left transalm. There remained by "D" Coy 9th B.W. who had been in BETHUNE since 24th maintaining fora raid to be carried out early tomorrow. — Intermittent bombardment throughout the day in left batches — Capt. W. STOREY-WILSON wounded — Shrapnel arm. | |
| | June 27 | 3.15am | Following artillery bombardment. "D" Company under 2/Lt W. ANDERSON attempted a raid on a small redoubt in the GERMAN line. The enemy were however undeterred by the bombardment and in position to repel any attack. The encounter developed into a bombing one merely. 2/Lt ANDERSON + 2 men alone penetrating the enemy's line. The enemy losses probably [about the] 3 died after being brought back to our line. Were 17 wounded of whom same. 2/Lt ANDERSON shot three with his revolver. | |
| | June 28 | | Enemy shelled TENTH AVENUE and CURLEY CRESCENT from 1.45am to 2.15am in retaliation for a fire attack from our front line at 1.0am. Batt. Hqrs were struck — no casualties. — at 1.30pm Batt. was relieved by 8/10 Gt. L.I. and proceeded into Divisional Reserve Billets at BETHUNE. Strength 10 all ranks joined. | |
| BETHUNE | June 30 | | 2/Lt J. ALLAN rejoined from wounded — 2/Lt F. PROUDFOOT joined Batt. for duty. | |
| | July 1 | | CAPT. R.F.D. BRUCE + 9 other ranks joined for duty. | |
| | July 6 | | Battalion left BETHUNE and proceeded to relieve 13th R. SCOTS. in HOHENZOLLERN SECTION. R Sub sector. 46 I.B. or R. + 8/10 Gordons on L. | |

S.R. Money
Cmdg 9th Black Watch

Casualties during June, 1916.

|  | Officers. | Other Ranks. |
|---|---|---|
| KILLED. | - | 4. |
| DIED OF WOUNDS. | - | 4. |
| WOUNDED. | 2. | 45. |
| MISSING. | - | - |
| EVACUATED. | 3. | 60. |
| RETURNED FROM HOSP. | 1. | 31. |
| IN HOSPITAL. | 1. | 23. |
| LEAVE. | 3. | 54. |

# WAR DIARY or INTELLIGENCE SUMMARY

**9th. (S) Bn. THE BLACK WATCH.**

Army Form C. 2118

**JULY 1916**

| Place | Date | Hour | Summary of Events and Information | Remarks and references to Appendices |
|---|---|---|---|---|
| BETHUNE | 1916 5 July | — | Battalion in Divisional Reserve. Intended in Tobacco Factory. | |
| HOHENZOLLERN SECTION R.SUB SECTOR | 6 July | 6.45pm | Battalion left BETHUNE and marched from to the trenches, relieving the 13th R.SCOTS in the trenches of the 12 H.L.I. 46th BRIGADE being on our R. and 8/10 GORDONS on our left. On taking over the trenches the Battalion occupies are in a very bad state, this being one of the most disturbed parts of the line. Repairs done at night are blown down next day. This is especially the case with our dug heads. Enemy Guns were not very active, but his minen werfer, T.M's, Rifle Grenade. At 7.0 pm we 4 aerial darts were. All our dugouts have one trench Korn in, 4 claimed 2 hits. Her a mine in HAIRPIN CRATERS successfully. Our own claimed 2 hits. Quiet day on our front, but intermittent activity from minenwerger T.M's, rifle grenades. 4 T.M's Capt. G.A. RUSK. The enemy dead. He retaliated with Rifle Grenades, to where we replied with slightly wounded by minenwerger, Lieut H.E. EGYWELL miles others shown sent to SAILLY LABOURSE & Lieut EGLINGTON brought up. Capt. G.A. RUSK |  |
| | 8 July | | The usual T.M. and aerial dart activity to which we duly retaliated. Capt. J.M.S. DUKE, Lieut N.A. GRANT & 2 Lieut. B.M. WILSON joined the Battalion from home ETAPLES. All belong to 5th Battn T.F. | |
| | 9 July | | Intermittent shelling of F.L.S. to where we replied with a quiet morning. In afternoon T.M's and rifle grenades. | |
| | 10 July | | At 11.30 pm heavy bombardment was opened in connection with T.M's and rifle grenades. We answered with T.M's & Rifle Grenades & M.G. fire. Enemy attacked on our F.L.S. but before doing a good deal of damage & Manning was attacked on our 8th SEAFORTHS on our left. 2 Lieut N. BARTMANN slightly wounded. | |

9th. (S) Bn. THE BLACK WATCH.

# WAR DIARY or INTELLIGENCE SUMMARY

**Army Form C. 2118**

**9th. (S) Bn. THE BLACK WATCH.**  
**JULY 1916**

| Place | Date | Hour | Summary of Events and Information | Remarks and references to Appendices |
|---|---|---|---|---|
| HOHENZOLLERN SECTION RIGHT SUB-SECTION | 11th July | | A normal day. Slight shelling & minenwerfer on RABBIT RUN and KULLUCH ALLEY — Rifle grenades and 60 W.T.Ms. | Relief |
| | 12 July | | Quiet — T.M.s and dart still troublesome over our front. | |
| | 13 July | | Enemy T.M.s & Minenwerfer active all night long. Much damage to CROWN TRENCH and Left by of HAIRPIN SAP. At 3.0.pm. we blew a mine near ALEXANDER SAP but as no crater was formed, we did not occupy till up. About 7.0.pm enemy blew a mine under Sap 2&3 at HAIRPIN, but did no damage. 2/Lieut D.M. WILSON wounded arrange- | |
| BRIGADE SUPPORT CANNON ST. | 14 July | 12 a.m. | The Battalion was relieved by 7 (S) CAMERON HIGHLANDERS and proceeded to take up position in Brigade Support in CANNON STREET | |
| HOHENZOLLERN SECTION CENTRE SUB-SECTION | 18 July | 11.30 a.m. | The Battalion relieved 8/10 GORDON HIGHLANDERS in CENTRE SUB-SECTION. On our right 7 CAMERON HIGHLANDERS on our left 8th SEAFORTH HIGHLANDERS. A bombardment of enemy front & support trenches carried out from 2.0 pm to 6.0 pm when a large mine was sprung by us, blowing up BORDER REDOUBT & ALEXANDER SAP. | |
| | 19 July | | Retaliation given in a better line with a great fort enemy bombarded our F.L.S. with 77 mm 4.2" & 5.9" shells, dem- during the night. KAISERIN TRENCH and VIGO STREET. In suffered no casualties. From again the enemy retaliated from 3.50 p.m. the enemy was bombarded. We retaliated fully. Heavy but — intermittent bombardment during the night. From our F.L.S. suffered | |
| | 20 July | | A quiet day — Intermittent bombardment during the night, beyond the crater, we fort at 6.0 am enemy blew a mine outside but 83 relayed G.R.F.C. no casualties. Lieut H.E. REYNELL struck the strength on transfer | |
| | 21 July | | The night passed off quietly except in left Coy area where very active working parties were employed opposite with Track. holding normal occurred, during the day. | |
| HOUCHIN | 22 July | 6.30 pm | The Battalion was relieved by 2nd LINCOLNS and proceeded to billets in HOUCHIN. | |
| LATHIEULOYE | 23 July | 3.0 pm | The 44th I.B. marched Westwards. The Battalion from billets at LATHIEULOYE after a march of 14 miles. 2/Lieut T.E. REID & 2/Lieut W.H. CUTHBERT joined from 3rd Batt. Total casualties during 7.7.16 — 22-7-16 4 Officers wounded. 7 O.R. Killed & 40 wounded. Total 51 | |

9th. (S) Bn. THE BLACK WATCH.

**CONFIDENTIAL**

9th (S) Bn. The Black Watch

**WAR DIARY** JULY 1916

**INTELLIGENCE SUMMARY**

Army Form C. 2118

Instructions regarding War Diaries and Intelligence Summaries are contained in F.S. Regs., Part II. and the Staff Manual respectively. Title Pages will be prepared in manuscript.

*(Erase heading not required.)*

| Place | Date | Hour | Summary of Events and Information | Remarks and references to Appendices |
|---|---|---|---|---|
| MAGNICOURT SUR CANCHÉ | 26 July 1916 | 11.0am | Battalion left LATHIEULOYE 8.0 am and marched South into the 44th Brigade arriving at MAGNICOURT SUR CANCHÉ even after 11.0am and going into billets there. | |
| OCCOCHES | 27 July | 2.30pm | Battalion left MAGNICOURT SUR CANCHÉ 8.0 am and marched South into the 44th Brigade arriving at OCCOCHES at 2.30 pm. after a march of 14 miles and going into billets there. | |
| LONGUEVILLETTE | 28 July | 11.0am | Battalion left OCCOCHES 8.0 am and marched South into the 44th Brigade arriving at LONGUEVILLETTE at 11.0 am and going into billets there. | |
| | 29 July | | 2nd Lieut. W. DOW joined the battalion from the base at ETAPLES. | |
| NADURS | 30 July 1916 | 9.0am | Battalion left LONGUEVILLETTE at 4.0 am and marched South into the 44th Brigade arriving at NADURS at 9.0 am going into billets there. | |
| | | | 2/Lieut J.D.A. MACFIE struck off the strength as Observer on probation to R.F.C. | |

S.A. Innes Lt Col
Cmdg 9th (S) Bn. THE BLACK WATCH

**CONFIDENTIAL.**

Headquarters,
    15th Division.

    Herewith War Diary for the month of JULY. Please acknowledge receipt.

                                              Lieut. Colonel,

1-8-1916.        Commanding 9th (S) Battalion, The Black Watch.

Miss Kells.

B 12

Confidential

War Diary

of

9th (S) Bn. The Black Watch.

From :— 1st July 1916.
To :— 31st July 1916.

( Volume     )

The Artillery shooting was most excellent, 211 rounds were fired by B and D Batteries, nearly all landing in or close to the target.

About 7.45 P.M. O.C. B Coy informed me that enemy working parties were very busy in (a) evidently repairing the damage done in the afternoon.

I sent the Artillery Observing Officer down to observe the fire from the front trench and again got in touch with O.C. 70th Battery, arranging with him to open fire at 8.15 P.M. first on (a) and then on whole of enemy front line in H.25.D finishing up, after a gap of 15 minutes, with two salvoes on (a). This was done, 73 rounds were fired and again as far as could be seen from the front trenches the shooting was splendid.

I do not know what damage was done.

The enemy did not attempt to continue the repair of trenches in (a) during the night.

J Stewart Lt. Col.
Comdg 9th Black Watch

27-2-16.

Notes for O.C. Companies, Officer i/c Transport
Machine Gun, & Headquarters details.

---

When the Battalion arrives at PHILOSOPHE the
following programme will be carried out, during
the three days, and also during the four days at
NOEUX-les-MINES.

---

**1st. Day.** Baths, ensuring that all get one.
Clean arms, equipment, clothing & boots.

**2nd. Day.** Return all grocery portion of Iron Rations
to Q.M. Stores, and demand on a separate indent
numbers to replace. Any Iron Rations or bags or
portions of Iron Rations required to be demanded
to complete every Officer, W.O., N.C.O., and man
of the Battalion.
Inspect field dressing, and Iodine Ampouls, and
demand from Q.M. on a seperate indent those
required to complete deficiencies. All ranks
must be in possession of these, and carried in
the proper places. Inspect Identity Discs, and
submit rolls in block capitals giving full number,
rank, name, initial and religion. All ranks
must be in possession of an Identity Disc.

**3rd. Day.** Inspection of Arms, equipment, clothing
and necessaries. Articles for repair to be noted
and all repairs to be carried out at NOEUX-les-MINES
in workshops (tailor, shoemaker, and armourer) in
the order H.Q.A.C. Hd.Qrs. and M. Gun.
The workshops will be opened on arrival in long
rest billets and O.C. Companies and other details
will ensure that all repairs to Arms, equipment,
and clothing are carried on, and kept in
serviceable condition. It is observed that N.C.O.'s
and men are deficient of buttons from their service
dress jackets and greatcoats which tends to give
them a slovenly appearance in their dress. A
supply of buttons is kept in the Tailors Shop for

(over)

Contd.
replacing. Separate indents for articles to replace
unserviceable, and on payment, to be sent to the
Q.M. on completion of the inspections and with
the least possible delay.
Battalion equipment, i.e. periscopes, saws, wire-
cutters, hedging gloves, binoculars, range finders,
snipers rifles, steel helmets, very pistols,
wirebreakers, will be inspected by the C.O. personally
at an hour to be fixed later. C.S.M's will be present
and ensure that every article is produced.
As all officers ought to know the various articles
comprising a field service kit, i.e. arms, equipment,
and clothing a list of articles comprising these
is attached for their information. It should be
noted that some of the items starred are winter
issues only.
Inspection of Smoke Helmets, and goggles. All ranks
should be in possession of one P. and one P.H.
Helmet.
Range finders in possession of Machine Gun Section
will be produced at the inspection of Battalion
equipment.    The Officer I/C of signallers, &
Machine Gun will send a detailed list of equipment
in their possession to the Adjutant by 10 A.M. 22nd.

SECRET

## Defence Orders

LEFT Subsection. PUITS 14 BIS
                    Section
Ref. Trench map. 1/10000. 36 C. NW 3
                    (Edition 6)

1. Front from CHALK PIT ALLEY (exclusive) to POSEN ALLEY (inclusive); this is held by three Companies, C on the Right B in the Centre and D on the left, each finding its own support.

   A Company is in Battn Reserve in the Reserve Trench between CHALK PIT ALLEY and POSEN ALLEY.

2. The 10th Gordon Highlanders are on our right – the 6th Camerons (45th I.B.) on our left

   The 7th Camerons are in Brigade Support in 10th AVENUE, GUN TRENCH and keeps at NORTHERN SAP REDOUBT and 65 METRE PT REDOUBT

3. The 70th Brigade RFA covers our front and assistance from heavy artillery can be obtained through Artillery observation officers or through 44th Bde Hd Qrs

4. Action in case of attack
   a. The front line will be held at all costs
   b. If attacked Artillery support will be immediately called for by means of the SOS signal - 5 RED rockets in quick succession. This is to be done even if Coys are in telephonic communication and will be repeated by Batt Hd Qrs
   c. As required OC Coys will reinforce their front line from their supports and reinforcements will be sent up from Coy in Batt Reserve on receipt of orders from OC Batt
   d. OC Coys will report at once by telephone and runners (in pairs) as soon as possible after an attack takes place

and will keep the CO constantly informed as regards the progress of the fight.

e. If the front line is penetrated at any spot OsC Coys on either side will take immediate steps to dislodge the enemy by counter attack with grenadiers; instant and immediate action is required and everything depends on the initiative of the Coy and Platoon Commanders on the spot

f. The loss of a portion of the line does not entail the withdrawal of the troops on the flanks of the position penetrated. It is the duty of the latter to assist the counter attack by bombing down the trenches occupied by the enemy.

5. Should the line held by the Brigade on our left be penetrated OC A Coy will on receipt of

orders from OC Batt occupy that part of POSEN ALLEY East of the Reserve Trench

6. No opportunity must be lost by grenadiers in repelling an enemy attack - instant and resolute action will keep the enemy from establishing himself in any part of our line, should he penetrate even a small portion of it

Stewart Lt Col
Commanding 9th Batt the Black Watch

26/2/16.

Ref Map 1/10,000: 36 C; N.W.3; Edition 6.

Report on Artillery retaliation on enemy front line trenches in H 25 B and D on Feb 26th 1916.

About 3.50 P.M. O.C. "B" Coy informed me that his part of the line, about dumbbell H 25.4 was being fairly heavily bombarded by enemy rifle grenades and Trench Mortars; He also told one that our artillery were replying on enemy line directly in front.

I got in touch with O.C. 70th Battery and asked him to carry out retaliation on enemy trenches to the NORTH and SOUTH as I judged that enemy's Trench Mortars would probably be firing from one or other of the flanks.

I asked that fire be opened ~~simultaneously~~ simultaneously on enemy trenches at

(a) From H 25 D 2½.4½ to H 25 D 7.7.
    and
(b) From H 25 B 6.3. to H 25 B 4.7.
and that the heavies cooperate.

This arrangement was carried out shortly after 4 P.M. with I think very satisfactory results; The T.M. which by this time was thought to be firing from some spot in the (a) sector at once ceased fire and has not re-opened since.

SECRET.

Operation Order No.45 by Major A.D. Carmichael
Commanding 9th (S) Battn. The Black Watch.
Ref. Map 36B. 1/20,000  Friday, 26-5-16.
-------------------------------------------

1.  The 9th Black Watch will be relieved by the 7th Cameron Hrs. in
the right Sub Section of the HOHENZOLLERN SECTION on 27-5-16 as follows:-
    C. Coy. 9th B.W. will be relieved by B. Coy 7th C.H. on the right.
    D. Coy. 9th B.W.    "    "    "    "  A. Coy 7th C.H. in centre.
    A. Coy. 9th B.W.    "    "    "    "  D. Coy 7th C.H. on left.
    B. Coy. 9th B.W.    "    "    "    "  C. Coy 7th C.H. in reserve.
    Hd.Qrs. Coy.9th B.W. "   "    "    "  Hd.Qrs.7th C.H.
    The relieving Coys 7th C.H. will come up in the following order
A.B.D.C.

2.  On relief Coys. 9th B.W. will move in the following order :-
1st.  B. Coy via STANSFIELD ROAD & HULLUCH ALLEY to RAILWAY RESERVE
TRENCH north of BARTS ALLEY and one platoon to CENTRAL KEEP near
Junction of BARTS ALLEY & RAILWAY RESERVE TRENCH.
2nd.  H.Qrs. via STANSFIELD ROAD, HULLUCH ALLEY, VILLAGE LINE, &
CENTRAL KEEP ALLEY to junction RAILWAY & CENTRAL ALLEY, point G.3.C.9.2.
3rd.  D. Coy via ST. ELIE AVENUE, STANSFIELD ROAD & HULLUCH ALLEY to
LANCASHIRE TRENCH in the centre.
4th.  C. Coy by same route as D. Coy to LANCASHIRE TRENCH on left.
5th.  A. Coy via HULLUCH ALLEY, O.B.1. STANSFIELD ROAD, HULLUCH ALLEY,
to LANCASHIRE TRENCH on the right and one platoon in JUNCTION KEEP,
near junction of HULLUCH ALLEY & STANSFIELD ROAD.
Companies will move with suitable intervals between platoons.

3. Separate orders are being issued to Lewis Gun Section.

4. Guides 4 per Coy. from D.A.B. Coys. and 1 from H.Q. will meet A.B.C.
   Coys. and H.Q.,7th Camerons Highlanders at junction of HULLUCH ALLEY
   and RAILWAY at 9 A.M.
   C Coy. Guides (4) will meet B Coy. 7th Cameron Highlanders at junction
   of HULLUCH ALLEY ans RAILWAY RESERVE TRENCH at 9 A.M.
   Route :- B Coy. C.H. by HULLUCH ALLEY, O.B.I, FOSSEWAY and GOEBEN ALLEY.
            A Coy. C.H. by HULLUCH ALLEY, O.B.I, and FOSSEWAY.
            D Coy. C.H. by HULLUCH ALLEY.
            C Coy. C.H. by HULLUCH ALLEY, O.B.I, and STANSFIELD ROAD.

5. On relief Coys. and H.Q. Details will pick up one guide each at
   junction of STANSFIELD ROAD and HULLUCH ALLEY.

6. One guide per Coy., less B Coy. will be at Battalion Headquarters at
   7 A.M. to meet parties taking over Trench Stores.
   One guide B Coy., to meet party taking over Trench Stores from B Coy.
   will be at junction of HULLUCH ALLEY and RAILWAY at 6.30 A.M.

7. Coy. Signallers will move with their Companies.

8. The Trenches, dugouts and shelters must be left clean before relief.
   Attention is drawn to the fact that latrines are not always found
   sanitary after a relief.

9. O.C. Coys. will report by telephone directly their Coys. have moved
   off, and also when they arrive in position in support.
10. Trench Store lists will be handed to Headquarters by 6 P.M. on 27th inst.

                (Sgd) L.G.Morrison, 2nd Lieut.and A/Adjt.
                      9th Black Watch.
    Copy.No.1. A.Coy.  Copy No.5. M.G.O.  Copy No.9.
         2. B.Coy.          6. B.S.M.         10. File.
         3. C.Coy.          7. C.O?
         4. D.Coy.          8.

<u>SECRET.</u>  Operation Order No.42 by Lieut. J. Stewart.   Copy No.....
             Commanding 9th (S) Battalion, The Black Watch.
   Ref. France 36 B & C                              Tuesday, 10-5-16.
   -------------------------------------------

1. The 44th I.B. will be relieved by the 46th I.B. in the QUARRIES Section on 11-5-16.

2. The 9th B.W. in Brigade Reserve in NOYELLES and VERMELLES will be relieved by the 12th H.L.I.   H.Q. and 2 Coys. arriving at VERMELLES at 12.15 P.M.   Billeting parties of the 12th H.L.I. will be at H.Q. at NOYELLES and VERMELLES at 9.30 A.M on 11-5-16

3. On relief the 9th B.W. will move into billets at SAILLY LABOURSE by platoons at 200 paces intervals.   H.Q., B. and A. Coys., and L.G. detachment via main road LENS - BETHUNE.   C and D Coys. and T.M. detachment via Cross Roads L.6.0.

4. Billeting party under Lieut. Reynell will move on 10-5-16 and has received separate orders.

5. Duties at VERMELLES as under will be relieved as soon as possible 12th H.L.I. have moved into billets.   They will assemble at the Brewery, VERMELLES on being relieved and will be marched to SAILLY by a Sgt. to be detailed by O.C. C. Coy.
    1 N.C.O. and 1 man at Baths VERMELLES.
    1 N.C.O. and 3 men at Level Crossing, HULLUCH ROAD.
         do.        at Strombus Horn, VERMELLES.
         do.        Guard at Brigade Bomb Store.
    1 N.C.O. and 8 bombers, detonating party at Bomb store.
    4 men at Soup Kitchen, VERMELLES.
   1 N.C.O. and 4 men at BATHS, NOYELLES, will proceed direct to SAILLY LABOURSE on being relieved.

6. Officers Mess Cart will call at Company Messes at 9.30 A.M. VERMELLES and 10.15 A.M. at NOYELLES. Officers kits and blankets, rolled in tens as usual, for Coys. at VERMELLES to be at C. Coy. H.Q. at 9 A.M. Coys. at NOYELLES to be at Q.M. Stores at 9.30 A.M.

7. Strict attention will be paid to march discipline.   The platoon commander will march in rear of his platoon; a senior N.C.O. in the front.   Men who have to fall out will not try to catch up their own platoon but will join the next platoon that passes.

                (sgd)   S. Norie Miller, Capt. and Adjt.
                        9th Black Watch.

Copy No. 1. to A Coy.          Copy No. 9. to M.O.
         2.    B Coy.                   10. O.C.H.Q.
         3.    D Coy.                   11. to C.O.
         4.    D Coy.                   12. to 2nd in Command.
         5. M.G.O.                      13.
         6. T.O.                        14  File.
         7. Q.Mr.
         8. B.S.M.

44th Brigade.
15th Division.
------------

1/9th BATTALION

BLACK WATCH

AUGUST 1916

Attached:- Report on Operations 17/18th

CONFIDENTIAL.

44th Infantry Brigade.

Herewith War Diary for the month of August 1916.

Please acknowledge receipt.

3rd September 1916.   Cmdg. 9th (S) Battn. Black Watch
                                                   Lt-Colonel

# WAR DIARY / INTELLIGENCE SUMMARY

**Army Form C. 2118**

9th (S) Bn. THE BLACK WATCH.

| Place | Date | Hour | Summary of Events and Information | Remarks and references to Appendices |
|---|---|---|---|---|
| NAOURS | 1 August | | Battalion in billets in NAOURS, together with Hqrs & 4 regts of 44th Infantry Brigade. | |
| | 2 August | | A draft of 40 O.R. arrived from 18 I.B.D. C.O. and Capt BINNIE inspected the line between POZIERES and BAZENTIN LE PETIT. | |
| MIRVAUX | 4 August | 7.30am | Battalion left NAOURS at 4.0 am and marched southwards into billets there. | |
| LA HOUSSOYE | 5 August | 10.0am | Battalion left MIRVAUX at 7.0 am & marched southwards with 44 I.B. to LA HOUSSOYE going into billets there. | |
| | 6 Aug | | Battn. marched to BAZIEUX and met the 1st Battn. who were bivouacked there. | |
| ALBERT | 8 Aug | 6.30am | Battn. marched to ALBERT with 44th I.B. and relieved 12 D.L.I. 68 I.B. in Divisional Reserve on the BAZENTIN-LE-PETIT – POZIÈRES sector. Only 20 Officers went with the Bn. The remainder, 14 in number, proceeded under Major CARMICHAEL to a reinforcement camp. Total 20 Officers 589 O.R. | |
| O.B.1. (X 26 a & c) ALBERT map | 12 Aug | 8.0pm | Battn. moved forward into Brigade Support to 45th I.B. We were conducting an attack during the night 12/13 Aug. on SWITCH TRENCH in conjunction with 46th Brigade & ANZAC Divn on our left. The attack was precempt at but held up on R. | |

# WAR DIARY or INTELLIGENCE SUMMARY

**Army Form C. 2118**

9th. (S) Bn. THE BLACK WATCH.

| Place | Date | Hour | Summary of Events and Information | Remarks and references to Appendices |
|---|---|---|---|---|
| BÉCOURT | 1916 13 Aug | | Battn. in trenches in Divisional Reserve Brigade. | |
| CONTALMAISON | 14 Aug | 7.0 am | Battn. moved into dugouts in CONTALMAISON in relief of 11th ARGYLLS. One Platoon garrisoning strong post at CONTALMAISON VILLA, with L.Gun. 2 Coys (less 1 platoon) in GOURLAY TRENCH. | |
| FIRING LINE | 16 Aug | 5.0 am | Battn. relieved 8/10 GORDON HIGHS in the front line. On our R. 10/11 H.L.I. on our L. 4th ANZAC DIVISION. 2/Lieuts C.K. YOUNG and H.B. JOHNSTONE joined the Battn. commissioned in the field. A draft of 38 O.R. joined 1st line Transport in ALBERT. The fighting was of a curious nature, largely above the ground wielded of the unreal trench warfare. Towards mid-day the shelling became intense, especially on support + communication lines, but the casualties suffered were slight. Towards evening shelling increased, and reserve line was bombarded heavily. W1 12:30 am | |
| | 17 Aug | 2:30 am | After a lull of 2 hours recce line was again bombarded. An uneventful night save for the heavy shelling. | |
| | | 8.55 am | An attack on SWITCH LINE + ELBOW was undertaken by 7th CAMERONS from our support line. It succeeded and about 200 of trench passed into our possession. All the CAMERON officers being casualties CAPT BINNIE, 9th BLACK WATCH took command + order A Coy (9 BW) into the N (later also E) the position was made by bombing down the ELBOW was continued and | |
| | | 12 noon | of consolidation. When an counter-attack by bombing from the N of the ELBOW, a flash was well. The enemy were held with the help of a Stokes gun + mfs grenades. CAPT BINNIE being left to continue | |
| | | 12:30 pm 1:0 pm | the succeeded in re-occupying it + about 50 yds as well. The enemy were held with the help of a Stokes gun + mfs grenades. CAPT BINNIE being left to continue the consolidation of the captured trench + prepare to co-operate in a counter-attack to retake the ELBOW. | |

9th. (S) Bn. THE BLACK WATCH.

# WAR DIARY or INTELLIGENCE SUMMARY

Army Form C. 2118

9th. (S) Bn. THE BLACK WATCH.

| Place | Date | Hour | Summary of Events and Information | Remarks and references to Appendices |
|---|---|---|---|---|
| FIRING LINE 1m. N. of CONTALMAISON | 17 Aug 1916 | 2.0 pm | Owing to heavy shelling MUNSTER ALLEY had to be cleared of troops in the centre. Counter-attack against ELBOW launched by 3 coy CAMERONS, 2 platoon SEAFORTHS on R. & 2 coy BLACK WATCH on left. It was completely successful. | |
| | | 10 pm | Heavy bombardment commenced & continued till 9.0 pm when all troops had to be dispersed on account of the intensity of the fire. This bombardment continued most of the night. (The Reserve Line was bombarded all night with a constant barrage being maintained till about 5 am.) | |
| | | 9.0 pm | | |
| | | | 5.9, 4.2 & 7.8 mm | |
| CONTALMAISON | 18 Aug | 11.30 am | Relief by 8th SEAFORTHS commenced & was completed by 7.0 am. The Mission taken by the 9th BLACK WATCH was 1 Officer, about 179 Regt, 1 Corpl & 6 O.R., 179th Regt. A run & Corpl duelled with a German machine fire were captured by "B" Coy. but the officer was trained in the shelling & not recovered. There were 2 hours firing of the Battn. Bel. Wounded not by direct hits. The losses were: 1 Officer 2/Lt R.B.A. MACDONALD Killed, 6 Officers; CAPT. F.A. BEAR M., R.A.M.C., LIEUT. D.C. EGLINTON, 2/LIEUT. J.F.M. MACRAE, A.F. WATSON, R.J. McMURRAY, J.S. STRANG. Wounded — 25 men Killed 113 Wounded 12 missing, a total of 157. | |
| SCOTS REDOUBT | 19 Aug | 7.10 am | Battn. relieved by the 8/10 GORDON HIGHLANDERS who took over "B" Battn. left Brigade, & becoming "D" Battn. left Brigade, marched to SCOTS REDOUBT. | |
| PEAKE WOOD | 20 Aug | 7.0 am | Battn. relieved by 8 "K" SEAFORTHS who took over duties of "D" Battn. & relieved "C" CAMERONS as "C" Battn. in PEAKE WOOD. | |
| | | 11.0 pm | For 4 hours enemy shelled CONTALMAISON with gas shells, only portions of 2 coy were affected & none seriously. | |

9th. (8) Bn. THE BLACK WATCH.

# WAR DIARY or INTELLIGENCE SUMMARY

Army Form C. 2118

(Erase heading not required.)

| Place | Date | Hour | Summary of Events and Information | Remarks and references to Appendices |
|---|---|---|---|---|
| PEAKE WOOD | 1916 22 AUG | 8.0 am | Batln in Brigade Reserve as C. Battalion. Left Brigade XX Division. Enemy Wright. West emplaced shelled for 2 hours into CONTALMAISON. Our 2 Companies there were retiring for helmets for 1 hour. Casualties 3 men slightly gassed. | |
| CONTALMAISON FIRING LINE | 23 AUG 24 AUG | 5.0 am | Battalion moved to CONTALMAISON as B Battalion in Brigade Reserve, a draft of 157 mostly from 2/8 BLACKWATCH arrived. A further draft of 105 reached 1st Transport, mostly from 2/6 & 2/6 R.S. Battalion relieved 7th CAMERONS in the firing line, left section, XV Division III Corps on our R. 6th CAMERONS, 45th Brigade, on our L. 19 AUSTRALIAN INFANTRY. The trenches in the first to occupy 5 small strong points about 150 x in front of our front line. There were free from fire all day. The enemy was quiet during the morning but towards afternoon he shelled front & support line intermittently. Then from 7.0 pm – midnight the shelling was heavy with 8", 5.9", 4.2" & high explosives. The garrison of BUTTERWORTH TRENCH had to be moved up at one period to avoid shelling. Many men were buried & dug out. Reserve line was heavily shelled with 5.9" for ¾ hour about 7 pm. This was followed at 9.0 pm by shrapnel & gas shells in large numbers. The Coy carried to a second Kers trench over F.L.S. and helmets had to be worn for 3 hours. Till 4.0 am enemy continued occasional shrapnel & H.E. 2/Lt D.O. TWEEDIE went down with shell shock. 2/Lieut T.B. ALLISON attached to 44th L.M. Battery. | |
| | 25 AUG | | A quiet morning. During the night the enemy shelling did considerable damage to CAMERON TRENCH, HIGHLAND TRENCH, BUTTERWORTH TRENCH & ARGYLL ALLEY. About noon intermittent shelling continued & continued all afternoon. The support line was chiefly troubled by M.G. & rifle grenades. Reserve line only shelled | |

9th. (S) Bn. THE BLACK WATCH.

Army Form C. 2118

# WAR DIARY
## or
## INTELLIGENCE SUMMARY
*(Erase heading not required.)*

Instructions regarding War Diaries and Intelligence Summaries are contained in F.S. Regs., Part II. and the Staff Manual respectively. Title Pages will be prepared in manuscript.

| Place | Date | Hour | Summary of Events and Information | Remarks and references to Appendices |
|---|---|---|---|---|
| 1916 FIRING LINE | 25 Aug | | at intervals in short bursts. One 5.9 shell found the trench and killed one man & wounded another. 2/Lt H.B. JOHNSTONE wounded on a working party. 4/Lts. J.M. BROWN, J.E. DRUMMOND, & G.B. MACKIE joined from I.B.D. | |
| SCOTS REDOUBT | 26 Aug | 7.30am | Battalion was relieved in F.L.S. by 8th SEAFORTHS and proceeded to take up a position in "D" Battn. in SCOTS REDOUBT. At noon a heavy burst of Shelling with 5.9" was experienced. Intense for 15' & then lighter for ½ hour. 2 men wounded. | |
| | 27 Aug | | A quiet day, gone for intermittent shelling for ½ hour in evening. | |
| PEAKE WOOD | 28 Aug | 8.00am | Battalion took up position of "A" Battalion at PEAKE WOOD. There was a good deal of shelling throughout the day, especially about 3 o 40 pm & at 9.30 pm. | |
| ALBERT | 30 Aug | 9.45am | Battalion relieved by 27th NORTHUMBERLAND FUSILIERS and proceeded to 1m E of ALBERT, the 4th Regt. taking up Divisional Reserve in relief of 103rd I.B. Advance party of 20 O.R. joined from 3rd Battalion. | |
| | 31 Aug | | Day spent in drying all kit & equipment and in straightening up camping ground. Total casualties since Battn went into the line 9 Officers & 240 men of whom 34 were sick. | |

J.A. Innes M???
Comdg 9th Battn The Black Watch

9th. (8) Bn. THE BLACK WATCH.

44th I.B.   APPENDIX H4

Hepworth please find a diary of events during the period between 8·0 am 17th Aug 1916 and 7·0 am 18th Aug 1916

8·30 am  Dispositions Assaulting troops 3 Coys 7th CAMERONS in position in BUTTERWORTH & HIGHLAND TR — 9th BLACK WATCH 1 Coy withdrawn into the Loop from BUTTERWORTH & GLOSTER SAP., ½ Coy CAMERON TR, 1 Coy MUNSTER ALLEY, 1 Coy in & around the LOOP & ½ Coy in reserve in GOURLAY TR.

A L/Cpl & 2 men crawled out to shell hole 40× in front of MUNSTER ALLEY, from which place a M.G. had been noticed firing.

Finding the gun unmanned they brought it into MUNSTER ALLEY, where it is partly buried in a heavily shelled area but is capable of being salved in daylight.

8·55 am  Intense barrage by our artillery on enemy's line.

9·0 am  Assaulting troops, 3 coys 7 CAMERONS, went over & gained their objective. X6 a 9.3 to S.1 d 4.9 of SWITCH TR, with heavy officer casualties.

9·15 am  During our attack on SWITCH. a party of 4 Germans with M.G. on MARTINPUICH Ry stood up. Lewis gun was turned on them

|  |  |
|---|---|
| 2/ | and they were seen to fall 277 |
| 9.20am | 9 Prisoners brought down ARGYLL ALLEY & 7th CAMERON runner informed CAPT BINNIE that all the officers of his regt were hit. On going up CAPT BINNIE found men consolidating on both sides of SWITCH and he took command of about 2 companies. |
| 9.30am | CAPT BINNIE decided to construct a new trench on enemy's side of SWITCH LINE; at the same time a platoon was withdrawn from CAMERON TR to construct a sap linking GORDON ALLEY with the new front line |
| 9.45am | Work done on strong point about letter X on map, which had been finished to a depth of 3-4 ft. (Under the bombardment it has all been flattened out.) |
| 10.15am | Consolidation of SWITCH proceeded under heavy machine gun & rifle fire. The sap in front line being well marked out, the line was thinned out & the tracing of a second C.T. commenced. |
| 12 noon | This work was proceeding when sounds of bombing were heard on R. near SWITCH ELBOW. Good targets were offered by enemy |

3/        in MARTINPUICH WOOD, walking about. They were frequently fired on by Lewis & M.Gs.

           Enemy commenced bombardment with 8" shells on L. of front line & working party ceased work.

12.10pm   CAPT BINNIE proceeded to GLOSTER SAP to investigate conditions there, & found the enemy had driven in our posts, & were bombing down SWITCH, having retaken about 60ˣ.

12.30pm   Block was constructed in S.1.d.2.9 and enemy were held with aid of Stokes gun & rifle grenades.

12.45pm   Finding that CAPT MACRAE of 7ᵗʰ CAMERONS was still alive, CAPT BINNIE arranged with him to make a counter attack to recover lost portion of trench.

1.0pm   When arrangements were being made, COL MARSH arrived & took over command. From then on CAPT BINNIE centered his attention on constructing trenches as shewn in sketch from GORDON ALLEY to about S.1.b.1.½.

2.0pm   Centre of MUNSTER ALLEY cleared of troops owing to heavy shelling.

H.Q.
A H I B.

## Situation Report

Supplementary to Diary of Events already submitted.—

At about 12.10 a.m. the enemy attempted a bombing raid on our Sap at X.6.A.6½.4. M.G. & rapid fire was opened & the enemy retired without doing any damage.

Shone Miller
Capt & Adjt
for O.C. 9th Black Watch.

8/8/16
3.45 p.m.

2.50 pm. Enemy seen advancing to L. of MARTINPUICH wood. Artillery informed, who dispersed them.
3.30 pm Shelled by our own shrapnel.
4.0 pm Our counter attack launched against SWITCH ELBOW, & was successful, as we occupied it.
5.0 pm Heavy shelling, gradually increasing in intensity till 9.0 pm. when bombardment was so furious thatwork was impossible. It continued intermittently throughout the whole night
8.0 pm Heavy bombardment of MUNSTER ALLEY ceased.
10.0 pm. Resumed with greater intensity than ever

18 Aug 1916
12.30 am R. Platoon in MUNSTER ALLEY relieved by 8th SEAFORTHS
7.0 am Relief Completed

Prisoners Taken by 9th B.W. 1 officer Lt. 179th Regt, 1 corpl + 6 O.R. 179th Regt. of whom the officer & corpl died of wounds.
The officer had no papers. Those of Cpl + 1 private are sent herewith. The remaining prisoners' papers were sent down with them.
Lewis Guns

5.

One gun knocked out by direct hit which killed all the team save No1. Over half of 8 teams are casualties. 1 Vickers knocked out in CAMERON TR & 3 in MUNSTER ALLEY buried.

Reserve Line very heavily bombarded & regularly traversed by 5.9", 4.2" and pipsqueaks & occasional 8".

Casualties:
Officers Killed 1
     2 Lieut R.B.A. MACDONALD
     Wounded 6
Capt F.A. BEARN R.A.M.C.
Lieut D.C. EGLINGTON
2/Lt J.F.N. MACRAE
" A.F. WATSON
" R.J. MCMURRAY
" J.S. STRANG

O.R. Killed 27    Total 170
   Wounded 112
   Missing 24

pm
18 August 1916

S.A. Innes Lt Col
Cmdg 9th The Black Watch

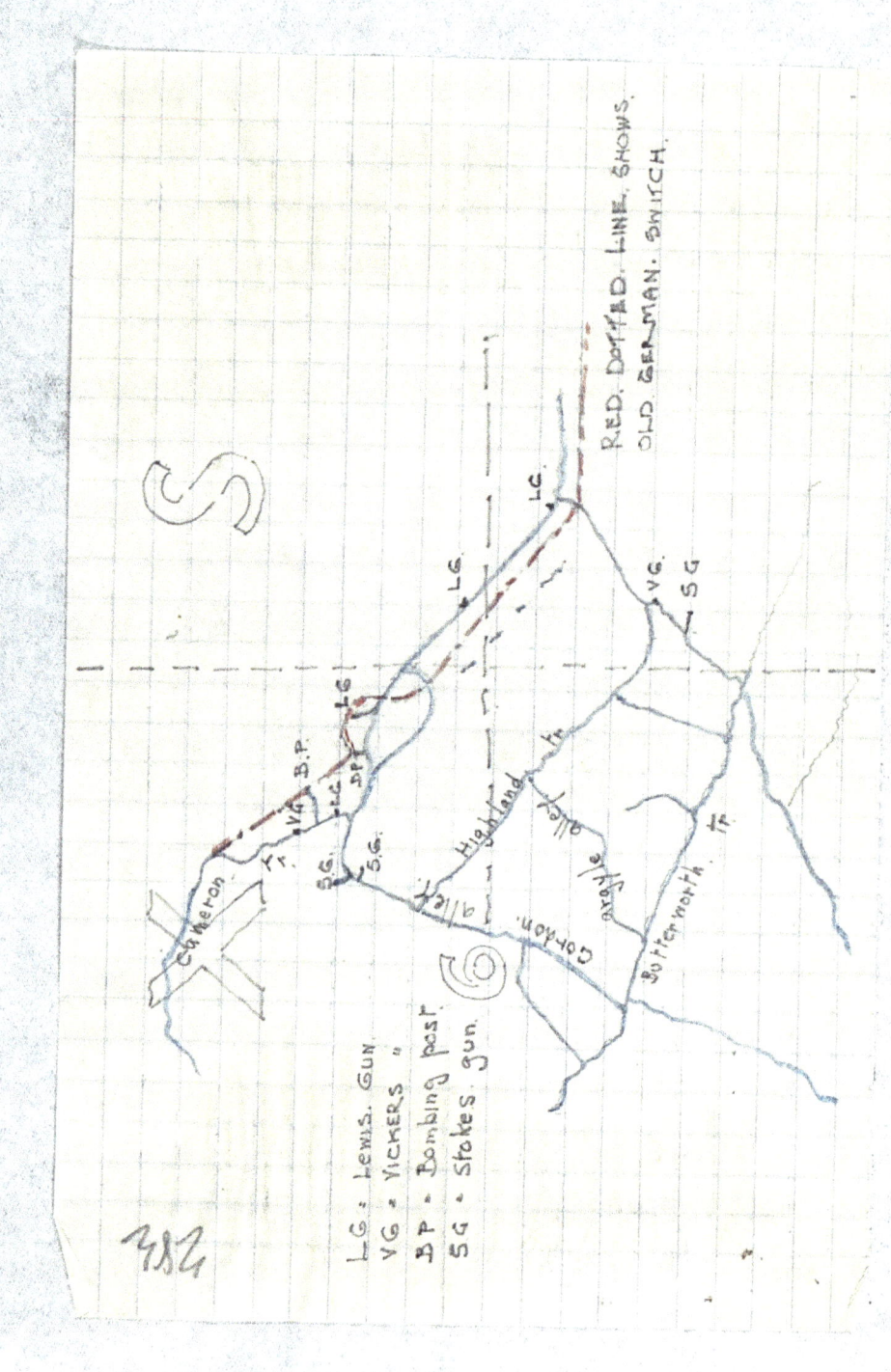

B 14

44/15. Vol 15

CONFIDENTIAL

WAR DIARY

of

9th. (S) Bn. THE BLACK WATCH.

from 1 Sept 16 to 30. Sept 16

(Vol XI)

# WAR DIARY or INTELLIGENCE SUMMARY

Army Form C. 2118

| Place | Date | Hour | Summary of Events and Information | Remarks and references to Appendices |
|---|---|---|---|---|
| ALBERT | 1916 1 Sep 2 Sep | | Battalion in Bivouac 1m E. of ALBERT in Divisional Reserve. 2/Lieut. G.H. GORDON and 15 O.R. joined from I.B.D. | |
| SHELTER WOOD | 4 Sept | 7.30 | Battn. left ALBERT and proceeded to Relieve 7th Bn. of Lincolns tog. with 1 Coy. 4th to 4 & 1/13 at SHELTER WOOD. | |
| FRONT LINE | 6 Sept | 7.30pm | Batt'n relieved 7 CAMERONS in R. Sector of the line. Field went continued towards the Relief meanwhile. HIGH WOOD and BAZENTIN LE PETIT on our R. 1/ GLOUCESTERS 3rd Brigade 1st Division on our L. 7 CAMERONS. The Sector is a very difficult one to hold as so long as HIGH WOOD is in enemy hands our front line can only be got at by night. When in that state no work of any sort can be done. | |
| | 7 Sept | | Quiet night with occasional shelling, the trenches when it rains in a terrible mess. Unsuccessful with enemy [...] been done to them. Rest little to work filling bags. BETHELL SAP was [...] Head & [...] and SIMPSONS were pushed out to join up with the [...] 59 & 77 mm [...] in the [...] Capt. J.B. ROBERTSON seriously wounded. 2 O.R. [...] Wind killing, 6 men wounded. AT MEARNS tonight it is up to take | |
| | 8 Sept | | [...] At 6.30pm a bombing attack was made on [...] Enemy trench from [...] NW corner of HIGH WOOD. At 3.30am enemy airplane flew low overhead and [...] our front. [...] BETHELL SAP. [...] [illegible] [...] machine gun & [...] led to [illegible] [...] HUMBLE ROAD B. Coy. J.E. DRUMMOND was slightly wounded. At 6.30pm also a bomb contentment B Coy under Capt. STIRLING in [...] supported by D Coy Capt. BRUCE in support [...] the enemy trench successfully carried out. A total of 70 German prisoners killed, 30 taken prisoners. The enemy line garrisoned with our [...] 2 machine guns were captured [...] [illegible] | |

1875 Wt. W593/826 1,000,000 4/15 I.B.C. I.B.C. A.D.S.S./Forms/C. 2118.
9th. (S) Bn. THE BLACK WATCH.

# WAR DIARY
## or
## INTELLIGENCE SUMMARY
*(Erase heading not required.)*

Army Form C. 2118

Instructions regarding War Diaries and Intelligence Summaries are contained in F.S. Regs., Part II. and the Staff Manual respectively. Title Pages will be prepared in manuscript.

| Place | Date | Hour | Summary of Events and Information | Remarks and references to Appendices |
|---|---|---|---|---|
| FRICOURT & LINE | 8 Sept (contd) | | Shelled but was untouched. It however started and a bombardment was made by ID Coy at optional trench but G5's practiced 750 pm & light Machine gun took up position B.2 & T.I. + about 750 pm tried to attack Fritz I went on was completed. The GLOUCESTER Regt on our R. front line. The prisoners were completed. On went up to fall back and then an enemy attack was taken enemy come into our signalling with 48 lt R Stirling to Capt R STIRLING & Coll W B RINNIE were wounded. 2/Lt G Irvine betrayed wounded. 2/Lt G R killed. 14 Somersets wounded. & Lieut J B IRELAND was many wounded. 59 wounded. TOTAL 100. Our & G5 during the night in trench consolidated themselves in parties of the enemy & snipers were rather troublesome from ShelHole. A heavy trench was made by our front trench kept up till 11.30 pm & of our support trenches turn till 4.0 am on & G were knocked out G5 cleared out from a hill. | |
| | 9 Sept | | The morning passed with a bombardment by our heavy artillery of enemy's front trench. O Coy relieved B & D Coy in front line at 4.45 pm. the I & M burn on the R. made another attack on HIGH WOOD. All L.G's in 13 ETHEL'S SAP no hanging German Casualties were inflicted on the enemy. The relief of the battalion in the line by 10 & 6th NORTHUMBERLAND FUSILIERS, 149th Brigade, 50th Division was commenced | |
| ALBERT | 10 Sept | 4.0 am | The front line was relieved by 10 & 15 " & by R.W. FORSTER. The Gulbien pushed back in ALBERT & R.W. FORSTER front pushed party. Battalion arrived in ALBERT. The day was spent in re-equipping & refitting the Coy with ammunition. Boots clothing & cleared of casualties reported from 6 officers + 119 OR. Lieut F R WILSON rejoined the battn from the Camp in the trenches party. | |
| SHELTER WOOD | 11 Sept | 10 am | Battalion proceeded to take of route in Sufflot Battalion in SHELTER WOOD march while on a memorial parade. A strap. 30 OR J F N MACRAE sent on a trip to join the battn | 3/hour |
| ALBERT | 13 Sept | 12 am | Battalion left Sufflot and proceeded to ALBERT ale. 44+113 ORs going into dinnes | |

# WAR DIARY or INTELLIGENCE SUMMARY

Army Form C. 2118

| Place | Date 1916 | Hour | Summary of Events and Information | Remarks and references to Appendices |
|---|---|---|---|---|
| ALBERT SCOTS REDOUBT | 14 Sept | 9.0 pm | Bn. fell in & moved to SCOTS REDOUBT & 9.0 pm. 2nd Battalion arrived in Reserve Trenches. | |
| MARTIN PUICH | 17/9 | 7 pm | Bn. ordered to take over trenches 9th H.L.I. in front of MARTIN PUICH with 2 R. & SEAFORTHS on right, CANADIAN Division on left. The Bn was heavily shelled during the relief & suffered several casualties. | |
| | 18/9 | | After taking over trenches the enemy opened heavy artillery fire & attempted an attack which was beaten off. The day was spent in consolidating the position won, but could not be carried out owing to heavy shelling & 150' ahead of the trenches taken. Programme arranged as shells & wire in field by 2 am. | |
| BÉCOURT | 19/9/16 | 2 am | Bn. withdrew to BÉCOURT for the 2 days. 7 killed 37 wounded. 2 N.Y.N.S. Canadians for the command of the right. Casualties in trenches at 5 O.R. killed 10 wounded. At... moved to ALBERT | |
| LAVIÉVILLE | | 2.30 pm | Bn. at LAVIÉVILLE after 4th days. Relief reached. Canadians history written Major G. Forsyth & MacGREGOR & Co. 3/15 R. McROBERTS & Co. ... left to join the Bn. ... was joined in the line by Lieut... on ... Comm... left the line. | |
| FRANVILLERS | 20 Sept | 12.30 pm | Bn. at ... Bn marched NW in camp to FRANVILLERS arrived at ... | 7 Officers killed, 4 wounded, 15 Sick 6 missing 23 | 49 294 " 62 7 Missing 456 |

9th (8) Bn. THE BLACK WATCH

# WAR DIARY or INTELLIGENCE SUMMARY

Army Form C. 2118

| Place | Date | Hour | Summary of Events and Information | Remarks and references to Appendices |
|---|---|---|---|---|
| FRAMMILLERS | 21/9/16 | | 2/Lieut R.A.M. HASTINGS joined from 11th Bn. 2/Lt. IRELAND was wounded by falling missile. S/4724 Pte T. BEATTIE S/4902 Cpl R BROWN S/4416 Cpl J. CASHMORE S/6628 Sgt T FOSTER S/7979 CQMS M A JACK S/5360 Pte W ROBERTSON S/6629 Sgt J. SAINT DERS S/6603 Pte H THOMSON all rec'd garnet scrawl S/11458 for gallantry on 17 Aug 1916 S/3967 Sgt G SIMPSON S/4571 Sgt W CHRISTIE S/11458 Sgt J BOOTH, S/3995 Cpl McCLUCKIE, S/9047 Cpl J McAULEY S/10001 Cpl F McKAY S/4754 Pte D SULLIVAN S/9613 Pte T. SMITH, S/9995 Pte T WARD, S/4779 Pte T FLETCHER S/9461 Pte R MILNE S/5360 Pte W ROBERTSON | |
| | 22 Sept | | 2/Lieuts R.T. CLARK, J CALLAM, J WILSON joined from 3rd Bn. Capt W. B. BINNIE reported Mentum Camp for service ordered on 17 Aug. | |
| | 25 Sept | | S/4794 Pte T BEATTIE to M.U. Middf. for service on 8 Sept. S/4362 Pte D WALLACE. S/9324 Pte J PUMAR, S/5127 L/Cpl W MURRAY awarded M.M. for B.W. | |
| | 29 Sept | | 2/Lt C. G. MACDOWALL joined battalion for duty from 11th Battn. | |

30 September 1916

J.R. Munro Lt.Col.
Commanding 9th Bn. The Black Watch.

9th (S) Bn. THE BLACK WATCH.

Confidential

War Diary

9th Black Watch.

1/10/16

31/10/16.

Volume 16

# WAR DIARY
## INTELLIGENCE SUMMARY

Army Form C. 2118

| Place | Date | Hour | Summary of Events and Information | Remarks and references to Appendices |
|---|---|---|---|---|
| FRANVILLERS | 1916 1 Oct. | | Battalion in Corps Reserve with 44 I.B. since 20 September 1916. Captain N. F. NORMAN R.A.M.C. and 2/Lt C. K. YOUNG evacuated sick. Captain E. GORDON R.A.M.C. assumed medical charge of the Battn. | |
| | 2 Oct. | | No. S/4096 Pte W. COSBAN awarded D.C.M. and S/4343 Pte R. McQUEEN awarded M.M. both for Gallantry on 8 Sept 16. 2/Lt S. GRAHAM joined the Battn from a Cadet Unit. | |
| BECOURT. | 6 Oct. | 5.30 p.m. | Battn marched to BECOURT with remainder of 44 I.B. & bivouaced there. | |
| LE SARS | 8 Oct. | | Battn left 3.0 a.m. and proceeded to relieve 13 D.L.I., 68th Brigade, 23rd Division in LE SARS area. The march was very long and the relief was only completed at 4.0 a.m. on our R. are 8/10 GORDONS, on our L. 6th CAMERONS. 45th I.B. were being attached. Our L. were Canadians, mostly with 5.9" & Maxmens. Battn holding salient at N.E. half of LE SARS village, with to strong points. Subject to much artillery fire, that did not suffer unduly considering the time was spent in lengthy work, cleaning weather, consolidating & improving up the strong points. Water and rations present great difficulties so they have to be brought about 4 miles, and carried up by relieving parties. | |
| | 9 Oct. | | A fairly quiet day. We had intermittent shelling with 5.9" of LE SARS and our strong point outside it. Towards afternoon 77 mm got to work on the strong point as well, with the result that several casualties occurred. | |
| | 10 Oct. | | | |

T. R. TURNBULL Lt Col
9th (S) Bn. THE BLACK WATCH

# WAR DIARY
## INTELLIGENCE SUMMARY
*(Erase heading not required.)*

Army Form C. 2118

| Place | Date | Hour | Summary of Events and Information | Remarks and references to Appendices |
|---|---|---|---|---|
| LE SARS | 1916 10 Oct | 10.30 pm | At 10.30 pm the relief of the Battn by 7th CAMERONS commenced. Owing to very slow effort that forced quietly was completed by 3.35 a.m. The Battn from Trench into support in STARFISH LINE. 2 Coy TYNE TR. ½ Coy 1½ Coys TANGLE N. & HERS MARTIN STREET. Casualties incurred there. Our heavy M.G. killed 1 officer. O.R. 4 killed | |
| MARTIN TRENCH | 11 Oct | | tot̄ɑl 53. Our have 1 officer killed 1 officer, 36 wounded, 11 missing, total 53. | |
| | 12 Oct | | Occasional shelling throughout the battalion. Men were employed in deepening CRESCENT ALLEY, MARTIN Trenches and collection of salvage, as well as repairing their own trenches. Captain J.M. REID & J. CULLEN reported on arrival from I.B.D. | |
| | 13 Oct | | Usual slight shelling took place. Major A.D. CARMICHAEL proceeded to ENGLAND for a course of instruction for officers ordered to be selected for command of Battn The Battn were relieved in 2nd support by the 10th SCOTTISH RIFLES and 2/Lieut J.B THIRD proceeded to SCOTS REDOUBT in Divisional Reserve area | |
| SCOTS REDOUBT | 14 Oct | 10.0 pm | joined from I.B.D. | |
| MARTIN TRENCH | 18 Oct | 8.0 pm | 44 + 5 I.Bs relieve 46 K I.B. in the line. Battn relieved 6 SEAFORTHS ½ Coy Battn in 2nd support in STARFISH, TYNE & TANGLE Trenches. H.Qrs in MARTIN TRENCH. | |
| CRESCENT ALLEY | 19 Oct | 9.0 pm | Battn relieved 8/10 GORDON HIGHS in support in CRESCENT ALLEY. PRUE TRENCH and O.G.1. Very wet – mud everywhere – a dark night – Relief was carried out under great difficulties – D.G.1 Coy had to dig out many of their men who were stuck in the mud. There were no casualties. | |

9th. (S) Bn. THE BLACK WATCH.

**Army Form C. 2118**

# WAR DIARY
## or
## INTELLIGENCE SUMMARY
*(Erase heading not required.)*

| Place | Date | Hour | Summary of Events and Information | Remarks and references to Appendices |
|---|---|---|---|---|
| CRESCENT ALLEY | 1916 20 Oct | | Night passed off quietly — O.G.1 shelled at intervals — Carrying parties in during trenches at much hunter. | |
| | 21 Oct | | O.G.1 shelled intermittently — remainder works an odd shrapnel or two. The weather cleared, and 7 degrees of frost during the night. | |
| | 22 Oct | | Another fire day — Frost again during night — CRESCENT ALLEY shelled from 9.0 — 10.0 pm with 5.9 at intervals. Captain W. REID, 9/t G.C. LESLIE, & 2/Lt J.F.M.L. WILKIE joined from I.B.D. | |
| LE SARS | 23 Oct | 11.4 A | The batln. relieved 7th CAMERON HIGHRS in Front Line, R. Sector, L. Division on 5th R. 9th Division on account of rain coming on, but on arrival the relief was stopped & north half companies Front Line & support off trenches were shelled into a quiet night. Much work was hindered as gas masks stopped. mostly the day. Trenches in very bad, and our sanitary park storm in the day almost unmanned. Relief of the Battln by 8/10 SEAFORTHS commenced at 8.0 pm. Relief in completed by 11.35 pm. | |
| SCOTS REDOUBT | 24 Oct | 8.30 am | at SCOTS REDOUBT in Divisional Reserve. The weather was appalling, the men very heavy, & Lot company reached here at 6.0 am after 8 hour walk of 4½ miles of ground. Casualties in this time 1 killed & 5 wounded. had the second occasion on which the batln. had to withdraw on account of weather conditions, when prevented to carry out and participate in a general attack. | |

Army Form C. 2118.

# WAR DIARY
## or
## INTELLIGENCE SUMMARY.
*(Erase heading not required.)*

| Place | Date | Hour | Summary of Events and Information | Remarks and references to Appendices |
|---|---|---|---|---|
| SCOTS REDOUBT | 1916 26 Oct | | The battalion was employed cleaning up arms, equipment etc, drying their clothes, repair boots etc. | |
| | 27 Oct | | Batln. was to have gone into the line in preparation for an attack, but it was postponed on account of bad weather. | |
| | 28 Oct | | Employed on salvage work & carrying parties. Batln. was again to have proceeded up to front line, but owing to bad weather move was further postponed. | |
| CRESCENT ALLEY | 31 Oct | 6.0 pm | Battn. moved up to 1st Support in CRESCENT ALLEY in relief of 12th H.L.I. Lieut D.A.D. BROWN sentenced by G.C.M. to be dismissed the service. Sentence duly promulgated. | |

S.A. Innes Ker
Cmdg 9th (S) Battn. The Black Watch.

CONFIDENTIAL

Vol 17

B16

9th. (S) Bn. THE BLACK WATCH.

War Diary
November 1916.

Vol 17.

# WAR DIARY or INTELLIGENCE SUMMARY

Army Form C. 2118.

| Place | Date | Hour | Summary of Events and Information | Remarks and references to Appendices |
|---|---|---|---|---|
| | 1916 | | | |
| CRESCENT ALLEY | 1 Nov. | | The enemy kept up intermittent shelling of try in front in O.G.1. Enemy aeroplane was employed in watching parties in LE SARS S. TRENCH. Working parties were greatly hampered by wet. The trenches continually falling in. | |
| BÉCOURT | 2 Nov. | 11.0 pm | A heavy enemy barrage put on O.G.1 about 7.0 pm but night. Intermittent shelling throughout the day. At 8.30 pm 6th GLOUCESTERS 48TH DIVN relieved the batth in its support & we moved back into Reserve at BÉCOURT under canvas. Casualties whilst in the line during the 2nd tour 50tr - 2 Nov. Killed: 10/L, 7 O.R. Wounded 68 O.R. Missing 3. Total 79. | |
| BRESLE | 5 Nov. | 3.30 pm | Battalion left BÉCOURT and marched via ALBERT to BRESLE where the 4th & 1.B. went into rest billets, 2 battalions under canvas. | |
| | 6 Nov. | | Taken up with cleaning rifles, equipment &c., replacing clothing, boots. Inspection of head, organs, teeth, feet & cycle. | |
| | 7 Nov. | | Platoon training by Coy commanders. Specialists under their own officers. | |

9th. (8) Bn. THE BLACK WATCH.

Army Form C. 2118.

# WAR DIARY
## or
## INTELLIGENCE SUMMARY.

(Erase heading not required.)

Instructions regarding War Diaries and Intelligence Summaries are contained in F. S. Regs., Part II. and the Staff Manual respectively. Title pages will be prepared in manuscript.

| Place | Date | Hour | Summary of Events and Information | Remarks and references to Appendices |
|---|---|---|---|---|
| BRESLE | 1916 | | | |
| | 13 Nov. | | Major H.F.F. MURRAY arrived from NIGG for duty with the Battn. | |
| | 20 Nov. | | Lt Gen. Sir W.P. PULTENEY, G.O.C. III CORPS addressed the Battalion on their work twice coming to the SOMME front, 300 men of the Battalion went to BECOURT to work on roads, hutting etc. remaining there. | |
| | 25 Nov. | | 2nd Lts O.C. FRASER, A.D. McDIARMID, W. FERGUSON, & R.O.S. WILSON joined from 11th Battn. | |
| | 27 Nov. | | Hqrs & 'C' Coy inspected by G.O.C. 15th Division, Maj Gen McCRACKEN DSO. MIL. MEDAL was awarded to No 11214 Sergt WILLIAM GOWARD for gallantry at MARTINPUICH on 15 Sept 1916. Military Cross awarded to Lieut & Qmr W. CLARK | |
| | 28 Nov. | | | |
| | 30 Nov. | | orders received that Bn would move to ALBERT on 1st Dec. | |

J. Munro Lt. Col.
Commanding 9th Bn. The Black Watch.

9th. (S) Bn. THE BLACK WATCH.

Secret
Confidential

Vol 18

B17

9TH (S) BATTN  THE  BLACK WATCH

WAR DIARY

DECEMBER
1916

Vol. XVIII

1 Jan 1917

J A Hunter
Cmdt 9th Black Watch

# WAR DIARY
## or
## INTELLIGENCE SUMMARY.
*(Erase heading not required.)*

Army Form C. 2118.

| Place | Date | Hour | Summary of Events and Information | Remarks and references to Appendices |
|---|---|---|---|---|
| | 1916 | | | |
| ALBERT | 1 Dec. | 11.0 am | 44th I. Brigade marched from BRESLE where they had been in rest since 5 November to ALBERT, arriving about 11.0 am the Battn going into billets in RUE FÉLIX FAURE. | |
| | 6 Dec. | | Battn employed on fatigues 2 days in every four. The Town is shelled every afternoon for about an hour, a large proportion of the shells being duds. 2 Lieut G.B. MACKIE evacuated sick to England 25 Nov. 16. | |
| | 11 Dec. | | Major J.M. GILLATT, Royal Scots struck off the strength on leaving to assume Command of 16 Royal Scots. The Battalion paraded 22 officers & 11 O.R. for inspection by G.O.C. 15th Divn. who expressed himself very pleased with their turn out, kit and general appearance. A draft of 199 O.R. arrived from NIGG and joined the Battalion. | |
| | 13 Dec | | Major A.H.d'A. DENNISTOUN, 3rd attached to Battalion. Transferred from 12th H.L.I. | |
| SHELTER WOOD | 16 Dec | 10.30 am | 44th I.B. moved into Divisional Reserve at SHELTER WOOD & Scots Redoubt. The Battn was in tents and without boards 8-12 inches of mud in front at night. Work done was roadmaking in the camp itself. | |

9th (S) Bn THE BLACK WATCH.

# WAR DIARY or INTELLIGENCE SUMMARY.

Army Form C. 2118.

| Place | Date | Hour | Summary of Events and Information | Remarks and references to Appendices |
|---|---|---|---|---|
| SHELTER WOOD | 19-6 18 Dec | | Battn still employed road making. 300x of road were cleared of mud debris & drainage cleared out & chalk laid on. Then filled up the chalk had to be carried on trap 1/2 mile which lengthened the task. | |
| CONTALMAISON | 19 Dec | 3.30pm | 4th I.B. relieved 46 L.I.B. in L Sector. 15th Durh: Front. The Battn went into 2nd Support at NIUA CAMP relieving 13 R Scot. CONTALMAISON was shelled for about an hour from 4.30 - 5.30 pm. also the road Hut Hge to the CUTTING in CONTALMAISON. | |
| | 20 Dec | | A quiet day. 1/2 Battn employed on working Parties. Remainder in draining and improving camp. | |
| | 21 Dec | | Working parties as before. CONTALMAISON and vicinity shelled 6-8 pm & 10-11 pm. | |
| | 22 Dec | | Very wet. Battn employed draining & clearing camp. 150 men on working parties. 2/Lieut J. M. BROWN wounded whilst on way up to inspect the line. | |
| 26TH AVENUE | 23 Dec | 6.30 | Battn relieved 8 SEAFORTH HIGHRS in front line. Left Battn left section. 4th CAMERONS on R. 7th CAMERONS on L. 4th GORDONS. Sit Domain. The weather was wet, but with a high wind which dried the ground a good deal between the showers. A very rapid relief was effected. | |

9th (3) Bn. THE BLACK WATCH.

# WAR DIARY
## INTELLIGENCE SUMMARY
*(Erase heading not required.)*

Army Form C. 2118.

Instructions regarding War Diaries and Intelligence Summaries are contained in F. S. Regs., Part II. and the Staff Manual respectively. Title pages will be prepared in manuscript.

| Place | Date | Hour | Summary of Events and Information | Remarks and references to Appendices |
|---|---|---|---|---|
| 26TH AVENUE | 1916 24 Dec | | A quiet night. Suspected that a relief of the enemy was taking place, as artillery rate was increased to 6/72 rds per hour. No officers searched. 2 Patrols were sent out, both getting in touch with the enemy. 2 Pats for centres wandering & misstepped. Many materiel was carried up and trenches partially cleared of mud. Where the men were actually living. | |
| | 25 Dec | | A quiet night. Not very wet. 150+ wire was almost finished and 20+ more half finished. Our artillery kept up the same bombard- ment throughout the night as last night. From 11.0 to 11.30 am 3 intense bombardments of enemy line took place. In afternoon enemy retaliated shelling FLERS LINE, DESTREMONT FARM, 26TH AVENUE & valley nearby from 3-4 pm. 6-8 pm & 10-11 pm. 2/Lt GRAHAM slightly wounded. | |
| | 26 Dec | | Enemy artillery was more active on our support trenches lines during the night. Wiring was continued during the night, 100 yards being completed in addition to that already in hand | |

8th. (S) Bn. THE BLACK WATCH.

# WAR DIARY
## or
## INTELLIGENCE SUMMARY.
(Erase heading not required.)

Army Form C. 2118.

| Place | Date | Hour | Summary of Events and Information | Remarks and references to Appendices |
|---|---|---|---|---|
| | 1916 | | | |
| 28TH AVENUE | 26 Dec | | Hand. No material for further work was available. Our front support lines were shelled intermittently. DESIRE (MONT FARM) and trench cross trench heavily camouflaged for Alfred. Line suffered one casualty. | |
| | 27 Dec | | A quiet night. 65 x bombs completed NOF CABLE TRENCH in front of her trench filled in Pits, trench boarded. During the afternoon intermittent shelling of trench trench. At 5.0 pm relief of Batn. | |
| SCOTS REDOUBT NORTH | | 11.0 pm | by 7/8 K.O.S.B.'s commenced & finished at 11.0 pm. About 6.45 pm the enemy shelled MARTIN PUICH & trench trench trench very heavily with gas - shell & shrapnel. 3 companies were caught in the gas but came through very luckily in relieved, with only 2 casualties 2/Lt RAM HASTINGS & 1 man wounded. The former slightly remaining at duty. Tear gas & shell gas were mixed, & there was hard frost the next day. The gas hung about a long time. 3 or 4 men complained of the after effects. Bn. proceeded a relief to SCOTS REDOUBT NORTH, arriving at 1.30 am, the rear party the camp being handed by 10th SCOTISH RIFLES. 4/4th I.B. with relieved in the line by 4 & 4 I.B. & proceeded into Divn. Reserve 9th. (S) Bn. THE BLACK WATCH. | |

T2134. Wt. W708—776. 500000. 4/15. Sir J. C. & S.

# WAR DIARY
## INTELLIGENCE SUMMARY
(Erase heading not required.)

Army Form C. 2118.

| Place | Date | Hour | Summary of Events and Information | Remarks and references to Appendices |
|---|---|---|---|---|
| | 1916 | | | |
| SCOTS REDOUBT | 28 Dec | | A cold damp day. Men employed in cleaning rifles, ammunition & resting. Total casualties during Dec. 3 O.R.s wounded, 1 O.R. killed, 1 O.R. | |
| NORTH | | | wounded & 3 cases trench feet. | |
| | 30 Dec | | Bn. employed laying trench boards, draining the camp, filling shell holes and generally making it more habitable. 2/Lt J.F.M WILKIE evacuated 21st to England. | |
| PIONEER CAMP | 31 Dec | 4.30pm | Bn. employed as duty Battn. on numerous working parties. At 4.0 pm left SCOTS REDOUBT and proceeded to PIONEER CAMP in relief of 6th CAMERONS as Reserve Bn. in R. Sector, R. Divn. Section. 44th I.B. relieved 45th I.B. | |

S.A. Munro Lt.C.
Cmdg 9th Black Watch.

31st December 1917

4/5' 9TH (S) BATTN.
The Black Watch.
January, 1917

CONFIDENTIAL

Vol 19

9TH (S) BN. THE BLACK WATCH

WAR DIARY

JANUARY 1917

117/113

S Athur ... on
Cmdg 9th Black Watch

Army Form C. 2118.

# WAR DIARY or INTELLIGENCE SUMMARY.
(Erase heading not required.)

9th (S) Bn. THE BLACK WATCH

118

| Place | Date | Hour | Summary of Events and Information | Remarks and references to Appendices |
|---|---|---|---|---|
| | 1917 | | | |
| PIONEER CAMP | 1 Jan | | Battn. in Brigade Reserve, R. Sector, 15th Divn Front, III Corps, 4th Army | |
| SEVEN ELMS | 2 Jan | 7.15 pm | Battn. relieved 8 SEAFORTH HIGHRS in support at SEVEN ELMS (ICO3), 2 Coys STAR-FISH TRENCH, 1 Coy PRUE TRENCH. Before relief Battn employed on Brigade working parties, and cleaning up camp. Opening drains & laying trench boards. | |
| | 3 Jan | | A quiet night. PRUE TRENCH shelled with shrapnel & H.E. from 10 - 10.30 pm and again 5.30 - 6.0 am causing 7 casualties. Battn employed on working parties improving front line & reserve line. A draft of 112 O.R. arrived from ETAPLES. | |
| FLERS SWITCH | 4 Jan | 9.15 pm | A quiet night. Slight shelling of PRUE TRENCH, E. end. Battn. relieved 8/10 GORDON HIGHRS and R. Battn (R Sector, L Sector III Corps) on our R. 50th Divn, 6th NORTHUMBERLAND FUSILIERS on our L. 8th SEAFORTH HIGHRS. Front line Coys employed improving their posn. Reserve Coy. working in Support line. | |
| | 5 Jan | | A quiet night, but from noon an enemy artillery activity increased con-siderably. FLERS LINE & rally leading towards the BUTTE and BUTTE Alley were shelled a good deal. In the afternoon a bright moon in front line much interfered with by the bright moonlight which gave great chance. | |

# WAR DIARY or INTELLIGENCE SUMMARY

Army Form C. 2118.

| Place | Date | Hour | Summary of Events and Information | Remarks and references to Appendices |
|---|---|---|---|---|
| FLERS SWITCH | 5 Jan 1917 | | Rifles and Machine Guns 110* rounds were carried out. Trenches were hard & frosted. Enemy's Bank Stores filled up. Mr. G.H. GORDON slightly wounded. Following New Year Honours were announced :- D.S.O. MAJ (TEMP LT-COL) S.A. INNES, CAPT F.A. BEARN RFA. M.C. 3/3849 R.S.M. G.D. BEDSON, Mention - MAJ (TEMP. LT-COL), S.A. INNES, TEMP. MAJ. A.D. CARMICHAEL TEMP CAPT S. NORIE-MILLER, TEMP 2/LIEUTS. J.F.N. MACRAE, G.B. MACKIE & TEMP. QMR & HON. LT. W. CLARK. | |
| | 6 Jan | | Hostile artillery became active early in the day especially on support line & Reserve Crystler. Afternoon it increased in intensity on the same localities. Only one party was affected. Our heavies carried out 2 bombardments of BUTTE TRENCH but without any retaliation. Bright moonlight gave enemy snipers & machine gunners too good a target for any amount of work to be carried out. Aircraft of 17 O.R joined the Bath from ETAPLES. Intercompany relief no effected wit 1 casualty. | |
| | 7 Jan | | A quiet night in front. trepid man shot. Enemy artillery shelled FLERS LINE & Br Nys heavily throughout daylight. Construction of further posts in front commenced. | 119 |

**Army Form C. 2118.**

# WAR DIARY
## INTELLIGENCE SUMMARY.
*(Erase heading not required.)*

Instructions regarding War Diaries and Intelligence Summaries are contained in F. S. Regs., Part II. and the Staff Manual respectively. Title pages will be prepared in manuscript.

| Place | Date | Hour | Summary of Events and Information | Remarks and references to Appendices |
|---|---|---|---|---|
| FLERS SWITCH | 1917 7 Jan | | A quiet day in front. Intermittent shelling of FLERS LINE & BOX TRENCH 9 p.m. The frost gave way to rain & weather was very mild. 130 yards French wire were put out in front line, 2 posts were dug and one improved. Work continued on revetment of posts and clearing out drains. Enemy aeroplane very active. | |
| | 8 Jan | | Battle wire active on that part of enemy's artillery on the support reserve line but a quiet night in front. From 10-1.30 Bn. H.Q.s were shelled. Enemy's 9" and 5.9" guns used. In the afternoon MARTINPUICH to BAZENTIN were shelled heavily with 5.9" & 4.2". Bn H.Qrs shelter C.J. opened up on the I.B. The 7/6 K.O.S.B. relieved the Batt. in front lines, the 4th & 1.B. | |
| SHELTER WOOD SOUTH | | 11.30 pm | relieving us 4.4 I.B. & Batt. came back into Divn Reserve at SHELTER WOOD SOUTH. Consolidating trenches. 2 O.R. killed, 1 Offr, 12 O.R. wounded. Batts. resting and cleaning themselves & their equipment. Relief was complete | |
| | 9 Jan | | | |
| | 10 Jan | | —do— and supplying small working parties. | |
| | 11 Jan | | —do— | |
| TWENTY SIXTH AVENUE | 12 Jan | 9 & 11 p.m | The 4/4/5 I.Bde. relieved the 45/5 I Bde. in the Right section, Left section IIV front the Bn. relieved the 13th Royal Scots in the right Bn. frontage. The relief was complete | 120 |

6th (S) Bn THE BLACK WATCH.

| Place | Date | Hour | Summary of Events and Information |
|---|---|---|---|
| | 1917 Jan | | |
| | | 9:40 pm | On the right of the Bn. are the 46th I Bde. on the left are the 8th Seaforths others of 44th I Bde. Coys. were engaged in cleaning mud out of the trenches & posts occupied and carrying on with the work in connection with same. |
| | 13 Jan. | | Work carried on in parties of two, teaching fire tactics, trench head layers, wiring and revetting. Three Coys. engaged in carrying material to support Coy. supplied as many men as were available to assist working parties of 9th Gordon Hrs. diggers new trench between O.G.1 & O.G.2 in this line. Bn. H.Q. DESTREMONT FARM and neighborhood now shelled in retaliation for our artillery strafes of the BUTTE. nights very dark until moon rises. |
| | 14 Jan. | | A party of 5 enemy approached one of our posts they were observed and our L.G. was turned on to them; result not known, buoyant to the fact that they were challenged, one of them however returned and gave himself up; he belonged to the 64th T.I.R. he was asked at N Coy. H.Q. if he would like a cigarette and said "no thanks!" lady smoke again; the evening could be slow owing to the fact that the Dump had been over night glean, men not fatheoming. Until the moon rises any movement is difficult owing to referenced in getting about owing to the intense cloudiness. Rumours of firing are continued and |

Army Form C. 2118.

# WAR DIARY
## or
## INTELLIGENCE SUMMARY.
*(Erase heading not required.)*

122

| Place | Date | Hour | Summary of Events and Information | Remarks and references to Appendices |
|---|---|---|---|---|
| | 1917 Jan | | | |
| | 15 | | enlarging of same. An whole Coy. relief was carried out N night; the relief was completed at 12.46 am. Stown for writing, revetting, trench heads, did not arrive so that the work was severely hampered. There was a good deal of shelling in the vicinity of Bn. H.Q. DESTREMONT FARM & LE SARS, with 5.9 H.E. amongst which were some tear shells. | |
| ACID DROP CAMP | 16th | | Battⁿ moved to ACID DROP CAMP as Bde Reserve on relief in front line by 7th Bn. Cameron Highlanders. | |
| | 17th 18th | | Battⁿ remained at ACID DROP CAMP and furnished various Brigade working parties. | |
| VILLA CAMP | 19th | | Battⁿ proceeded to VILLA CAMP. Two companies detached to MARTIN PUICH, the whole Bn. furnished Batt⁵ in support to 13th Worcesters furnished for Bg. | |
| | 20th | | No change. Working parties furnished as on previous day. | |
| SHELTER WOOD SOUTH | 21–23. | | Bn. moved to SHELTER WOOD SOUTH on 13th becoming Bde in Div Reserve. Working parties furnished under Bde instructions. | |

Army Form C. 2118.

# WAR DIARY
## or
## ~~INTELLIGENCE SUMMARY.~~
*(Erase heading not required.)*

Instructions regarding War Diaries and Intelligence Summaries are contained in F.S. Regs., Part II. and the Staff Manual respectively. Title pages will be prepared in manuscript.

123

| Place | Date | Hour | Summary of Events and Information | Remarks and references to Appendices |
|---|---|---|---|---|
| | 1917 Jan | | | |
| FLERS SWITCH | 24-1-17 11.15pm | | Bn. took over Bt. Sector from 11th & 2nd A. & S. H. at 11.15 p.m. Slight casualties from shell during relief. 9/5 D.O.W. and 7 men slightly wounded. A and D. Coys. Front line. C & H. Qts. B. | |
| | 25-1-17 | | Heavy trench mortar played on right part of D Coy. One O.R. mortally wounded. MAXWELL SUPPORT badly damaged. Garrison withdrawn about 20 yards. During the night the post was improved and material carried up. One hand kindled by the frozen state of the ground. Patrol proceeded in direction of BUTTE DE WARLENCOURT but nearly superior forces of enemy withdrew without casualty. | |
| | 26-1-17 | | "B" and "C" Companies took over from "A" and "D" in the evening. A patrol went out from "B" Company and encountered a hostile patrol near LE SARS STATION. Shots were exchanged. Our patrol returned without casualty having effected its purpose. | |
| | 27-1-17 | | Hostile Artillery and Aerial Scouts caused a few casualties. Hin activity probably due to it being the Kaiser's birthday. In the evening several strong parties of the enemy were seen and dispersed by our Lewis Guns and R.F.A. Went of the night was quiet. Considerable enemy artillery activity on our front line front and Bt. H.Qts. | |
| PIONEER CAMP | 28-1-17 8.2pm | | Bn. handed over to 8/10th Gordons and moved to Bde Reserve at PIONEER CAMP. Battalion was shelled, 1 killed, 3 wounded. | |
| | 29/30-1-17 | | Bn. used at Pioneer Camp and furnished Bde working parties, as Bn. in Reserve, R. Sector. | |
| SEVEN ELMS | 31-1-17 | | Bn. moved to Bde Support at SEVEN ELMS, taking over from 4th Cameron Highlanders. | |

9th. (S) Bn. THE BLACK WATCH

T2134. Wt. W708—776. 500000. 4/15. Sir J. C. & S.

Army Form C. 2118.

# WAR DIARY
## or
## INTELLIGENCE SUMMARY.
*(Erase heading not required.)*

| Place | Date | Hour | Summary of Events and Information | Remarks and references to Appendices |
|---|---|---|---|---|
| SEVEN ELMS | 31 Jan 1917 | | Battn in Support - Furnishing working parties. 2/Lieut J.W. BARR joined on 9th Jan from No 18 I.B.D., CAPT. W. B. BINNIE m.c. and 2/LIEUT. A. F. WATSON rejoined the Battn, after being wounded, from Home. 2/LIEUT. J. ALLAN evacuated sick to ENGLAND 23rd Jan. 1917. | 124 / 1B |

S A Innes Lt Col
Cmg 9th (S) Bn. The Black Watch

8. Head quarters will move to RUE de TURENNE. leaving present Head quarters at 12 midnight.

9. Spare Officers will be accommodated at RUE de TURENNE.

10. A cyclist orderly will be at H 19 b 3.3. by Tank in Northumberland lane at 9 a.m. daily to collect reports and messages
    This orderly will leave not later than 10 a.m

16/12/17.

K Barrett
M.C Capt
Comdg. 144 M.G.Coy

Copies to.
1. O.C
2. Lt Winn
3. " Jenkins
4. " Fell
5. " Smith
6. " Taylor
7. " Littlejohn
8. T.O
9. File
10. War Diary
11. War Diary
12. 46 M.G Coy.

to guide the teams of 46 Coy.

On relief teams in 2, 3, positions will return to BAUDIMON BARRACKS. Guns from positions 11, 12, will move to positions nos. 2, 3A.

e. Guides for 4, 5, 6, 7. positions will be at TANK DUMP at 6.pm on 13th inst to guide in teams of 46 Coy.
On relief Lt Smith will be responsible that teams from Nos 5, 6 7 positions move to G.S.1 G.S.2. I 9.
Gun from No 4 position will report at H 14 b 3.3. Corrugated iron shelter by the Tank in Northumberland Lane. Lt Bell will direct them to I 9 position.

Below will be found a table showing positions of guns & Officers in Charge.

been handed over Lt Smith will return with the Officer of 46 Coy (Lt Arch) and take over positions I.9, I.10, G.S.1 G.S.2.

On the morning 17th inst, Lt Jell will visit the Officer of 46 Coy who lives at H.17.b.3.3. (by Tank in Northumberland (ave)) and will take over positions I.1, I.2, I.3, I.6, I.7.

Lts Jell & Smith must see that not only they but also the Officers they are relieving thoroughly understand the system of relief.

C. The gun in TRENT TRENCH will change places with No I.10 position — this will be completed by 6 p.m. on the 17th inst.

D. Guns 2, 13, 11, 12 will have guides at CAMEL X roads at 6 p.m. on the 17th inst.

| Gun from Position No. in Reserve at Hqrs. | Move to Position No. | MAP. REFERENCE. | OFFICER IN CHARGE. |
|---|---|---|---|
| 3 guns | S. 15. | Along | Lt. JENKINS. |
|  | S. 16. | INVERGORDON TRENCH |  |
|  | S. 17. |  |  |
| 8 | 1 | H 17 d 00·90 | Lt. FELL. |
| 10 | 2 | H 17 b 20·20 |  |
| 14 | 3 | H 17 b 40·25 |  |
| 15 | 6 | H 11 c 95·20 |  |
| TRENT TRENCH | 10 | In TRENT TRENCH | Lt. SMITH |
| 2 | ARRAS |  |  |
| 11 | CORPS LINE 2 | H 16 d 50·20 | Lt. LITTLEJOHN. |
| 12 | " " 3A | H 16 d 80·40 |  |
| 13 | ARRAS |  |  |
| 5 | GS. 1 | H 6 c 45·55 | Lt. SMITH. |
| 6 | GS. 2 | H 6 a 45·25 |  |
| 7 | 9 | In TRENT TRENCH |  |
| 4 | 4 | H 11 c 80·80 | Lt. FELL. |

4. As soon as relief is complete and guns are in position in their new places, "Relief Complete" will be sent to present Headquarters.

5. As soon as teams are in position in their new places all teams shall be reduced to 3 men — a suitable number of N.C.O's being retained. The remainder, N.C.O's & men, will move to BAUDIMONT BARRACKS, & report to C.S.M. Officers will report names and positions of N.C.O's retained with their "relief complete".

6. Tripods & belt boxes will be handed over with the ordinary trench stores & receipts obtained. Lists of all trench stores (a) handed over to (b) taken over from, 46 M.G. Coy will be sent to present Headquarters with "relief complete".

7. All movement by day will be in very small parties, not more than one gun team at a time.

SECRET

Operation Order 6 [Bn Diary]
by
Capt. K.V. Barrett. M.C.
Cmdg. 44th Machine Gun Coy.

1. The 46th M.G. Coy will relieve the 44th M.G. Coy in the left sector 15th Div. On relief 44th Coy will move to positions in Divisional reserve. This relief will be carried out on 17th/18th December.

2. Nos 1 of 46 Coy will be at the CAMEL X roads at 5.45 p.m. on 16th inst — these will be collected by ration parties.

3. The relief will be carried out as follows:—

   a. The three guns at present in reserve will move at 11 a.m. on the 17th inst. to positions S 15, 16, 17. in INVERGORDON TRENCH, and relieve 3 guns of 46 Coy who are moving to the positions vacated by them.

b. Guns 8, 10, 14, 15, will have guides at the CAMEL X roads at 2 pm on the 17th inst to guide in teams of 46 Bty.

On relief these teams will move to CAMEL X roads where they will meet an N.C.O of 46 Bty who will guide them to positions I1, I2, I3, I6.

In order to facilitate the relief Officers of 46 Bty are going us to take over on the afternoon of the 16 inst as follows:—

1 Officer will meet Lt Dell at No 15 position at 2 pm to take over Nos 14, 15 positions.

1 Officer will meet Lt Smith at No. 10 position to take over nos. 7, 8, 10 positions at 3 p.m.

As soon as these positions have

OPERATION ORDER No 1. War Diary

BY

CAPT. K. V. BARRETT. V.C.

CMDG N° 44 M.G. Coy

(SGD) KB/1917

1. The H.H. Coy. M.G. Corps will relieve the H.B.C. Company on night of 1/2nd Dec 1917.

2. Positions will be taken up as follows:-

   "A" Section in Reserve in SHRAPNEL SWITCH.

   "B" Section.
      N° 5 Team to N° 2 Position
      " 6 "  "  "  14   "
      " 7 "  "  "  11   "
      " 8 "  "  "  12   "

   "C" Section
      N° 9 Team to N° 3 Position
      " 10 "  "  "  15   "
      " 11 "  "  "  16   "
      " 12 "  "  "       "

O.O.B. CON.

"D"-SECTION

| Nº 13 TEAM to | Nº 4 POSITION. |
|---|---|
| " 14 " | " 5 " |
| " 15 " | " 6 " |
| " 16 " | " 7 " |

LIEUT. TAYLOR will be in charge of positions 2, 11, and 12.

LIEUT SMITH. positions 4, 5, 6, and 7.

LIEUT LITTLEJOHN positions 8, and 10.

LIEUT JENKINS positions TRENT TRENCH. and 14, 15 reserve Section.

III. Tripods and Belt boxes will be taken over by B, C, and D. Sections.

"A" Section will take in with them 4 Tripods and 110 belt boxes.

(Continued)

O.O 61 cont

(v) Units of Trench Stores taken over are to be at H.Q. by 8:30 am 2nd Dec 1917.

(vi) Officers will report daily at Battn HQ in whose sector their guns are.

(vii) All Officers will send by 6 pm 2nd Dec. a DETAILED report on am of a rough sketch map of each of their gun positions and its field of fire.

(viii) C.H.) are situated in gun pits just in Lear of SUNKEN ROAD. at H.17.c.1.7

9TH (S.) BATTN,
The Black Watch.

February, 1917.

9th (S) Bn. The Blackwatch Vol 20

WAR DIARY
1st installment
28th February 1917

125
///

J Bowllo Shaw
Lt. Col.
9th Blackwatch

Army Form C. 2118.

# WAR DIARY
## or
## INTELLIGENCE SUMMARY.
*(Erase heading not required.)*

| Place | Date | Hour | Summary of Events and Information | Remarks and references to Appendices |
|---|---|---|---|---|
| | 1917 | | | |
| SEVEN ELMS | 1 Feb | | Battn in support R. Subsector R. Section to Section III Corps | |
| BECOURT CAMP | 2 Feb | 11pm | Battn relieved by 19th Bn Australian Infantry and proceeded to A Camp. The 13th Division relieved by 2nd AUSTRALIAN Division. | |
| | | | 2/LIEUT. W. DOW. died of wounds received 24th Jan 1917 at 45 Z C.C.S. + buried at DERNANCOURT. | |
| BRESLE | 4 Feb | 4.0 pm | Battn left BECOURT and marched via ALBERT & MILLENCOURT to BRESLE where they went into billets. On the road they were bombed by hostile aeroplanes. but only 2 horses were slightly wounded. | |
| | | | The details from HENENCOURT reinforcement camp rejoined Battn. | |
| | | | Total casualties during the last tour in the line 15th Dec — 2 Feb were | |
| | 5 Feb | | Officers. Killed 1 Wounded 3 Sick 9 O.R. K. 9 W. 36 Sick 178 Total 236. | |
| | | | The New Year's Dinner was held. over 700 being present. A draft of 2 Officers 2/Lieuts T. BYERS & T. EDWARDS & 80 O.R. joined from No 18 I.B.D. 2/Lieut W. FERGUSON evacuated sick to ENGLAND 30 Jan 17 | |
| | 8 Feb | | | |
| | 11 Feb | | 2/Lieut J.L. BURTON and 42 O.R. joined Battn from No 18 I.B.D. | |
| VADENCOURT | 13 Feb | 11.30 am | Battn left BRESLE at 10.0 am and marched to VADENCOURT CHATEAU from | |

126

(8) Bn. THE BLACK WATCH.

**Army Form C. 2118.**

# WAR DIARY
## or
## INTELLIGENCE SUMMARY.
*(Erase heading not required.)*

| Place | Date | Hour | Summary of Events and Information | Remarks and references to Appendices |
|---|---|---|---|---|
| | 1917 | | | |
| VADENCOURT | 13 Feb | | into billets there | |
| BEAUVAL | 14" | | Bn. marched from VADENCOURT to BEAUVAL, where it was billeted. | |
| OUTREBOIS | 15" | | Bn. marched from BEAUVAL to OUTREBOIS  " | |
| LIGNY | 16" | | Bn. marched from OUTREBOIS to LIGNY  " | |
| CROISETTE | 17" | | Bn. marched from LIGNY to CROISETTE  " | |
| BUNEVILLE | 18/23" | | Bn. marched to BUNEVILLE on 18th, on which day 2/Lt W. ANDERSON and M. DUGGAN joined from No. 18 I.B.D. Company training was undergone till the 23rd, when the Bn. moved to billets at AMBRINES. Capt J. CULLEN remained left in BUNEVILLE as Town Major. | |
| AMBRINES | 24/28" | | The Bn. was reorganised in accordance with instructions from G.H.Q. The Bn. was employed on Brigade fatigue. Training was carried on in accordance with divisional scheme by all available men. Capt J.M. REID rejoined Bn. from III Corps. M.T. on February 28th. | 127 2B |

WWMurray /Major

Commdg. 9(S) Bn. The Black Watch

Vol 21

WAR DIARY

March 1917

9' Black Watch

15 Fri

CONFIDENTIAL

13 20

# WAR DIARY or INTELLIGENCE SUMMARY

Army Form C. 2118.

| Place | Date | Hour | Summary of Events and Information | Remarks and references to Appendices |
|---|---|---|---|---|
| AMBRINES | March 1st to March 8th | | Bn. remained at AMBRINES. Bn. fatigue party of Capt. J.M. REID and 113 O.R. furnished. EDL 4th Coy. training was gone through on 1st – 3rd; IX Bn. training commenced on 6th; the Bn. was inspected by the C. in C. Field Marshal Sir Douglas Haig on March 6th. O. draft of 30 men joined the Bn. from the base on 5th. 2/Lt. HUMBLE rejoined on 6th. Capt. MEARNS, 2/Lt. T.W. HUNTER and 2/Lt. A. D. McDIARMID re-joined and 2/Lt. E. E. DALE joined the Bn. from the Base on 8th. 2/Lt. DALE was posted to "A" Company. Capt. and Adjt. S. NORIE MILLER rejoined the Bn. on 2nd. | |
| ARRAS | 10 Mar | 9.35 pm | Battn. marched via HERMAVILLE and BAUDIMONT GATE to billets in ARRAS relieving the 11th A. & S.H. and "D" (Reserve) Battn., & lent to 4/5th L.B. | |
| | 11 Mar | 10 am | Battn. relieved 13 R. SCOTS in I 3 Sector Left Sub-section, on our R. 8/10 GORDONS, on our L. 8th BLACK WATCH, 26th & 39th Division. Capt. A. H. MEARNS struck off the strength on proceeding to R.F.C. on 10th Mar & Capt. J.M.S. DUKE struck off on 10th March on taking up duty as Staff Captain 9(?) | |
| | 12 Mar | | Enemy was not very active. No or little(?) front or support but reserve line shelled between 1 & 5 pm about 10.30 pm & during the night. | |

# WAR DIARY
## or
## INTELLIGENCE SUMMARY.
(Erase heading not required.)

Army Form C. 2118.

| Place | Date | Hour | Summary of Events and Information | Remarks and references to Appendices |
|---|---|---|---|---|
| | 1917 | | | |
| ARRAS | 13 Mar | | The night passed off quietly. Work was done on F.L. and I.C. Ts, but the rain interfered considerably with operations. R. Coy was subjected to intermittent T.M. fire throughout the morning. At 5.0 pm S.O.S. was put up on our R. and our trenches, front & support, being subjected to heavy fire from the enemy. After about an hour normal conditions prevailed. The Bn. had only 1 casualty, a corporal killed. | |
| | 14 Mar | | A quiet night. The usual intermittent bombardment of our R. Coy with T.Ms. in the morning. At 1.50 pm our artillery, Stokes, Medium & Heavy T.Ms. carried out a 20 min bombardment of BLANGY and vicinity. The enemy replied vigorously on our front & support trenches. The men were withdrawn under cover & our casualties were slight. At 7.30 pm an intense bombardment by T.Ms. aerial darts and rifle grenades was opened on our front line. Our Stokes retaliated. Enemy working parties were dispersed by our Lewis guns. The remainder of the night passed quietly. | |
| | 15 Mar | 9.30 am | Battn. was relieved in L. Sector, L. Subsection, by 8th (S) Bn THE BLACK WATCH. 9th (S) Bn SEAFORTHS and | |

Army Form C. 2118.

# WAR DIARY
## or
## INTELLIGENCE SUMMARY.
(Erase heading not required.)

Instructions regarding War Diaries and Intelligence Summaries are contained in F. S. Regs., Part II. and the Staff Manual respectively. Title pages will be prepared in manuscript.

| Place | Date | Hour | Summary of Events and Information | Remarks and references to Appendices |
|---|---|---|---|---|
| | 1917 | | | |
| ARRAS | 15 Mar | | returned to billets in ARRAS in cellars, as "D" Batt in reserve. | |
| | 19 Mar | | Capt W. STOREY-WILSON awarded Italian Silver Medal for Military Valour. | |
| | 20 Mar | | ARRAS shelled heavily from 7-0 pm to 8-30 pm. | |
| | 21 Mar | | ARRAS shelled almost all day chiefly with 5.9". | |
| | 22 Mar | | A draft of 41 O.R. arrived from No 18 I.B.D. to join the battalion. Lieut F.R. WILSON evacuated sick to ENGLAND 15th March 1917 | |
| DUISANS | 26 Mar | 11.0 pm | Batt relieved by 7th CAMERONS and marched back to No 1 Camp at DUISANS. The night was quiet & there were no casualties. | |
| | 27 Mar | | A draft of 83 O.R. arrived from No 18 I.B.D. on 27, and of 27 O.R. from No 18 I.B.D. on 29. Mt J. ADDISON joined the Bn on 25th. | |
| | 30 Mar | | The Batt. was inspected and addressed by the Corps Commander | |
| | 31 Mar | | After the inspection the Bn marched past in fours. Batt. employed on washing parties. | |

S. A. Innes Ker Col
Cmdg. 9th Bn The Black Watch

9th (S) Bn. THE BLACK WATCH.

CONFIDENTIAL

WAR DIARY

APRIL 1917

9TH BN. THE BLACK WATCH

# WAR DIARY
## or
## INTELLIGENCE SUMMARY.
(Erase heading not required.)

Army Form C. 2118.

| Place | Date | Hour | Summary of Events and Information | Remarks and references to Appendices |
|---|---|---|---|---|
| DUISANS | 1917 3/4 April | 10.30pm | Battn in Reserve at DUISANS. Returned to ACQ carried out. Battn marched via ST CATHERINES and relieved 7 CAMERONS in L. Sub sector. The 8/10 GORDONS being on our R. and the 6/7 R.S.F. 45th I.B. on our left. There was only casualty coming in | |
| | 4 April | | at 6.0 a.m. the bombardment started, followed by a discharge from Gas Bombs at 6.15 a.m. which appeared to be very successfully scattered over RAILWAY TRIANGLE. Retaliation was very slight by day, and Artillery at night. | |
| | 5 April | | Retaliation at night for 2½ days bombardment was heavy, at 7.0 a.m. a practice barrage enemy front trenches failed to draw any response. Raids were carried out at noon on the L. and at | |
| | 6 April | | 10.15 pm on the R. again at 3.25 a.m. the shelling which had been continued to Reserve line + Bn Hqrs was very heavy all over + lasted all night through, that our casualties were only 1 killed + 1 wounded was remarkable. | |
| | 7 April | | Shelling by the enemy was only intermittent and our bombardment | |

Army Form C. 2118.

# WAR DIARY
## or
## INTELLIGENCE SUMMARY.
(Erase heading not required.)

Instructions regarding War Diaries and Intelligence Summaries are contained in F. S. Regs., Part II. and the Staff Manual respectively. Title pages will be prepared in manuscript.

| Place | Date | Hour | Summary of Events and Information | Remarks and references to Appendices |
|---|---|---|---|---|
| | 1917 | | | |
| FRONT LINE | 7 April | | Continued as before. A very successful patrol was carried out by 2/Lt S. GRAHAM at 3 am. He penetrated both I.N.C.O. into the enemy front line & gained valuable information & only just missed bringing back a prisoner. | |
| | 8 April | | At 1.0 am a raid was carried out by 2 Platoons of B Coy under 2/Lts R.K. McROBERTS & J.L. BURTON on the Enemy line S. of the Railway to DOUAI. Parties of platoon reached the enemy front & support trenches but there remained from going further by the trenches being filled with concertina wire. By the time the line cut only 10 minutes remained before our barrage came back to the front line again. 2 Boys who were located, 1 prisoner was taken & enemy killed. The former was apparently killed when being escorted back. An 2 of his escort were wounded by a shell stayed by an explosion at very short range. Total Casualties were 5 O.R. Wounded. 2 2/O.R. Missing. | |

T2134. Wt. W708—776. 500000. 4/15. Sir J. C. & S.   8th. (S) Bn. THE BLACK WATCH.

**Army Form C. 2118.**

**WAR DIARY**
or
**INTELLIGENCE SUMMARY.**
(Erase heading not required.)

CONFIDENTIAL

Instructions regarding War Diaries and Intelligence Summaries are contained in F. S. Regs., Part II. and the Staff Manual respectively. Title pages will be prepared in manuscript.

| Place | Date | Hour | Summary of Events and Information | Remarks and references to Appendices |
|---|---|---|---|---|
| FRONT LINE | 1917 8 April 10 p.m. | | Gas was liberated from 4 "Stokes" shells on to enemy F.L.S. | |
| | 9 April 5.30 a.m. | | Batt. was all in position in jumping-off trenches by 3.10 am in order to admit of troops in rear moving up. At 5.30 am gas was again put into the enemy lines. The whole line advanced on a front of 1200 yds with slight losses & reached 1st objective at about 5.45 am. Barrage was put down promptly & about 1 minute on our F.L.S. | |
| | 7.10 am | | At 7.10 the advance to the second objective was commenced. The attack was held up by hostile M.G. fire from the E. arm of the RAILWAY TRIANGLE for about 3 hours. The support Bn. Gs. (A Tank advanced and the second objective was reached about 1.30 pm. Consolidation began at once commenced. At 2.10 p.m. the 46th Regt advanced through 44 I.B. & 45 I.B. to attack the 3rd Objective. The 7th Cameron relieved 9th Bn in front line & 9 B.W. came into reserve in HERMES TRENCH. | |
| HERMES TRENCH. | | | Casualties were over 200. Prisoners & Machine guns taken. Large consignments war material, mortars, sundry ammunition, maps plans, medical. | |

9th. (S) Bn. THE BLACK WATCH.

**CONFIDENTIAL**

Army Form C. 2118.

# WAR DIARY
## or
## INTELLIGENCE SUMMARY.
*(Erase heading not required.)*

| Place | Date | Hour | Summary of Events and Information | Remarks and references to Appendices |
|---|---|---|---|---|
| HERMES TRENCH | 1917 9 Apr. | | The casualties were 3 Officers killed, 12 wounded, OR K. 38. W. 176. M. 12. Total 241 out of a strength of 17 Officers & 618 OR. The Officers killed were:— 2/Lt. O.C. FRASER, Capt. H.J. COLLINS C.F., 2/Lt. D.W.H. CUTHBERT, wounded:— Capt. & Adjt. S. NORIE-MILLER, W. STOREY-WILSON, 2/Lieut. T.W. HUNTER, E.M. REID, T.E. REID, J. CALLAN, R.K. McROBERTS, A. MARSHALL, F. PROUDFOOT, J.W. BARR, H.S. MUIR, R.M. DINWIDDIE. | |
| | | 10 p.m. | The Battn remained in Reserve, and were employed in burying dead, collecting salvage, and furnishing working parties to wiring parties. | |
| FEUCHY | 11 p.m. 5:00am | | At 3.5 am Battn. was ordered to move to FEUCHY to support an attack by 45 & 46 Bydes. They arrived at 5:30 pm & orders received there all day. At 11.30 pm orders were received to move into ARRAS in anticipation of relief by 17th Division. | |
| ARRAS | 10 Apr 2:30 am | | Battn arrived in ARRAS & billeted in the Grande Place. Later in the day they moved to the SCHRAMM Barracks. Battn received congratulatory messages from C in C, Army, Corps & Divisional Commanders on their excellent performance on 9th April. | |

Army Form C. 2118.

# WAR DIARY
## or
## INTELLIGENCE SUMMARY.
*(Erase heading not required.)*

| Place | Date | Hour | Summary of Events and Information | Remarks and references to Appendices |
|---|---|---|---|---|
| | 1917 | | | |
| ARRAS | 18 April | | Bn. in cellars in GRANDE PLACE, refitting after action of 9th April. 2nd Lieut. T.F.REID died of wounds received on 9th at No.1 RED CROSS HOSPITAL. | |
| WANCOURT – FEUCHY – LINE | 19 April 11.30 AM | | Batt. relieved 1/K.O.S.B., 29th Division in support 8/10 GORDONS taking over front line on R. of Divisional Sectr. On our L/F R.S. FUSILIERS, 45 I.B. on our L. 4 YORKS REGT. 150th I.B. | |
| | 20 April | | During the day the trenches were deepened. Hostile shelling continued. About 9.30 pm in retaliation for an attempt to avenge a post on our left the enemy put a barrage down on our support trench line which caused a few casualties and seriously interfered with working parties in front. | |
| | 21 April | | A fine cold day with good observation towards enemy trenches. Artillery on both sides was very active especially on ours. 2/Lt R.K. NARDBERTS evacuated to England 11 April. | |
| | 22 April | | A quiet day. Artillery harassment continued. First preparations were made for attack. | |
| WANCOURT MARLIÈRE | 23 April 3.00 AM | | Batt. stood to at 2.30 am to man the front line of trenches & then moved forward to... | |

9th. (S) Bn. THE BLACK WATCH.

**Army Form C. 2118.**

# WAR DIARY
## —or—
## INTELLIGENCE SUMMARY.
*(Erase heading not required.)*

Instructions regarding War Diaries and Intelligence Summaries are contained in F.S. Regs., Part II. and the Staff Manual respectively. Title pages will be prepared in manuscript.

| Place | Date | Hour | Summary of Events and Information | Remarks and references to Appendices |
|---|---|---|---|---|
| | 1917 | | MARLIÈRE. All were in position by 4:30 am. Zero hour was 4:45 am. | |
| MARLIÈRE | 22 April | 4:45am | The Batt. was to attack the R. Front, moving up however in support of 4/5 and 1/8 SEAFORTHS who were to take GUÉMAPPE. The 7 CAMERONS were on L and 8/10 Gordons in reserve. The attack was held up soon after the start by M. Gun fire from LH flank, and as the storms of the Bayelles in interior R. COEUIL dependent on our flank being secure, whereas 50 Bgn on R or 45/B at L ceased to make progress, so did 44 I.B. do likewise. The Seaforths here moved to get through GUÉMAPPE or even into it until about 11.0 am when the M.G. which had been covering the trouble was knocked out by the Scots. An advance of about 500 yards was then made. When the M. gun trouble commenced, and the attackers were compelled to ensure GUÉMAPPE. A move partly of about 70, chiefly Black Watch under Capt MORRISON however remained in their trenches to N of village, and though their flanks were quite open, they managed to maintain themselves there for 4 hours until ordered to withdraw to O.G.1 and straggled to their pits. The shelling was heavy | |

9th. (S) Bn. THE BLACK WATCH.

**Army Form C. 2118.**

**WAR DIARY**
or
**INTELLIGENCE SUMMARY.**
(Erase heading not required.)

| Place | Date | Hour | Summary of Events and Information | Remarks and references to Appendices |
|---|---|---|---|---|
| | 1917 | | | |
| MARLIERE | 23 April | | On there particular trenches as our own artillery not knowing the Black Watch had not retired to O.G.1 put a barrage upon them. Turning the next hour the situation remained much the same one for the shelling which was intense at 6.0 p.m. a second attack was ordered by Capt. Morrison with all the troops he could muster in Immediate reserve, viz. some 70 men of Stirling, Black Watch, Seaforths & Cameron. The leader & Ranger in killed in the first few yards but the attack succeeded in recovering all ground lost and a little more besides. The 46 I.B. came through & CA when 300 of 1st Objective which they could have easily reached had the barrage not melted according to original order. | |
| N.15.a | 24 April 2.30 a.m. | | The 9th B.W. consolidated & kept watch but brought here withdrawn to bivouac at N-15.a. where they arrived about 2.30 a.m. The Officers killed were 4. Capt. & G Morrison — Lieut. O.L. Bearn — 2/Lts A.F. Watson & J. Wilson. 1 died of wounds 2/Lt W. Anderson, 6 wounded 2/Lts C.K. Young, J.N. Humble, J.B. Third, G.C. Leslie, R.A.M. Hastings, J.L. Burton (on duty). O.R. — K.5 — W.155 — M.12 | |

9th. (S) Bn. THE BLACK WATCH.

**Army Form C. 2118.**

**WAR DIARY**
or
**INTELLIGENCE SUMMARY.**
(Erase heading not required.)

| Place | Date | Hour | Summary of Events and Information | Remarks and references to Appendices |
|---|---|---|---|---|
| | 1917 | | | |
| N.15.a | 24 April | | The enemy were 3rd BAVARIAN DIV. and 1st Jaeger Btn. belonged chiefly to 16th Regt. The fighting throughout seven divisions the shelling and the Coy. Officer were relieved from 16.6.6. the to the were employed chiefly in a trench that night | |
| BROWN LINE | 25 April | 7am | Battn. moved up to the BROWN LINE the day being spent in re-equipping & for no particular for advance. | |
| Between MARLIÈRE & GUÉMAPPE | | 4.0pm | A4th & V45 LBs relieved 46th I.B. in the Sum Sector. 9th B Watch were on R. between R. COJEUL and point 500* N.7.d. 1500* E. of GUÉMAPPE on our R. 11/6 Divn & our L. 7th CAMERONS. Front line consisted of short length of trench unconnected with, but within sight of each other. There were no at behind the BLUE LINE the objective ordered. A proposed reconnaissance in force to take CAVALRY FARM & 2 adjoining trenches at 2.30pm was considered impracticable and unordered. The night passed quietly only a few shrapnel being put over in front and Battn. Hqrs. in Henin shelled with 5.9, 4.2 & high explosive, but intermed. throughout the night CAVALRY FARM & adjoining trenches were bombarded by the heavy artillery | |
| | 26 April | | | |

9th (S) Bn. THE BLACK WATCH.

**CONFIDENTIAL**

Army Form C. 2118.

# WAR DIARY
## INTELLIGENCE SUMMARY.
*(Erase heading not required.)*

Instructions regarding War Diaries and Intelligence Summaries are contained in F.S. Regs., Part II. and the Staff Manual respectively. Title pages will be prepared in manuscript.

| Place | Date | Hour | Summary of Events and Information | Remarks and references to Appendices |
|---|---|---|---|---|
| Between MARLIÈRE & GUÉMAPPE | 1917 26 April | | In preparation for an attack on then by 45 I.B. on L. 7 Camerons on Centre & 9th B.W. on Right. The operation presented considerable difficulty as from the line in which touch recommenced & the advance to be made turned from S.0. on R. to 30° in some places. The result the wiring & digging of the 45 I.B. reached their objective & established 2 posts in N. Trench. 7 Camerons noted the farm but failed at L.5 trench next to M.G. fire. 9th B.W. pushed at fort on R. went too far on each up L. 7 Lot trench. All started to consolidate but the Enemy counter attacking drove out 45 I.B. & 7 Camerons & left B.W. had 300 in front of our front line & to the our 2/Lt A.D. McDIARMID and 2/Lt T.B. ALLISON, 2/Lt A.4.T.M.B. wounded | |
| | 27/4/17 | | The difficulty of the situation which had arisen lay in the fact that movement by day into the trenches and on to forming were completely cut off from the start, by all they had power over the ground at night. It was discovered that 2/Lt J.L. BURTON and about 20 men were missing which may include casualties yet to be reported. Enemy artillery was very active especially in early morning and continuous on GUÉMAPPE & ranks | |

9th. (S) Bn. THE BLACK WATCH.

# WAR DIARY
## INTELLIGENCE SUMMARY

Army Form C. 2118.

| Place | Date | Hour | Summary of Events and Information | Remarks and references to Appendices |
|---|---|---|---|---|
| Between MARLIERE & GUÉMAPPE | 1917 27 April | | Battn. H.qrs. at abt midnight the 8/10 Gordons relieved the Battn in R. Sector & Battn came back to DRAGOON TRENCH and SPEAR LANE strength reduced to 2 officers with exp. + 130 OR. Battn H.qr.s at N.B. Moore | |
| ARRAS | 28 April | 9.30 pm | Battn was relieved by 2 coys 1/LONDON Regt and proceeded back to ARRAS arriving about 11.50 pm | |
| SIMENCOURT | 29 April | 5.45 pm | Battn left ARRAS at 3.15 pm and marched via BERNEVILLE to SIMENCOURT where the whole 44th IB went into billet | |
| | 30 April | | Total casualties in the 2nd phase 23rd – 28th April – Officers – killed 1, missing 7, wounded Total 13. O.R. killed 28, missing 27, wounded 175. Total 230 grand total 243 all ranks. Total 1st Phase 15 officers 242 OR = 257 Total casualties in April 28 officers & 472 OR | |

S.P. Innes Lt Col
Cmdg 9th (S) Bn The Black Watch

9th. (S) Bn. THE BLACK WATCH.

Headquarters,

44th Infantry Brigade.

BB706

Narrative of Events from 23rd to 28th April 1917
with special reference to 9th Bn. The Black Watch.

| | |
|---|---|
| 23rd April. 3-30.am. | The Battalion started at 2-30.am. to move into Jumping Off trenches. One shell caused 19 casualties in one platoon. Headquarters moved forward to MAHLIERE. All were in position at 4-30.am. |
| 4-45.am. | At "Zero" hour 7th Camerons commenced the attack, but in the darkness held rather too much to the North, with the result that troops following them were also slightly misdirected. The 9th Black Watch, instead of waiting for half an hour as they should have done, commenced going over at about "Zero" plus 6 minutes, filling up the gap between Camerons and Seaforths. The result of this was an intermingling of units from the start, and probably slightly increased the casualties when held up at the SUNKEN ROAD by machine gun fire. |
| 11.am. | A Stokes Gun came into action and overcame one of the machine guns. Sgt. GIBB of "B" Coy. singlehanded worked his way round through the end of the trench and knocked out the crew of another, and the line advanced, about 60 prisoners being taken.<br>The advance was continued to just E. of GUEMAPPE village, when owing to machine gun fire the attack was driven back again. A mixed party of about 70, chiefly Black Watch, under Captain Morrison, remained however in their trenches to the North of the village, DRAGOON LANE and the bank of road to the West of it, and, though their flanks were quite open, they managed to maintain themselves for over 4 hours until ordered to withdraw to O.G. 1 and straighten out the line. The shelling was heavy on these particular trenches, as our own artillery, not knowing that the whole line had not retired, put a barrage upon them. When this retiral took place some 10 or 12 men refused and an officer of the Camerons refused to leave the position they occupied. All were found still holding the position later in the day when the advance was resumed. A small party of one officer and about 12 other ranks of the Black Watch also remained in GUEMAPPE throughout the day. |
| 2.pm. | For the next 4 hours the situation remained much the same, save for the hostile shelling which was intense. |
| 6.pm. | About 5-45.pm. a second attack was organised by Captain Morrison with all the troops he could muster in the vicinity, about 70 Black Watch, Seaforths and Camerons. The leader was unfortunately killed in the first few yards, but the attack succeeded in recovering all the ground lost and a little more besides. |
| 6-15.pm. | 46th Inf. Bde. came through and got within 300 yards of the first objective, which they could easily have reached had the barrage not rested short of it according to order. |
| 24th April 2-30.am. | 9th Black Watch consolidated and about midnight were withdrawn to bivouac about N.15.a.<br><br>The enemy were 3rd Bavarian Division 18th Regiment and were men of very fine physique. |
| 25th April 7.am. | The battalion moved to the BROWN LINE, the day being spent in re-equipping. |

2.

**25th April.**
**11 p.m.**
The 9th Black Watch took over the Right Sector of the Divisional Front from 46th Brigade: on our right 14th Div. on our left 7th Camerons. The front line consisted of short lines of trench not connected with, but in sight of each other. These were just behind the BLUE LINE.

**26th April.**
**10-30 p.m.**
Attack on CAVALRY FARM and neighbouring trenches.
The operation presented considerable difficulty, as the ground was not well reconnoitred and the advance to be made by the battalion, co-operating with the attack, varied from 50 yards on the right to 300 yards on the left. The result was that the battalion was enabled to push out posts from the Bridge on River COJEUL Northwards for 150 yards, which were in touch with our own line, and for 250 yards further North, which were out of touch and over the crest. The Black Watch left and centre went too far forward, as the Camerons attack on the trench South of CAMBRAI Road failed, consequently touch with the left was never gained.

**27th April.**
Movement by day was impossible and the posts on centre and left were cut off. At dusk patrols were sent out and no trace of the missing posts could be found. From information subsequently received a post of 12 men and survivors Lewis Gun team were rushed by the enemy about 8-30 am.
2/Lt. BURTON, O.C. Front Company, was last seen about 3-30 am. supervising the consolidation, his intention being to return to his Company Headquarters before dawn, but that he did not do so, points to his having become a casualty from the heavy machine gun fire which was maintained throughout the night.
The Battalion was relieved by the 8/10th Gordons and returned to DRAGOON TRENCH and SPEAR LANE.

**Stokes Guns.**
Were used on 2 occasions with great success, - (1) When the advance was held up at the SUNKEN ROAD West of GUEMAPPE and (2) Covering the advance on the night of the 25th. 26th?

**Rifle Grenades.**
Were not made use of owing, I consider, to the very intense machine gun fire which was maintained.

**Rations.**
I consider the hardships undergone by the men on the 25th and 26th would have been very much lessened had a sufficient supply of Tommies' Cookers been available for men in front line trenches. 24 were available for the whole battalion, but only 12 could be sent up during these two days, communication by daylight being impossible. The second 12 were received too late to be sent up under cover of darkness/night.
The cold on these nights was intense and to exhausted men a hot drink would have been a very great reviver.

**Capture**
One Enemy M. Gun. was taken & returned through railhead to Base.

*[signature]*
Lieut. Colonel,
30. 4. 17. Commanding 9th Bn. The Black Watch.

REPORT ON RAID CARRIED OUT ON 8TH APRIL 1917 at 10 AM  Ref. 1 51 B
10000 NW 3

1. **Strength & Objectives.** "A" platoon.  Enemy Support Line
   G 24 d 4.2½  to 3.5½.  "B" Platoon.  Enemy Front & Control
   Trenches,  G 24 d 2.2½  to 1.4½.

2. **Object.** To obtain identification, damage dug-outs and gain information about wire and state of trenches.

3. Our barrage appeared to be weak, but No Man's Land was crossed without hindrance.

4. Very soon after Zero clusters of orange lights were put up and the enemy put a barrage on his own front line and No Man's Land as the raiders arrived.

5. The trenches were much knocked about and the control trench was filled with concertina wire which took so long to cut through that there was not time to penetrate into the Support Line before our barrage would have again been put on it.

6. The front line was searched and 2 dug-outs were dealt with. From one of them a prisoner was taken, and one man was bombed inside, and presumably killed.

7. While being escorted by three men past a large crater in the front line a gun or mortar of some sort was discharged.
   Two of the escort were wounded, the prisoner pitched forward and the third man was so dazed by the explosion that he could see nothing for 2 or 3 minutes.  The escort were only able to get back to our own lines still somewhat dazed 10 minutes after the raid was over.

8. The front line was explored to the railway but nobody was seen.

9. **Casualties.** 5 O.R. wounded, 1 killed, 1 missing.

10. **Conclusions.** (1) The raid failed to reach the support line owing to the insufficient time being allowed to get through the concertina wire in front system.  (2) That identification was not taken from the prisoner at once on capture was due to forgetfulness, one of the last instructions given to the raiding officers being that immediate steps should be taken to obtain such.  (3) The gaps in front line wire are good, but bridges will be required to cross trench filled with wire.

SECRET.        Operation Order No.151 by Lieut. Col S.A. Innes. D.S.O.
               Commanding 9th (S) Battalion, The Black Watch.
               Ref; 1/10,000 VIS-EN-ARTOIS.    22-4-17.
----------------------------------------------------------------

1. At Zero hour on Z day, 44th I.B. will attack COTEUL river to
   N.18.a.9.8.  45th I.B. will be on our left. 4th Yorks Regt, 150th
   Brigade on our Right - 46th I.B. in reserve.
   1st Objective.  BLUE LINE.)  as already
   2nd.Objective.  RED  LINE.)  detailed.

2. 8th Seaforths will attack and consolidate GUEMAPPE. 7th Camerons
   on left and 9th Black Watch on right will attack the BLUE LINE,
   and RED LINE.
   Dividing line between Battalions, on BLUE LINE O.14.c.7.8. on RED
   LINE O.15.D.1.8.
   8/10th Gordons will be in Reserve.

3. 1 hour before Zero 9th B.W. will be in BRITISH Front line trench in
   order Right to Left D,C,A,B. - Battn. H.Q. at N.17.D.1.2.

4. 9th. B.W. will advance. A. Coy on Right, B. Coy on left, in two
   waves at 80 yards distance. Right of A. Coy will direct. These
   two Companies will maintain a distance of 200 yards from the
   Reserve Coy of the 7th Camerons. C. Coy in Support will move in
   Artillery Formation 250 yards in rear of A. and B Coys and D Coy
   in Reserve in Artillery Formation in rear of C. Coy.

5. Coys will move North of GUEMAPPE, on reaching the E end of the
   village A and B Coys will incline to the Right until Right flank
   rests on River COTEUL.  They will continue the advance to the
   BLUE LINE, relieve the Support Coy of the 7th Camerons and
   consolidate between the river and O.14.c.7.8. pushing out covering
   parties before doing so.  C. and D. Coys will conform to the line
   of advance on clearing GUEMAPPE.    Should it be necessary owing
   to M.G. Fire to deploy they will do so into two waves at 80 yards
   distance.  They will not close up on the leading Coys, except to
   reinforce, and when halted behind the first objective, will at
   once dig in to obtain cover, putting out covering parties.

6. At Zero plus 7 hours the advance on the 2nd. Objective will commence
   Formation of A and B Coys as before, C and D Coys, each Coy in two
   waves at 80 yards distance between waves and 250 yards distance
   between Front and Support Coys, and Reserve Coys. On reaching
   2nd Objective covering parties will be put out and the position
   at once consolidated.     If C and D Coys have not already reinforced
   they will dig in near where they are halted.

7. D. Coy will be prepared to form a defensive flank should the Brigade
   on our Right be held up.   91st Coy R.E. will throw 4 bridges over
   River COTEUIL in O.13.c.

8. Strong points will be constructed by the R.E. about O.14.a.1.1. and
   O.8.c. N.E. behind the Crest - also O.15.a.7.3. and  O.9.B.3.2.

9. At Zero the Artillery barrage will lift at a rate of 100 yards in 4
   minutes.  There will also be a M.G. Barrage.

10. Tanks will co-operate on the attack on GUEMAPPE and afterwards
    will deal with buildings in O.14.a. and St ROHART factory.

11. One Stokes Mortar will be attached to Battn, and will advance
    behind the Support (C) Coy.

12. Two Vickers Guns will be attached to the Battn, and will advance
    behind the Reserve (D) Coy.

13. Flares will be lit when called on by Contact Aeroplanes either by
    KLAXON or White lights about 7 A.M. and 2 P.M. Five flares will be
    lit per 100 yards of Front by troops in Front Line any by covering
    parties only.

                                            over.

14. A Battalion reserve of 10 boxes S.A.A. will be with the R.S.M. at Battn. H.Q. (N.17 D.12. till the first objective is captured).

15. Dumps will be established as under :-
    A.R. "A"   N.16.D.2.0.
    A.R. "B"   N.18.a.1½.2.
    A.R. "C"   about O.14.c.4.8.
    A.R. "D"   about O.15.c.5.8.
    R.E. Dump N.22.b.7.6.

16. Prisoners to Divnl. Collecting Stn. N.10.A.2.2. where they together with all documents will be handed over to A.P.M. and a receipt obtained. The escort will at once return.

17. Advanced Dressing Stn. at N.17.D.1.2. Walking wounded via CAMBRAI Rd. to ARRAS.

18. Reports till 1st Objective is captured to Bn. H.Q. N.17.D.1.2. and thereafter through forward Bde Stn. about O.14.a.2.3. till capture of 2nd. Objective.

19. Zero hour and arrangements for synchronising of watches will be issued later.

(Sgd) SL Norie Miller, Capt.& Adjt.
K.S.

Copies.
No.1. O.C.A. Coy.
    2. O.C.B. Coy.
    3. O.C.C. Coy.
    4. O.C.D. Coy.
    5. O.i/c T.M.
    6. O.1/c M.G.
    7. War Diary.
    8. File.

By runner.

SECRET.

O.O. No. 154 by Lieutenant Colonel S.A. INNES, D.S.O.,
Commanding 9th. (S) Battalion The Black Watch.

Reference :- GUEMAPPE 1/10,000, 2nd. Edition.        26-4-17.

---

1. The enemy are still holding out in CAVALRY FARM trench N.E. from point 53 and S.W. from point 93, both on CAMBRAI ROAD.

2. 44th. I.B. and 45th. I.B. on night 26/27th. April will capture FARM and trenches and establish themselves on the BLUE LINE – Bridge over River in O.14.c. to point 93 on CAMBRAI ROAD, northwards.

3. 9th. Black Watch will be on the Right, 7th. Camerons on the Left – dividing line E. and W. through O.14 central. (45th. I.B. will attack North of the Road.) 8th. Seaforths in Support, 8/10th. Gordons in Reserve.

4. ARTILLERY. During 26th. Heavy Artillery are carrying out continuous bombardment of FARM and enemy trenches. At 10-30 P.M. Divisional Artillery will open intense fire on the FARM and trench NORTH of it. At 10-33 P.M. this fire will rake back and rest on trench in O.14.a. S.E. till 10-36 P.M. when it will lift on to LANYARD TRENCH and form a box to cover the attack.

5. 9th. Black Watch will be drawn up in two waves, No 1 Company in Front line, No 2 Company in Support. At 10-30 P.M. leading waves will get out of their trenches and at 10-33 P.M. 7th. Camerons will rush the FARM and trench to the E. of it. 9th. Black Watch will advance and secure the Crest of the spur in O.14.d.

8th. Seaforths will occupy the line vacated by the Camerons and one Company Gordons will occupy line vacated by the Black Watch. After the FARM and spur have been captured, covering parties with L.Gs. will be pushed out to cover consolidation which will commence at once.

SECRET.           /over.

Page 2 (Continued)

6. Stokes attached to 9th. Black Watch will form a barrage to cover the advance of the Battalion.

7. Officer 1/c. Vickers Guns attached 9th. Black Watch will select f fresh sites for guns in the new position to which they will move when the position has been consolidated.

8. Advanced report centre has been established in dug-out S. side of a house in O.13.a.4.o.
   Report will be handed in here or at Battalion Headquarters.

9. Aid post is at cave in MARLIERE.

10. Pass word as arranged yesterday.


Copy No 1. 2nd. Lt. BURTON.
     2. " BYERS.
     3. " McDIARMID.
     4. " DALE.
     5. Officer 1/c. M.G. Detachment.
     6. War Diary.
     7. File.


26-4-17.
                                                      Captain and Adjutant,
              9th. (S) Battalion The Black Watch.

B22  44/15

9th Royal Highlanders.

May 1917

CONFIDENTIAL.

Army Form C. 2118.

9 Royal Highlanders Vol 23

# WAR DIARY
## or
## INTELLIGENCE SUMMARY.
(Erase heading not required.)

Instructions regarding War Diaries and Intelligence Summaries are contained in F. S. Regs., Part II. and the Staff Manual respectively. Title pages will be prepared in manuscript.

| Place | Date | Hour | Summary of Events and Information | Remarks and references to Appendices |
|---|---|---|---|---|
| SIMENCOURT | 1917 1 May | | Battalion in Corps Reserve. 44th I.B. in SIMENCOURT in billets. 2/Lt D.G. HODGE evacuated to U.K. 17th April. The following joined the Battn. from FREVENT, together with 2 drafts of 136 r's O.R. Tho. J.E. DRUMMOND, G.R.M. KERR, R.J. McMURRAY, C.J.B. RITCHIE, A. GRAHAM, G.E.R. YOUNG, E.M. DRUMMOND, J.H. FRASER, A.D. TATHAM. | |
| | 4 May | | 2/Lt G.F. YOUNG joined the Battn. from FREVENT. | |
| | 5 May 7 May | | Lt.Col. S.A. INNES D.S.O. was admitted to Hospital; MAJOR H.F.F. MURRAY assumed command of the Bn. | |
| | 8 May | | The Battn. moved by route march to GRAND RULLECOURT, where it was billeted. It then became part of the 8th XVIIIth Corps. Bn. training was continued. | |
| GRAND RULLECOURT | 9 May 10 May | | The Bn. received a draft of 21 O.R. from the Depot Bn. at FREVENT. 2nd Lt F. PROUDFOOT was awarded the Military Cross and No 3/1007 — 9th Sgt A. BLACK the Distinguished Conduct Medal as an immediate Reward for their conduct on April 9th. | |
| | 11 May | | The following officers joined the Bn. from No. 8 I.B. Depot and were posted to Coys as shewn:— Capt J. DONALDSON "C"; LIEUT. J.S. STRANG "A"; 2/Lt J. TAYLOR "B"; J.G. SCOULAR "C"; C.F.J. NEISH "D"; W.R. TOVANI "B"; R. STEVENSON "A"; W.K. McGREGOR "C"; N. G. JOHNSTONE "B"; J.C. DEAS "B"; A.W. McLEOD "D"; T.B. ANDERSON "D". | |

9th. (S) Bn. THE BLACK WATCH.

**WAR DIARY**
or
**INTELLIGENCE SUMMARY.**
(Erase heading not required.)

Army Form C. 2118.

| Place | Date | Hour | Summary of Events and Information | Remarks and references to Appendices |
|---|---|---|---|---|
| GRAND RULLECOURT | May 13th | | 1/5th (Scottish) Divisional Horse Show and Football Tournament held at LE CAUROY. The Batt'n won the football tournament, and obtained 1st Prize for Pack Ponies and 3rd Prize for Mules in Limber. | |
| | May 18th | | The Bn. received a reinforcement of 17 O.R. All of which were men who had been wounded while with this Batt'n. 2/Lt W. MARCHBANK joined from 3/5th Bn. 2/Lt T. CULLEN rejoined Bn. on 20th | |
| LIGNY S/ CANCHE VIEIL HESDIN | May 9th | | 2/Lt J.C. WOODBURN joined from Depot Bn. The Bn. moved to LIGNY-SUR-CANCHE where it was billetted. | |
| VIEIL HESDIN | 22nd | | The Bn. moved to VIEIL HESDIN and, with the rest of 118th Bde, joined the XIXth Corps. | |
| VIEIL HESDIN | 24th 20th 31st | | CAPT. J. CULLEN appointed TOWN MAJOR, VIEIL HESDIN. Draft of 18 O.R. arrived from 18th I.B.D. Honours were awarded as follows, for services during the Battle of ARRAS:- MAJOR (T/ ) S.A. INNES, BAR TO D.S.O., 2/Lt T. BYERS, T/2 Lt T.B. ALLISON (a22nd T.M. Batt'n) S/9803 C.S.M. J. McKERCHER and 9/4926 C.S.M. J. PRICE, MIL.CROSSES, 9/4317 2/9262 J. SANDILANDS, D.C.M.. Batt'n training was carried out from arrival in VIEIL HESDIN till end of the month. | |

9th. (S) Bn. THE BLACK WATCH.

9th Black Watch
Vol. 8

15

44   B7

Vol 24

B23

9TH S. BATTN
THE BLACK WATCH
WAR DIARY
JUNE 1917

CONFIDENTIAL

Army Form C. 2118.

# WAR DIARY
## or
## INTELLIGENCE SUMMARY.
*(Erase heading not required.)*

| Place | Date | Hour | Summary of Events and Information | Remarks and references to Appendices |
|---|---|---|---|---|
| VIEIL HESDIN | JUNE 4th | | 44th 1.B. Sports. R.A.M.S. MUNRO.J. was presented Hon. X's and Q'M' and posted to 8/10 Gordon Highlanders. | |
| | | | 2/Lt. T. RITCHIE arrived from 1st Bn. on receiving this joint commission and was posted to "B" Coy. | |
| | 8th | | Lt. Col. SA INNES D.S.O returned from sick and resumed command of the Battalion. Following honours have been awarded CAPT. H.J COLLINS C.F. | |
| | | | Mentioi 7/Lt H.S. MUIR M.C. 3/3731 R.Q.M.S. J MUNRO., D.C.M. | |
| | | | S/4701 CPL. T. PARK., MÉDAILLE MILITAIRE | |
| | 13th | | 2/Lt M DUGGAN received a C of W (Shell shock) on 23rd April. A draft of 14 | |
| | | | O.R. arrived from 18 I.B.D. on 11th to join the Batn. | |
| | 16th | | Draft arrived on 15th 22 O.R. on 16th 36 O.R. on 17th 29 O.R. total from | |
| | | | No 19 I.B.D, & 4 O.R. from No 18 I.B.D | |
| HERNICOURT | 21st | 10.00am | 44th I.B. Commenced march Northwards – Bn marched to billet in HERNICOURT | |
| PERNES | 22nd | 9.0am | Bn marched to billet in PERNES | |
| ST HILAIRE | 23rd | noon | Bn marched to billet in ST HILAIRE | |
| STEENBECQUE | 25th | 1.0pm | Bn marched to billet in & around STEENBECQUE | |

9th. (S) Bn. THE BLACK WATCH.

# WAR DIARY or INTELLIGENCE SUMMARY.

Army Form C. 2118.

| Place | Date | Hour | Summary of Events and Information | Remarks and references to Appendices |
|---|---|---|---|---|
| | 1917 | | | |
| CAESTRE | 26 June | 10:00 am | Battn marched to Tillet in and around CAESTRE. | |
| TORONTO CAMP | 27 June | 10:00 am | Battn marched to TORONTO CAMP, entering Fifth Army area, and were inspected on the march by Acting G.O.C. 15th Division Maj. Gen. H.F. THUILLIER C.B. C.M.G. 2/Lts F. PROUDFOOT M.C., T. MACGREGOR and D.O. TWEEDIE joined the Battn from No 18. I.B.D. | |
| 2 mls S.W. of YPRES | 29 June | 11:00 pm | Battn moved up into billets in Reserve trenches. 7/8 K.O.S.B.'s and Cameron Camp mainly under 46th I.B. Draft of 20 O.R. joined on 28th from No 18 I.B.D. | |
| MENIN ROAD | | 10 pm | Battn moved up into support trenches in relief of 10/11 H.L.I., 46 I.B. | |
| ½m SE YPRES | 30 June | 1 | 1 Coy HALF MOON TR., 2 Coy ECOLE, 1 Coy CONVENT. Intermittent shelling all day of whole area by 4.2, 5.9, 8" & 12". A 17" gun firing armour piercing shell fired at the CONVENT throughout the day. 2/Lt DUGGAN evacuated to England 20 June. Lt & QMR W. CLARK M.C. struck off strength 28 June 1917. Captain R.H. ROBERTSON struck off the establishment 27 March 1917. | |

S.A. Munro Lt Col
Commanding 9th Bn. The Black Watch

9th (S) Bn. THE BLACK WATCH.

B 24    44/15

9ᵗʰ Royal Highlanders.

July 1917.

Confidential

44/15

WAR DIARY

9TH (S) BATTN. THE BLACK WATCH

JULY 1917

# WAR DIARY / INTELLIGENCE SUMMARY

Army Form C. 2118.

No 25

| Place | Date | Hour | Summary of Events and Information | Remarks and references to Appendices |
|---|---|---|---|---|
| YPRES MENIN ROAD | 2/7 | | Battn in support 2 Coys in ECOLE, 1 Coy in CONVENT HQ in HALF MOON TRENCH. | |
| YPRES | 3 July | 2 am | Battn relieved 12 H.L.I. in L. in trisector R. Sinclair XIX Corps front. | |
| DRAGOON FM | | | On our R 8/10 G. Highr. on our L 9 Lncrsh. Estd from a g'nd recce carried out with O.C.s 2 killed + 1 wounded + a little T.M. at stand to. Manned the front line + support. | |
| | 3 July | | Very quiet. RETIRE rd + reserve line shelled all day intermittently A/f at times. | |
| | 4 July | | A quiet night in front but very lively behind reserve lines DRAGOON FARM + DUMPS were full of 5-9 shells. I am told great work. Where 3 dumps were hit off in the Support line shelled for 1 hour. A few T.Ms sent over on us at 7.0 pm | |
| MENIN ROAD | 6 July | 1 am | A quiet night in front Intermittent shelling. Keep on Bn front. Battn relieved by 7 Cameron Hrs and moved back to bivouac at MENIN RD Iso bygne. Very stickey throughout day. Lut W.K. MacGregor wounded. | |
| | 7 July | | Quiet morning ECOLE + Bn HQ shelled heavily during afternoon. HALF MOON TR. also shelled. Lut T. EDWARDS wounded. | |

Army Form C. 2118.

# WAR DIARY
## INTELLIGENCE SUMMARY.
*(Erase heading not required.)*

Instructions regarding War Diaries and Intelligence Summaries are contained in F.S. Regs., Part II. and the Staff Manual respectively. Title pages will be prepared in manuscript.

CONFIDENTIAL

| Place | Date | Hour | Summary of Events and Information | Remarks and references to Appendices |
|---|---|---|---|---|
| MENIN RD YPRES | 8 July 1917 | | Quiet day - rain - Vicinity of Box 17 S/n shelled for 1hr with 5.9 during afternoon. | |
| TORONTO CAMP RUBROUCK | 9 July | 4.30 pm | Capt W.B. BINNIE M.C. rejoined Battn. 2/Lt McGuire 3 July '17 P/Ld released fm 13 R Scots and returned to TORONTO CAMP | |
| | 10 July | 6.0 pm | Bn marched to POPERINGHE where it entrained and was railed to ARNEKE marching thence to billets in RUBROUCK. | |
| | 12 July | | 2/Lt J.C. STEPHEN joined the Battn fm 18 I.B.D. | |
| | 13 July | | 2/Lt P.C. KERR joined the Bn + S.S.O.R. for duty. 2/Lt V.K. MACGREGOR evacuated to UK 9 July 1917 | |
| 1 m N of WINNEZEELE | 21 July | 10.0 am | 44th Mixed Brigade consisting of 9th BLACK WATCH 8/10 GORDONS 7/8 K.O.S.Bs, 10/11 H.L.I. & 1/2 44 M.G. Coy & T.M. Batty marched to WINNIE ZEELE area to canped there | |
| 2 m S.E. of WATOU | 22 July | 9.30 am | Battn marched into camp near WATOU Military Medal awarded to No. S/9458 Pte J. KEATINGS & S/6618 Pte A. BLACK for gallantry | |
| TORONTO CAMP | 23 July | 5.0 am | Battn marched via Suntel Road N. of POPERINGHE to TORONTO CAMP | |
| | 24 July | | a draft of 36 O.R. joined Battn. from No 18 I.B.D. | |
| 1 m W of YPRES | 25 July | 11.0 pm | Battn marched to trenches in area 1m W of YPRES | |

9th. (S) Bn. THE BLACK WATCH.

**Army Form C. 2118.**

# WAR DIARY
## INTELLIGENCE SUMMARY.
*(Erase heading not required.)*

| Place | Date | Hour | Summary of Events and Information | Remarks and references to Appendices |
|---|---|---|---|---|
| 1m W. of YPRES | 1917 | | | |
| | 26 July | | Battn in Bivouacs 1m W. of YPRES. | |
| CAMBRIDGE TRENCH | 30 July | 2.30am | Battn relieved 8/10 Gordons in left subsection R sector, 15 Bn front. On our R. 8/10 GORDONS on our L. 7/8 K O S B S. The relief was carried out with only 2 casualties despite the fact that C.T.'s were shelled fairly heavily. | |
| | 31 July | 12.5am | Battn in position in jumping off trenches for the attack. Only 4 casualties were caused during the 4 hour waiting previously without protection. | |
| | | 3.50am | Zero hour. The Battn moved No Mans Land and went right up to the Reserve line without a casualty hardly. From there on the fighting was the objective were reached in continuous. The opposition from the chiefly to machine & M Guns in shell holes & in small concrete emplacements built into them. | |
| | | 4.45am | First Objective reached. Coys re-organized in shell holes. Liaison established on R. with Canadian Bayart. Prisoners captured from 94 & 95 Regts. 3s.D. Division. | |
| | | 5.30am | Advance on Second Objective commenced. Tanks co-operated but were knocked out or broken down before it was reached with 2 exceptions | |

9th. (S) Bn. THE BLACK WATCH.

# WAR DIARY / INTELLIGENCE SUMMARY

Army Form C. 2118.

| Place | Date | Hour | Summary of Events and Information | Remarks and references to Appendices |
|---|---|---|---|---|
| FREZEN BERG | 1917 July 31 | | Above 2 tanks were of great assistance at the taking of the FREZENBERG Redoubt. The infantry advance consisted of sectional rushes against a screen of covered shell holes until the actual redoubt itself was reached. Here 50-60 prisoners were taken & the two M.G. crews bayoneted or shot. About 100 of the second objective established themselves. Those suffering about 35% Cas. (N.C.) The supporting companies (The reserve & C Coy) were up with the Redoubt staff. Left shoulder consolidation was at once commenced and liaison established with the flanks. | |
| | | 8.5 am | A local counter attack developed against our front. Strength about 3 companies but was driven off by M.G. & I.G. fire. Total casualties being coming under our view. The losses were heavy. | |
| | | 10.2 am | The 4-5th I.B. commenced the attack on the Third objective passing through the 4-4th & 4-6th I.B's. They were very successful & made ground rapidly but unfortunately did not mop up the ground behind them leaving M.G.'s snipers to open up in front. | |

9th. (S) Bn. THE BLACK WATCH.

# WAR DIARY or INTELLIGENCE SUMMARY

Army Form C. 2118.

9th. (S) Bn. THE BLACK WATCH.

| Place | Date | Hour | Summary of Events and Information | Remarks and references to Appendices |
|---|---|---|---|---|
| FREZENBERG | 1917 31 July | About 9.30am | The enemy brought down fresh battns into action & distinctly became very heavy & continued so throughout the day. This shelling combined with the sniping & machine gunning rendered reorganization impossible. Any movement of single individuals even in small numbers of casualties here caused by sniping & shelling which enfiladed parts of our line. | |
| | | 10 p.m. | 8th Division on our R. reported not going beyond second Objective. 45 I.B. had to withdraw from third Objective after being on a line 500x ahead of fourth Objective. | |
| | | 4.0 pm | Strong counter attack against 8th Division and our R. front developed. 8th Divn retired about 500x. 45th conforming and 44 I.B. left holding Second Objective with posts ahead 200–300x. The attack on division died about 5.0 pm. Shelling & trench mortaring continued heavy. At intervals an enemy aeroplane flew over our line unmolested (save that it was fired at by Lewis guns) & fired very lights indicating the position of troops to their own. | |

# WAR DIARY

## INTELLIGENCE SUMMARY

Army Form C. 2118.

9th. (S) Bn. THE BLACK WATCH.

| Place | Date | Hour | Summary of Events and Information | Remarks and references to Appendices |
|---|---|---|---|---|
| FREZENBERG | 1917 31 July | | Promptly shelled. Things continued very much the same all night, when orders were received that Battn was to be relieved by 8" SEAFORTHS. Relief commenced but was not completed till the following morning. The following officers were casualties. Killed 2/Lt J. TAYLOR. Wounded Capt N.A. GRANT, 2Lt E.M. DRUMMOND, J.H. FRASER, C.F. INEISH, W.R. TOVANI, W. MARCHBANK, T. McGREGOR, R.B. ANDERSON. Wounded (at duty) Lt-Col. S.A. INNES D.S.O. & CAPT & ADJT S. NORIE-MILLER. The Battn mustered only 7 Officers & 137 O.R. but there were many stragglers to come in, & R. had got third up with their baths. Estimated casualties to mark this Strength (inc) were Killed 30 – Wounded 150. | A-137 O.R. A-326 O.R. |

S.A. Innes Lt-Col.

SECRET.                                                    COPY NO.

OPERATION ORDER No.178 by LT. COL. S.A. INNES, D.S.O.
COMMANDING 9th (SERVICE) BATTALION THE BLACK WATCH.
Reference ZILLEBEKE, ZONNEBEKE & ST. JULIEN 1/10000. 28th JULY 1917.

1. 15th Division will assault at Zero hour on Zero day. On the R. will be the 8th Division and on the L. 55th Division.
2. 44th I.B. will be on the R., 46th I.B. on the L., and 45th I.B. in reserve.
3. There are 3 objectives known as the BLUE, BLACK & GREEN lines respectively, the location of which has already been communicated. 44th & 46th I.Bs will capture and consolidate BLUE & BLACK lines. 45th I.B. will capture and consolidate GREEN line. There will be a halt of ½ hour on BLUE line and of 4 hours on BLACK line.
4. The assault will be covered by a creeping shrapnel barrage which will advance at the rate of 100x in 4'.
5. In the attack on the Black line 4 tanks will operate on 44th I.B. front and 2 tanks on 46th I.B. front. An indirect M.G. barrage will also be put down.
6. 44th I.B. will attack, 8/10 Gordons on R. from YPRES&ROULERS Ry. inclusive to junction I 5-2a5; 9th Black Watch on L. from junction I 5 2a5, to junction I 5 5a6.. 8th Seaforths will be in support, 7th Camerons in reserve. The assaulting Bns. will capture the BLUE & BLACK lines and will consolidate the latter. The BLUE line will be occupied by 8th Seaforths as soon as vacated by the leading Bns.
7. The boundries of the Battn. front of attack are as follows :-
On the R. Junction of I 5 2a5 - ICE LANE - WILDE WOOD - DOUGLAS VILLA - Road join D 25 d 35.55, all inclusive, to 8/10 Gordons.
On the L. Junction of I 5 5a6 - House 60x S. of FREZENBERG X roads inclusive - I 25 central.
8. 9th Black Watch will attack on a front of 2 Companies, each Company on a front of 2 platoons, A on R., B on L., in 2 waves at 70x distance, each wave consisting of 2 lines at 15x distance, - D Company in support at 100x distance in 2 similar waves - C Company in reserve in Artillery formation at 100x distance.
7/8 K.O.S.B. will be on the L.
9. At Zero hour the assaulting and support Battns. will cross No Man's Land at once, halting under the barrage and taking up the distances detailed when the barrage moves forward.
10. Moppers Up for the enemy front line system will be found from Support Battn. and will advance in rear of 1st and 2nd waves of D Coy.
11. 1 Stokes Gun and 2 Vickers will be attached to the Battalion, and will advance in rear of C Company.
12. On reaching the BLUE line a picquet of 10 men and a Lewis Gun will be put out by A and B Companies respectively with patrols ahead of them as far as the barrage will permit. Companies will reorganise for the advance to the BLACK line. Liaison will be established with units on R. & L. on enemy reserve line and on HANEBEEK Brook. C Coy. will move up on the R. of D Coy. Companies when they advance will do so, A & B Coys. in 1 wave of 2 lines at 15x distance, C & D at 250 yards distance, in 1 wave of 2 lines at 15x distance; touch between these waves being maintained by connecting files.
13. Moppers up for FREZENBERG front & support lines will be found by both C & D Coys, and will advance in rear of the 2nd & 1st line of A & B Coys respectively. These parties will keep touch to their R.
14. On reaching BLACK line, picquets and patrols will be put out as before detailed, and the position will be consolidated - A Company constructing a cruciform strong point about D 25 d 05.45 and B Company a similar strong point about D 25 c 85.90. A Vickers gun will be placed in each of these posts. C & D Coys., if they have not already reinforced, will consolidate in the position they occupy. Liaison will be established with units on R. & L.
15. The following dumps are arranged for:-
A.R.A...........I 10 d 70.75.
A.R.A.I.(Rations) I 9c 6.5.
A.R.B...........I 10 b 95.75.
A.R.C...about I 5 c 9.7.
A.R.D...........I 1 a central. J 1 a central

15(Continued) A.R.A.I. contains only rations and filled water bottles. The latter will only be issued in exchange for empties. The remaining dumps will contain S.A.A., No. 5 & 23 Mx. grenades, flares, Stokes shells and Very lights.

16. Prisoners under escort of 1 man to 10 prisoners will be sent to the ROCHE and handed over to A.P.M., a receipt being obtained. Escorts will rejoin unit at once. Pay-books, Identity discs and decorations will not be removed from prisoners.

17. Reports to Battalion Headquarters, Junction of PICCADILLY and CAMBRIDGE trenches, I 5 a 0.2. After capture of BLUE line, to Brigade forward station which will be along the boundary line between 9th Black Watch and 8/10 Gordons.
Message dogs are being employed, and should not be detained.
Runners will carry all messages in top right hand pocket.

18. A contact aeroplane will work with the Division, marked with a black bar behind the right lower wing. White flares will be lit by the leading Infantry (a) When called for by means of Klaxon Horn and Very lights. This call will probably only be made when the Infantry are believed to be on the BLUE, BLACK or GREEN line. (b) When the Infantry consider it advisable to make known the position of the front line.
Flares should be lit at the bottom of a trench or shell-hole if possible, in clusters of 3 at 10x interval.

19. Regimental Aid Post will be at I 5 c 9.2, near Battalion Headquarters. Walking cases by route marked by signboards, round the E. of Ypres to VLAMERTINGHE MILL dressing station. They will be met as far as possible on this route by 'bus.

20. Orders re Zero hour and synchronisation of watches will be notified later.

(Sd.) S. Morie Miller, Capt. & Adjt.,
9th (S) Bn. The Black Watch.

Copies :- 1 - 4 Companies.
5. O.C. H.Q.Details.
6 F.O. & I.H.
7. O.C., 44th T.M.Battery.
8 O.C., 44th M.G.Company.
9 Captain Binnie.
10 R.S.M.
11 File
12 War Diary.

9th. (S) Bn. THE BLACK WATCH.

WAR DIARY
August 1917.

Army Form C. 2118.

# WAR DIARY
## or
## INTELLIGENCE SUMMARY.
(Erase heading not required.)

| Place | Date | Hour | Summary of Events and Information | Remarks and references to Appendices |
|---|---|---|---|---|
| | 1917 | | | |
| O.G.1. VERLORENHOEK | 1 Aug | 3.0 am | The Battalion relieved from the front line by 8 SEAFORTHS returned to O.G. line in reserve. They re-organised and were employed in carrying ammunition to the front line, through 2 very heavy barrages at WILDE WOOD & FREZENBERG REDOUBT. Captain W.B. BINNIE M.C. took over command about 3.0 pm. At 4.30 pm the Battn. stood to to repel a counter attack, but there was not ordered forward. 2/Lt J.E. WOOD BURN wounded (shell shock) O.G. lines were shelled throughout the day. | |
| | 2 Aug | | The Battn. was again employed carrying ammunition to front line to 15th Batn. during night. 2/Lt J.E. DRUMMOND was wounded and several other casualties occurred. Shelling of O.G. lines was severe. | |
| | | 3 am | O.G. lines again heavily shelled. | |
| Ens W.4 YPRES | | 3.0 pm | The Batt.n relieved by 4/5 L.B. and marched to bivouac 2 mile W. of YPRES. | |
| WINNEZEELE | 4 Aug | 6.0 am | Batt.n transported by bus to WINNEZEELE area. Being formed by details from TRAINED camp & going into training there. 15 Division merged into the 16 Division on relief by 16 Division. | |

A.D.S.S./Forms/C. 2118. 9th. (S) Bn. THE BLACK WATCH.

# WAR DIARY

## INTELLIGENCE SUMMARY

Army Form C. 2118.

| Place | Date | Hour | Summary of Events and Information | Remarks and references to Appendices |
|---|---|---|---|---|
| | 1917 | | | |
| WINNEZEELE | 5 Aug | | A draft of 46 O.R. arrived from No 18 I.B.D. The body of 2/Lt J.L. BURTON O/4066 was found near where he was last seen on 27 April 1917. Handed to 1/4 YORKS. Batt. agreeable to G.O.C 15th Divn., who conveyed his own, the Corps Army Commanders, appreciation & thanks for the good work done by the Battn during the recent operations. | |
| | 9 Aug | | 2/Lt T. CALVERT I.D.O.R. joined Btn from No 18 I.B.D. | |
| | 10 Aug | | CAPT GRANT evacuated to U.K. on 2nd Aug & 2/Lt TOVANI on 3 Aug. | |
| | 13 Aug | | A draft of 38 O.R. arrived from No 18 I.B.D. Lt & Qr W. CLARK M.C. returned from sick in U.K. | |
| | 16 Aug | | 2/Lt G R M KERR rejoined from light duty at base. | |
| POPERINGHE | 17 Aug | 6-9 pm | Battn marched to POPERINGHE & companies will remainder of 44 I.B. 2/Lt G. C. LESLIE died of wounds received on 23rd April 1917 on 15 Aug 1917. | |
| TORONTO CAMP | 19 Aug | 9.0 pm | Battn marched to billets in TORONTO CAMP. One other 3 trailor of I 44 I.B. from forward to trenches 2 ms W of YPRES. Enemy aeroplane active throughout all round. Engaged by our A.A. batteries but with apparently no effect. | |

# WAR DIARY or INTELLIGENCE SUMMARY.

Army Form C. 2118.

(Erase heading not required.)

| Place | Date | Hour | Summary of Events and Information | Remarks and references to Appendices |
|---|---|---|---|---|
| TORONTO CAMP | 1917 20 Aug | | Battn moved forward to bivouacs 1m W. of YPRES as reserve Battn att 1.B. who took over the left subsection R. sector XIX Corps front. | |
| 1m W. YPRES | | | Strength of Battn Going out 14 Officers & 442 O.R. | |
| O.G. LINE | 21 Aug | 11.0 pm | Battn relieved 8/10 GORDONS as reserve Battn. in O.G. line. Relief was carried out without casualties but shortly after arrival, a heavy | |
| | 22 Aug | 12.30 am | open shell & T.M.E. was put down about 30 casualties resulting. | |
| | | 4.45 am | 6/SEAFORTHS and 7/CAMERONS carried out an attack on the GREEN LINE but 8/10 GORDONS in support. The attack failed owing to M.G. fire from strong concrete emplacement. 7/& C.J.B. RITCHIE slightly wounded & at duty. | |
| POMMERN REDOUBT | | 11.0 pm | About 8.0 pm Battn was ordered to move forward to counter-attack and about midnight relieved 7 CAMERONS in firing line. On our R. 8/10 GORDONS on our | |
| | 23 Aug | 1.30 am | L 18d I.B. At 1.30 am an attack was launched against HILL 35 & GALLIPOLI by A & C companies. The ground was unknown to all ranks, the night pitch dark & O.C. M.G. fire intense, and direction could not be maintained & men & officers have been lost throughout. An advance of over 200x was made but owing to heavy M.G. & rifle fire | |

9th. (S) Bn. THE BLACK WATCH.

# WAR DIARY / INTELLIGENCE SUMMARY

Army Form C. 2118.

| Place | Date | Hour | Summary of Events and Information | Remarks and references to Appendices |
|---|---|---|---|---|
| POMMERN REDOUBT | 1917 23 Aug | | The wire withdrawn 100" & consolidation effected. CAPT. J. DONALDSON was killed + about 40 casualties O.O.R. occurred. 2/Lt G.R.M. KERR wounded (gassed). The day was passed in connecting up shell holes + finding connection between the companies. | |
| | | 11.0am | While H.Qrs were having breakfast a 5.9" came into the trench + burst there killing 12 + wounding 9 amongst the former were MAJR H.F.F. MURRAY in command, & 2/Lt R. STEVENSON & amongst the latter 2/Lt G.E.R. YOUNG, assistant adjt. Intermittent shelling of POMMERN REDOUBT all day. Snipers and M.G.un being active. | |
| | 24 Aug | 7.30am | Intermittent shelling throughout the night. About 7.30 to 8.30 am our heavies shelled the enemy's front line trenches resumed several casualties. They did this at intervals throughout the day despite further enemy shelling. One shell killed 7 men in C Coy alone. 2/Lt J. Brown took over command of Bttln, + 2/Lt J.C. STEPHEN the duties of adjutant. Kept being intermittent shelling in SQUARE FARM. | CAPT J. DONALDSON 2/Lt G.R.M. KERR CAPT W.B. BINNIE M.C. |

9th. (S) Bn. THE BLACK WATCH.

# WAR DIARY
## INTELLIGENCE SUMMARY.
*(Erase heading not required.)*

Army Form C. 2118

| Place | Date | Hour | Summary of Events and Information | Remarks and references to Appendices |
|---|---|---|---|---|
| POMMERN REDOUBT | 1917 25 Aug | | A quiet day with intermittent shelling, but towards evening our own heavies were again troublesome causing casualties in C Company. | |
| | | 10.0 pm | About 10.0 pm a force of 170 all ranks drawn from all 4 Companies commenced to get into position to attack recaption Hill 35 v GALLIPOLI. Zero hour was 11.0 pm but the attack was not launched till 11.5 pm. It succeeded on the L. in getting to the outskirts of GALLIPOLI, but on R. was held up by M.G. fire from a strong point. A second strong point was handed over in the darkness and caused casualties resulting in the falling back of the R. flank. The L/ft was forced back by an enemy counter attack but regained all ground up to 150 × in front of our old line. 4 Prts were established. 2 prisoners were taken. Casualties Capt G.F. YOUNG, 2/Lt S. GRAHAM & C.J.B. RITCHIE & about 60 O.R. | |
| | 26 Aug | 2.0 am | Consolidation of ground won was carried on throughout the hour of darkness. The shelling was light, but M.G. & rifle fire were very troublesome & hindered the operation. Capt J.S. STRANG was wounded. | |

9th. (S) Bn. THE BLACK WATCH.

Army Form C. 2118.

# WAR DIARY
## INTELLIGENCE SUMMARY.
*(Erase heading not required.)*

| Place | Date | Hour | Summary of Events and Information | Remarks and references to Appendices |
|---|---|---|---|---|
| POMMERN REDOUBT | 1917 26Aug | | The day proved fairly quiet, but during the afternoon our lines again commenced to fall short. | |
| | | 8.30pm | 8.30-9.0 p.m. the enemy put down a very heavy barrage on POMMERN REDOUBT. The relief of the Battn by 10/11 H.L.I. commenced at 9.0 p.m. & was concluded at 3.0 a.m. Only 5 casualties occurred. The Battn moved back into bivouacs 1m.W. of YPRES. | |
| 1m W YPRES | 27 Aug | 9.0pm | A quiet day into light shelling which caused no casualties. | |
| TORONTO CAMP | | 6.0pm | The Battn moved back to TORONTO CAMP. Strength 7 Officers & 245 O.R. Major MURRAY, Capt. DONALDSON & 2/Lt R. STEVENSON were buried with full military honours in BRANDHOEK military cemetery. The following officers were evacuated to U.K. 4 Aug. 2Lts R.B.ANDERSON & E.M. DRUMMOND. 14 Aug. 2Lts T. McGREGOR & C.G. MACDOWALL. 15 Aug. 2/Lieut MARCHBANK. 19 Aug. 2Lt J.H. FRASER & C.F.I. NEISH. 21st Aug. 2Lt D.O. TWEEDIE. The following officer & 18 O.R. joined Battn on 25th Aug from No 18 I.B.D:- Lieut. J.I. BUCHAN, D.S.O. & F.A.K.D. Viscount DRUMLANRIG, 2/Lts C.K. YOUNG, G.H. GORDON & J.M. BROWN. | |

9th. (S) Bn. THE BLACK WATCH.

**WAR DIARY** or **INTELLIGENCE SUMMARY.**

Army Form C. 2118.

| Place | Date | Hour | Summary of Events and Information | Remarks and references to Appendices |
|---|---|---|---|---|
| TORONTO CAMP | 1917 28 Aug | | The following awards were made in connection with operations on 31 July 1917. Bar to Military Medal S/17979 Pte A. JACK. — Military Medal 3759 Sergt C. OGILVIE, S/4109 Cpl J.H. DAVIDSON, S/9937 Sergt C. CODY, S/17082 Pte W. MOFFAT, S/4342 Cpl W. SHARPLES, S/8435 Cpl G. WRIGHT, S/12320 Pte A. STONE, S/4246 Pte J. GRANT. | |
| | 29 Aug 6.0 pm | | 44th I.B. relieved in the line by 46th I.B. and returned to BRANDHOEK No 2 area. | |
| No 2 Area WATOU | 30 Aug 6.0 pm | | 44 I.B. marched back to WATOU No 2 AREA arriving from 5.0 pm onwards. G.O.C. V Army, Sir H. Gough, inspected the Bn. on the march (but from a distance), then on the first wash down & turnout cheered and congratulated them. A draft of 1 O/r & 215 O.R. arrived from No 16 I.B.D. under Lieut L. McKENZIE. 2/Lt T. RITCHIE struck off on appointment as Inst. XIX Corps School. 2/Lt P.E. KERR & 25 O.R. arrived from No 16 I.B.D. The following honours were announced in connection with Operations on 31st July 1917. BAR to M.C. 2/Lt F. PROUDFOOT. M.C. — MILITARY CROSSES — 2/Lt J.E. DRUMMOND, W.R. TOVANI & S/4539 Coy Sergt Major J. McCALL — D.C.M. | |
| | 31 Aug | | | |

9th. (S) Bn. THE BLACK WATCH.

# WAR DIARY
## INTELLIGENCE SUMMARY

| Place | Date | Hour | Summary of Events and Information | Remarks and references to Appendices |
|---|---|---|---|---|
| WATOU No 2 Area | 1917 3/Aug | | S/16555 Cpl. A JOHNSTONE, — M.M. S/11798 Cpl J.A.DUNCAN. M.M. The following promotions appeared in London Gazette of 29 Aug 1917. To be Captains (Temporary) J.S STRANG. & T.W. HUNTER, to date 27/3/17. To be Lieutenants (Temporary) F.PROUDFOOT.M.C. to date 27/3/17 — S GRAHAM & R.O.S. WILSON to date 24/4/17. Total Battle losses to date in second phase of YPRES fighting K. 3 Offrs. 85 O.R. W. 7 Offrs. 143 O.R. M. 1/2 O.R. Total 200. S.R. Innes Lt.Col Comdg 9th Battn. the Black Watch | |

B 26

9th (S) Batt The Black Watch

War Diary

September 1917

Vol 27

**Army Form C. 2118.**

# WAR DIARY
## of
## INTELLIGENCE SUMMARY.
*(Erase heading not required.)*

| Place | Date | Hour | Summary of Events and Information | Remarks and references to Appendices |
|---|---|---|---|---|
| WATOU No1 Area | 1917 1st Sept | | Battn. in Camp "Hillet" in MILL CAMP. 2 ms. S. of WATOU. | |
| CAESTRE | 2 Sept | 1.45 pm | Battn. marched to CAESTRE and after 3 hour halt entrained there proceeding via | |
| ARRAS | | 8.30 pm | HAZEBROUCK and ST POL to ARRAS. They arrived there at 8.30 pm and de- | |
| MONTENESCOURT | 3 Sept | 1.30 am | trained & marched to MONTENESCOURT reaching billet about 1.30 a.m. | |
| | | | A draft of 68 O.R. arrived to join the Battn from No 18 I.B.D. The following have been awarded the Military Medal for gallantry on 31/7/17. S/240240 Pte GEORGE GOUK – S/3814 L/cpl RICHARD ROSS – S/9499 Pte WILLIAM BROWN – S/40820 Pte JOHN JOHNSON – S/240171 A/cpl HARRY BROWN. | |
| BLANGY. BAROSSA CAMP. | 7 Sept | 12 noon | Battn. marched via ARRAS to BLANGY ST LAURENT, BAROSSA CAMP. the 44th I.B. becoming Divisional Reserve R. Sector, XVII Corps. LIEUT J.W. MORRIS, M.O. R.A.M.C. U.S.A. joined Battn. as M.O. %C vice CAPT E. GORDON, R.A.M.C. who proceeded to U.K. on duty 8 Sept. 2/Lt J.C. WOODBURN evacuated U.K. 30 Aug 1917. 2/Lt J.G. SCOUAR having proceeded to U.K. recalled by W.O. is struck off from 6 Sept 1917, the establishment. | |
| BAROSSA CAMP | Sept 7-13 | | Battn. training at BAROSSA CAMP and finding working parties of 100 O.R. daily. | |

9th. (S) Bn. THE BLACK WATCH.

Army Form C. 2118.

# WAR DIARY
## or
## INTELLIGENCE SUMMARY.
(Erase heading not required.)

Instructions regarding War Diaries and Intelligence Summaries are contained in F. S. Regs., Part II. and the Staff Manual respectively. Title pages will be prepared in manuscript.

| Place | Date | Hour | Summary of Events and Information | Remarks and references to Appendices |
|---|---|---|---|---|
| BAROSSA CAMP | Sept 8th | | Major W.B. BINNIE, M.C. proceeded on leave to BOULOGNE. | |
| | 10th | | Lt.Col. S.A. INNES, D.S.O. proceeded to Third Army School (C.O.'s Course), Capt S. NORIE-MILLER taking over command of the Batt. | |
| STIRLING CAMP H.13.d.8.6 (FRANCE 51B) | 14th | | Batn. moved into position as Support Batt. of Left Brigade. Divisional Sector. Hqrs and 2 Coys (A+C) being in Bungalows on railway embankment, H.13.d.8.6. – the remaining 2 Coys (B+D), under command of Capt. I.I. BUCHAN, D.S.O., being in shelters and dugout about H.23 central, S. of FAMPOUX. | |
| Do. | 15th | | Major W.B. Binnie M.C. returned from leave and took over Command. Lieut. R&S Milson invalided to U.K. on 25th Aug., | |
| | Do. | | | |
| | 22nd | | at STIRLING CAMP continued training the two forward Companies finding working parties in the Front line. | |
| | 17th – 18th | | 2nd Lieut. J.E. Drummond M.C. returned from hospital (wounded). Intel. Company relief took place. A & C. Companies relieving B & D Companies. 2 Lieuts E.W.D. Wilson and J.E.M. Dobran joined the Battn. from J.R.B. | |
| | 20th | | 2 O.R. Killed & 3 O.R. wounded in working party in Front line | |

9th. (S) Bn. THE BLACK WATCH.

# WAR DIARY or INTELLIGENCE SUMMARY.

Army Form C. 2118.

| Place | Date | Hour | Summary of Events and Information | Remarks and references to Appendices |
|---|---|---|---|---|
| | 22nd | | Battalion moved into the line relieving 5/10 Gordon High. Left Sub-Sector Left Sector of Divisional Front. Relief completed without incident at 10.10 p.m. 3 O.R. wounded in the morning. | |
| | 23rd | | 5th Seaforth High.s on the right S of River Scarpe. 2/6. Warwicks. 61st Division on the left. 2nd Lieuts. A.W. Macdonald, G.N. Cook, J.G. Malcolm, C.W. Bellamy & 51 O.R. joined battalion from 18th I.B.D. | |
| | 24th | 4.30 AM | Enemy put down a heavy T.M. barrage on our Left Front and Battn on Left and at 4.45 AM attempted to raid. Raid was repelled by Rifle & L/G fire. One prisoner taken by Left Battn. Our casualties 5 O.R. wounded of whom 1 died of wounds on 29th. | |
| | 25th | | Normal day. T.M.s and Rifle grenades on our Front. | |
| | 26th | | Normal day. T.M.s and Rifle grenades again active on our Front. | |
| | 27th | 10 mm | Slight shelling of Support line. 1 O.R. killed in Battn Observation Post. at 12.30 pm an enemy heavy T.M. fell in No 3 Post killing 6 O.R. | |
| | 28th | | Lieut. F.A.K.D. Vincent Dunklening slightly wounded by Rifle Grenade while on patrol. (at duty) of The Black Watch. 2 pm to 3 pm our artillery | |

# WAR DIARY
## INTELLIGENCE SUMMARY

Army Form C. 2118.

| Place | Date | Hour | Summary of Events and Information | Remarks and references to Appendices |
|---|---|---|---|---|
| | 28th | | and T.M⁵ all calibres bombarded enemy front line in retaliation for T.M. activity. 1. O.R Wounded. | |
| | 29th | | Sharpened. | |
| | 26th/27th | | Inter-Coy relief took place D and B. Coys relieving A & C Coys in front line. Relief completed without incident. | |
| | 30. | | Enemy T.M⁵ very active. 2. O.R killed with Rifle grenade and 2 O.R wounded at 10.30 pm enemy put out gas in form of T.M bombs & Rifle grenades the gas lingered in trenches till about 1.30 A.M. 4 O.R killed and 7 O.R wounded all ranks stood to arms but no attack developed. | |
| | 1. | | Enemy again put out gas T.M Bombs causing casualties 4 O.R Wounded. Day was very quiet. Enemy raided forward post of Regt Battalion (5th Bn Seaforths) 5 O.R missing. Battalion sent out patrol but no sign of enemy could be seen. Relief of Battalion commenced at 9.p.m. by 7/8. K.O.S.B 13⁵ relief completed at 2.30 A.M without incident. Battalion march back to RIFLE CAMP. | |

Wm B. Binnie Major
Command'g 9 B/W.

9th. (S) Bn. THE BLACK WATCH.

B 27

9th. (S) Bn. THE BLACK WATCH.

WAR DIARY

OCTOBER 1917

S. A. Innes Lt Col.
Commanding 9th Bn. The Black Watch.

Vol 28

# WAR DIARY
## INTELLIGENCE SUMMARY

Army Form C. 2118.

**CONFIDENTIAL**

Instructions regarding War Diaries and Intelligence Summaries are contained in F.S. Regs., Part II. and the Staff Manual respectively. Title pages will be prepared in manuscript.

| Place | Date | Hour | Summary of Events and Information | Remarks and references to Appendices |
|---|---|---|---|---|
| RIFLE CAMP. G.24.b.9.8. | 3rd Oct. | | Battalion in Reserve. Cleaning equipment, Baths etc. | |
| | 4th Oct. | | Battalion in Reserve. Training. Honours. a/Major W.B. Binnie M.C. Bar to Military Cross, Military Cross. 2nd Lieut J. Addison. 2/Lieut S. Graham, N.G. Johnstone, 2/Captain J.S. Strong, 2/Calvert, 2/Lieuts S. Graham, N.G. Johnstone, 2/Captain J.S. Strong, Honours. Bar to M.M. | |
| | 5th Oct. | | Battalion in Reserve. Working & training. Honours. Bar to M.M. S/3814 Pte (L/Cpl) R. Ross. S/11888 Sgt. J. Mullen. Y.M.M. 26533 Cpl. Pte J. Ross S/5639 Pte J. Somerville, S/40822 Pte W. Kennedy. S/1397 Pte G. N. Mc Isaac. S/9428 Pte (A/Cpl) J. Smith. 267324 Cpl. W. Rankin. S/9399 Sgt. W. Murphy. 2694 Pte R. Duffy. attach T.M. Battery. | |
| | 6 Oct. | | Battalion in Reserve. Working & training. | |
| | 8 Oct. | | S/4750 Pte J. BEVERIDGE awarded M. Medal. Capt. W. STOREY-WILSON Capt W.P. CAMPBELL. 2/Lts H.S. MUIR M.C., E.P. WALCOTT, A. LEITCH, C. SCOTT. A. MORRISON. A.S.G LOXTON, A. SCOTT & W.A. FORREST joined the Battn. from No.16 I.B.D. 2/Lt W. REID hospitalised (U.K.) 15 Sept 1917. | |
| WILDERNESS CAMP | 9 Oct. | 4.0 p.m | Battn. moved to WILDERNESS CAMP in reserve. 44 I.B. moved into line. R. detached centre through Corps. 9th (S) Bn. THE BLACK WATCH | |

# WAR DIARY or INTELLIGENCE SUMMARY

Army Form C. 2118.

| Place | Date | Hour | Summary of Events and Information | Remarks and references to Appendices |
|---|---|---|---|---|
| WILDERNESS CAMP | 1917 10 Oct | | Maj. (Temp. Lt Col) S.A. INNES D.S.O. to command the Battalion vice Lt Col T.O. LLOYD, C.M.G. to retain his temporary rank, to date 4 Sept 17. A draft of 81 O.R. arrived to join the Battn from No 28 I.B.D. | |
| | 11 Oct | | 2/Lt W.J. LESLIE assumed rank of Lieut on from 3 Oct 1917. | |
| | 13 Oct | | Battn took over support battalion relieving 8/SEAFORTH HIGHRS. | |
| I'm N.W. MONCHY LE PREUX | 17 Oct | 11am | Battn relieved 8/10 GORDONS in Left Sector, Right Brigade, of Divisional front. On our right 8 SEAFORTHS, on our Left 6/7 R.S.FUSILIERS, 45 I.B. The relief passed off quietly, as did the remainder of the day. A few T.M.s were sent over on our left coy, but did little or no damage. Usual patrols and working parties. | |
| | 18 Oct | | Our artillery active at intervals throughout the night, also enemy T.Ms, and sniped during the day to the enemy. E. M.Gs swept our parapets at intervals. The day was very quiet, MONCHY coming in for attention but artillery left our sector almost alone. After stand to at night, 20 armed dark were sent over on R.Coy front. Usual patrols and working parties. Shelton claims 2 hits. | |

**Army Form C. 2118.**

# WAR DIARY
## or
## INTELLIGENCE SUMMARY.
*(Erase heading not required.)*

| Place | Date | Hour | Summary of Events and Information | Remarks and references to Appendices |
|---|---|---|---|---|
| I.M.N.W. MONCHY LE PREUX | 1917 19 Oct | | A quiet night. Patrols were sent out to examine state of enemy wire. Slight T.M. and 77mm activity at intervals throughout the day. A few aerial darts were sent over. Our T.Ms replied energetically. Our artillery active. Work done — Front line cleared, berm made, French trench filled. New bogies opened up. 16th RIFLE TRENCH re-dug. 2/Lt P.C. SNYTHE 6th BLACK WATCH. | |
| | | Lt Lt | A quiet night, save for slight T.M. activity by the enemy. During the day enemy artillery were slightly more active with 77 mm. shrapnel + H.E. on our support line + RIFLE TRENCH. Work was done on F. line, new bogies + general maintenance of front trenches made. | |
| | 21 Oct. | | An inter company relief was carried out successfully by 11.0 am. Throughout the quiet, our patrols discovered the enemy working on his wire and opened fire with Lewis gun + communicated with the artillery also. The enemy artillery was slightly more active; a few 77mm falling in LONE AVENUE + RIFLE SUPPORT TRENCH. Also a few medium T.Ms on SCABBARD + HARNESS Tou Leon on new BOYAU | |

9th. (S) Bn. THE BLACK WATCH.

**Army Form C. 2118.**

# WAR DIARY
## INTELLIGENCE SUMMARY.
*(Erase heading not required.)*

**CONFIDENTIAL**

Instructions regarding War Diaries and Intelligence Summaries are contained in F. S. Regs., Part II. and the Staff Manual respectively. Title pages will be prepared in manuscript.

| Place | Date | Hour | Summary of Events and Information | Remarks and references to Appendices |
|---|---|---|---|---|
| Tk. N.W. of MONCHY LE PREUX | 1917 21st |  | Work was continued on F. Line, mainly relaying duckboards, on new BOYAU, and on WELFORD RESERVE. | |
|  | 22nd |  | The division on our left (61st) carried out a raid immediately N. of ROEUX and in retaliation our trenches were shelled with 77 cm + 10 cm. Some damage being caused. The enemy artillery were slightly more active on our F.L system at intervals shelling RIFLE SUPPORT, LONE AVENUE and HAPPY VALLEY. Work was continued as before, and BAYONET TRENCH was taken in hand for reconstruction. | |
|  | 23rd |  | Some 7.7 cm shells fell behind our front line also some aerial darts. The day passed off quietly save for shelling of LONE AVENUE at intervals. Duckboards were laid in new BOYAU & BAYONET TRENCH had rear wall almost completed. Artillery on both sides was fairly active during the evening. After medium T.M.s fell round SCABBARD & HARNESS ALLEYS. Enemy MG's crept our parapet at intervals during the night, but our wiring parties completed their tasks into one man killed the only casualty. | |
|  | 24th |  | A quiet day till evening when enemy artillery shelled our F.L.S with | |

9th. (S) Bn. THE BLACK WATCH.

**Army Form C. 2118.**

# WAR DIARY
## INTELLIGENCE SUMMARY.
*(Erase heading not required.)*

| Place | Date | Hour | Summary of Events and Information | Remarks and references to Appendices |
|---|---|---|---|---|
| 1m N.W of MONCHY LE PREUX | 1917 | 24:00 | 7.7, 4.2, & 15 cm. shells. LONE AVENUE received 2 direct hits at least. The B'n at dinner on our left carried out 2 raids during the afternoon from which the enemy retaliated feebly. One escaped prisoner was re-captured early this morning, he having come over to our lines again considering that life amongst his own people was not as comfortable as in our cages. Work on the same trench as before was continued. The front line duckboards being completed. The weather broke and with the rain the trenches started to fall in & a number of places. Enemy artillery normal. T.M.'s quiet. Another wet night, but a quiet one. X top wire was laid up and | |
| | | 23:00 | concealed. BAYONET TRENCH rear face was completed & half the front as well. Enemy shelled LONE AVENUE with 7.7m 4.2 & 5.9 falling 2 direct hits. Otherwise little activity. Patrols heard enemy working on front line & T.M.'s & L.G.'s were turned on to him. | |
| ARRAS | 10/11 | 9.30 p.m. | H.L.I. relieved B'n in front line, and 44 I.B. moved into British Reserve in ARRAS on relief by 46 th I.B. | |

9th. (S) Bn. THE BLACK WATCH.

**Army Form C. 2118.**

# WAR DIARY
## INTELLIGENCE SUMMARY.
*(Erase heading not required.)*

| Place | Date | Hour | Summary of Events and Information | Remarks and references to Appendices |
|---|---|---|---|---|
| ARRAS | 1917 | | | |
| | 26 Oct | | Battn in BAUDIMONT BARRACKS employed, repairing, cleaning equipment. | |
| | | | 2/Lt D. KINNOCH, J. McVEIGH, & W. F. DUNDAS, joined from 1st Div Depot Bn. | |
| | 29 Oct | | 2/Lt F. READ joined the Battn for duty from No 18 I.B.D. | |
| | 31 Oct | | Battn still in BAUDIMONT BARRACKS. | |

S.A.Innes(?) 

9th. (S) Bn. THE BLACK WATCH.

9th Royal Highlanders

November 1917.

CONFIDENTIAL

# WAR DIARY

## 9th. (S) Bn. THE BLACK WATCH.

### NOVEMBER 1917

Commanding 9th Bn. The Black Watch

**Army Form C. 2118.**

# WAR DIARY and INTELLIGENCE SUMMARY.

(Erase heading not required.)

| Place | Date | Hour | Summary of Events and Information | Remarks and references to Appendices |
|---|---|---|---|---|
| | 1917 | | | |
| ARRAS | 1 Nov | | Battn in BAUDIMONT BARRACKS in Divisional Reserve. Capt & A/Lt. Col S. NORIE-MILLER proceeded to U.K. on termination of his appointment and posting for duty at home. (A.G. A1075/O.I.) of 27.10.17. 2/Lt T RITCHIE struck off the strength 26 July 1917 on posting to establishment of XIX Corps School. | |
| RIFLE CAMP | 2 Nov | 4.0 p.m. | Battn moved to RIFLE CAMP and became Reserve Battn. 44 I.B. taking over Left Sector 15th Divisional Front. A draft of 31 O.R. arrived to join Battn from 15th Divl Depot Battn. Mr J.E. DROMMUND M.C. granted permission to assume appointment of Adjutant of the Battn vice Capt S. NORIE-MILLER, to date 18 October 1917, with acting rank of Captain and pay of Lieutenant. | |
| FAMPOUX | 6 Nov | 4.0 p.m. | Battn moved into Support in Railway Cutting near FAMPOUX, relieving 8 SEAFORTH Hldrs. Employed daily in large working parties over 500 every outgoing every 24 hours. | |
| ROEUX | 10 Nov | | Battn relieved 8/10 GORDONS in L. atrecdor on our R. 8/SEAFORTHS on our L. 2/4 OX & BUCKS LI. 184th Brigade. The Relief was effected | |

**Army Form C. 2118.**

**WAR DIARY**
or
**INTELLIGENCE SUMMARY.**
(Erase heading not required.)

| Place | Date | Hour | Summary of Events and Information | Remarks and references to Appendices |
|---|---|---|---|---|
| ROEUX | 1917 10 Nov | | Early exploded by the enemy, who shelled the canal bank, causing 18 Cas rather. One patrol went out towards enemy's trenches, arriving to an T.M. shelling enemy front line. The trenches were in a bad state owing to weather. A few trench mortar shells fell in ROEUX between 4.30 am. and intermittent light T.M. fire after ca. 7.0 am. A quiet morning and afternoon. Towards evening T.M. act. was renewed on the enemy's part. | |
| | 11 Nov | | | |
| | 12 Nov | about 3.0 am. a few shell bombardment of our front at FAMPOUX and flat trench over our lines, causing 8 slight casualties. The usual T.M. activity during the small hours and our trenches were swept by M.G. fire. Work done was entirely confined to cleaning trenches & refitting them. B. General F.J. MARSHALL handed over command of 44 I.B. to B. General E. HILLIAM, C.M.G., D.S.O. and proceeded to U.K. to take up command of Senior Officers School ALDERSHOT. Both employed in cleaning trenches, installing chains and in improving posts along the front line. | |

Army Form C. 2118.

# WAR DIARY

## INTELLIGENCE SUMMARY.

(Erase heading not required.)

| Place | Date | Hour | Summary of Events and Information | Remarks and references to Appendices |
|---|---|---|---|---|
| ROEUX | 1917 13 Nov. | | About 2.0 am enemy again carried out a still further bombardment of Hqrs. + Battens: area, causing a few casualties. He fired again soft feathersly over our line. T. reflectors were worn for about 2 hours. Nothing ominous resulted. A few shells dropped short in ROEUX. Enemy shelling light on CORONA SUPPORT, GORDON TRENCH and CEYLON AVENUE during morning. A few light + medium T.M's fell about CABBAGE & COLOMBO during afternoon & evening. M.G's active on both sides at night. Patrols sent out to examine wire. Our artillery were cutting all day on CRUST. Snipers claim 2 hits. | |
| | 14 Nov. | | A quiet night. Severe M.G fire hostile went out but could do nothing owing to our M.G's being in NO MAN'S LAND a very quiet day all hands were completing the loopholed raid on CRUST. About 7.0 p.m a German was observed close to No 16 Post, he was fired at afterwards & our wire had both got in it and scaling ladders in position it was decided to cancel the raid. The wire was put out afterwards and remained in NO MAN'S LAND from 1 – 5 am meeting with very little opposition. Wiring of ground between No 3 & 15 Pats was commenced + No 13 Post was connected by a trench with GORDON TRENCH. Usual work of trench maintenance continued. | |
| | 15 Nov. | | During the night an inter-company relief was carried out quietly. A very quiet day. Enemy snipers active. Usual work on maintenance of trenches. | |
| | 16 Nov. | | Enemy artillery generally inactive after a few T.M's fell in ROEUX a quiet night till 4:30 am when in retaliation for a raid on our left our F.K.S. too active in bombardment for about an hour & a half. One direct hit on No 10 Post. Wire put in. 150 yards being put in. Wiring between posts 3 & 15 was completed. Enemy artillery generally more active throughout the day. 3 direct hits on CEYLON AVENUE + some in GORDON TRENCH. | |

9th. (S) Bn. THE BLACK WATCH.

Army Form C. 2118.

# WAR DIARY
## or
## INTELLIGENCE SUMMARY.
*(Erase heading not required.)*

CONFIDENTIAL

Instructions regarding War Diaries and Intelligence Summaries are contained in F. S. Regs., Part II. and the Staff Manual respectively. Title pages will be prepared in manuscript.

| Place | Date | Hour | Summary of Events and Information | Remarks and references to Appendices |
|---|---|---|---|---|
| ROEUX | 1917 17 Nov | 4.30 am | a raid by 6 SEAFORTHS on our R. drew forth retaliation. 6/5 GLOU-CESTERS relieved on our L. Enemy artillery fairly active throughout the day with 77, 10 + 15 cm. Trench Mortars between 3 + 15A huts & on our front. Pats. 1.B. drew retaliation. | |
| | 18 Nov | | Quiet night. Pats. for the usual M.G. fire. Patrols went out to hour in No MAN'S LAND but saw no sign of the enemy. Strong pts. were held working in this Fortlin. At 3.0 p.m. enemy [?] along the entire army front. Retaliation was severe for an hour + intermittent thereafter on the afternoon. The 44 I.B. have relieved by 46 I.B. in L. Sector & the Battn. were relieved by 7/6 K.O.S.Bs. with drawing to BAUDIMONT BARRACKS. ARRAS. | |
| ARRAS | 19 Nov | 8.35 pm | 2/Lt E.E. DALE dismissed by sentence of G.C.M. 5/10/17. The following promoted to Lieut. vary in date:- A. GRAHAM, C.M. BELLAMY, J.D.A. MACFIE, E.M. REID, T. McGREGOR, R.W. PORTER, J.M. BROWN, M. DUGGAN, J.G. WOODBURN, A. MARSHALL, J.N. HUMBLE, T.B. ALLISON, G.H. GORDON, A.D. TATHAM, A.D. MACDIARMID, G.B. MACKIE, C.G. MACDOWALL. Lt T.B. ALLISON, M.E. invalided out of the Service on account of wounds. a draft of 2.5. O.R. arrived from Depot Battn. 2/Lt R. STEVENSON (mick i.a.) to be Lt 1/7/17. | |
| | 20 Nov | | a draft of 21 O.R. arrived from Depot Battn. 2/Lt G.R.M. KERR classified unfit G.S. 22/10/17. | |
| | 24 Nov | | Captain W.P. CAMPBELL posted to 1/6 BLACK WATCH to strength the strength from 3 Oct 1917. | |
| In N.W. of MONCHY-LE-PREUX | 26 Nov | 6.15 pm | Battn. proceeded by tram to ATHIES LOCK and marched thence to relieve 11 A + S. HIGHRS. in L. Section R. Sub sector 15th Divisl. Front. A.4. I.B. relieved 45 I.B. On our R. 8/SEAFORTHS on our L. 12/H.L.I. 46 I.B. Relief was accomplished without any hitch. During the night heard enemy moving over M.G. fire from enemy sounded quietly. A few T. M.S. fell in HARNESS, SCABBARD & LINK ALLEYS Targets at intervals. | |

9th. (S) Bn. THE BLACK WATCH.

Army Form C. 2118.

# WAR DIARY
## or
## INTELLIGENCE SUMMARY.
(Erase heading not required.)

Instructions regarding War Diaries and Intelligence Summaries are contained in F.S. Regs., Part II. and the Staff Manual respectively. Title pages will be prepared in manuscript.

| Place | Date | Hour | Summary of Events and Information | Remarks and references to Appendices |
|---|---|---|---|---|
| IN N.W. of MONCHY LE PREUX | 1917 27 Nov | | At 3.0 am patrols went out from both front coys. & M.Gr fire interested much movement on U.R. No enemy were seen & Major Strahan had a covering party went on the L. That B W.D. WILSON Harry Strahan but a covering party went on the L. 2.6 Km reconnoitred. He saw 2 enemy in a large crater near HARNESS, LAKE and without hesitation, made a rush in on them & succeeded in taking them prisoners. They belonged to 1/133 I.R Regt. 24th Division. The capture was of the utmost importance as the capture of Army intimated the prisoners say that identifications were urgently required from this sector. The thanks of Brigade & Divisional Commanders were felt expressed. A very quiet morning. In afternoon about 2.30-4.30 both T.M. & Artillery were very active on our front & opposite lines T.M. & HARNESS ALLEY were also a LONE AVENUE. B/W. RIFLE SUPPORT & HARNESS ALLEY were them in several places. WELFORD RESERVE also received some attention. Batt. was employed in repairing trenches during them & MGs did trade to Our Artillery was active during the night. The enemy responded with T.M's & 5.9 on WELFORD RESERVE about 1.0 am Patrols were unable to more about owing to enemy M.G. activity. The enemy was shelled Monchy and R. Bn sector. In afternoon about from the afternoon MONCHY and R. Bn sector. Inf shell 77mm & 10cm. and a few 15 cm on WELFORD RESERVE. but chiefly 77mm. (Batt. was relieved by 1/ HAMPSHIRE Regt. 11th 13 | |
| | 28 Nov | 7.30 pm | At 7.30 pm the 44th I.B. withdrew to Divisional Reserve at ARRAS. 4 Division withdrew to BAUDIMONT BARRACKS ARRAS. Batt. CLARK. M.C. is granted the hon. rank of Captain. | |
| ARRAS. | 30 Nov | | Batt in ARRAS. Training & cleaning equipment etc. 4.9 Sept. 1917. | |

S.D. Munro Lt.Col
9th (S) Bn. THE BLACK WATCH.

Miss West

B 29

9th Royal Highlanders.

December 1917.

Confidential

9th Battn The Black Watch

WAR DIARY

DECEMBER 1917

# WAR DIARY / INTELLIGENCE SUMMARY

Army Form C. 2118.

**9th (S) Bn. THE BLACK WATCH**

| Place | Date | Hour | Summary of Events and Information | Remarks and references to Appendices |
|---|---|---|---|---|
| ARRAS | 1917 1 Dec | 8.55pm | Battalion in BAUDIMONT BARRACKS, in Divisional Reserve, preparatory to not moved relieving 4/5 I.B. The front companies were three GORDON HIGHLANDERS not moved. The remainder marching in all the body, and 6/7 R.S.Fs were relieved by 6/10 GORDONS. We with the Battn. on our R. 7/ CAMERONS on our L. Outposts of support line relieved 7.30 and 8.0 pm. passed quietly, save for slight shelling of support line. During the day Patrols went out towards morning but encountered no Marshals. During the day parties were employed in repairing + cleaning trenches and in carrying up material after aerial darts, and Right T.Ms fell on our L. Front Coy about 9.0 am. 2/Lt. J.N. MENZIES posted to the Battn. from 1/7 /Battn. and Lt. W.J. DUFFY M.C. transferred from 7/ CAMERONS. CHALK RESERVE shelled with 4.2" 7.0 – 8.0 pm. | |
| | 2 Dec | | Patrols went out from L. Coy investigating size of mine and from R. Coy which encountered 3 of the enemy who continued work two continued opening up new ret and spread debris out of BOYAUX. The day passed quietly a few darts falling on support line. About 8.0 pm intermittently throughout the afternoon CHALK RESERVE was shelled with 4.2s. | |
| | 3 Dec | | Throughout the afternoon our front Coys R. Front Coy in front of a quiet night. Patrols were out from line, line. R. Coy carried along the front an enemy patrol with L.G. fire, also work of deepening + enemy when our own deepening continued a few dark fell on an Mt. support line + CHALK trenches was resumed. Shelled with 4.2" for about half an hour. | |
| | 4 Dec | | RESERVE was shelled with 4.2" for about half an hour. Patrols were out on both company fronts but no enemy were encountered. | |
| | 5 Dec | 8.30pm | A quiet night. No news and a car from him arrived on to them. During the morning we also They were from working parties carrying this support line. R.E. T.S. the 8/SEAFORTHS tried among the front and deepening of CHALK by 77 + 10 cm shells. at intervals quiet save for shelling of CHALK by 5/ BLACK WATCH were withdrawn to support in HUDSON behind the Battn. and PUDDING TRENCHES. | |
| NORTHUMBERLAND LANE | 6 Dec | | Battn. resting, cleaning up, baths and working parties. | |

Army Form C. 2118.

# WAR DIARY / INTELLIGENCE SUMMARY.

(Erase heading not required.)

| Place | Date 1917 | Hour | Summary of Events and Information | Remarks and references to Appendices |
|---|---|---|---|---|
| NORTHUMBERLAND LANE 1m N. of ROEUX | 7 Dec | | Battn. in Support. Resting and working Parties. 2/Lt B.W. MACHIN slightly wounded. 3 Sec. | |
| | 9 Dec | 6.45 pm | Battn moved up into centre sub-section, which it left on 5th Dec. in relief of 8/SEAFORTHS who side-slipped to left. On our R. 7th CAMERONS. The night passed off very quietly. Patrols were out examining wire, but met with no opposition. Working parties were out cleaning trenches in F.L.S. which had fallen in owing to the heavy rain following a spell of severe. Weather was declared and rations of rum were issued from | |
| | 10 Dec | | 6 a.m. to 9.30 am. Enemy aeroplanes were very active from 6.45 am onwards. At one time, from over ad. hunt 8 S.A. circled over our lines repeatedly. Guns apparently. About 10.0 am hostile artillery + T.M.s were very active, especially on R. front & left front line + CHILI AVENUE, several direct hits on the trench being obtained. Towards afternoon the activity decreased. On the forward area interested on the back areas CONRAD + CHALK Trenches receiving a good number of 15 C.m. A quiet night, but a good deal of M.G. fire. One man being killed at Stand To during the morning. A few 4.2 's fell on CHALK RESERVE Near hair shelters on nostly on the North Bank. 2 patrols went out, but Sent activity was contained. + work on cleaning trenches was | |
| | 11 Dec | | still forward. The night was quiet but enemy aeroplanes were out over their lines & during the day were unusually quiet, not heard working in their front line. Two patrols of 4 machines each activity was kept mainly on the enemy's front. Our A.A. guns fired retained up & down our line to & fro as the SCARPE. On them in afternoon only. Work was continued on shelter in CHALK and on CLAN ALLEY also cleaning trenches in front line + clearing trenches generally. | |
| | 12 Dec | | | |

9th. (S) Bn. THE BLACK WATCH.

**WAR DIARY**
or
**INTELLIGENCE SUMMARY**

Army Form C. 2118.

| Place | Date | Hour | Summary of Events and Information | Remarks and references to Appendices |
|---|---|---|---|---|
| 1 m. N. of ROEUX | 1917 13 Dec | | The enemy was more active all along our front but kept T.M's & acted daily. Several direct hits were obtained on COSTA ALLEY. Front line & CHARLIE SUPPORT. 3 patrols were sent out but encountered no opposition. at 9.45 pm an enemy patrol came towards N6 & SAP. one man falling in. It was fired on & was thought to have been hit, L.G. & rifle fire were directed on the patrol but without success. An inter company relief was carried out, troops was continued on CLAW & shelters in CHALK and the shelters were cleared. | |
| | 14 Dec | | A machine gun alarm was held at 2.0 am but only eventuated. Temp Captain Whitt commanding 4th T.M.Battery was killed 15 Aug 1917. Lt N. G. JOHNSTONE promoted quietly on our front. Patrols went out the night at 6.45 am the enemy sent down a heavy barrage & light M.G. fire on our L.G. front which & also a C.T. of Port a far dart & light T.M's on a party of about 20 worked up to our wire and endeavoured to bomb. he did not succeed in penetrating our defences. R. Under cover of his rifle & L.G. fire he had 4 men wounded, one disappeared & was driven off and they rather the day & perhaps men died. T.M's were very active on our R. throughout but no action followed. Work was continued on shelters in CHALK & on COIN & CLAW & floors in COSTA were cleared. | |
| | 15 Dec | | A very quiet night. Patrols were laying out as cement parties and also in front for an enemy patrol but with no success. Enemy available men was employed in digging a new trench connecting Sap at Port 30 & 32, and a post opposite the enemy will spend with 7.7 cm on front line, COSTA & CHARLIE. Also W/2 on CAULDRON TRENCH. Otherwise a quiet afternoon & evening. | |
| | 16 Dec | | Work was continued on the new trench and very foot half progress made, an amount defect of 5 feet being reached. A good deal of T.M. and M.G./ activity both. Our patrols sent out patrols in the distance & L.G./patrol was turned on to it. | |

9th. (S) Bn. THE BLACK WATCH.

**Army Form C. 2118.**

# WAR DIARY
## INTELLIGENCE SUMMARY
*(Erase heading not required.)*

| Place | Date | Hour | Summary of Events and Information | Remarks and references to Appendices |
|---|---|---|---|---|
| 1m. N of ROEUX | 1917 16 Dec | | Enemy artillery activity very considerable. Salvoes of 7.7 & 10 cm were fired throughout the day on our front & support, reserve lines. Direct hits on the telephone wires wanted from trenches to searching afternoon. No damage resulted. | |
| | 17 Dec | | During the night salvoes of 7.7cm were fired on our front & support lines, also about 50 rounds of light T.Ms. which were continued in deepening and enlarging the new trench. Wiring also in accordance with plan in CHALK Patrols were out but saw nothing. The early morning was quiet. Some time was found for a few rifle grenades. About noon 7.7, 10 & 15 cm were fired intermittently for 3 or 4 hours on our front, support & reserve lines. The Bn. was relieved in the centre sub-sector by the 12th H.L.I., the 4/6 I.B. relieving the 44 I.B. the latter withdrawing to Divisional Reserve in ARRAS. The 9th B.W. going into BAUDIMONT BARRACKS | |
| ARRAS | | 8.10pm | | |
| ROEUX | 23 Dec | 6.40pm | 4/4 I.B. relieved 4/5 I.B. in R. Brigade Section. 9" B.W. relieving 6/7 R.S.F. in L. Sub sector. On our R. 8/ SEAFORTHS, on our L. 12/ H.L.I. 4/6 I.B. The relief was effected quietly. During a strafe S. of the SCARPE the S.O.S. was put up there and our 18 hrs retaliating on our front, fell short flowing in our front line between CORFU & COCOA TRENCHES in 6 places, one shell being trained to fim M.G.C. 18th Dec. 2/Lt A.F. LAKEMAN proceeded to join 2/Lt C.K. YOUNG proceeded to join M.G.C. 18th Dec. The following Mentions in Despatches appeared in gazette of 18 Dec 1917. Lt-Col. S.A. INNES, D.S.O. MAJOR A.H.O. DENNISTOUN, CAPTAIN W. CLARK, M.C. S/11256 C.Q.M.S. NAESMITH, S/6319 Sergt A. STEELE. 2/Lt W.F. DUNDAS Tank Corps 22 Dec. | |
| | 24 Dec | | to U.K. Nick 14th Dec. save for rifle grenades and aerial darts on our front & support lines. A quiet night. Bright moon, so no work could be done, nor could patrols be sent out. Coys were employed cleaning trenches where blown in, and improving strong points. | |

8th. (S) Bn. THE BLACK WATCH.

# WAR DIARY
## INTELLIGENCE SUMMARY

**Army Form C. 2118.**

| Place | Date | Hour | Summary of Events and Information | Remarks and references to Appendices |
|---|---|---|---|---|
| ROEUX | 1917 24 Dec | | During the morning there was intermittent light T.M. shelling and rifle grenades and aerial darts on our front & support line. The day was very cold & visibility was poor. During the afternoon it became milder & a mist started. Lieut. VISCT. DRUMLANRIG wounded. No 18249 Pte R.A. GREIG awarded Military Medal. | |
| | 25 Dec | | A quiet night, milder, and misty at times, permitting of a little wire being put out. COCOA ALLEY was cleared and deepened and work on the front line, support line & Strong Points continued throughout the day. A few dart, rifle grenade & light T.M. shells fell at intervals. | |
| | 26 Dec | | Save for some heavy T.M's in ROEUX and light T.M's darts & rifle grenades on front & support line during the night about 2–3 a.m. it passed off quietly. The snow & slight moonlight prevented any patrolling or wiring. Work was continued in Strong Points and clearing COCOA ALLEY. About 11.0 a.m enemy activity increased chiefly with T.M's on support line. ROEUX was shelled for half an hour with 7.7 a.m. | |
| | 27 Dec | | A very quiet night, and very cold. No patrols were possible and no wiring. N end of CORONA SUPPORT was deepened. During the morning the enemy T.M's & 7.7 cm were much more active than usual | |

9th. (S) Bn. THE BLACK WATCH.

Army Form C. 2118.

# WAR DIARY
## INTELLIGENCE SUMMARY.
*(Erase heading not required.)*

| Place | Date | Hour | Summary of Events and Information | Remarks and references to Appendices |
|---|---|---|---|---|
| ROEUX | 1917 27 Dec | | On our Centre Coy L/Corp. CEYLON also came in for some attention from 10cm. About 4.0 pm again at 4.30pm enemy bombardments with T.M. & 7.7cm, on front line system & 4.2" in support & 10/15cm. on back areas broke out. Our artillery retaliated and all became | |
| | | 9.30pm | quiet again after half an hour. The 8/10 GORDON HIGHS relieved the batt. in the L Sub Sector, the R Coy of SEAFORTHS, being relieved by a company of 7th CAMERONS. The batt. withdrew without opposition to CUTTING in railway at FAMPOUX, 1 Coy in LANCER AVENUE & 2 Coys in CORDITE & CRUMP respectively. | |
| FAMPOUX CUTTING | 30 Dec | | Capt N G JOHNSTONE M.C. & Lieut A. GRAHAM. attached 44th T.M.B. were killed by a premature explosion in a Stokes gun. 2 O.R. were killed & 10/pr & 1 O.R. wounded at the same time 2/Lt T. RITCHIE rejoined the Batt. from XIX Corps School. | |
| | 31 Dec | | The Battalion was employed on various working parties throughout the Brigade Sector. Batt. in Support. Employed on working parties | |

J.R. Wauchope
Capt 9th Batt. Black Watch

9th. (S) Bn. THE BLACK WATCH.

Army Form C. 2118.

# WAR DIARY
## INTELLIGENCE SUMMARY
*(Erase heading not required.)*

| Place | Date | Hour | Summary of Events and Information | Remarks and references to Appendices |
|---|---|---|---|---|
| FAMPOUX CUTTING | 1918 1 Jan | | Battn in support. Right Brigade XVII Corps Front. Battn employed daily in wiring front & support the Brigade area | |
| ARRAS | 2 Jan | 10:30pm | 1st Scots Guards relieved 2nd Battn. Battn withdrew to BARDIRN BARRACKS ARRAS GUARDS DIVISION relieved 15th DIVISION & withdrew to Corps Reserve. 2nd GUARDS BRIGADE relieved 44th I.B. Lt.Col S.A. INNES, D.S.O. assumed command of 4th I.B. on 29 Dec 1917 during the absence on leave of Brig. Genl E. HILAM, CMG, DSO. CAPT W. STOREY was | |
| | 5 Jan | | assumed command of Battn till 5 Jan 1918 when MAJOR V.B. BINNIE M.C. returned from leave. LT R.J. McMURRAY left (on 6 Septembers) 5 Oct 1917. LT G.F. YOUNG relinquishes acting rank of Capt 6 Sept 1917. 2/Lt B.W. MACHIN expires to 1/K 31 Dec 1917. 2/Lt J. STUART & W.W. MITCHELL join II. Battn from 3rd Battn for duty. | |
| | 14th | | Lt.Col S.A. INNES, D.S.O. resumed command of the Battn. T.L.P. PROUDFOOT M.C. return (?) to Battn and (Captain whilst commanding Coy 31 Oct 1917.) T/Lt C. MEETHE | |
| | 15 Jan | | acting captain (acting Major) 2/f 15 November 1917. A New Year dinner was held in E.F.C. Canteen building to 811 men a great success. The Brigadier addressed them | |

9th. (S) Bn. THE BLACK WATCH.

Headquarters
15th Division

Ref attached.

Original copy was
forwarded to Officer i/c Records.
please. Error very much
regretted.

44/15.

/s/ ——
Lieut.
for O.C.
9th. (S) Bn. THE BLACK WATCH.

> ORDERLY ROOM.
> No. F 81
> DATE 10/2/18
> 9th (SER.) Bn. THE BLACK WATCH

Army Form C. 2118.

# WAR DIARY
## INTELLIGENCE SUMMARY
(Erase heading not required.)

| Place | Date | Hour | Summary of Events and Information | Remarks and references to Appendices |
|---|---|---|---|---|
| ARRAS | 1915 | | | |
| | 15 Jan | | The Bn was inspected in marching order by G.O.C. Major Gen. H.L. REED. V.C. C.B. DMG. 29 officers & 757 being on parade. He expressed himself as well pleased with the appearance of the Battalion. | |
| | 22 Jan | | Capt R.J. McMURRAY to U.K. sick. | |
| | | | 5 Jan 1916. Lieut K.T. DRUMLANRIG to U.K. 9 Jan 1916. | |
| | 23 Jan | | Capt J.I. BUCHAN. D.S.O. appointed A.D.C. to B. Gen.1 13-1-18 vice Capt J.E. DRUMMOND. M.C. to BASE—sick. 2nd Lt G.E.R. YOUNG. relinquishes his Commission on account of ill-health. 21-1-18. Lt Col S.A. INNES. D.S.O. proceeded to BERTHANGLES on 5 days Course with Y.& 6 Squadron R.F.C. Major W.B. BINNIE ; M.C. assumed temporary command of the Bn during Col S.A. INNES' absence from today. | |
| | 26 Jan | | Bn took part in Divisional Excercise near AGNY. Dinner & mess served in the field and Bn returned to ARRAS. about 4 pm. | |
| | 30 Jan | | LIEUT. W.F. DUFFY ; M.G. to U.K.-sick. 20 January 1915. | |
| | 31 Jan | | Bn took part in Brigade Exercise. Acting assaulting Bn with 8th Seaforth Hrs. The Corps Comm[anding] & Lt Gen. Sir CHARLES FERGUSSON. BT. K.C.B. K.C.M.G. M.V.O. D.S.O. being present expressed himself as well pleased with the operations. | |

W.B. Binnie. Major
(S) Bn. THE BLACK WATCH.

Transferred from 44' Bde
to 46 Bde 7.2.18.

WAR DIARY
9th. (S) Bn. THE BLACK WATCH.
FEBRUARY
1918

46/15

CONFIDENTIAL.

# WAR DIARY / INTELLIGENCE SUMMARY

Army Form C. 2118.

CONFIDENTIAL

| Place | Date | Hour | Summary of Events and Information | Remarks and references to Appendices |
|---|---|---|---|---|
| S. Bank of RIVER SCARPE | 9th Feb. | | "B" Coy moved up from Duffort, and relieved 2 Coys of 1st Irish Guards taking over extreme left of Brigade front, which now rests on S. Bank of SCARPE. Enemy T.M.s are active on our front line, and 4.5" on Reserve Line, near WELFORD RESERVE at intervals during the day. One or two direct hits being obtained. | |
| " | 10th Feb. | | Enemy normally quiet. Weather conditions improving. Less overland traffic is necessary. Lt. A.K. HAMILTON reported for duty with Bn from U.K. Posted to "C" Coy. | |
| " | 11th Feb. | | Enemy making a practice of Shelling Comm. trenches and Reserve Line during Stand-to hour. Q direct hit on WELFORD RESERVE at 5 p.m. and 2 men of "C" Coy were Killed. No. 43244 L/Cpl W. TAYLOR "A" Coy died of wounds 10-2-18. | |
| " | 12th Feb. | | Enemy very quiet during the past 24 hours. Coy Patrols went out into No Man's Land and found everything below normal. About 10 p.m. a few shells landed near Bn. Stn. Or which moved to contain Gas. Lt. A.K. HAMILTON reported for duty. | |
| " | 13th Feb. | | Relieved by 10th Scottish Rifles. Relief was completed without a hitch and Bn. moved back to Reserve Billets at ECOLE des JEUNNES FILLES: ARRAS. Men came on about 6 p.m. and made the trenches very dirty for our feeling out to Reserve. | |

9th. (S). Bn. THE BLACK WATCH.

# WAR DIARY / INTELLIGENCE SUMMARY

Army Form C. 2118.

9th (S) Bn. THE BLACK WATCH

9 Royal Scots Vol 32

B 31

| Place | Date | Hour | Summary of Events and Information | Remarks and references to Appendices |
|---|---|---|---|---|
| ARRAS | 3 Feb | | Bn. in BAUDIMONT BARRACKS. Bn. Training carried out under orders of Brigadier 44th I.B. | |
| | 4 Feb | | Bn. took part in Brigade "Platoon v Lewis Gun Competition". Brigadier L. HILLIAM offered a silver cup to the winning teams. "D" Coy won the Lewis Gun Competition and were presented with the cup. 15th Division took over from 4th Div - 44th I.B. relieved 13th I.B. and 1 Bn 11th Bgde in Right Sector Divisional Front. | |
| | 5 Feb | | 9 R.S. Bn. moved into Reserve at BOIS DES BOEUFS relieving 1 Bn. Rifle Brigade. | |
| BOIS DES BOEUFS | 6 Feb | | 10 Officers & 300 men were employed in clearing GORDON AVENUE which was in very bad condition due to recent rains. | |
| MONCHY SECTOR | 7 Feb | | Bn transferred into 46th I.B. and moved forward to take over Left Sub Sector of Centre Section, Div Front. x 3652 Sgt MONKLEY J. awarded CROIX DE GUERRE. (with A.M.S. 3rd Army H.R./915 of 28-1-18) x Bn relieved 6th Cameron H[igh]rs. 5 men "A" Coy & 1 "B" Coy killed, and 3 men wounded. "C" Coy casualties: 1 man "A" Coy by enemy MINENWERFER and "D" Coy by aerial dart. Owing to the muddy condition of the trenches, communication trenches are very little used at present and over land tracks are used up to the Front line system. | |
| | 8 Feb | | | |

**Army Form C. 2118.**

# WAR DIARY
## or
## INTELLIGENCE SUMMARY.
*(Erase heading not required.)*

Instructions regarding War Diaries and Intelligence Summaries are contained in F. S. Regs., Part II. and the Staff Manual respectively. Title pages will be prepared in manuscript.

| Place | Date | Hour | Summary of Events and Information | Remarks and references to Appendices |
|---|---|---|---|---|
| ARRAS | 14th Feb |  | Bn. engaged in cleaning up equipment Kit &c. Bn. Cys handed for Baths & change of under-clothing which are always welcome. Weather was good. |  |
| " | 15th Feb |  | Training resumed under O.C. Coys. Coys were also busy in trying to improve the billets which are not so comfortable as those we had at BAUDIMONT BARRACKS. 2/Lt. R.T. CLARK left for U.K. on 6 months tour of duty. |  |
| " | 16th Feb |  | CAPT. J.S. STRANG: M.O. rejoined the Bn. today and took over Command of "C" Coy from Lt. P.C. SMYTHE. CAPT. T.D. BYERS returned from Rest Camp where he has been since 4th January. |  |
| " | 17th Feb |  | Temp Capt (A/Major) W.B. BINNIE: M.C. to be 2nd in Command and to be Temp Major to fill establishment from 24th August 1914. Capt W.R. BRAND: C.F. having been transferred to the Base for a tour of duty, Capt W.T. MORTON: C.F. took over duties as Presbyterian Chaplain to the Bn. 7/Lt. M. DUGGAN relinquishes his Commission on account of ill-health contracted on Active Service (M.S. 9510 of 10-2-18.) |  |
| " | 19th |  | Moved off from ARRAS by 2 Bns at 3.15 pm and 5.4 pm to relieve 1/8th Co. S.B. in Brigade Support. Bn. H.Q. and O.R.s were accommodated beside "C" Coy in HAPPY VALLEY. |  |

9th. (S) Bn. THE BLACK WATCH.

**Army Form C. 2118.**

# WAR DIARY
## INTELLIGENCE SUMMARY.
*(Erase heading not required.)*

| Place | Date | Hour | Summary of Events and Information | Remarks and references to Appendices |
|---|---|---|---|---|
| | 19th | | "B" Coy were in position as Right Support Coy – "C" Coy Left Support and "A" v "D" Coys Rear Support Coys in CALIFORNIA TRENCH. The Germans (10) fired in the VALLEY, about 6am, but caused no damage. B being Right Coy with working parties – supplying 4 Officers and 320 O.R. daily. | |
| S. of SCARPE & | 21st | | Bn. in Support in HAPPY VALLEY. Working parties. 1 321. O.R. from 6 U.K. Lieutenant P. Smyth. 2nd Lt. A.S.G. Laxton. Captain T. Trevstan M.C. Captain W J Morton C.F. | |
| | 22nd | | Bn. in Support in HAPPY VALLEY. Captain & Adjutant J. Buchan D.S.O. evacuating Sick | |
| | 23rd | | Bn. in Support in HAPPY VALLEY. Working parties | |
| | 24th | | Bn. in Support in HAPPY VALLEY. Working parties. | |
| | 25th | | Bn. relieved 7/8. K.O.S.B's in LEFT SECTION. Two men of "A" Coy killed by an aerial dart. Company dispositions as follows C Coy Right Front. A Coy Centre Coy. D Coy Left Front Company. B Coy in Battalion Support. Relief Completed at 9.45 pm. | |

**9th. (S) Bn. THE BLACK WATCH.**

# WAR DIARY
## INTELLIGENCE SUMMARY

Army Form C. 2118.

| Place | Date | Hour | Summary of Events and Information | Remarks and references to Appendices |
|---|---|---|---|---|
| | 26th | | Weather frosty & clear. Enemy TM's very active. A TM duel commenced at 9 am and lasted till 12 noon. About 150 TM's were fired by our TM Batteries. Artillery twice called on to assist 9.0. casualties but trenches badly damaged. Officers patrol under 2nd Lt. A. Scott entered enemy front line at ARCHIE TR. It was found unoccupied. | |
| | 27th | | Weather clear. Enemy TM's again active. Artillery retaliated twice to enemy TM fire. Enemy seem to be trying & Retaliation scheme with their 4.2's & 5.9's to our TM fire, twice when our TM's were firing salvos were fired on to our FRONT and SUPPORT LINES. Sgt Wilson A Cy, dangerly wounded. Patrols during night report No Man's Land clear of the enemy. Enemy FRONT LINE again found unoccupied. | |
| | 2 | | | |
| | 28th | | Weather misty & slight rain. Line very quiet, only two TM's were fired during the forenoon. 2nd Lt. D. Kinnoch, A Cy, evacuated sick. A battalion of the "Guards" raided the enemy FRONT LINE | |

9th. (S) Bn. THE BLACK WATCH.

Army Form C. 2118.

# WAR DIARY
## or
## INTELLIGENCE SUMMARY.
(Erase heading not required.)

| Place | Date | Hour | Summary of Events and Information | Remarks and references to Appendices |
|---|---|---|---|---|
| WELFORD RESERVE | 1918 28th Feb | | N. of the SCARPE at the NOSE.. 12 prisoners + 1 M.G. being taken. Slight casualties suffered. Enemy retaliation came down on our support line very weak — no casualties.  Following Officers were evacuated sick. Lt DUFFY 20 Jan, Lt J.M BROWN 28 Jan. Lt W.J. LESLIE 28 Feb, all to U.K. Leut Visct DRUMMANRIG posted to U.K. to date 9 Jan. Capt J.I. BUCHAN D.S.O. to be adjutant vice 2/Lt J.E. DRUMMOND 12 Jan. 2/Lt J.E. DRUMMOND to be Lieut 7 Jan. | |

S.O.Humphren
Adj 9th Bn The Black Watch

9th. (S) Bn. THE BLACK WATCH.

46th Brigade.

15th Division.

--------

9th BATTALION

THE BLACK WATCH

MARCH 1918

Appendices attached:-

Report on Operations 27th-29th March.

(6339) Wt. W160/M3016 1,500,000 10/17 McA & W Ltd (E1898) Forms W3091.   Army Form W.3091.

**Cover for Documents.**

**Nature of Enclosures.**

9TH (S) BATTALION

THE BLACK WATCH.

WAR DIARY
for
MARCH 1918.

VOLUME XXXIII.

Notes, or Letters written.

# WAR DIARY
## INTELLIGENCE SUMMARY

9th. (S) Bn. THE BLACK WATCH.

| Place | Date | Hour | Summary of Events and Information | Remarks and references to Appendices |
|---|---|---|---|---|
| | 1918 | | | |
| ARRAS | 3 March | 11.30 pm | ARRAS being late. Batt. billeted in ECOLE in ARRAS. Lt Col S. A. INNES resumed command of Batt. on 2nd March on return from leave. Batt. in reserve 4th–10th March. Training and 2 nights digging cable trench. | |
| WELLFORD RESERVE | 10 Mar | 11.5 pm | Batt. relieved 7/8 K.O.S.B's in front line 46 I.B. sector. A quiet relief. On our R. 6th CAMERONS, 45 I.B. on our L. 1 COLDSTREAM GDS. | |
| | 11 Mar | | The night passed quietly and throughout the day the enemy were generally inactive on front area. About 6.0 p.m. a few 5.9" fell near LONE AVENUE and rear defences were shelled at intervals. A heavy trench bombardment of T.M's 4.2" heavies on ROEUX took place 5–6 p.m. to which our guns replied. Army to inform us received from a prisoner special precautionary measures were taken to resist an attack expected on 13th. Enemy were generally quiet till 7.30 p.m. when a few 4.2 & 7.7 mm were sent over our reserve line WELLFORD. Front system received a few light T.M's round Batt. | |
| | 12 Mar | | From midnight onwards at intervals of about 1 hour harassing fire by our guns & M.G's to carried out on depth over whole enemy system. At times the bombardment was intense. The enemy replied very feebly on the | |

# WAR DIARY
## INTELLIGENCE SUMMARY.
*(Erase heading not required.)*

Army Form C. 2118.

| Place | Date | Hour | Summary of Events and Information | Remarks and references to Appendices |
|---|---|---|---|---|
| WELLFORD RESERVE | 1918 13 Mar | | Front occupied by 7th Battalion, had a talk on plans, his reply was much keener. About 5.0 am however, 77 cm & 10 cm were asleep on our Rifle Front. Several direct hits on trenches being obtained. Lys- T.Ms were also used frequently on forward area. The day dawned clear and quiet although harm over the front by 7.30 am. During the day enemy was intermittently active on back area and about 10 pm shelled HAPPY VALLEY with 4.2 & 5.9 doing a certain amount of damage. After 5.9 fell round WELLFORD with a further shell hold was continued. | |
| | 14 Mar | | A quiet night. Slight shelling of WELLFORD and HAPPY VALLEY with 4.2 during morning. Stand to. Very little activity throughout the day. Our artillery carried out a good deal of harassing fire. Towards evening, ROEUX and FAMPOUX were shelled with 5.9 of shell. | |
| | 15 Mar | | The road harassing fire was carried out by our artillery. Front system very quiet all day. WELLFORD & LONE AVENUE shelled with 5.9 from 9.30 – 10.0 a.m. Took no extra enemy opposition. Enemy shell hole & general upkeep. | |
| | 16 Mar | | The night passed quietly, a few heavies falling near our front line system | |

8th. (S) Bn. THE BLACK WATCH.

**Army Form C.2118.**

# WAR DIARY
## INTELLIGENCE SUMMARY.
*(Erase heading not required)*

| Place | Date | Hour | Summary of Events and Information | Remarks and references to Appendices |
|---|---|---|---|---|
| WELLFORD RESERVE | 1918 16 Mar | | A.2" & 77mm & light T.Ms in the front support but no damage resulted. The day passed quietly, and our artillery were intermittently active. The Battn. was relieved in front line by 10th SCOTTISH RIFLES and proceeded to support | |
| JOHNSON AVENUE | | 9.45pm 11.30pm | reserve 78 K.O.S.Bs. Gas shell were put into HAPPY VALLEY & FAMPOUX. Battn. employed on minor working parties throughout the front system. Mr W.W. MITCHELL evacuated to U.K. sick. | |
| | 17 Mar | | 11 March 1918 Battn. employed on working parties to its almost working capacity. | |
| | 20 Mar | 5.5am | Enemy suddenly opened an intense barrage of shells on HAPPY VALLEY, ORANGE HILL & FAMPOUX. It went on W and the heaviest took place in the valley over 2 Coy & 147th in occupation. The continued rearing of rocks. About 10.0am the Bn. came out of 7 117 am. rather gradually down by stealth by the enemy reports developed to the S. along front of VI, V & IV Corps. The enemy refugs stating an advance of about 3000 yards had been made into our lines. | |
| | 21 Mar | | 2 raids about WANCOURT were brought off on hearing of this, about 9.45am shelling throughout the day active on Tullercourt Vaulx area, but little in front. | |

**9th. (S) Bn. THE BLACK WATCH.**

Army Form C. 2118.

# WAR DIARY
## INTELLIGENCE SUMMARY.
*(Erase heading not required.)*

8th. (S) Bn. THE BLACK WATCH.

| Place | Date | Hour | Summary of Events and Information | Remarks and references to Appendices |
|---|---|---|---|---|
| Johnston Trench | 22 March | | Intermittent shelling during the day. Captain T. CHIVERS wounded. | |
| | | 11 p.m. | Intermittent shelling. Orders recd. to relieve the 9th Black Watch tomorrow towards dusk in our usual | |
| | 23 | 3 a.m. | Recce of the left of front. Flit plans. Filed today. New dispositions were taken up by the bn. as follows:- Dep held a line of shell-holes from JAMAICA Trench to CHINSTRAP Lane Parallel L and about 200 yds N.W. of JOHNSON Avenue. A Coy in support to D Coy and manned a trench running from K Post to CHINSTRAP Lane in a N. Easterly direction. C Coy in the right manner as earlier but shallow trench from JAMAICA Trench just S of K Post to JERUSALEM Trench. B Coy in reserve took up position in the BRONX LINE; Bn. Hd Qrs in HALIFAX TRENCH. One Coy of the 10th Patriot Rifles formed a rear guard and manned BAYONET TRENCH, MUSKET RESERVE and CURB SWITCH SOUTH. | |

# WAR DIARY
## INTELLIGENCE SUMMARY.
*(Erase heading not required.)*

Army Form C. 2118.

| Place | Date | Hour | Summary of Events and Information | Remarks and references to Appendices |
|---|---|---|---|---|
| | 24 | | The enemy was very quiet during the forenoon, and it was about 10 o'clock before he commenced to occupy the ground evacuated by us. The 10th Scottish Rifles withdrew according to plan and our Artillery was very active. The enemy suffered considerable casualties during the day as he seemed about seeing in the open. The Bn. was relieved by the 7/8th K.O.S.B. at night and proceeded to the Army Line with Bn. and Bn. H.Q. in WILDERNESS CAMP. Lieut-Colonel J.A.INNES.D.S.O. proceeded to Hospital and Major L.S.BINNIE took over the Bn. | |
| | 25 | | Work was carried out improving the ARMY LINE. B fer 59" shells fire in the vicinity of WILDERNESS CAMP. A draft of 67 O.R. arrived from Base Depot and were taken on the strength of the Bn. Details. Fairly quiet during the day, a little shelling by the enemy. Enemy aircraft over vicinity of WILDERNESS CAMP. | |

9th. (S) Bn. THE BLACK WATCH.

# WAR DIARY
## INTELLIGENCE SUMMARY

Army Form C.-2118.

| Place | Date | Hour | Summary of Events and Information | Remarks and references to Appendices |
|---|---|---|---|---|
| | 26 | | Intermittent shelling of back areas. WILDERNESS CAMP received attention and Bn and Coy HQrs moved out and dug in for the rest of day in the open - dug-outs. | |
| | 27 | | Quiet day. Fire trenches intermittently shelling during the day. Relieved 10th Scottish Rifles 12 m.n. Dropp 16.O.R. reported. | |
| | 28 | | Enemy attacked after at 7.30 a.m. after heavy preliminary bombardment, delivered attack report on intermittent rate, attacked. The following were the Officer Casualties killed. 2nd Lieut. J. McVEIGH. Died of wounds Lieut L. MAKENZIE. Wounded and Missing 2nd Lieut A. FORREST and Lieut E.R.M. WALCOTT. Missing Lieut J.W.MORRIS M.O.R.C. U.S.A. Wounded Major W.B. BINNIE M.C. Capt. J.S. STRANG M.C. 2nd Lieut BEMGOVAN. 2nd Lieut. A.S.G. LOXTON. Wounded at duty Capt W. STOREY-WILSON. Other Ranks Killed 19. Wounded 122. Missing 76. | |
| | 29 | | Situation became normal. Intermittent shelling during the day. In the evening the Bn relieved the 9th (S) Bn. THE BLACK WATCH. | |

| Place | Date | Hour | Summary of Events and Information | Remarks and references to Appendices |
|---|---|---|---|---|
| | 30. | | over that part of the line immediately South of the CAMBRAI ROAD. | |
| | 31. | | Normal day. Bn. H.Q. Female ESTAMINET CORNER. Sig. nets applied. Intermittent shelling throughout the day. At night Bns A&B Coys were relieved by the 7th R. SEAFORTH HIGHRS. and C and D Coys by the 8/10th GORDON HIGHRS. The Bn. on relief withdrew to IMPERIAL CAVES just E of ARRAS. | |

W Storey Wilson. Capt
Ag.
9th. (S.) Bn. THE BLACK WATCH.

9th (S) Bn The Black Watch        HQ 46th Inf Bde

Report on Operations from

Midday 27th March to Midday 29th March 1918

At midday the 27th March the 9th
Bn The Black Watch were in position
in the Army Line. Relieved the
10th Scottish Rifles in the front
system about midnight 24th/25th
March, with the following dispositions
"A" and "B" Companies in the front line
(JERUSALEM TRENCH)
"D" Coy in Support line (CROMARTY TR).
2 Platoons "C" Coy in Reserve (INVERGORDON TR)
2 Platoons "C" Coy escort to Vickers M. Guns
200x W. of FEUCHY CHAPEL ROAD.
The following readjustment commenced
about 3 am
1 Platoon "A" Coy and 1 Platoon "B" Coy
withdrew to CROMARTY TR.
"D" Coy withdrew to INVERGORDON TR.
2 Platoons "C" Coy withdrew to HALIFAX TR
THE BROWN LINE
This readjustment was not quite
completed when the bombardment
of the front system commenced.

2.

At 3 a.m. a heavy barrage was opened on our artillery and communications. This continued until 4.45 a.m. when an exceptionally heavy barrage of Trench Mortars and artillery opened out on our front system.

The enemy attacked at 7.30 a.m. The right flank of his main attack came about the centre of the right front company (B Coy). The enemy was apparently lying out in No Mans Land prior to 3000 hour as he was at our wire as soon as the barrage lifted.

He broke through on the right of 'B' Coy and immediately commenced bombing Northwards along our front line.

A block was formed and the enemy was held with the assistance of a Stokes Mortar. This block however had shortly to be abandoned owing to its being shelled by our own artillery, and another block was formed further to the NORTH.

The left front Company (A Coy) with the assistance of the remainder of the 'B' Coy, which was by this time rather disorganised, formed a defensive flank along the C.T. in H.35.a. where it held out till about 8.45 am when it was shelled out by our artillery and was forced to withdraw to PELVES LANE where in conjunction with the 7/8th KOSB's a defensive flank was formed. This flank line inflicted severe casualties on the enemy from both its positions.

The support Coy ("D" Coy) very shortly found its right flank "in the air". The company in front had been driven to the North along the front and support lines and the 45th Bde on the right had retired. The officers of this company had all become casualties and it had suffered much more severely than the two forward companies, but after holding on for over half an hour it was driven out by a combined rush from from both front and right flank.

By 8 am large numbers of the 45th Bde on the right were retiring in a N.W. direction and quite disorganised. They were rallied at Halifax trench and came under the orders of the O.C. 9th Black Watch.

About 8.15 am the support company retired on this line and reorganisation of the Brown line, now front line commenced. The Brown line was now too thickly held so a support line was established – in old trench about 100ˣ E. of FEUCHY CHAPEL ROAD and a reserve line in line with the Vicker's M Guns about 200ˣ W of FEUCHY CHAPEL RD.

By 9.30 am the enemy had broken through the BROWN LINE, on the right and had bombed along the trench and driven the front line back on the support line.

Enemy artillery had by this time almost ceased in front of the Army line but their M Guns were in action and were inflicting rather severe casualties on our front and support lines.

This line E of FEUCHY CHAPEL RD held out till 12.45 pm when the right flank was again driven in, and the front and support lines retired in a rather disorderly manner on the Army line.

A rear guard was formed and took up a position in front of the Vickers gun line and covered their withdrawal to the Army line.

OC 9th Black Watch assumed command of the army line from H32a cent to H26c cent and reorganised the Batt in that part of the line.

In the course of the afternoon the situation became normal and the two companies which had been holding a defensive flank along PELVES LANE withdrew to the army line in conjunction with the 4th Div on our left.

The enemy made no further attack but settled down with his front line along the valley in H33a.

After dusk an outpost line was established from H32 + 22 N2 a. 4,2. The night of the 28th/29th March was fairly quiet except for a little shelling of the back areas.

The total casualties suffered by the Batt were. Officers. Killed 2 Wounded 4. Wounded & missing 2. Missing 1.
O.R. Killed 19. Wounded 122. Missing 76.

8/4/18.     Alltony Wilson Capt.
Then Commanding 9th Black Watch

15th Division.
46th Infantry Brigade

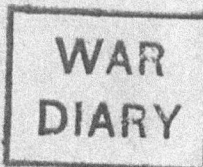

9th BATTALION

THE ROYAL HIGHLANDERS.

APRIL 1 9 1 8

B.33

CONFIDENTIAL.

WAR DIARY

of

9th BN. THE ROYAL HIGHLANDERS.

Vol......

From 1-4-18    To 30-4-18.

**WAR DIARY**
**INTELLIGENCE SUMMARY.**

Army Form C. 2118.

| Place | Date | Hour | Summary of Events and Information | Remarks and references to Appendices |
|---|---|---|---|---|
| IMPERIAL CAVES. ARRAS. | 1918 April 1st | | Lt. Col. R.M. Dudgeon D.S.O., M.C. assumed command of the Batt. vice Lt. Col. S.A. Innes DSO hospital sick. 2nd Lt G.N. Cooke to U.K. sick. Lt A.K. Hamilton assumed command of "B" Coy. Lt A Marshall assumes command of "C" Coy. | A.W.W. |
| " | 2nd | | The men were employed during the day in cleaning up. Companies were reorganised. Lieut B.B. Mc Clean M.O.R.C. U.S.A. attached for duty as Medical Officer as from 29/3/18. | A.W.W. |
| | 3rd | | Lt. Col. S.A. Innes D.S.O. to U.K. sick. All available men employed from 8p. to 12 midnight deepening and making fire steps in the Batt. battle positions in Blangy system. Capt. T. Calvert M.C. wounded (gas). Capt and Adj. J.J. Basham D.S.O. rejoined Batt. from sick leave. Work was carried out as on the previous night. | A.W.W. |
| | 4th | | 2nd Lt J. Ballan to be Lieut (Temporary) 7.1.18. London Gazette dt 1/3/18. Work was continued from 8p. to 12 mn on Blangy system. | A.W.W. |
| FRONT LINE E of ARRAS. | 5th | 10p/- | The Batt. relieved the 10th Scottish Rifles — the front line N. of CAMBRAI RD and was disposed as follows. "C" Coy in line. It shall hold. 500yd E of Army line. "D" Coy in army line. A Coy - support line of Army line. "B" Coy in reserve trenches. The relief was carried out without interruption from the enemy. 2nd Lts R.T. Clark and E.W.D. Wilson to be Lieuts (Temporary) 7.1.18. London Gazette dt 1.3.18. Casualties one man missing. | A.W.W. |

9th. (S) Bn. THE BLACK WATCH.

# WAR DIARY or INTELLIGENCE SUMMARY.

Army Form C. 2118.

9th. (S) Bn. THE BLACK WATCH.

| Place | Date 1916. | Hour | Summary of Events and Information | Remarks and references to Appendices |
|---|---|---|---|---|
| FRONT LINE ARRAS. E of ARRAS. | 6th | | Intermittent shelling during the day of front, support and reserve lines. | |
| | | 9 p.m. | A patrol of 1 Off. & 12 O.R. proceeded east along PURVES LANE for 300 yds but saw no sign of the enemy. The night was very quiet - rain fell heavily all night. Work was confined to improvement of trenches held by companies. | |
| | 7th | | Generally a quiet day; a few shells fell round Battn. H.Q. and reserve company area. About 11 a.m. firm continued all day and "C" Coy in shell holes were suffering rather badly from it fire. Work on company areas was carried on during the night. | |
| | 8th | | 2nd Lt. P.E. Kerr to England wounded (gas) — shell hole line. "B" Coy relieved "C" Coy. | |
| | 9th | 9 p.m. | Quiet day. A patrol of 1 Off & 12 ORs patrolled our front but saw no sign of the enemy. Work was continued on trenches occupied by companies. | |
| | 10th | | Intermittent shelling throughout the day but quiet at night. | |
| | | 9 p.m. | "C" Coy relieved "B" Coy in shell hole line. Weather improved greatly. Work carried on on trenches occupied by companies. | |
| | 11th | 6 a.m. | A general bombardment of our area for about half an hour, but generally a quiet day. | |

# WAR DIARY / INTELLIGENCE SUMMARY

Army Form C. 2118.

| Place | Date | Hour | Summary of Events and Information | Remarks and references to Appendices |
|---|---|---|---|---|
| FRONT LINE E of ARRAS | 1918 APRIL 11th | | Night quiet. 2nd Lt Snodgar and two officers of the 10th Scottish Rifles while out selecting positions for new shell hole runs into an enemy post and were fired upon. An artillery officer who was also with them was wounded. Work was carried on improving trenches held by companies. | |
| | 12th | 9 p.m. | "B" Coy relieved "C" Coy in shell hole line. Generally a quiet day. A patrol of 1 Off & 12 O.R. proceeded to investigate post which had been located on the previous night and were fired on by 2 x M.Gun. The night was quiet. | |
| | 13th | | Enemy in enemy artillery during the day. Night very quiet. 351149 I/Cpl John Gallagher, 18731 Pte Alexander Ross Robertson, 290695 I/Cpl John Glink, and 43489 Pte Alfred Rowley awarded military medals for gallantry in the field on 28/3/18. Work on trenches occupied by companies continued. | |
| | 14th | 11 p.m. | Quiet day. The Batt was relieved by two companies 11th A&SH and one company 6th Cameron and on relief moved back to Blangy dugouts with HQrs in IMPERIAL CAVES. | |

29th (S) Bn. THE BLACK WATCH.

Army Form C. 2118.

# WAR DIARY
## INTELLIGENCE SUMMARY.
*(Erase heading not required.)*

| Place | Date 1918 | Hour | Summary of Events and Information | Remarks and references to Appendices |
|---|---|---|---|---|
| BLANGY SYSTEM. | APRIL 15th | 11am | Batt. moved back to billets in ARRAS via. the underground passages. | |
| | | 8 pm | Batt. marched to Y.HUTS. ETRUN. arriving about 10.30 pm. 2nd Lt C Scott. to U.K. Sick. | |
| Y HUTS. ETRUN | 16th | | A draft of 51 O.R. arrived from home depôt and were taken on the strength of the Batt. The day was spent in cleaning up and refitting. 2nd Lt I.T Reid to U.K. Sick. Baths were allotted to the Batt. (Rifles were inspected by the Armourer Sergt. and refitting was continued. | |
| | 17th | | 2nd Lt J Stuart transferred from "C" to "B" Coy. training was carried out under company arrangements. Lewis Gunners under their own instructors. | |
| | 18th | | 2nd Lt A Marshall transferred from "B" Coy. and assumes command of "D" Coy. Training carried out under Company arrangements. Range allotted to Batt. | |
| | 19th | | The Batt relieved the 6th Cameron = Blangy System in the Support. H Gun in | |
| BLANGY SYSTEM. | 20th | | IMPERIAL CAVES. | |
| | 21st | | Lt. B.B. McClean M.O.R.C. U.S.A. to Newft. aid. Work was carried out improving trenches occupied by companies. | |
| | 22nd | | Lt A.K. Hamilton, Lt A Marshall, Lt E.W.D Wilson awarded the Military Cross for gallantry in the field on 28/3/18. | |

9th. (S) Bn. THE BLACK WATCH.

# WAR DIARY

## INTELLIGENCE SUMMARY.

Army Form C. 2118.

| Place | Date 1918. | Hour | Summary of Events and Information | Remarks and references to Appendices |
|---|---|---|---|---|
| BLANGY SYSTEM. | APRIL 22nd | | Capt J.S. Gutchrist R.A.M.C. posted to the Batt for duty as Medical Officer with effect from 20/4/18. Quiet day. Work was continued on trenches occupied by the Battalion. | |
| Y HUTS ETRUN. | 23rd | | The Batt moved back to Y HUTS about 2.30 p.m. Lt D.A. Grant reported for duty and posted to "C" Coy. Lt Col R.M. Bridgman D.S.O. M.C. struck off the strength of the Batt. Major R.A. Bullock resumed command of the Bn. Major A.H.O. Donnerston struck off the strength of the Batt having proceeded to U.K. to take command of the 3rd Blackwatch. | |
| BURBURÉ. | 24th 25th | | The Batt moved by Bus to BURBURÉ. arriving about 2 p.m. 2nd Lt B.A. Harley and C.H. Collins taken on the strength and posted to "C" and "B" Coys respectively. The following message from Lt General Commanding 17th Corps received by G.O.C. 15th Division. " I wish to express to you and to all ranks in the division my great regrets at your departure from the XVII Corps. We have now been associated for many months and I had hoped that we might have seen this battle through together, that however is not to be, and I can only hope that the fortune of war may some day bring us together again. | |

A.D.S.S./Forms/C. 2/9th. (S) Bn. THE BLACK WATCH.

Army Form C. 2118.

# WAR DIARY
## INTELLIGENCE SUMMARY.
(Erase heading not required.)

Instructions regarding War Diaries and Intelligence Summaries are contained in F. S. Regs., Part II. and the Staff Manual respectively. Title pages will be prepared in manuscript.

| Place | Date 1918 | Hour | Summary of Events and Information | Remarks and references to Appendices |
|---|---|---|---|---|
| BURBURE | APRIL 25th | | The Division has a great reputation and may well be proud of it. I trust that the honour of Scotland is safe in its keeping, and that those who are now serving will from themselves worthy of those gallant men who have won glory for the Division in the past. I wish you all good luck and success from the bottom of my heart." | |
| " | 26th | | Training was carried out as follows. Platoon drill 9 a.m. to 10 a.m. P.T. & B.F. 10·15a.m–11·15a.m. Coy drill 11·30 a.m. to 12·30 p.m. | |
| " | 27th | | Range allotted to the Batt. when not on Range companies were employed on Platoon and Coy drill and at P.T. & B.F. 9678 L/Cpl John Smith awarded star to military medal for gallantry in the field on 28/3/18. | |
| " | 28th | | Sunday. Divine Service. Lieut W.T. Wilkin having reported for duty is taken on the strength and posted to "D" Coy. | |
| " | 29th | | Orders received that the Batt. will move to ARRAS at 11 a.m. Batt. paraded and marched to PERNES station, entrained and all was in order to move when the order was cancelled & the Batt. marched back to BURBURE. | |

9th. (S) Bn. THE BLACK WATCH.

# WAR DIARY

## INTELLIGENCE SUMMARY.

*(Erase heading not required.)*

Army Form C. 2118.

| Place | Date | Hour | Summary of Events and Information | Remarks and references to Appendices |
|---|---|---|---|---|
| BURDORE | April 29th | | 2nd Lts R. Strachan and W.F. Drumbies having reported for duty on return on the strength and posted to "A" and "C" Coys respectively. Capt J.S. Strong M.C. previously reported wounded now reported wounded and missing on 28/3/18. | |
| | 30th | | Training was carried out as follows. Platoon drill, PT and BF and the company on an advanced guard. Lewis gunners inspected on the range during the afternoon by the Brigadier. | |

30/4/18 —

W Strong Lt Col
for Commanding
9th (S) Bn. The Black Watch

Vol 35

B. 34

(6339) Wt. W160/M3016 1,500,000 10/17 McA & W Ltd (E1898) Forms W3091.   Army Form W.3091.

## Cover for Documents.

### Nature of Enclosures.

War Diary
9th Bn The Black Watch
1st to 15th May
1918.

Reduced to T.C. 19.5.18

### Notes, or Letters written.

To UK with 16 Div in June. Reformed
& joined 47 Bde 16 Di 30.7.18.

**Army Form C. 2118**

# WAR DIARY
## INTELLIGENCE SUMMARY.
*(Erase heading not required.)*

| Place | Date | Hour | Summary of Events and Information | Remarks and references to Appendices |
|---|---|---|---|---|
| BURBURE | 1st May 1918 | | In ARMY RESERVE: Coy. received in monastery, Ad's Guards, P.T. v B.F. and bathed by Coys at RAIMBERT. | NB. |
| " | 2nd | | Received orders to be transferred to 19 & Corps. Coys. carried out training on Bn. parade ground. | U. |
| " | 3rd | | Bn. is transferred to XIII Corps. Bn. entrained at PERNES at 9 p.m. and detrained at MAROEUIL at 12 mn. Infantry May 1918. | U. |
| ARRAS | 4th | | Bn. marches from MAROEUIL to LILLUS — BRITMONT BARRACKS areas arriving at area at 2 a.m. | U. |
| | | 9 a.m. | Bn. left BARRS to go into the line as Bn. in Brigade Support, taking over from 10th Canadian Infy. Bn. Bn. HQ established at H.14.a.2.70. | U. |
| | | | 2/Lt. D. KINNOCH — A. Coy. wounded sick. Bn. in Brigade Support. Heavy shelling in vicinity of Bn. HQ during the day. | U. |
| FAMPOUX Sector | 5th | | Bn. in Brigade Support. Intermittent hostile shelling during the day. | U. |
| " | 6th | | No. 9749 L/C L. DOUGLAS and N. 10250 L/Cpl D. GILLIES, both of "D" Coy. wounded and died of wounds. | U. |

9th. (8) Bn. THE BLACK WATCH.

**CONFIDENTIAL.**

Army Form C. 2118.

Instructions regarding War Diaries and Intelligence Summaries are contained in F. S. Regs., Part II. and the Staff Manual respectively. Title pages will be prepared in manuscript.

# WAR DIARY
# or
# INTELLIGENCE SUMMARY.
*(Erase heading not required.)*

| Place | Date | Hour | Summary of Events and Information | Remarks and references to Appendices |
|---|---|---|---|---|
| Harbour Labe | 6th. | | No. 9517 Sgt. G. SIMPSON "D" Coy, promoted B.S.M. of "D" Coy, vice B.S.M. R. DOUGANS died of wounds. | Nil. |
| " | 7th. | | Bn. in Brigade Support. Bn. Hd. moved to STUBERNIC CAMP 4.15.O.9.2. No. 43370 Sgt. Summer J. LEVACK transferred from 8/10th Gordon Highrs. to 9th.(S) Bn. Black Watch, and posted to "A" Coy. | Nil. |
| " | 8th. | | Bn. in Brigade Support. No. 8976 A/L/S.H. D.C. BARCLAY reverts to substantive rank of L./Sgt. | Nil. |
| " | 9th. | | Bn. in Brigade Support. The following officers joined for duty:— | Nil. |
| | | | Lieut. R. INCH } to "A" Coy. | |
| | | | 2/Lt. D.M. CUNNINGHAM } to "A" Coy. | |
| | | | 2/Lt. R.G. TAIT } to "B" Coy. | |
| | | | 2/Lt. W. MACGREGOR } to "B" Coy. | |
| | | | 2/Lt. T. EDWARDS } to C. Coy. | |
| | | | 2/Lt. W. MALCOLM } to "D" Coy. | |
| | | | 2/Lt. R. HUGHES } to "D" Coy. | |
| | | | No. 7923 R.S.M. R. DEWAR joined for duty. Posted to "A" Coy. | |

9th. (S) Bn. THE BLACK WATCH.

# WAR DIARY
## INTELLIGENCE SUMMARY
*(Erase heading not required.)*

Army Form C. 2118.

| Place | Date | Hour | Summary of Events and Information | Remarks and references to Appendices |
|---|---|---|---|---|
| FAMPOUX Sector | 10th | | Projects relieved into Divisional Reserve. Bn. moved back to WAKEFIELD CAMP (C.6.a.3.8.) arriving about 12 m.n. (Men being ending party). Tackers party reached WAKEFIELD CAMP at noon 11th May, 1918. | M. |
| WAKEFIELD CAMP | 11th | | Resc. Sgt. E Roe reported Sgt. Bernad Lgt. & Cpl. C Simpson "Wounded" Owing to the enemy dog the impression was held and men were given opportunities to get cleaned up and have their hair cut. Specialists found work. Their instructors for training. | M. |
| WAKEFIELD CAMP | 12th | | To the evening the L.o. held a Lecture to officers. Runners behind gunner, Platoon footballl competition. Bn. provided covering party to wire under 73rd (Fr.) Bg. Rft. - Strength 4 Offrs. 150 O.R. Party paraded at 7.30.p.m. returning to Camp at 3 a.m. 13.5.18. L.I.H Motto: "LiRoy" exercised. | M. |
| WAKEFIELD CAMP | 13th | 9.30 a.m. – 11.30 a.m. | Training under Bog. Commander. Programme: Rifle Exercises of Section leading on extended order. Use of ground and selection of fire positions. Battle of MAFEKING (from 12.30 p.m. one other to 6 p.m. Equipment | M. |

9th. (S) Bn. THE BLACK WATCH.

# WAR DIARY

## INTELLIGENCE SUMMARY

*(Erase heading not required.)*

Army Form C. 2118.

| Place | Date | Hour | Summary of Events and Information | Remarks and references to Appendices |
|---|---|---|---|---|
| WIMEREUX CAMP | 14th | | Bn. provided a fatigue party of 2 Offrs. 300 O.R. to work under 91st F.C. R.E. from 8.30 a.m. to 12.30 p.m. During the morning C.O. sent parties to the Gas Chamber at CORNWOOD CAMP. Co. Comdrs. and Plat. Sdrs. P.o. B.T. and fur arrival lecturers specialists attended made them an Instruction. 9 a.m. Conference of Coy. Offrs. by Brit. Commander. Afternoon. Football. 9th Bat. v. 11th Wt. Regt. Draw. The evening was free. (Field firing). | M. |
| WIMEREUX CAMP | 15th | | 8.30 a.m. – 1 p.m. Battn. at ST CATHERINE during the morning. In the afternoon platoons had tactical exercises for the benefit of the Offrs. & NCOs. Lieut. J. D. Wrench and Lt. T. Wynne rejoined the Bn. | M. |

W. R. Wease
Lieut. Colonel
Commdg. 9th (S) Bn the Black Watch

9th. (S) Bn. THE BLACK WATCH.

16TH DIVISION
44TH INFY BDE

4-5TH BN ROY. HDRS (BLK WATCH)

MAY 1918 - APL 1919

from 39 DIV
118 Bde

McInde,
Jan 1918

Army Form W.3091.

**Cover for Documents.**

Nature of Enclosures.

War Diary.
4/5th Bn. Black Watch
16th – 31st May.
1918.

Notes, or Letters written.

Secret.

Proposals for Raid to be carried out
by 4/5th Bn The Black Watch

Ref: FEUCHY TRENCH                    26.6.18
MAP 1/5000

1./ Objects of the Raid.
   (a) To obtain an identification
   (b) To capture or destroy any enemy Machine guns or other material that may be found.

2./ Portion of the Enemy line to be raided
Front line trench from CAMEL AVENUE (inclusive) H11d.53.01 to H11d.63.29 and sunken road immediately East of this trench.

3./ Troops to be employed
Two officers & 75 O R (Three Platoons)

4./ Preliminary Artillery & Trench Mortar Preparation
        nil.

5./ Artillery Support
At zero.
18 Pounder shrapnel barrage from H17.b.56.78 to H11d.80.70
6 guns from H17.b.56.78 to H11d.53.01
8 guns from H11d.53.01 to H11d.63.29
10 guns from H11d.63.29 to H11d.80.70
1 4.5 How. Battery on Sunken Road from ~~Road Junction~~ H17.d.61.29 to H17.b.56.78

all known enemy machine gun or T.M. emplacements which could bring fire to bear on Raiders to be bombarded by 4.5 Hows.

A feint barrage of 18 prs to be put on HAZARD Trench from H11b59.21 to HYDERABAD Trench at H11b78.55

1. 4.5" How on Trench Junction H11d80.72
1.    "    "    "    "    "    "    H11b91.05
1.    "    "    "    "    "    "    H12a00.32

2. 6 inch Hows on hollow about H18a2.4

At zero +½ minutes shrapnel barrage from H17b56.78 to H11d80.70 will lift to line H17b56.78 - Trench junctn H17b91.89 thence along ZION ALLEY to Trench Jctn H12a10.40 - H11d80.70

All other guns & Hows remain on their former targets.

At zero +25 fire will slacken & gradually cease.

6.- Action of the Infantry
(a) The Raiding Party will form up in front of our wire with their right on CAMEL AVENUE at H17b16.95 & left at H11d15.30

The forming up will be covered by a covering party

The formation will be in two lines at 15 paces distance.

(b.) At zero they will advance to close behind the shrapnel barrage and at zero + 4 when the barrage lifts will rush the trench.

The leading line will go straight on to the SUNKEN ROAD, the rear line remaining in the trench.

(c.) Special Precautions

The right Platoon will send a Bombing party & Lewis Gun section up CAMEL AVENUE to the sunken road, where the L. Gun section will take up a position to sweep the road to the south.

The left Platoon will send a bombing party on arriving at the enemy trench up the trench to establish a block about H 11 d 6 4. 3 9

(d.) At Zero + 20 min. at a given light signal the raiders will withdraw from the enemy lines.

(e.) Any prisoners captured to be sent straight back, an N.C.O & two men from each platoon to be told off previously for this duty.

2/ Time of Zero & Date of Raid.

The raid to take place either on the night 31st/1st or 1st/2nd June.

Zero hour to be just after the moon has risen viz 1 am 31st/1st or 2.15 am 1st/2nd

SECRET

4/5th Black Watch Operation Order No 2

Copy No 1

Ref PONT DU JOUR }
and FEUCHY TRENCH }
Maps 1/10.000.

1. (a) "C" Coy 4/5th Black Watch will carry out a raid on the enemy's trenches at H.11.d and the SUNKEN ROAD immediately East of it on the night 30/31st May 1918.

   (b) 1st objective: Trench from H.11.d.53.00 (CAMEL AVENUE inclusive) to H.11.d.63.29.
   2nd objective: SUNKEN ROAD from H.17.b.60.99 to H.11.d.70.30.

   (c) The object of the raid is to capture prisoners and destroy any hostile machine guns or other material that may be found.

2. (a) The raid will be carried out by 2 Officers and 75 other ranks (3 platoons less 1 Lewis Gun Section)

   (b) The raiding party will be divided into three parties as follows:—
      (1) Party "A" (Raiding party) — 2 Off. + 53 other ranks
      (2) Party "B" (Right blocking party) — 1 NCO + 10 other ranks (4 Lewis Bombers and 6 Rifle Grenadiers)
      (3) Party "C" (Left blocking party) Same as for Party "B"

3. (a) At Zero minus 15 minutes these parties will be formed up in front of our wire :—
   A covering party will cover the assembly.

3 (a) Continued:-
   The formation will be in two waves at 15 paces distance, blocking parties in file on either flank between the two waves.
   The Right blocking party will be in CAMEL AVENUE.
(b) At Zero hour the artillery barrage will be put down on the hostile trench and the raiders will move forward close up under the barrage.
   At Zero hour plus 5 minutes the barrage will lift and the raiders will rush the trench.
   The leading wave will go straight forward to the SUNKEN ROAD and mop it up and make prisoners any enemy found there.
   The rear wave will halt in the trench and act as above.
(c) Party "B" will take up positions as follows:-
   (1) The Lewis Gunners will push forward & establish their gun in a position about H.17.b.60.98 from which the SUNKEN ROAD can be enfiladed.
   (2) The rifle grenadiers will halt in CAMEL AVENUE at H.11.d.55.00. and will fire a rifle grenade barrage into the SUNKEN ROAD at H.17.b.60.80.
(d) Party "C" will advance to the enemy's trench and establish a block at H.11.d.64.34.
4 (a) At Zero plus 20 minutes, on a blue very light being fired low across the front of the Raiding party, the Raiders will withdraw from the enemy's lines.
  (b) At Zero plus 25 minutes artillery will slacken rate of fire and cease at Zero plus 40 minutes.
5. Artillery and Machine Gun arrangements have been

5. (Continued)
explained to all concerned.

Stokes Mortars will cooperate as follows:-

2 Mortars – on block at H.11.d.49.00.
   Hurricane fire Zero to Zero plus 2 minutes.
   These mortars will cease fire at Zero plus 2 minutes.

3 Mortars:- on STAFFORD LANE H.17.b.60.45 to H.17.b.60.75.
   Zero to Zero plus 40 – 5 rounds per Mortar per minute.

1 Mortar – on suspected hostile post H.11.d.59.69.
   Zero to Zero plus 5 rapid fire.
   Zero plus 5 to Zero plus 40 – 5 rounds per Mortar per minute.

6(a) The raiding party will move from VICTORY CAMP to a dugout in LEMON TRENCH under arrangements to be issued later.

(b) A hot meal will be issued in LEMON TRENCH at 10.30 pm.

(c) The move forward from LEMON TRENCH will commence at 11.30 pm.

(d) The raiding party on their return will be accommodated in the same dugout.

7.(a) Any prisoners taken will be sent straight back to Advanced Report Centre H.10.d.70.30 (Coy HQ LEMON TRENCH).

(b) Identification of any dead enemy found will be taken.

7(c) Any Machine Guns or Trench Mortars captured will be brought back or, if this is impossible, will be destroyed.

8.(a) The Raiding party will be equipped as follows:—
Steel Helmet
Rifle & Bayonet fixed
Skeleton Equipment.
30 rounds S.A.A. (10 rounds in the magazine 10 rounds in each side pocket of the jacket.)
2 — No.23. Mills Grenades.
Rifle Grenadiers will each carry 6 rodded No.23 Mills Grenades. 2 carriers to carry 12 grenades each.
A proportion of wire cutters S.A. No.1 Mk.1 will be issued to the Raiders and fixed on their rifles.
Each officer and two N.C.O's will carry a Very Pistol & coloured cartridge.

(b) All documents or means of identification must be removed from personnel of the raiding party.

(c) Special identity discs will be issued to all ranks taking part in the raid. On completion of the raid these discs will be handed in to "O.C." "X" Company who will personally check them with the Nominal Roll of the Raiders. This will be done in the Raiders' dugout.

(d) All ranks taking part in the operation must be warned only to give their Number, rank and name if captured & no other information at all

9. The M.O. 4/5th Black Watch will establish an Aid Post at Right Battalion RAP - H.16.c.8.6.
10. Watches will be Synchronised at 11pm in raiders' dugout.
11. Zero hour will be notified later.
12. The Advanced Report Centre will be at HQ dugout (LEMON TRENCH) - H.10.d.70.30.

J B Buchan. Capt. & adjt
for O.C. 4/5th Black Watch

29/5/18

Distribution:-
1. G.O.C.
2. C.O.
3. O.C. Raid
4. 7/8th K.O.S.B.
5-6 Coys & HQ
7. War Diary
8. File.

Secret. 9

46th Inf Bde

26.5.18

1/ Herewith scheme for proposed raid to be carried out by the Bn. under my command.

2/ If this raid is to be carried out shortly, I should like the platoons who are to carry it out to go back to the Transport lines on relief tomorrow night, to enable them to practice. Could this be arranged please?

[signature] Lt Col.
N.F.M.R.

**WAR DIARY**
or
**INTELLIGENCE SUMMARY.**
*(Erase heading not required.)*

Army Form C. 2118.

Sheet A.4.1

| Place | Date | Hour | Summary of Events and Information | Remarks and references to Appendices |
|---|---|---|---|---|
| | 1918 | | | |
| Trenches | Jany. 2 | — | The Battalion was relieved in The Right Sub-Sector by the 2nd Irish Guards. The Relief took place without incident, and on completing the Battalion returned to Billets in The GRANARY, ARRAS. | O.O.137. |
| ARRAS | 4 | — | The following Officers joined the Battalion and were taken on the Strength accordingly:— 2/Lieut A.G.G. WATSON. 2/Lieut J.W.T. LEITH M.C. 2/Lieut J.F. MARTIN. | |
| " | 6 | — | The following Warrant Officer & men were rewarded the "Distinguished Conduct Medal" for gallantry in action during recent operations:— 907529 C.S.M. W.L. SMITH. 90 S/11651 PTE J. McEWAN. | Appx A. |
| " | 12 | — | Major CHARLES REID assumed temporary Command of the Battalion during the absence of Lt. Col: The LORD DUDLEY GORDON D.S.O. | |
| " | 13 | — | Lt. Col: The LORD DUDLEY GORDON D.S.O. appointed to Command the Battalion with effect from 21/12/17. (Authority A.G. 2158/360(0) dated 1/1/18) | |

Army Form C. 2118.

# WAR DIARY
## or
## INTELLIGENCE SUMMARY.
(Erase heading not required.)

Sheet 442

Instructions regarding War Diaries and Intelligence Summaries are contained in F. S. Regs., Part II. and the Staff Manual respectively. Title pages will be prepared in manuscript.

| Place | Date | Hour | Summary of Events and Information | Remarks and references to Appendices |
|---|---|---|---|---|
| ARRAS | 1916 Jany 15 | — | The Battalion carried out a "Field Firing Practice" on the WAILLY RANGE. The practice was done by two Companies at a time and proved a great success. Live ammunition was used. | S.F.O. App 15a |
| " | 17 | — | The undermentioned Officers joined the Battalion and were taken on the Strength accordingly. 2/Lt. A. Campbell. 2/Lt. A.J.F. Duncan. | |
| " | 18 | — | The Battalion was inspected by the BOTTE du TIR by the Divisional Commander | |
| " | 25 | — | The following Officer joined the Battalion and were taken on the strength accordingly 2/Lt. G. G. Cruickshanks. | App 15 |
| " | 29 | " | To celebrate the anniversary of the Raid by the BUTTE de WARLENCOURT which was carried out by the Battalion, the THEATRE in ARRAS was engaged, and the Battalion attended an excellent performance given by the "JOCKS". | |

Army Form C. 2118.

Sheet 443.

# WAR DIARY
## or
## INTELLIGENCE SUMMARY.
*(Erase heading not required.)*

| Place | Date | Hour | Summary of Events and Information | Remarks and references to Appendices |
|---|---|---|---|---|
| ARRAS | 1918 Jan 31 | — | The Battalion received a warning order from their Brigade to be prepared to relieve the Battalions of the 10th Division on 5th February 1918. The unit was reconnoitred the same day by the Commanding Officer, O.C. Coys and 2i/c Commands of Companies. | Act 3 |

# WAR DIARY
## or
## INTELLIGENCE SUMMARY

**Army Form C. 2118**

CONFIDENTIAL.

WAR DIARY

OF

4/5th BATTALION THE BLACK WATCH (R.H.)

from 1/6/18 to 30/6/18

Vol. ............

9th. (S) Bn. THE BLACK WATCH.

4/5 Black Watch
4/15
Vol 33

26.11

**WAR DIARY**

**INTELLIGENCE SUMMARY.**

War Diary
of the Black Watch
4/5th Battn
for
May, 1918.
Volume V.

Wauchope? Lt. Col.
Comdg 4/5th Bn The Black Watch.

4/6/18

# WAR DIARY
## or
## INTELLIGENCE SUMMARY.

Army Form C. 2118.

| Place | Date | Hour | Summary of Events and Information | Remarks and references to Appendices |
|---|---|---|---|---|
| | 1/5th | | The details of the Battalion were billeted in various gym., musketry and Physical training was carried out. | |
| | 6th | | On the withdrawal from the line of Gen. Hubback's Composite Brigade, the Battalion was reformed at GANSPETTE. Major (a/Lt.Col.) I. CRUICKSHANK. assumed command. | |
| | 7/11th | | The reorganising and equipping of the Battalion was carried out. Owing to the Battalion being very weak it was organised into two companies "A" Coy. under command of Capt. D. MAXWELL, M.C. and "B" Coy. under command of Lieut. R.E. BADENOCH. | |
| | 12th | | The Battalion was inspected by Brig-Gen. G.B. HUBBACK, C.M.G. Commanding 118th Inf. Brigade. | |
| | 13th | | Orders were received that the Battalion was to be transferred from the 39th Division to 15th Division. This order was subsequently postponed for 24 hours. | |
| | 14th | | The Battalion was inspected by Major General C.A. BLACKLOCK, C.M.G., D.S.O. commanding 39th Division. After the inspection medals ribands were presented to the following Officers, W.Os and men for gallantry and devotion to duty. | |

| Place | Date | Hour | Summary of Events and Information | Remarks and references to Appendices |
|---|---|---|---|---|
| MILITARY CROSS. 2/Lt. A FRASER. | | | | |
| | | | D.C.M. N⁰ 201211 L/M A. ANDERSON. 201115 Pte. D. HEDZEY. | |
| | | | MILITARY MEDAL N⁰ 240991 L.S.M. W. STEWART. 240345 Pte. R.S. HUTCHESON. | |
| | 15th | | The Battalion moved off at 3 p.m. to WATTEN Station to entrain. The band of the 1/6th Sheshire Regt. played the Battalion out. The Commanding Officer 1/6th Sheshire Regt. had very kindly arranged tea for the Battalion at the Station. | |
| | | | The Battalion detrained at BARLIN at 12.5 a.m and proceeded by light Railway to ANZIN and thence by route march to MADAGASCAR Camp. arriving there at 5.30 am when it came under command of Brig. Gen. LUMSDEN D.S.O. commanding 46th Inft. Brigade. | |
| | 16th | | The 4/5th Battalion was ordered to absorb the 9th Bn. The Black Watch and moved to WAKEFIELD camp for this purpose. The strengths of this Battalion at this time were as follows:- | |
| | | | 4/5 Bn. The Black Watch. 19 offrs. 350 O.Rs. ⎫ these figures include all 9th Bn. The Black Watch. 42 offrs. 642 O.Rs. ⎭ detailed and attached personnel | |

| Place | Date | Hour | Summary of Events and Information | Remarks and references to Appendices |
|---|---|---|---|---|
| | 16th contd | | The Battalion thus formed was named the 4/5th Bn. the Black Watch. It paraded to the trail in the evening under the command of Major (A/Lt Col) J. CRUICKSHANK. | |
| | 17/15 | | The work of amalgamating the administration portion of the two Battalions was proceeded with. Major (A/Lt Col) R.A. BULLOCH, D.S.O. assumed command of the 4/5th Bn. the Black Watch. | |

# WAR DIARY or INTELLIGENCE SUMMARY.

*(Erase heading not required.)*

Army Form C. 2118.

| Place | Date | Hour | Summary of Events and Information | Remarks and references to Appendices |
|---|---|---|---|---|
| WAKEFIELD CAMP. | 1918 16th May | | Transferred to 15th Division, 46th Infantry Brigade, 16 vice 46 Bde 5/5/18. Amalgamation of 4/5th and 9th Battalions took over and started gth. Bn at WAKEFIELD CAMP. On completion of amalgamation Bn. moved into line, relieving 6th Seam Highrs in left Section (Right Front Bn) – Bn. H.Q. at H.18.c.50.50. Left WAKEFIELD CAMP for line at 8pm–Lieut Col J. L. MacIlwraith in command. Details moved to MADAGASCAR CAMP under command of Lt.Col. R.A. BULLOCH, D.S.O. | AA |
| FAUQUIN SECTOR | 17th. | | 2nd Lieut. D. KINNOCH – 'A' Coy. – to R.E.S. (S.S) Lt.Col. R.A. BULLOCH D.S.O. proceeded to fire and strike over Emmeard of Bn. from Lt.Col. J.L. MacIlwraith. (to DETAILS) CAPT. F. PROUDFOOT, M.C. – To Hospital, BASE (S) while at LE TOUQUET, in course. 1 man 'C' Coy. (R. Front Bn) wounded. | BB |
| FAUQUIN SECTOR | 18th. | | Other Ranks of 9th Bn. transferred to 4/5th Bn. 1 man 'B' Coy.,' 1 man 'C' Coy. (L. Front Coy) wounded (at duty) | CC |
| – do – | 19th. | | 10 Officers: Lt.Col. J MacIlwraith, Hon Capt. T. McLachlan, M.B. Capt. F. Proudfoot, M.C. Lieut. L.W. Bellamy, 2nd Lt. R. Kinnoch, 2nd Lt. L. Ritchie, 2nd Lt. O. Fraser, 2nd Lt. Fa Munges, 2nd Lt. J.P. MacDonald, 2nd Lt. A.D. MacDonald, & 59 O.R.'s transferred to 9th Black Watch. | DD |

4/5th Bn. THE BLACK WATCH.

Army Form C. 2118.

# WAR DIARY
## INTELLIGENCE SUMMARY.
*(Erase heading not required.)*

Instructions regarding War Diaries and Intelligence Summaries are contained in F. S. Regs., Part II. and the Staff Manual respectively. Title pages will be prepared in manuscript.

| Place | Date | Hour | Summary of Events and Information | Remarks and references to Appendices |
|---|---|---|---|---|
| FAMPOUX SECTOR. | 1918 20th May. | | Into: day relief: 'A' Coy. relieved 'B' Coy. (Left Front Coy.) 'D' Coy. relieved 'C' Coy. (Right Front Coy). | A/3 |
| - do - | 21st | | 1 man 'A' Coy. and 1 man 'C' Coy. wounded. Major J. Stewart Wilson assumed Command of 2nd in Comg. 2nd Lieut. W.G. Ramsay - wounded. Captain J. Gilchrist R.A.M.C. rejoined (S). | QB |
| - do - | 22nd | | 1 man of 7/8 Bn. killed. | B |
| - do - | 23rd | | Capt. & QM. McCleith, M.C. rejoined from leave. Lieut. R.E. BADENOCH - assumed Command of 'B' Coy. | QB QB |
| - do - | 24th | | P.R's of 4/5-7/3.45. re-posted to Companies 1 man of 'D' Coy. killed. | QB |
| - do - | 25th | | 2 men of 'C' Coy. and 1 man 'D' Coy. wounded. Lieut. J. Lovett took surplus transport to C.O.C.R. by march route. 201163 Pte. MacGregor W. - awarded Military Medal. (D.R.O. No 138.) | QB |
| - do - | 26th | | 242328 L/cpl. MacLean A. 'R' Coy. - awarded Bar to Military Medal. (D.R.O. No 62) | QB |
| - do - | 27th | | Bn. relieved from front line system by 7/8 K.O.S.B. Bn. relief Ren. Relief completed by 2am 28/5/18. | QB |
| | | | moves back to Brigade Reserve | |

(8) Bn. THE BLACK WATCH.

# WAR DIARY
## or
## INTELLIGENCE SUMMARY.
*(Erase heading not required.)*

Army Form C. 2118.

| Place | Date | Hour | Summary of Events and Information | Remarks and references to Appendices |
|---|---|---|---|---|
| | 1918 May | | | |
| FAMPOUX | | | | |
| SOUCHEZ | 27th (Boots) | | Balance of personnel surplus to 40 Officers and 900 O.R's proceeded to BASE Up 10 Officers and 52 O.R's. Names of Officers: Lieut A. Marshall, M.C. Lieut: P.L. Smythe, Lt. QM. Gordon, Lt. H.D. McLeod, Lt. P.A. Chapman, 2nd Lt. C.A. Hansen, 2nd Lt. C. Make, 2nd Lt. D.A. Silkes, proof t.w. Pladonyn 2nd Lt. antoracford | OB BB |
| -do- | 28th | | Lt. C.B. Smyth, 2nd Lt. Artz, killed. | BS |
| -do- | 29th | | To Brigade Reserve. 2nd Lieut A.W. Moss - leave to United Kingdom from 29-5-18 to 12-6-18. | BB |
| -do- | 30th | | In Brigade Reserve. 2nd Lt. A. Morrison, Lt. A.C. Grant, with Battalion, and 4539 Pte. Sgt. Majr. Metcalf, M.C. proceeds to 9 "Black Watch" training personnel 9th Division for duty vice 2nd Lt. R. Kinnoith (S), Capt. A.P. Brereton, M.C. and R.S.M. F.L. Barclay, R.D.M. respectively. | OB |
| -do- | 31st | | Party composed of 53 O.R's under 2nd Lieuts. Edwards and Lt. A.J. Kinnear supported by 2 stocking parties, consisting of 1 N.C.O. 9 10 men per party raided enemy trenches in the H.11.d. and SUNKEN ROAD (Ref. Sheet: PONT DU JOUR and FAMPOUX trench maps 1/10000) at 12-35 am on 1st June 1918. Party was held up by enemy wire & were heavily bombed. 2nd Lt. J. Edwards and 8 O.R's were slightly wounded. | OB |

(8) Bn. THE BLACK WATCH.

Army Form C. 2118.

# WAR DIARY
## INTELLIGENCE SUMMARY.
(Erase heading not required.)

Instructions regarding War Diaries and Intelligence Summaries are contained in F. S. Regs., Part II. and the Staff Manual respectively. Title pages will be prepared in manuscript.

| Place | Date | Hour | Summary of Events and Information | Remarks and references to Appendices |
|---|---|---|---|---|
| FAMPOUX SECTOR | 1918 May 31st | | Raid (Boche) after bombing the enemy from his wire Party withdrew to our trenches without further casualties. | AB |

M.R. Reese
Lt. Col.
Commdg. 4/5 Bn. The Black Watch.

9th (S) Bn. THE BLACK WATCH.

Army Form C. 2118.

# WAR DIARY
## or
## INTELLIGENCE SUMMARY.
(Erase heading not required.)

| Place | Date | Hour | Summary of Events and Information | Remarks and references to Appendices |
|---|---|---|---|---|
| Brigade Support | 1st June 1918 | | The day was quiet. Orders received that Battalion are to be relieved by 8th Seaforth Highlanders on night 2nd. This relief was duly carried out. There being no casualties. | |
| Wakefield Camp | 2nd June | | After the relief the Battalion took over Bivvies in WAKEFIELD CAMP, and the Battalion training was carried out during the day | |
| Do. | 3rd June | | Battalion carried out Range Practice, Bn Drill etc. The wearing of the Black Thistle on the shoulder of S.D. Jackets which is the 15th Divisional Sign of the Black Watch will be adopted by this Battalion. Lieut A.Y. Duncan transferred to Bgd Reinf (Wounded) | |
| Do. | 4th June | | The following Officers reported from the Divisional Reception Camp and are taken on the strength to-day. 2/Lieut J.H. Barnett & 2/Lt D. Lawson | 4/5-2 |

9th (19) Bn. THE BLACK WATCH.

Army Form C. 2118.

# WAR DIARY
## & INTELLIGENCE SUMMARY.
*(Erase heading not required.)*

Instructions regarding War Diaries and Intelligence Summaries are contained in F. S. Regs., Part II. and the Staff Manual respectively. Title pages will be prepared in manuscript.

| Place | Date | Hour | Summary of Events and Information | Remarks and references to Appendices |
|---|---|---|---|---|
| WAKEFIELD CAMP. | 4th June | | Capt. I. Prowfoot M.B., transferred to England (Sick) Battalion training was carried out during the day, viz:- Musketry, Gas Drill & Labour Drill. | |
| | | | **Honours & Rewards** | |
| | | | Bar to Military Cross:- Lieut (A/Capt) D. Maxwell M.C. | |
| | | | Military Cross 2/Lieut. G.R. Farrar | |
| | | | Bar to Distinguished Conduct Medal. M/240991 B.S.M. Stewart W.m D.C.M., M.M. | |
| | | | Distinguished Conduct Medal M/200501 Sergt. Keith J.L. | |
| | | | The above will be transferred from the 6/7 Infantry Brigade to 4/4 Infantry Brigade on night 4/5th June. | |
| | Do. 5th June | | 2/Lieut. J. Edwards transferred to England (Wounded) Range Practices were carried out at MAKDEUIL, also Sharp Drill, Arms Drill close Order Labour Drill & P.T. & B.F. - A draft of L & Other Ranks Worked from the Divisional Reception Camp, and are seen on strength today. | 4/5 |

9th (6) Bn. THE BLACK WATCH.

Army Form C. 2118.

# WAR DIARY
## or
## INTELLIGENCE SUMMARY.
*(Erase heading not required.)*

Instructions regarding War Diaries and Intelligence Summaries are contained in F. S. Regs., Part II. and the Staff Manual respectively. Title pages will be prepared in manuscript.

| Place | Date | Hour | Summary of Events and Information | Remarks and references to Appendices |
|---|---|---|---|---|
| WAKEFIELD CAMP. | 6th June | | 4th B of Battalion were inspected by the Commanding Officers. Training was carried out under Company arrangements. Wylie Battalion relieved the 4th Camerons Highlanders in the FRONT LINE of the FAMPOUX SECTOR in the LEFT SUB-SECTOR of the Brigade Area on the night of 6/7th. | |
| FAMPOUX SECTOR FRONT LINE LEFT SUB SECTOR | | | | |
| Do | 7th June | | Lieut (A/Capt.) D.K. Hamilton M.C. granted 21 days Sick Leave to England. The Day was quiet. | |
| Do | 8th June | | Horace & Rewards. <br> The Military Cross — Lt. (A/Capt.) J.R. Sheep <br> The Military Cross — Lt. (A/Capt.) G.H. G.P. Penney <br> The Military Cross — 2/Lt. D.B. Skinner <br> Major J.S.Y. Rogers, D.S.O. R.A.M.C. transferred to 9th Black Watch. <br> Training Staff. 10 Other Ranks "A" Coy & 1 Other Rank "D" Coy. Wounded. | 4/5-B |

9th (S.) Bn. THE BLACK WATCH.

# WAR DIARY or INTELLIGENCE SUMMARY

**Army Form C. 2118**

(Erase heading not required.)

Instructions regarding War Diaries and Intelligence Summaries are contained in F.S. Regs., Part II. and the Staff Manual respectively. Title pages will be prepared in manuscript.

| Place | Date | Hour | Summary of Events and Information | Remarks and references to Appendices |
|---|---|---|---|---|
| Do | 9th June | | The Enemy shelled our trenches, but the casualties were slight, there being 1 Other Rank killed & 1 Wounded, "B" Coy, 5 Other Ranks Wounded and 1 evacuated to hospital sick, "A" Coy, 1 Other Rank Wounded, "D" Coy. Capt. W.J. Wills R.A.M.C. is taken on the strength from today vice Major J.L. Rogers D.S.O. R.A.M.C. | |
| Do | 10th June | | The following Officers are entitled to wear the Badges of Rank of Lieut:– 2/Lt. S. Cameron & 2/Lt. W.K. McGregor. Lieut. R.S. Cunningham Marshalled & 2 Other Ranks killed "B" Coy. Enemy fairly active with T.M. No casualties resulted. Honours & Rewards | |
| Do | 11th June | | Mentioned in Despatches. Major (Lt. Col.) L.G. Innes D.S.O. 2/Lieut. 2/Lt. E. Larton, No. 1180 L/Sergt. D. Buchan Lt. D.W. Cunningham, Died of wounds received whilst The following N.C.Os. are struck off the strength on proceeding to U.K. for Commission :– No. 16553 Sergt Johnstone J. D.C.M., 202684 Cpl. J. Reid. The day was quiet. 2 Other Ranks Wounded, 1 Other Rank E. Coy Wounded. | |

4/5 (9th) Bn. THE BLACK WATCH.

# WAR DIARY
## or
## INTELLIGENCE SUMMARY.
(Erase heading not required.)

Army Form C. 2118.

**4/5 (5) Bn. THE BLACK WATCH.**

| Place | Date | Hour | Summary of Events and Information | Remarks and references to Appendices |
|---|---|---|---|---|
| Do | 12th June | | The Battalion were relieved in the front line by the 5th Gordon Highlanders and we relieved the Battalion in the Brigade Support on night 12/13th. The reliefs were completed by midnight, there being no casualties. | |
| BRIGADE SUPPORT RAILWAY CUTTING | 13th June | | Battalion in support and furnished Brigade Working parties. | |
| Do | 14th June | | Lieut W.K. McGregor Wounded. Except for occasional shelling of support lines, the day was moderately quiet. | |
| Do | 15th June | | Capt W.J. Wills R.A.M.C. admitted to Hospital (Sick). Enemy Aeroplanes active, but prevented from coming very far over due to our A.A. Lewis Gun and Anti-Aircraft Batteries firing at them. | |
| Do | 6.15 June | | A Raid on the Enemy trench from W.5.d.4/60 to W.5.d.7.k was carried out on the night 16/17 by 2 & 4 Platoons of 6 Coy, & Platoon 2 & 4 of 5 Coy, and 32 other ranks of "B" Coy, which was very successful. Objective gained & Prisoners were captured. | |

Army Form C. 2118.

# WAR DIARY
## INTELLIGENCE SUMMARY.
(Erase heading not required.)

| Place | Date | Hour | Summary of Events and Information | Remarks and references to Appendices |
|---|---|---|---|---|
| Do | 16" | | Our casualties being 1 Other Rank Wounded and 1 Other Rank Missing. 2nd Lt. G. Markwyn O.R.C., U.S.D. is taken onto the strength from to-day vice Capt. W.F. Will R.A.M.C. | |
| Do | 17" | | Enemy artillery active chiefly on backareas. Gas shelling of our Battery positions at "Morning Star" & to " Our planes active on reconnaissance and bomb Battery work. | |
| Do | 18" | | Orders received that the Battalion are to be relieved on Brigade Support by 10/13th Royal Scots on night of 18/19". The Relief was duly carried out. Our casualties, 1 Other Rank of "B" Coy. Wounded by Enemy shelling. | |
| PORTSMOUTH CAMP | 19" | | After the relief we took over Billets in Portsmouth Camp, and same was completed by 7am. The following Officers were admitted to Hospital Sick:- Capt. W. Spens, 2/Lieut. J.W. Garnett, 2/Lieut J. Hurst, also 2 Other Ranks. A draft of 1 Other Rank also reported from the Divisional Reception Camp and are taken on the strength from to-day. | |
| Do | 20" | | Battalion cleaning also carried out during the day. Sig. Majors Geo. Laird, s.b. 4/5" | |

9th (G.) Bn. THE BLACK WATCH

# WAR DIARY or INTELLIGENCE SUMMARY

Army Form C. 2118.

| Place | Date | Hour | Summary of Events and Information | Remarks and references to Appendices |
|---|---|---|---|---|
| D | 20th | | The following Officers struck off from Divisional Reception Camps and the strength from to-day:- Lieut. B. Hunter, 2/Lieut. J. Adams, 2/Lieut. G. Herbert & 2/Lieut. J. Nesbit. The following admitted to hospital (Sick):- 2/Lieut. J.C.L. Harvey, 2/Lieut. D.B. Shally, 2/Lieut. R. Shally, 2/Lieut. W. Malcolm also 25 Other Ranks of "C" Coy. Lt Col. R.D. Bullock D.S.O. ceased command (temporary) of 44th Infantry Brigade vice Brigadier General R.D. Thomson C.M.G., D.S.O. Major R.J. Stewart D.S.O. ceased command (temporarily) of Battalion vice Lt Col. R.D. Bullock D.S.O. to H.Q. Brigade. An epidemic of fever seems to be raging in and about Bethune in the Environs at present. | |
| D | 21st | | Battalion training was carried out during the day viz., Wiring, Bombing, Lewis Gun firing on the Range, also Drill, etc. The following are admitted to hospital (Sick):- 11 Other Ranks "C" Coy & 1 Other Rank "B" Coy. | |
| D | 22nd | | Battalion training was carried out during the day viz., Musketry, Bombing, Drill, &c. 1 Other Rank of "C" Coy. Evacuated to hospital Sick. | |

9th (S) Bn. THE BLACK WATCH.

Army Form C. 2118.

# WAR DIARY
## or
## INTELLIGENCE SUMMARY.
*(Erase heading not required.)*

CONFIDENTIAL

Instructions regarding War Diaries and Intelligence Summaries are contained in F. S. Regs., Part II. and the Staff Manual respectively. Title pages will be prepared in manuscript.

| Place | Date | Hour | Summary of Events and Information | Remarks and references to Appendices |
|---|---|---|---|---|
| Do | 23rd | | Battalion training was carried out during the day. viz:- Gas Drill Musketry, P. & P.T. etc. Evacuated to Hospital (Sick) 1 Other Rank of "A" Coy | |
| Do | 24th | | Battalion training was carried out during the day. viz. During Bombing Gas Drill etc. Evacuated to Hospital (Sick) 7 Other Ranks "A" Coy & 1 Other Rank "B" Coy. Lieut W.J. Wilkie, admitted to hospital (sick) | |
| Do | 25th | | Battalion training was carried out during the day. viz Live Grenade firing, Bayonet Drill etc. Evacuated to Hospital (Sick) 3 Other Ranks of "D" Coy. The following Officer reported from 1st Corps School and was taken on the strength from today — Lieut R.M. Leslie. The Battalion relieved the 9th Royal Scots in trenches of the | |
| RIGHT SECTION | 26th | | RIGHT SECTION of the 15th Divl Front — relief was slightly held up owing to difficulty in taking over cooked potatoes from TAMPOUX but was organised and successful without casualties by 1.20 a.m. 1/Officer Patrol 2 N.C.O.'s & 4 men. Army Detailed to Battalion following N.C.O. & 4 men are Struck off the strength on proceeding to U.K. for Commission 3433 Sergt. Boggarth J., & 202490 Sergt. McPherson D. 4/5(?) Bn. THE BLACK WATCH. | |

# WAR DIARY or INTELLIGENCE SUMMARY

Army Form C. 2118.

| Place | Date | Hour | Summary of Events and Information | Remarks and references to Appendices |
|---|---|---|---|---|
| | 26th | | The following are evacuated to Hospital (sick) 4, other Ranks. "B" Coy 4 Other Ranks. "C" Coy 2. Other Ranks. "B" Coy 4. Other Ranks. 9 Other Ranks. by Wounded. | |
| | 27th | | Very quiet day. Front line being held by Eastern ruin of FAMPOUX VILLAGE. 1 Other Rank "B" Coy evacuated to hospital (sick). In the morning the enemy shelled over trenches but the remainder of the day was quiet. A draft of 29 Other Ranks reported from the Divisional Reception Camp and are taken on the strength from to-day. Enemy shelled ATHIES ROAD near CAM VALLEY from 2.30 a.m. to 3.30 a.m. No casualties reported. | |
| | 28th | | A draft of 25 Other Ranks reported from the Divisional Reception Camp, and are taken on the strength from to-day. 1 Other Rank "B" Coy Wounded (Gas) as result of Gas shelling. Enemy light F.M. slightly active — No casualties. 1 Other Rank "B" Coy Wounded (Gas) as result of Gas shelling. | |
| | 29th | | | |
| | 30th | | Very quiet — American Officer and N.C.Os attached to Battalion to return to American Army. 4/5 9th (S) Bn. THE BLACK WATCH. | |

Army Form C. 2118.

# WAR DIARY
## or
## INTELLIGENCE SUMMARY.
*(Erase heading not required.)*

Instructions regarding War Diaries and Intelligence Summaries are contained in F. S. Regs., Part II. and the Staff Manual respectively. Title pages will be prepared in manuscript.

| Place | Date | Hour | Summary of Events and Information | Remarks and references to Appendices |
|---|---|---|---|---|
| In the Field | 1st July 1915 | | | |

Wm Stewart Major
Cmdg 9/5 The Black Watch R.H.

T2134. Wt. W708—776. 500000. 4/15. Sir J. C. & S.

9th. (S) Bn. THE BLACK WATCH.

Army Form C. 2118.

# WAR DIARY
## INTELLIGENCE SUMMARY.
(Erase heading not required.)

# WAR DIARY
## OF
### 4/5th BATTALION THE BLACK WATCH (R.H.)

FROM 1st JULY, 1918. TO 31st JULY, 1918.

**CONFIDENTIAL.**

Army Form C. 2118.

# WAR DIARY
## INTELLIGENCE SUMMARY.
*(Erase heading not required.)*

Instructions regarding War Diaries and Intelligence Summaries are contained in F. S. Regs., Part II. and the Staff Manual respectively. Title pages will be prepared in manuscript.

| Place | Date | Hour | Summary of Events and Information | Remarks and references to Appendices |
|---|---|---|---|---|
| FRONT LINE FAMPOUX SECTOR (North) | 1/7/18 | | A draft of 11 Other Ranks were taken on the strength from to-day. 2 Other Ranks were admitted to hospital (Sick). The day was comparatively quiet. | |
| --- Do. --- | 2 | | The Enemy shelled our trenches during the morning - casualties very slight - 2 men Wounded. The remainder of the day was fairly quiet. A draft of 2 Other Ranks are taken on the strength from to-day. Capt. J.CULLEN is struck off the strength on taking over Command of the 15th Divisional Reception Camp. Lieut. R.M.LESLIE and 12 Other Ranks admitted to hospital (Sick). | |
| --- Do. --- | 3 | | T/Capt. (A/Major) W.STOREY WILSON is struck off strength on proceeding to U.K.to attend Senior Officer's Course at ALDERSHOT. 2/Lieut.J.P.McDONALD is struck off strength on proceeding to Base Depot,CALAIS. Draft of 10 Other Ranks are taken on the strength from to-day. 2/Lieut.D.SYME,Wounded and 3 Other Ranks Wounded - result of shelling. | |
| --- Do. --- | 4 | | 2/Lieut.D.SYME, died of Wounds at Dressing Station. Draft of 7 Other Ranks are taken on the strength from to-day. Enemy Artillery fairly active during the early morning - the result being 1 Other Rank slightly Wounded. | |
| --- Do. --- | 5 | | Draft of 5 Other Ranks are taken on strength from to-day. 1 Other Rank,Wounded - result of shelling. Lt.Col.R.A.BULLOCH,D.S.O. ceases to Command 44th Infantry Brigade,while Major A.J.STEWART,D.S.O. ceases to Command Battalion. The Battalion were relieved by the 8th Battalion Seaforth Highlanders in the FRONT LINE on night 5/6th.,and took over the position as Brigade Support at STIRLING CAMP. | |

Army Form C. 2118.

# WAR DIARY
## *or*
## INTELLIGENCE SUMMARY.
*(Erase heading not required.)*

Instructions regarding War Diaries and Intelligence Summaries are contained in F. S. Regs., Part II. and the Staff Manual respectively. Title pages will be prepared in manuscript.

| Place | Date | Hour | Summary of Events and Information | Remarks and references to Appendices |
|---|---|---|---|---|
| SUPPORT BATTALION. STIRLING CAMP. | 6 | | The relief was completed by 1.am. Enemy Artillery active during relief – 1 man Wounded. Draft of 10 Other Ranks are taken on strength from to-day. 3 Other Ranks admitted to hospital (Sick). | |
| ---Do.--- | 7 | | Enemy Artillery active at intervals during the day, but no casualties occurred. 2/Lieut.J.A.RITCHIE reported from the 15th Divisional Reception Camp, and is taken on strength from to-day. Capt.T.BYERS,M.C. rejoined from to-day. | |
| ---Do.--- | 8 | | Draft of 6 Other Ranks are taken on strength from to-day. The day was quiet. | |
| ---Do.--- | 9 | | The following Officers reported from the 15th Divisional Reception Camp and are taken on the strength from to-day:- 2/Lieuts. A.G.BAKER, M.J.BETT, and P.A.BROWNE, also 25 Other Ranks. The Enemy Artillery fairly active during the day – Casualties - Nil. | |
| ---Do.--- | 10 | | During the Afternoon the Enemy shelled our position fairly heavy – 1 Other Rank, Wounded. | |
| ---Do.--- | 11 | | 6 Other Ranks rejoined from hospital to-day. 1 Other Rank, admitted to hospital (Sick). The day was comparatively quiet. | |

Army Form C. 2118.

# WAR DIARY

## INTELLIGENCE SUMMARY.

(Erase heading not required.)

Instructions regarding War Diaries and Intelligence Summaries are contained in F. S. Regs., Part II. and the Staff Manual respectively. Title pages will be prepared in manuscript.

| Place | Date | Hour | Summary of Events and Information | Remarks and references to Appendices |
|---|---|---|---|---|
| SUPPORT BATTALION. STIRLING CAMP. | 12 | | Capt. A.K.HAMILTON,M.C. is struck off the strength to-day, having proceeded to U.K.(Sick) 2 Other Ranks rejoined from hospital to-day. Enemy Artillery active during night. | |
| ---Do.--- | 13 | | The Battalion were relieved by the 1st Canadian Battalion, 1st Canadian Brigade on night 13/14th The relief being completed by midnight, and without a casualty. | |
| ARRAS. | 14 | | After relief the Battalion proceeded to Billets in ARRAS, arriving about 1.am. Left ARRAS about 6.am. for SAVY area by the Light Railway, arriving at SAVY about 10.am. - then by Route March to BERLES, where Billets were taken over. Draft of 6 Other Ranks are taken on strength from to-day. 238009 Sergt. C.WALLER is struck off strength, having proceeded to U.K. for Commission. | |
| BILLETS in BERLES. | 15 | | 2/Lieut. H.KINNEAR reported from Base Depot, is taken on strength from to-day. 7 Other Ranks rejoined from hospital. Orders received for the Battalion to be prepared to move at short notice. | |
| ---Do.--- | 16 | | The Battalion left BERLES about 5.30 am., and proceeded by Route March to TINCQUES, arriving at 7.30 am. During the march a severe thunder storm was encountered. The Battalion commenced to entrain at TINCQUES Station at 10.30 am., and same was completed by 1.pm. Journey commenced at 1.30 pm. Destination unknown. | |

Army Form C. 2118.

# WAR DIARY
## INTELLIGENCE SUMMARY.

*(Erase heading not required.)*

| Place | Date | Hour | Summary of Events and Information | Remarks and references to Appendices |
|---|---|---|---|---|
| BILLETS in MONCHY ST. ELOI. | 17th | | The Battalion detrained at LAIGNEVILLE Station about 7.am., and proceeded by Route March to MONCHY ST. ELOI, where Billets were taken over on arrival. | |
| --Do.-- | 18th | | Remained here all day, and the day was spent in cleaning up, and preparing for further orders. 2/Lieut.J.C.T.HARVEY is struck off the strength having been evacuated (Sick) to ENGLAND. | |
| --Do.-- | 19th | | Orders received at 1.15 am. for the Battalion to be ready to move by Bus at short notice. Embussing commenced at 7.am. in French Motor Lorries on the MONCHY ST. ELOI - SAULAY ROAD. The journey started at 8.30 am.,and arrived at CUISE LA MOTTE (Southern France) at 6.30 pm., where the Battalion was Billeted. | |
| BILLETS in CUISE LA MOTTE | 20th | | Remained here all day - still on short notice. No.11160 L/Sergt. A.BUCHAN is struck off the strength, having proceeded to U.K. for Commission | |
| --Do.-- | 21th | | Moved by Route March at 6.30 am. to CHELLES area, and arrived at ROY ST. NICHOLAS about 8.30 am. Billets were obtained for Battalion, and remained here all day resting. At 11.40 pm. orders were received for the Battalion to move forward by Route March to ST. PIERRE AIGLE. C.Q.M.Sergt.A.GREENWAY was Killed by a bomb dropped from an Enemy Aeroplane at COEUVRES, while on duty with advanced Billeting Party | |

Army Form C. 2118.

# WAR DIARY
## INTELLIGENCE SUMMARY.
*(Erase heading not required.)*

Instructions regarding War Diaries and Intelligence Summaries are contained in F.S. Regs., Part II. and the Staff Manual respectively. Title pages will be prepared in manuscript.

| Place | Date | Hour | Summary of Events and Information | Remarks and references to Appendices |
|---|---|---|---|---|
| ST. PIERRE AIGLE | 22nd | | Arrived at ST. PIERRE AIGLE about 4.am., and the Battalion Bivouaced in a wood. During the march Enemy Aircraft were active, and Bombs were dropped on ROUTE taken by Battalion - no casualties occurred, but the other Battalions of the Brigade - 5th Gordon Highlanders, and 8th Seaforth Highlanders had a number of casualties. The Battalion moved forward about 11.15 pm. into Divisional Reserve, which was situated in front of CHAUDUN Village. | |
| DIVISIONAL RESERVE near CHAUDON VILLAGE | 23rd | | The Battalion arrived at 2.am., and took up the position as Divisional Reserve - on arrival the Battalion commenced to dig themselves in - this was completed by 3. am. The Enemy heavily shelled our positions at intervals during the day, which resulted in -2 Other Ranks Killed and 6 Other Ranks Wounded all of Battalion Headquarters. | |
| --- Do. --- | 24th | | Enemy Artillery active during the day -2/Lieut. H.KINNEAR,Wounded, and 2 Other Ranks Wounded. Major J.S.Y.ROGERS,D.S.O.,R.A.M.C. rejoined Battalion to-day vice Lieut.L.MARTIN,who took over duties as M.O. to the 5th Gordon Highlanders.  Lieut.(A/Capt.)W.F.WILKIE is struck off strength on having been pronounced B.I. | |
| --- Do. --- | 25th | | The Enemy Artillery shelled our Trenches at intervals during the day,which resulted in 2 Other Ranks being Wounded. The Battalion relieved the 10th Scottish Rifles in the Right Brigade Front on night 25/26th. The Enemy shelling was very heavy when Battalion were moving from Reserve to Front Line - Casualties , Nil. | |
| FRONT LINE near LA POULERIE | | | | |

Army Form C. 2118.

# WAR DIARY
## or
## INTELLIGENCE SUMMARY.
*(Erase heading not required.)*

| Place | Date | Hour | Summary of Events and Information | Remarks and references to Appendices |
|---|---|---|---|---|
| FRONT LINE near LA FOULERIE | 26th | | The relief was completed by 2.am. Our Area was heavily shelled from 1.30 am. to 3.am. with 5.9s and Gas Shells -result being 20 other Ranks Killed, and 9 Other Ranks Wounded, 1 Other Rank died of Wounds at Dressing Station. The remainder of the day was fairly quiet. The Battalion were relieved by the 8th Argyle & Sutherland Highlanders on night 26/27th., and took up position as Brigade Support. 2/Lieuts.S.L.DAVIE & W.LAWSON are struck off strength on proceeding to Base,Calais, to join the 1st. Battalion Black Watch. | |
| BRIGADE SUPPORT VALLEY east of LA FOULERIE | 27th | | The relief was completed by 3.30 am. The Enemy shelled the Valley leading from the Front Line to the Support Line when the Battalion were moving back to take up the position as Brigade Support, but the casualties were slight.- 7 Other Ranks Wounded. The remainder of the day was fairly quiet. No.350166 Sergt.W.B.GOWANS is struck off strength on proceeding to U.K. for Commission. | |
| B. GERARD east of BUZANCY | 28th | | Battalion moved forward and took up the position about 3.am. in close Support for Attack. "B"Coy. under Lieut.BADENOCH attached to 8th Seaforth Highlanders,Right Front Battalion of Brigade,and replaced by a Coy. of 10th Scottish Rifles,46th Infantry Brigade attached to Battalion. The Brigade attacked about 12.30 pm., and reached their objective, taking the Village of BUZANCY, and capturing a considerable number of prisoners - about 180. Owing to the position on the flank, Brigade was forced to abandon the ground gained. Enemy barrage fairly heavy and "B"Coy. in front suffered considerable casualties from this and from Machine Gun fire. "C" & "D" Coys. in support also suffered from enemy shell fire.- 2/Lieut.J.STUART. Killed, 2/Lieut.R.G.TAIT. Wounded, and 2/Lieut.W.K.McGREGOR, Missing, (all of "B" Coy.). Other Ranks - Killed 21, Wounded 103 and Missing 27. Battalion re-assumed positions as before attack,"A" Coy. moving forward and "B" Coy. moving back to Railway Cutting at LA FOULERIE. Enemy shelling continued throughout the night on Battalion area. Following message received from G.O.C. 15th Division:- "Please let me congratulate you and your Brigade on the work of to-day. There is no question about the complete initial success, | |

Army Form C. 2118.

# WAR DIARY
## or
## INTELLIGENCE SUMMARY.

(Erase heading not required.)

| Place | Date | Hour | Summary of Events and Information | Remarks and references to Appendices |
|---|---|---|---|---|
| BRIGADE SUPPORT. B.GERARD east of BUZANCY. | 28th Contd. | | thanks to plans made in a short time by you and carried into effect by the HIGHLAND BRIGADE with great gallantry. The fact that the ground gained had to be given up was due as far as I can judge through no fault of the SCOTTISH DIVISION". Enemy heavily shelled Battalion area with Gas Shells, chiefly near Battalion Headquarters and "A" Coy., who were Support Coy. | |
| --- Do.--- | 29th | | Enemy shelling continued throughout the day and into the night, a considerable number of Gas Shells being included. Battalion remained in positions as on the evening of 28th. and there were very few casualties - Other Ranks:- Killed 1, Wounded 9. The Battalion were relieved by the French - 2nd Battalion - a portion of the 3rd Battalion of the 91st Regiment on night 29/30th. The relief commenced about 11.pm., and Battalion started to move back to CHAZELLE VALLEY. | |
| DIVISIONAL RESERVE CHAZELLE VALLEY | 30th | | Relief was completed by 4.am. without casualties, in spite of continued harrassing fire by enemy & considerable Gas Shelling. The day passed quietly in new positions. Other Ranks of "B" Coy. remaining were attached to "D" Coy. Lieut. BADENOCH was sent down to Battalion Details. | |
| --- Do.--- | 31st | | Quiet day. Enemy shelling being confined to roads near Battalion area. Orders received for Battalion to move forward, Brigade to be in Support for attack on 1st. August,1918. Move commenced about 10.pm. | |

Army Form C. 2118.

# WAR DIARY
## *or*
## INTELLIGENCE SUMMARY.

*(Erase heading not required.)*

Instructions regarding War Diaries and Intelligence Summaries are contained in F. S. Regs., Part II. and the Staff Manual respectively. Title pages will be prepared in manuscript.

| Place | Date | Hour | Summary of Events and Information | Remarks and references to Appendices |
|---|---|---|---|---|
| | | | | |

Army Form C. 2118.

# WAR DIARY
## INTELLIGENCE SUMMARY.
*(Erase heading not required.)*

CONFIDENTIAL. 4/5th BATTN. THE BLACK WATCH.

WAR DIARY.

FROM 1/8/18 TO 31/8/18

VOL.

98/35

30H
12 rue?

| Place | Date | Hour | Summary of Events and Information | Remarks and references to Appendices |
|---|---|---|---|---|
| | | | | |

Instructions regarding War Diaries and Intelligence Summaries are contained in F. S. Regs., Part II, and the Staff Manual respectively. Title pages will be prepared in manuscript.

**Army Form C. 2118.**

# WAR DIARY
## or
## INTELLIGENCE SUMMARY.

(Erase heading not required.)

Instructions regarding War Diaries and Intelligence Summaries are contained in F. S. Regs., Part II. and the Staff Manual respectively. Title pages will be prepared in manuscript.

| Place | Date | Hour | Summary of Events and Information | Remarks and references to Appendices |
|---|---|---|---|---|
| SUPPORT LINE NEAR LA RAPERIE | 1/8/18 | | The Battalion moved forward into position about 3 a.m., the 44th Infy. Bde. being in support. 45th and 46th Infy. Bde. attacked at 9 a.m. and 44th Infy. Bde. moved forward to have passed through 46th Infy. Bde. on their reaching their objectives. The attack was held up by a heavy barrage, especially Machine Guns, and the Battalion was ordered to re-occupy their original positions. Considerable casualties were suffered during the operations – viz:- Killed:- 2/Lieut. J.H.BARNETT, Wounded:- Capt. D.MAXWELL, M.C., 2/Lt. J.A.RITCHIE, 2/Lt. G. HERBERT, 2/Lt. J. VINT, 2/Lt. A. SCOTT, 2/Lt. P.A.BROWN and 2/Lt. W.MALCOLM.  Other Ranks :- Killed - 20, Wounded - 118 and Missing 6. There was intermittent shelling of our positions during the day and throughout the night. About midnight the Battalion took over the front line on Right Front of Brigade. | |
| FRONT LINE NEAR LA RAPERIE | 2nd | | Early in the morning word was received that enemy was retiring and that the French were advancing on our Right. Patrols were then sent out by "C" Company, who were in front under 2/Lt. G. FULLERTON. Battalion then continued to move forward, patrols of 5th GORDON HQRS. going through to locate enemy. Advance continued till about 3 p.m. French Cavalry patrols keeping touch with enemy, who shelled intermittently at long range. No casualties were suffered. Word received at night that French relieving Division would pass through our Division during the night. | |

Army Form C. 2118.

# WAR DIARY
## INTELLIGENCE SUMMARY.
(Erase heading not required.)

Instructions regarding War Diaries and Intelligence Summaries are contained in F. S. Regs., Part II. and the Staff Manual respectively. Title pages will be prepared in manuscript.

| Place | Date | Hour | Summary of Events and Information | Remarks and references to Appendices |
|---|---|---|---|---|
| LA RAPERIE. | 3rd. | | French relieving troops had passed through by 4 a.m., and Battalion moved back to LA RAPERIE, where Cookers were met, and Breakfast served. Burial party from Battalion Details collected Battalion dead, burying them together near the SUGAR REFINERY, LA RAPERIE. About 1.30 p.m. Battalion moved off, and continued to march back to DOMMIERS, where Battalion was billeted for the night. Capt. D. MAXWELL, M.C., and 1 Other Rank Died of Wounds to-day. | |
| DOMMIERS VILLAGE. | 4th. | | Battalion moved off about 9 a.m., and proceeded by March Route to entraining point - 1 kilo. beyond COEUVRES, where motor lorries were met. All were entrained by 1 p.m., and proceeded on journey, arriving at MOGNEVILLE at 4 p.m., where billets were obtained, and remained there all night. | |
| MOGNEVILLE VILLAGE. | 5th. | | Remained here all day and night. The day was spent in cleaning up, and resting. | |
| --do-- | 6th. | | Left this village about 11 a.m. and proceeded by March Route to CLERMONT, where the Battalion were entrained. Destination unknown. Departing at 6 p.m. | |

**WAR DIARY**

**INTELLIGENCE SUMMARY.**

(Erase heading not required.)

Army Form C. 2118.

| Place | Date | Hour | Summary of Events and Information | Remarks and references to Appendices |
|---|---|---|---|---|
| PENIN VILLAGE | 7th | | The journey was continued throughout the night - detraining at TINCQUES STATION about 2 hrs. then proceeded by March Route to PENIN Village, arrived there about 14 hr, where billets were taken over. | |
| Do | 8th | | About 12 noon, the King motored through this village - the Battalion lined both sides of the Road, and three cheers were given as he passed by. The remainder of the day was spent in cleaning up. 2/Lt. W.G. COUTTS, and a draft of 13 Other Ranks were taken on the strength. 2/Lt. J.P. RITCHIE and 2 Other Ranks, Died of Wounds. | |
| Do | 9th | | Enemy Aircraft fairly active during the night in this Area - several bombs being dropped. The day was spent in cleaning up. | |
| Do | 10th | | 2/Lt. H. KINNEAR rejoined today from Hospital. C.S.M. A. ANDERSON, awarded the MERITORIOUS SERVICE MEDAL for services rendered in the field. Training was carried out under company arrangements. | |
| Do | 11th | | A draft of 20 Other Ranks taken on strength. Refitting of equipment was carried out by Companies, also Training. | |

Army Form C. 2118.

# WAR DIARY
## INTELLIGENCE SUMMARY.
(Erase heading not required.)

| Place | Date | Hour | Summary of Events and Information | Remarks and references to Appendices |
|---|---|---|---|---|
| PENIN VILLAGE | 12th | | The Battalion paraded at 9.30 a.m. and proceeded by Route March to IZEL - LES - HAMEAU, arriving about 11 a.m., where the remainder of the Brigade were met. The Brigade was ordered to parade on the occasion of the presentation, by G.O.C. Division, of French decorations won during operations near BUZANCY for period 26/7/18 - 2/8/18. After the presentation the Brigade moved off by Battalions to their respective Billets.  Draft of 19:- Other Ranks taken on strength. The following Officers and Other Ranks of the Battalion were amongst the recipients of honours presented at the above parade. | |

Lt. Col. R.A. BULLOCH, D.S.O. — CHEVALIER OF THE LEGION OF HONOUR & CROIX DE GUERRE.
Major J.S.Y. ROGERS, D.S.O. — CROIX DE GUERRE.
Capt. & Adjt. J.I. BUCHAN, D.S.O. — CROIX DE GUERRE.

Sergt. A. DICKSON — MEDAILLE MILITAIRE & CROIX DE GUERRE.
Sergt. J. CAIRNS — CROIX DE GUERRE.
Sergt. S. MALCOLM — CROIX DE GUERRE.
Corpl. J. MOFFAT — CROIX DE GUERRE.
Corpl. J. DAVIDSON — CROIX DE GUERRE.
Pte. M. KIDD — CROIX DE GUERRE.
Pte. T. ROSS — CROIX DE GUERRE.
Pte. A. ROBERTSON — CROIX DE GUERRE.
Pte. J. GRAHAM — CROIX DE GUERRE.

Army Form C. 2118.

# WAR DIARY

## INTELLIGENCE SUMMARY.

(Erase heading not required.)

| Place | Date | Hour | Summary of Events and Information | Remarks and references to Appendices |
|---|---|---|---|---|
| PENIN VILLAGE | 13th | | Draft of 8 Other Ranks taken on strength. Training was carried out under Company arrangements. | |
| Do. | 14th | | Lt. Col. R.A. BULLOCH, D.S.O. assumed command (temporarily) of 44th Infy. Bde. vice Brigadier General N.A. THOMSON, C.M.G., D.S.O., while Major A.J. STEWART, D.S.O. assumed command (temporarily) of Battalion. <br><br> HONOURS & AWARDS. <br><br> The following N.C.Os. and Men have been awarded the MILITARY MEDAL :- <br> 240948 Sergt. J. STEPHEN, 350396 L/Cpl. H. MILL, 9822 L/Cpl. F. WILLETS, 291706 L/Cpl. A. BROUGH, 16528 Pte. W. STEWART, 12369 Pte. F. SAYLE, and 202613 Pte. W. ROBERTSON. | |
| Do. | 15th | | Orders received for the 44th Infy. Bde. to move forward into the Line - relieving the 167th Infy. Bde. on night 15/16th in the front line - NEUVILLE VITASSE Sector. The Battalion left PENIN at 3.30 p.m. and proceeded by March Route to HERMAVILLE, arriving about 5 p.m.; then by Light Railway - entraining at 6 p.m. and detraining at 9 p.m. at the village of WAILLY. The Battalion then formed up and marched to the Front Line - relieving the 1st Londons. The night was quiet during the relief. | |

# WAR DIARY

## INTELLIGENCE SUMMARY.

(Erase heading not required.)

Army Form C. 2118.

| Place | Date | Hour | Summary of Events and Information | Remarks and references to Appendices |
|---|---|---|---|---|
| FRONT LINE NEUVILLE VITASSE SECTOR | 16th | | The relief was completed by 3.45 a.m., which passed very successful. About 9.30 p.m. the enemy sent over a considerable number of Aerial Bombs - 2/Lt. H. Kinnear being wounded. Enemy Aircraft fairly active about midnight - several Bombs were dropped in our Battalion area. | |
| Do. | 17th | | In the early morning about 3 a.m. the enemy Artillery shelled our area with a few 5".9". At 5.30 am an enemy Plane was observed coming towards our line flying low, but was compelled to descend by our planes flying on their own line. Between 5 & 6 pm. 50-60 rounds of 4".2" were fired on our area, also a considerable number of Gas Shells were sent over to the Back Area. | |
| Do. | 18th | | During the early morning between 4 and 4.30 am, hostile Artillery were active firing a considerable number of 4.2" also a few T.Ms. Enemy Plane flew over our lines at 12.30 p.m., but was forced to return by heavy fire from our Lewis Guns. A prisoner was captured last night and states he is a deserter. He reports that the enemy are relieving all along our front. About 8 p.m. the Battalion sent out a patrol to investigate where the enemy were after going forward for about 800 yards they came across an enemy Machine Gun Post, which was occupied by 6 men, also a considerable number of men were observed about the enemy front line. The enemy fired on the patrol, but retaliation was given, inflicting considerable casualties. The enemy - Our patrol returned without a casualty. 2 out of 5 Aerial Bombs taken out the strength. Capt. S. Norie Miller, M.C. | |

# WAR DIARY

## INTELLIGENCE SUMMARY

Army Form C. 2118.

| Place | Date | Hour | Summary of Events and Information | Remarks and references to Appendices |
|---|---|---|---|---|
| FRONT LINE NEUVILLE VITASSE SECTOR. | 19th | | Early in the morning the Battalion sent out strong fighting patrols to make an attempt to gain ground occupied by the enemy - the patrols reached Hindenburg Line but was forced to abandon the ground gained owing to Artillery fire Machine Guns &c.  Our casualties were  Other Ranks - Killed 2, Wounded 4. The enemy Artillery put over a heavy bombardment on our front line at 4.30 a.m. and this continued until 9.30 a.m., which consisted of 4.2", 5.9" and a considerable number of Trench Mortars, also heavy machine gun fire - which resulted in :- Killed 4, Wounded 3 Other Ranks.  During the bombardment enemy planes were seen over our lines several times being chopped.  The remainder of the day was fairly quiet.  The following Officers are taken on the strength :- 2/Lt. S.A. NEILE, 2/Lt. T.C. BELL, 2/Lt. J. McGLADDERY, 2/Lt. G.G. WEIR and Capt. & QrMr W. CLARK, M.C., admitted to hospital (Sick.) 64 Other Ranks. | |
| - Do. - | 20th | | The enemy heavily shelled our front line from 3 to 4 a.m., also back areas with 4.2", 5.9" and a few Trench Mortars. During the bombardment several enemy planes were observed over our front line - they returned to their own lines immediately the bombardment ceased.  Authority has been granted for A.R.E. BAGENOCH M.C. to wear the badges of the rank of Captain.  Draft of 62 Other Ranks taken on the strength. | |

# WAR DIARY

## INTELLIGENCE SUMMARY.

*(Erase heading not required.)*

Army Form C. 2118.

| Place | Date | Hour | Summary of Events and Information | Remarks and references to Appendices |
|---|---|---|---|---|
| FRONT LINE NEUVILLE VITASSE SECTOR | 21st | | Between 2 and 3 a.m. our front line was heavily shelled with 3", 4.2", 5.9" also a considerable number of Trench Mortars. During the bombardment about 50 of the enemy attempted a raid between our "B" Coy. and the 9th Royal Scots on our right, but the enemy were driven off by Rifle and Lewis Gun fire – Casualties being 2/Lt. J.C.BELL, Missing, 1 Other Rank Wounded and 1 Other Rank Missing. The 5th Gordon Highrs. relieved the Battalion in the front line on night 21/22nd. On relief the Battalion moved back to Reserve.  2/Lt. W.G. Coates is struck off strength, on being transfered to 15th Can. Machine Gun Corps. | |
| RESERVE LINE | 22nd | | During relief enemy Aircraft active, several bombs being dropped in this area, but there were no casualties. Phosh? I am an enemy Plane was seen to come down in flames. Relief was completed by 2 a.m. The day was quiet. The Battalion were relieved in the line by the 28th Canadian Infy. Battalion about 11 p.m. After the relief the Battalion moved by March Route to DAINVILLE. | |
| " Do. " | | | | |
| DAINVILLE | 23rd | | Arrived at DAINVILLE about 1 a.m. where the Battalion rested. About 2:30 a.m. several bombs were dropped by enemy Planes in our neighbourhood. No Casualties. At 5 a.m. the Battalion proceeded by Light Railway, to destination unknown. Detraining near HERSIN, then by March Route to BOIS DU FROISSART CAMP, where huts were provided, and remained here all night. | |

Army Form C. 2118.

# WAR DIARY
## INTELLIGENCE SUMMARY.
*(Erase heading not required.)*

Instructions regarding War Diaries and Intelligence Summaries are contained in F. S. Regs., Part II. and the Staff Manual respectively. Title pages will be prepared in manuscript.

| Place | Date | Hour | Summary of Events and Information | Remarks and references to Appendices |
|---|---|---|---|---|
| BOIS DU FROISSART CAMP. | 24th | | The Battalion left Camp about 3 p.m. and moved forward by light Railway, detraining at GRENAY - then by Marel Trench to Brigade Support, HULLUCH Sector, arriving about 7.30 p.m., and relief was completed by 8.15 p.m. The night was quiet. | |
| SUPPORT LINE. HULLUCH SECTOR | 25th | | In the early morning the enemy Artillery heavily shelled our positions. Between 6 & 7 p.m. 8 enemy planes were observed coming towards our line, but they were forced to return to their own lines, by fire from our Anti-aircraft and Lewis Guns. | |
| Do. | 26th | | About 12 a.m. the enemy heavily shelled our area with 4.2"; also a considerable number of Trench Mortars, which resulted in 1 Other Rank being killed and 2 Wounded. 7 Other Ranks taken on strength. | |
| Do. | 27th | | At 5 a.m. our area was shelled with 4.2", also at intervals during the day. At 3 p.m. an enemy plane attempted to cross our lines, but was driven off by our Anti-aircraft Return. The following Officers are taken on the strength :- 2/Lt. J.N.DUNCAN, 2/Lt. J. HERALD, 2/Lt. H. HARRISON, 2/Lt. W.B. SHAND., 2/Lt. F.E. CATTO, 2/Lt. N.D. STEVENSON, 2/Lt. R.S. CLARK, Also 3 Other Ranks. | |
| Do. | 28th | | The Battalion relieved 1/5th Gordon Hrs. in the front line - relief was completed by 7.30 p.m. Hostile Artillery active at intervals during the day. Draft of 69 - Other Ranks are taken on strength. | |

Army Form C. 2118.

# WAR DIARY

## INTELLIGENCE SUMMARY.
(Erase heading not required.)

Instructions regarding War Diaries and Intelligence Summaries are contained in F. S. Regs., Part II. and the Staff Manual respectively. Title pages will be prepared in manuscript.

| Place | Date | Hour | Summary of Events and Information | Remarks and references to Appendices |
|---|---|---|---|---|
| FRONT LINE. HULLUCH SECTOR. | 29th | | Enemy Artillery active during the night and throughout the day at intervals on our front line. At 8.30 am 2 Enemy Planes were observed coming towards our line, but were soon driven off by Lewis & Machine Gun fire. | |
| Do. | 30th | | In the afternoon about 4 o'clock an Enemy Plane was sighted, and was making for our lines but was soon turned by one of our Planes. Enemy Artillery very active about 9 p.m. and at intervals throughout the night. | |
| Do. | 31st | | Early in the morning an Enemy Plane was observed coming towards our line, but was driven off by one of our Planes. Artillery fire of a harassing nature, took place throughout the night on our front. | |

HONOURS & AWARDS.

MILITARY CROSS
CAPT. R.E. BADENOCH.
LIEUT. R. INCH.
2/LIEUT. G. FULLERTON.
" A. SCOTT.

DISTINGUISHED CONDUCT MEDAL.
40340 SGT. J. DICKSON.
350225 " S. MALCOLM.
1368 L/CPL. W. SOMERVILLE.

[signature]
Lt. Col.
O.C. 4/5th Bn. the Black Watch.

Army Form C. 2118.

# WAR DIARY
## INTELLIGENCE SUMMARY.
*(Erase heading not required.)*

Instructions regarding War Diaries and Intelligence Summaries are contained in F. S. Regs., Part II. and the Staff Manual respectively. Title pages will be prepared in manuscript.

| Place | Date | Hour | Summary of Events and Information | Remarks and references to Appendices |
|---|---|---|---|---|
| | | | | |

Army Form C. 2118.

# WAR DIARY
## INTELLIGENCE SUMMARY.
*(Erase heading not required.)*

Vol 36

WAR DIARY.

4/5th BATTN. THE BLACK WATCH.

FROM 1/9/18 TO 30/9/18

VOL.

CONFIDENTIAL.

Army Form C. 2118.

# WAR DIARY
## OF
## INTELLIGENCE SUMMARY.
*(Erase heading not required.)*

Instructions regarding War Diaries and Intelligence Summaries are contained in F. S. Regs., Part II. and the Staff Manual respectively. Title pages will be prepared in manuscript.

| Place | Date | Hour | Summary of Events and Information | Remarks and references to Appendices |
|---|---|---|---|---|
| HULLUCH SECTOR — FRONT LINE. | 1/9/18. | | In the early morning about 1 o'clock the Enemy Shelled our Front Line with Shells of various calibre, principally 4.2s, also a considerable number of Gas Shells - Blue Cross & Lachrymatory. At 8 a.m. an Enemy Plane flew over our Lines, flying very low, but was soon driven off by fire from our Lewis & Machine Guns. The Day was fairly quiet. Hostile Artillery particularly active between 10 & 11 p.m., over 100 rounds being fired - 4.2s, 5.9s & a few Blue Cross Gas Shells. 2/Lieut. C.C. CULROSS joined. | |
| - Do.- | 2 | | Fairly quiet during the day. Enemy Plane observed about 7 a.m. coming towards our line, but was driven off by fire from our Lewis Guns. Hostile Artillery was fairly active throughout the night at irregular intervals. Lieut. J.C. LAING & 19 O.R. joined. | |
| - Do.- | 3 | | About 7 a.m. an Enemy Balloon was brought down in flames by one of our Planes on the left of HULLUCH. Considerable number of Enemy Planes flew over our lines at intervals during the morning, but were driven off by our Anti-aircraft and Machine Guns. Our Front Line was Shelled with 5.9s and 4.2s in the morning, and same continued throughout the day. Between 10 & 11 p.m. our area was Shelled with a few Gas Shells. 64 O.R. joined. | |
| - Do.- | 4 | | Hostile Artillery fairly quiet during the day, but rather active towards night. Enemy Plane was seen, flying low, making for our front, but was forced to return by fire from our Lewis Guns. | |

Army Form C. 2118.

# WAR DIARY
# INTELLIGENCE SUMMARY.
*(Erase heading not required.)*

| Place | Date | Hour | Summary of Events and Information | Remarks and references to Appendices |
|---|---|---|---|---|
| HULLUCH SECTOR — FRONT LINE. | 5 | | During a Raid which was carried out on our Right between 4 & 5 a.m. the Enemy put down a heavy Bombardment on our Front Line with 4.2s & 5.9s and a few Gas Shells; at the same time Enemy Air-craft was very active, several Bombs being dropped on our area, but no casualties were inflicted.  The remainder of the day was quiet. Lieut. J.DAVIDSON, 2/Lieut. W.RAE, and Lieut. I.M.BRUCE-GARDYNE M.C. joined. Lieut. R.E.BADENOCH M.C. to be acting Captain whilst Commanding a Company from 6th June 1918. | |
| - Do.- | 6 | | In the early morning our Trenches were heavily Shelled by 4.2s, 5.9s, Trench Mortars and a few Gas Shells.  At 11 p.m. a Raid was carried out by this Battalion, party consisting of 2/Lieut. J.McGLADDERY and 20 O.R. Objective reached. Party waited 4 hours, but no Enemy were encountered and Party returned about 2 a.m. on 7th.- no casualties. Lieut J.B.BALDWIN, M.O.R.C., U.S.A. joined.    Lieut F.I.McGRADY struck off strength on being appointed I.O. 118th I.B. Casualties - Wounded 1 O.R. | |
| - Do.- | 7 | | Battalion relieved in Front Line by 8th Seaforth Hgrs.- relief completed by 5 p.m. On relief the Battalion moved to Support -in MAZINGARBE Village, where Battalion were accommodated in Huts. | |
| MAZINGARBE | 8 | | The day was spent on cleaning up and Baths. | |
| - Do.- | 9 | | Training. 990.R. joined. Lieut. (A/Capt.) & Adjt. J.I.BUCHAN D.S.O. to be T/Capt. - 24th Aug.1917. | |

Army Form C. 2118.

# WAR DIARY
## INTELLIGENCE SUMMARY.
(Erase heading not required.)

Instructions regarding War Diaries and Intelligence Summaries are contained in F. S. Regs., Part II. and the Staff Manual respectively. Title pages will be prepared in manuscript.

| Place | Date | Hour | Summary of Events and Information | Remarks and references to Appendices |
|---|---|---|---|---|
| MAZINGARBE | 10 | | Training. Lt. Col. R.A.BULLOCH,D.S.O. ceased to Command 44th I.B. while Major A.J.STEWART,D.S.O. ceased to Command Battalion | |
| - Do.- | 11 | | Training continued. | |
| - Do.- | 12 | | Battalion left MAZINGARBE about 2 p.m., and proceeded by March Route to Front Line, HULLUCH Sector to relieve 5th Gordon Hgrs. As the Battalion were actively engaged with the Enemy, complete relief was not possible, but 2 Companies relieved, and came under orders of O.C. 5th Gordon Hgrs. | |
| HULLUCH SECTOR THE Quarries. | 13 | | Command of the sector was taken over at noon and posts of 5th Gordon Hgrs. pushed out into the old German Lines and North of the Quarries were taken over after dark. At 11 p.m. "C" Company on Right and "D" Company on Left endeavoured to establish posts along the line of GREASE trench in G.12.b.(FRANCE 44 A N.W. 3 1/20000),but met with opposition and complete line was not established. Casualties - Wounded 1 O.R. | |
| - Do.- | 14 | | Enemy counterattacked and drove "D" Company back to the QUARRIES, but line was re-established as previously held at 10.15 a.m. without opposition. 8th Seaforth Hgrs. on the Right took over a portion of the Front on re-adjustment of Boundaries at noon. During the Afternoon the Enemy counterattacked again and drove in our forward posts whicw were not re-established,our Line running along N.E. edge of the QUARRIES. Casualties- Killed 3 O.R., Wounded 19 O.R., Missing 5 O.R.,Evacuated (Sick) 2 O.R. | |

Army Form C. 2118.

# WAR DIARY

## INTELLIGENCE SUMMARY.

*(Erase heading not required.)*

Instructions regarding War Diaries and Intelligence Summaries are contained in F.S. Regs., Part II. and the Staff Manual respectively. Title pages will be prepared in manuscript.

| Place | Date | Hour | Summary of Events and Information | Remarks and references to Appendices |
|---|---|---|---|---|
| HULLUCH SECTOR THE QUARRIES | 15 | | The Enemy attacked in strength at 5.15 a.m., and drove our forward posts to the old British Front Line. A counterattack by 2 Platoons of "A" Company at 7.15 am. drove the Enemy back and Line was re-established along N.E. edge of QUARRIES. Casualties - Lt.J.N.DUNCAN Wounded, 2/Lt.C.C.CULROSS Wounded (Gas) O.R., Killed 2, Wounded 11. 9 O.R. joined. | |
| - Do.- | 16 | | At 5 a.m. "A" Company advanced in conjuction with 13th Royal Scots on left, and the forward posts in GREASE Trench were re-established and consolidation commenced with the assistance of the R.E. Owing to the posts on our left being forced back at 8 a.m. these posts withdrew temporarily, but on situation being restored they were re-established at 9.45 a.m., and consolidation continued. Casualties - O.R. Killed 2, Died of Wounds 2, Wounded 13. | |
| - Do.- | 17 | | "A" Company were relieved in the forward posts by "B" Company. Day passed fairly quietly. Casualties - O.R. Died of Wounds 1, Wounded 2, Evacuated (sick) 2. Capt.H.E.D.ORR-EWING and 7 O.R. joined. | |
| - Do.- | 18 | | At 5 a.m. Enemy attacked our posts under a T.M. Barrage, and the advanced posts were forced to withdraw, but were re-established almost immediately without opposition. Remainder of the day quiet. Casualties - O.R. Killed 3, Wounded 2, Evacuated (sick) 2. R.S.M. Dewar left for Commission. | |

Army Form C. 2118.

# WAR DIARY

## INTELLIGENCE SUMMARY.

*(Erase heading not required.)*

| Place | Date | Hour | Summary of Events and Information | Remarks and references to Appendices |
|---|---|---|---|---|
| HULLUCH SECTOR THE QUARRIES | 19 | | Day passed fairly quietly. | |
| - Do. - | 20 | | At 9.45 a.m. Enemy put down a heavy Barrage with 4.2s & T.Ms. for half an hour, and attacked our Posts and those of the Battalion on our left (10th Scottish Rifles)at 10.15 a.m. He drove in one of our posts temporarily but was driven back immediately. The rest of the day was quiet, and "D" Company relieved B Company on Left Front in Afternoon. Casualties -.O.R. Killed 1, Wounded 2, Evacuated (sick) 1. 9 O.R. joined. Transferred to England - Capt.& Qr.Mr.W.CLARK,M.C.(Sick) and Lt.J.M.DUNCAN, (Wounded) | |
| - Do. - | 21 | | Consolidation of Posts and Wiring were carried out with little interruption. R.S.M. Watson joined from 8th Black Watch. | |
| - Do, - | 22 | | Battalion was relieved by 8th Seaforth Hgrs.(2Coys)and 5th Gordon Hgrs.(1 Coy.) and moved into Support,Battalion Hd.Qrs. and 3 Coys. at MAZINGARBE, and 1 Coy.at LE RUTOIRE FARM. Total Casualties for Tour; Killed 11,Died of Wounds 3, Wounded 2 Officers & 47,Missing 4. | |
| MAZINGARBE | 23 | | Day was spent in cleaning up and Baths. | |
| - Do. - | 24 | | Training.  40 O.R. joined. | |

Army Form C. 2118.

# WAR DIARY
# INTELLIGENCE SUMMARY.
(Erase heading not required.)

Instructions regarding War Diaries and Intelligence Summaries are contained in F. S. Regs., Part II. and the Staff Manual respectively. Title pages will be prepared in manuscript.

| Place | Date | Hour | Summary of Events and Information | Remarks and references to Appendices |
|---|---|---|---|---|
| MAZINGARBE | 25 | | Training continued.   2 O.R. joined.   Evacuated (sick) 3 O.R. | |
| - Do. - | 26 | | Training continued.   Evacuated (sick) 3 O.R. | |
| - Do. - | 27 | | Battalion left at 2 p.m., and proceeded to Front Line, relieving 5th Gordon Hgrs.- Relief complete 7.10 p.m.   Evacuated (sick) 5 O.R. | |
| HULLUCH SECTOR ---- Front Line. | 28 | | Day quiet.   12 O.R. joined.   Evacuated (sick) 2 O.R. Major A.J.STEWART,D.S.O. left to assume Command of 9th Black Watch. | |
| - Do. - | 29 | | Preparation for a move forward to keep in touch with the Enemy, believed to be about to withdraw.   52 O.R. joined. | |
| - Do. - | 30 | | 6th Cameron Hgrs. On our Right carried out a Raid on Enemy Lines, and 8th Seaforth Hgrs. on our left and ourselves pushed out strong Patrols to ascertain the Enemy's strength. They came under heavy Machine Gun Fire, and returned an hour later except one Patrol, which was unable to get back, and waited in the old German Front Line until dusk, returning intact at 7.30 p.m.   3 O.R. rejoined from Hospital. Casualties - O.R. Killed 1, Wounded 1. | |

W Storey Wilson Major
for O.C. 4/5th Black Watch.

Army Form C. 2118.

# WAR DIARY
## *or*
# INTELLIGENCE SUMMARY.

*(Erase heading not required.)*

Instructions regarding War Diaries and Intelligence Summaries are contained in F. S. Regs., Part II. and the Staff Manual respectively. Title pages will be prepared in manuscript.

| Place | Date | Hour | Summary of Events and Information | Remarks and references to Appendices |
|---|---|---|---|---|
| | | | | |

**CONFIDENTIAL**

Army Form C.

# WAR DIARY
## or
## INTELLIGENCE SUMMARY.
*(Erase heading not required.)*

Vol 39

SECRET. & CONFIDENTIAL.

WAR DIARY.

4/5th Bn. The Black Watch.

from 1/10/18. to 31/10/18.

Vol. ———

**CONFIDENTIAL**

Army Form C. 2118.

Instructions regarding War Diaries and Intelligence Summaries are contained in F. S. Regs., Part II. and the Staff Manual respectively. Title pages will be prepared in manuscript.

# WAR DIARY
## or
## INTELLIGENCE SUMMARY.
*(Erase heading not required.)*

| Place | Date | Hour | Summary of Events and Information | Remarks and references to Appendices |
|---|---|---|---|---|
| HULLUCH SECTOR FRONT LINE | 1/10/18. | | Preparations for a move forward continued, as from information obtained, a withdrawal on the part of the Enemy appeared imminent. Draft of 9 Other Ranks joined. | |
| Do. | 2 | | Prisoner gave himself up at "K" Post to "C" Coy. at 06.15 hours - stated on examination that the Enemy had commenced withdrawal to Line of HAUTE DEULE Canal at 04.30 hours. Patrols pushed forward and occupied BLUE line at 09.30 hours (HULLUCH-PUITS 13.bis.) 2 Coys. then pushed forward to BLUE line - patrols meantime advancing to BROWN line (HULLUCH TRENCH). BROWN line was reached by noon and hastily consolidated, and held for the night. "B" Coy. on left, "D" Coy. on right with "C" Coy. in Support in BLUE line. "A" Coy. remained in reserve - Tunnels. Battn. Hd. Qrs. established in HULLUCH Tunnel at 16.30 hours. Casualties:- Killed 2 Other Ranks, Wounded 3 Other Ranks, Evacuated 2 Other Ranks. Rejoined from Hospital:- 2/Lieut.C.C.CULROSS and 1 Other Rank. | |
| Do. | 3 | | At dawn "B" & "D" Coys. pushed forward and established themselves in VENDIN À DOUVRIN = LA BASSEE line at 09.30 hours, and pushed forward patrols to make good "METALLURGIQUE WORKS". Right Coy. reached AQUEDUCT, but were obliged to withdraw to above mentioned line, owing to lack of Support on Right Flank. Platoon of Left Coy. reached S.W. corner of WORKS and came under heavy enfilade Machine Gun Fire. They were unable either to advance or withdraw. 15 of this Platoon are missing, and are believed to have been cut off and captured. Situation at dusk. - "B" & "D" Coys. firmly established in VENDIN - DOUVRIN - LA BASSEE LINE with posts established about 200 yards in front. "C" Coy. in Support in old BROWN LINE and "A" Coy. in HAY LOCALITY. Casualties:- Killed 2 Other Ranks, Wounded 5 Other Ranks, Missing 15 Other Ranks. Capt.H.E.D. ORR-EWING is struck off the strength on proceeding to Senior Officers' Course, ALDERSHOT. Rejoined from Hospital:- 3 Other Ranks. | |

**CONFIDENTIAL**

Army Form C. 2118.

Instructions regarding War Diaries and Intelligence Summaries are contained in F.S. Regs., Part II. and the Staff Manual respectively. Title pages will be prepared in manuscript.

# WAR DIARY
or
## INTELLIGENCE SUMMARY.
*(Erase heading not required.)*

| Place | Date | Hour | Summary of Events and Information | Remarks and references to Appendices |
|---|---|---|---|---|
| HULLUCH SECTOR — FRONT LINE. | 4 | | At 05.45 hours patrols pushed forward in conjunction with flank Units and established a line of posts along railway S.W. side METALLURGIQUE WORKS without opposition. "A" Coy. relieved "D" Coy. who took up position in BROWN LINE (HERCULES TRENCH). "C" Coy. relieved "B" Coy. who took up position in left of "D" Coy. Battalion H.Q. moved forward; and established H.Q. in HERCULES TRENCH. Casualties:- 1 Other Rank Wounded, 1 Other Rank Evacuated. Draft of 11 Other Ranks. Rejoined from Hospital:- 2/Lt. G.C. JOHNSON. | |
| - DO. - | 5 | | During night of 4/5th "A" Coy. (Right) were relieved by 6th Camerons and in turn relieved Right Coy. 8th Seaforths. Battalion Front now from junction HALSTEAD ALLEYE and DOUVRIN LINE to WINGLES ROAD inclusive. Out Post line pushed forward in early morning and now runs along S.E. side factory thence due North to MEURCHIN ROAD. 5th Gordons relieved 8th Seaforths on left. Casualties:- Lieut. J. Baldwin M.O. Gassed. Killed:- 1 Other Rank, Wounded 1Other Rank, Wounded (Gas) 3 Other Ranks. Joined:- Major W.STOREY WILSON,M.C.Z, Lieut. B.A. HARRISON,M.O.R.C.Z U.S.A., & 2 Other Ranks. | |
| - DO. - | 6 | | Enemy very quiet, apparently settling to hold line of Canal. Shelling which has not been heavy at any time during advance now practically Nil. Can walk round Out Post line without being fired on. "A" Coy. moved to forward Support. Reserve Platoons to WINGLES between WINGLES ROAD, and METALLURGIQUE WORKS. "D" Coy. moved into Support position in DOUVRIN LINE between WINGLES ROAD AND left of "C" Coy. Casualties:- 1 Other Rank Evacuated. Joined:- Lieut.C.H.P.C.PENNEYE M.C. & 2 Other Ranks. | |

**CONFIDENTIAL**

Army Form C. 2118.

# WAR DIARY
## or
## INTELLIGENCE SUMMARY

*(Erase heading not required.)*

Instructions regarding War Diaries and Intelligence Summaries are contained in F. S. Regs., Part II. and the Staff Manual respectively. Title pages will be prepared in manuscript.

| Place | Date | Hour | Summary of Events and Information | Remarks and references to Appendices |
|---|---|---|---|---|
| HULLUCH SECTOR FRONT LINE. | 7 | | Very quiet Day. Inter Coy. Relief afterz dark. "A" Coy. changed places with "D" Coy., and "C" Coy. with "B" Coy. Enemy's attempt to flood area between left Coy. and Canal not meeting with much success— MEURCHIN ROAD still dry although wood on either side submerged to depth of about 2 ft. 2/Lt. G. FULLERTON: M.C. to C.C.S. (S). 1 Other Rank Evacuated. Rejoined from Hospital:- 3 Other Ranks. | |
| Do. | 8 | | Some slight Shelling of METALLURGIQUE WORKS with 5.9s and 4.2s, otherwise day passed quietly. Some interesting Souvenirs obtained in Factory— "C" Coy. salved an excellent Piano and sent it back to Transport Lines. Capt. T. BYERS M.C. struck off strength on proceeding on 6 Months Tour of Duty at Home. 1 Other Rank Evacuated. | |
| Do. | 9 | | Rumour of Enemy withdrawal from Canal. Patrols sent out reported no change in Enemy dispositions. Advance Party from 8th Seaforths arrived this morning at Bn.H.Q. Relieved by 8th Seaforths during Afternoon and Evening, Battalion withdrew to Support— Coys. in Tunnels and H.Q. at junction of LIMBER TRENCH and LE RUTOIRE ALLEY. Major J.D. SIMPSON (Brigade Major) severely Wounded by Shell in HULLUCH ROAD. Joined:- Lt. L/P. DENROCHE SMITH , 2/Lt. J. WALLACE and 1 Other Rank. | |
| HULLUCH SECTOR SUPPORT LINE. | 10 | | Coy. spent the day resting and cleaning up. 2 Other Ranks Evacuated. | |

Army Form C. 2118.

# WAR DIARY
## or
## INTELLIGENCE SUMMARY.
*(Erase heading not required.)*

| Place | Date | Hour | Summary of Events and Information | Remarks and references to Appendices |
|---|---|---|---|---|
| HULLUCH SECTOR - SUPPORT LINE. | 11 | | "B" & "D" Coys. working on roads under R.Es., "A" & "C" Coys. for refitting. Lt.Col.R.A.BULLOCH D.S.O. left to take over G.S.O.1 at 15th Div. H.Q., whilst Major W.STOREY WILSON M.C. took over command of Battalion. Draft of 13 Other Ranks joined. 3 Other Ranks Evacuated. | |
| -Do.- | 12 | | "A" & "C" Coys. Working Parties, "B" & "D" Coys. for refitting. Major J.D.SIMPSON (Brigade Major) died of Wounds at C.C.S. at BARLIN. Brigade on Right reported to have captured VENDIN-le-VEIL, expect to advance to-morrow. Draft of 2 Other Ranks joined. 6 Other Ranks Evacuated. | |
| -Do.- | 13 | | Coys. attended Baths, remainder of day spent on Working Parties. Brigade Major buried at BARLIN. Draft of 3 Other Ranks joined 4 Other Ranks Evacuated. | |
| -Do.- | 14 | | Lt.B.A.HARRISON,M.O.R.C.,U.S.A. 4 Other Ranks Evacuated. Draft of 4 Other Ranks joined. | |
| -Do.- | 15 | | Enemy reported withdrawing from HAUTE-DEULE CANAL at dawn. Battalion stood to, and moved to vicinity of HERCULES TRENCH at mid-day. At 16.00 hours Battalion moved to WINGLES, and remained there over night. The 5th Gordons and 8th Seaforths being well East of Canal. 2/Lt J.O.ADAMS admitted to C.C.S. (S)and 2 Other Ranks Evacuated. | |

Army Form C. 2118.

# WAR DIARY
## or
## INTELLIGENCE SUMMARY.
*(Erase heading not required.)*

CONFIDENTIAL

Instructions regarding War Diaries and Intelligence Summaries are contained in F. S. Regs., Part II. and the Staff Manual respectively. Title pages will be prepared in manuscript.

| Place | Date | Hour | Summary of Events and Information | Remarks and references to Appendices |
|---|---|---|---|---|
| WINGLES SUPPORT LINE. | 16 | | At 07.00 hours "B" & "C" Coys. relieved Bridge-head Guards of Gordons. "A" & "D" Coys and Hd. Qrs. moved into Billets in MEURCHIN. 45th Brigade relieved 44th Brigade Out Post line during evening. 1 Other Rank Evacuated. | |
| MEURCHIN | 17 | | Battalion moved to CARVIN at 16.00 hours and remained there in Billets all night. 45th Brigade having taken over advanced Guard. A few civilians reached CARVIN in the evening having come through our out post line. 2 Other Ranks Evacuated. | |
| CARVIN | 18 | | Left CARVIN at 10.30 hours and moved to BOIS d' EPINOY, where Battalion was accomodated in Huts. 44th Brigade now Rear Brigade of Division. 2 Other Ranks Evacuated. | |
| BOIS d' EPINOY | 19 | | Battalion left BOIS d' EPINOY at 08.30 hours and arrived MARIGNIES at 13.30 hours. Battalion billeted in LA ROSIERE and LA VERDERIE. | |
| LA ROSIERE | 20 | | Battalion moved to HUCQUINVILLE, arriving there at 14.00 hours. 2/Lt.J.O.ADAMS transferred to ENGLAND (S). 1 Other Rank Evacuated. | |

**CONFIDENTIAL**

Instructions regarding War Diaries and Intelligence Summaries are contained in F. S. Regs., Part II. and the Staff Manual respectively. Title pages will be prepared in manuscript.

Army Form C. 2118.

# WAR DIARY
## or
## INTELLIGENCE SUMMARY.
(Erase heading not required.)

| Place | Date | Hour | Summary of Events and Information | Remarks and references to Appendices |
|---|---|---|---|---|
| HUCQUINVILLE | 21 | | Battalion left HUCQUINVILLE AT 10.30 hours and marched 17 Kilos. to L'ECUILLE. All Ranks are in excellent spirits, and no men have fallen out on the march since the beginning of the Advance. The Battalion received a rousing reception from the inhabitants of repatriated villages, notably in passing through MOUCHIN and an arrival at L'ECUILLE WHERE WOMEN and children broke into the ranks and presented flowers to the men, the C.O. & Adjt. each receiving a bouquet. 3 Other Ranks Evacuated. | |
| L'ECUILLE | 22 | | Battalion resting in L'ECUILLE. Village was heavily shelled during night with H.V. Casualties:- 1 Other Rank Killed, and 2 Other Ranks Wounded. | |
| Do. | 23 | | Heavy shelling during night. Coys. refitting. Draft of 13 Other Ranks joined. | |
| Do. | 24 | | In the early morning them Village was heavily shelled, 9 Horses being Killed at Transport Lines. Training under Coy. Arrangements. 4 Other Ranks Evacuated. | |
| Do. | 25 | | Training under Coy. Arrangements. C.Os. Birthday to-day. | |
| Do. | 26 | | Training and recreation. | |

# WAR DIARY
## or
## INTELLIGENCE SUMMARY.
(Erase heading not required.)

Army Form C. 2118.

| Place | Date | Hour | Summary of Events and Information | Remarks and references to Appendices |
|---|---|---|---|---|
| L' ECUILLE | 27 | | 3 Coys. working on roads under 9th Gordons. 4 Other Ranks Evacuated. HONOURS AND AWARDS. Bar to M.M. .. .. 291706 L/C. A. Brough M.M. Military Medal .. 268508 Sgt. G. Paton. Do. .. .. 24147 L/C. R. Sutherland Do. .. .. 13458 Pte. J. Reid | |
| Do. | 28 | | Training and Recreation. 2/Lt.G.FULLERTON M.C. rejoined from Hospital. Draft of 8 Other Ranks joined. Capt.R.F.D.BRUCE, Capt.& Q.M. W. DRON, and Lt. G.A.BUTLER joined. | |
| Do. | 29 | | Relieved 9th Royal Scots in Out-post line on Banks of SCHELDT. H.Q. in CHATEAU at WEZ VELVAIN. Out-post line runs from BRUYELLE along west Bank of River to the SUCRERIE. 4 Other Ranks Evacuated. | |
| ANTOING SECTOR Front Line. | 30 | | Battalion H.Q. heavily shelled during night with H.E. and Gas. "C" Coy. had over 50 Gas Casualties caused by concentration of Gas in their Billets, the result of a previous bombardment. Casualties:- 1 Other Rank Wounded, 53 Other Ranks Wounded (Gas). | |
| Do. | 31 | | Considerable shelling of Bn. H.Q. during night, mostly Gas Shells, Box Respirators had to be worn. Casualties:- 2/Lt.C.C.CULROSS Wounded. | |

5th Nov. 1918.
W Stacy Wilson Major
O.C. 4/5th Blackwatch.

**CONFIDENTIAL**

Army Form C. 2118.

# WAR DIARY
*or*
~~INTELLIGENCE SUMMARY.~~

(*Erase heading not required.*)

Instructions regarding War Diaries and Intelligence Summaries are contained in F. S. Regs., Part II. and the Staff Manual respectively. Title pages will be prepared in manuscript.

| Place | Date | Hour | Summary of Events and Information | Remarks and references to Appendices |
|---|---|---|---|---|
| | | | | |
| | | | | |

F3/251

Hd. Qrs.,
44th Infy Bde.

Herewith War Diary for period 1st to 30th November 1918

Please acknowledge receipt.

5/12/18

Buck__
Capt. & Adjt.
for O.C. 4/5th Black Watch

A.A.G.
   3rd Echelon

The attached War Diary of
4/5th Bn Black Watch is forwarded
to you

                F. Tinker
                   Maj BM
6.12.18.    for Bg Commdg.
                 44th Inf Bde

## "A" Form
### MESSAGES AND SIGNALS.

Army Form C. 2121
(in pads of 100.)

No. of Message ..................

Prefix ............ Code ............m. | Words. | Charge.
Office of Origin and Service Instructions.

This message is on a/c of .

....................................Service.

Recd. at ......... .m.

Sent
At................m.
To ....................
By ....................

(Signature of "Franking Officer.")

Date ....................
From ....................
By ....................

TO {

| Sender's Number. | Day of Month. | In reply to Number. | |
|---|---|---|---|
| * | | | AAA |

From
Place
Time

*The above may be forwarded as now corrected.* (Z)

.................................... Censor. Signature of Addressor or person authorised to telegraph in his name.

* This line should be erased if not required.

(1539). Wt. W3253/P511. 200,000 Pads. 2/18. H.C. & L., Ltd.

Army Form C. 2118.

44/13

WAR DIARY
or
INTELLIGENCE SUMMARY.
(Erase heading not required.)

4/5th Battn. THE BLACK WATCH

WAR DIARY.

FROM 1/11/18 TO 30/11/18

Vol. ———

CONFIDENTIAL.

53.11

Army Form C. 2118.

# WAR DIARY
## or
## INTELLIGENCE SUMMARY.

*(Erase heading not required.)*

Instructions regarding War Diaries and Intelligence Summaries are contained in F.S. Regs., Part II. and the Staff Manual respectively. Title pages will be prepared in manuscript.

| Place | Date | Hour | Summary of Events and Information | Remarks and references to Appendices |
|---|---|---|---|---|
| BRUXELLES.- JOUR.AIN-MERBES.- SECTOR FRONT LINE. | 1 11 18. | | No change in Dispositions. "D" Coy. advanced posts in BRUXELLES. 2.Lts. dislodged 2 Snipers near BRUXELLES CHATEAU. Draft of 6 Other Ranks joined. 1 Other Rank Evacuated to Hospital (Sick). Lieut.J.C.DRAS transferred to U.K. for Medical Board, ordered by War Office. | |
| Do. | 2 | | No change. "A" Coy. had inter-platoon relief. Heavy Gas Shelling on "C" Coy. & Bn.Hd.Qrs.- Blue Cross. Draft of 8 Other Ranks joined. 1 Other Rank Evacuated to Hospital (Sick). | |
| Do. | 3 | | Adjutant 8th Seaforth Higrs. came up to arrange relief. Enemy post in Fort BRUXELLES spotted and dealt with effectively. Draft of 3 Other Ranks joined. 2 Other Ranks Evacuated to Hospital (Sick). 1 Other Rank Died (Influenza). | |
| Do. | 4 | | Relieved by 8th Seaforth Higrs., relief completed by 17.30 hours. On relief the Battn. moved back into Support. Battn.Hd.Qrs.,"A","C" & "D".Coys.billeted in GUIGNIES. "B"Coy. in VELVAIN. "B"Coy.heavily Shelled during the night. Draft of 3 Other Ranks joined. | |
| GUIGNIES.- SUPPORT LINE. | 5 | | Day spent in cleaning up, issue and exchange of clothing of Battn. Gas Shelling on Battn. area during night. 1 Other Rank Evacuated to Hospital (Sick). | |

Army Form C. 2118.

# WAR DIARY

## INTELLIGENCE SUMMARY.

(Erase heading not required).

| Place | Date | Hour | Summary of Events and Information | Remarks and references to Appendices |
|---|---|---|---|---|
| QUIEVRES. SUPPORT LINE. | 6 | | Training carried out under Coy. arrangements, indoor work owing to rain. 3 Other Ranks Evacuated to Hospital (Sick); also 2 Other Ranks Wounded (Gas). | |
| -- Do. -- | 7 | | Training carried out under Coy arrangements, indoor work, weather still wet. Heavy Shelling on the whole Battn. area, including Gas Shells. Draft of 3 Other Ranks joined. 2 Other Ranks Evacuated to Hospital (Sick). HONOURS AND REWARDS. MILITARY MEDAL. 5985 C.Q.M.S. Smith W. -- Do. -- 6735 Sergt. Higgins J. -- Do. -- 4458 Corpl. Davidson J. | |
| -- Do. -- | 8 | | Received word that the Enemy were retiring about 10.00 hours, and got ready to move. Orders were received to move forward about 11.30 hours. The Battn. moved forward, and were in the new position by 12.45 hours. After remaining in this position for a few hours, we received word that the Enemy had not retired, and were ordered to resume our old positions. 1 Other Rank Evacuated to Hospital (Sick). | |
| -- Do. -- | 9 | | On orders from Brigade Battn moved forward at 06.30 hours to assembly positions near BRUXELLES, all in position by 09.00 hours. "A" & "B" Coys. moved forward to 1st Objective on line FONTENOY - GUERONDE. Objective reached about 11.00 hours. 1 Other Rank rejoined from Hospital. 1 Other Rank died of Influenza. At 14.30 hours new objective given line BERTINCROIX - WASMES, and reached by 17.00 hours. Battn. Hd. Qrs., "C" & "D" Coys. in reserve at FONTENOY. | |

CONFIDENTIAL.

Army Form C. 2118.

# WAR DIARY
## or
## INTELLIGENCE SUMMARY.
*(Erase heading not required.)*

Instructions regarding War Diaries and Intelligence Summaries are contained in F. S. Regs., Part II. and the Staff Manual respectively. Title pages will be prepared in manuscript.

| Place | Date | Hour | Summary of Events and Information | Remarks and references to Appendices |
|---|---|---|---|---|
| POMMEROY | 10 | | Move forward at 04.30 hours to Objective on line ELICQUY - AUBROIES reached. Same Coys in front. Bn.H.Q. & "D" Coy. in ELICQUY, "C" Coy.in AUBECIES. Cavalry and Cyclists on ahead. Orders received that K.O.S.Bs.were to pass through us to-morrow. This days March was a long one, but no men feel out. | |
| SUPPORT LINE. | | | | |
| ELICQUY | 11 | | K.O.S.Bs. passed through outpost line at 06.30 hours. Orders received to move at 10.45 hours to HUISSIGNIES. Wire received from Division at 09.00 hours stating that Hostilities were to cease at 11.00 hours. The Battn. proceeded by March Route to HUISSIGNIES, arriving about 14.00 hours, where Battn. were Billeted. | |
| HUISSIGNIES. | 12 | | The day was spent in cleaning up. Recreational Training in the afternoon. 2/Lt.F.E.CATTO admitted to Hospital, also 2 Other Ranks. | |
| -- Do. -- | 13 | | Battn. Parade at 09.00 hours - Steady Drill & Battn. falling in in Mass. Inter-Company Football Matches. | |
| -- Do. -- | 14 | | Battn. Parade at 09.15 hours - Steady Drill, P.T. & Battn. March Past. Football Match Versus 8th Seaforth Hgrs. - Result - 1 Goal each. Draft of 5 Other Ranks joined. | |

Army Form C. 2118.

# WAR DIARY
# INTELLIGENCE SUMMARY.

*(Erase heading not required.)*

Instructions regarding War Diaries and Intelligence Summaries are contained in F. S. Regs., Part II. and the Staff Manual respectively. Title pages will be prepared in manuscript.

| Place | Date | Hour | Summary of Events and Information | Remarks and references to Appendices |
|---|---|---|---|---|
| HUISSIGNIES. | 15. | | Clothing and Equipment Inspection. Inter-Platoon Football in the Afternoon. 2/Lt. W.CHALKER and 5 Other Ranks joined. 1 Other Rank Evacuated to Hospital (Sick) | |
| -- Do. -- | 16 | | Battn. Paraded at 09.15 hours for Steady Drill and P.T., also Lectures on Educational Scheme. Div. Band played to Battn. in the Afternoon. Draft of 5 Other Ranks joined. | |
| -- Do. -- | 17 | | Church Parade in Theatre. Lecture by 2% C.O. on Demobilization Scheme. Draft of 6 Other Ranks joined. 1 Other Rank Evacuated to Hospital (Sick). | |
| -- Do. -- | 18 | | Rehearsal of Inspection parade for G.O.C. 15th Div. Capt. W.F.MORTON,O.F. to U.K. Capt. D.CAMERON,C.F. taken on strength. Draft of 9 Other Ranks joined. | |
| -- Do. -- | 19 | | The Battn. were Inspected by the G.O.C., 15th Div. at 10.30 hours. Recreational Training in the Afternoon. | |
| -- Do. -- | 20 | | Training carried out under Coy.arrangements. 2 Other Ranks Evacuated to Hospital (Sick). | |

Army Form C. 2118.

# WAR DIARY
# INTELLIGENCE SUMMARY.

*(Erase heading not required.)*

| Place | Date | Hour | Summary of Events and Information | Remarks and references to Appendices |
|---|---|---|---|---|
| HUISSIGNIES | 21 | | The Battn. Paraded for Route March at 09.00 hours. Battn. Concert Party gave an entertainment at 18.00 hours in the Theatre. 2 Other Ranks Evacuated to Hospital (Sick). | |
| Do. | 22 | | Training carried out under Coy. arrangements. Draft of 10 Other Ranks joined. | |
| Do. | 23 | | The Battn Paraded for Route March at 09.00 hours. 2 Other Ranks Evacuated to Hospital (Sick). Draft of 2 Other Ranks joined. | |
| Do. | 24 | | Church Parade. Draft of 15 Other Ranks joined. 1 Other Rank Evacuated to Hospital (Sick). | |
| Do. | 25 | | The Battn. left HUISSIGNIES at 14.00 hours, and proceeded by March Route to CHIEVRES, arriving about 16.00 hours, where Battn. were Billeted. Lt. H.G.DONALD and 1 Other Rank joined. 1 Other Rank Evacuated to Hospital (Sick). | |
| Do. | 26 | | Brigade ceremonial parade in forenoon. Regtl. Football Team played 8th Seaforth Hgrs. in Brigade League. - Result - one goal each. Educational programme resumed, including classes in FRENCH - SPANISH - SHORTHAND Etc., also series of lectures. | |

Army Form C. 2118.

# WAR DIARY
## INTELLIGENCE SUMMARY.
*(Erase heading not required.)*

| Place | Date | Hour | Summary of Events and Information | Remarks and references to Appendices |
|---|---|---|---|---|
| CHIEVRES | 27 | | The day was spent in cleaning equipment, etc. Recreational Training in the Afternoon. Draft of 82 Other Ranks joined. 2 Other Ranks Evacuated to Hospital (Sick) | |
| -- Do. -- | 28 | | Training carried out under Coy. Arrangements. Football postponed owing to wet weather. 1 Other Rank Evacuated to Hospital (Sick). | |
| -- Do. -- | 29 | | Battn. paraded for Route March at 09.00 hours. In the Afternoon the Regtl. Football Team played it's April 1st. League Match. Result - Black Watch 2 Goal Gordons Nil. Lt.R.D.OGILVIE taken on the strength. Lt. H.D.DONALD admitted to Hospital. | |
| -- Do. -- | 30 | | Battn. Ceremonial parade at 09.15 hours. Officers Riding School in Afternoon. Draft of 17 Other Ranks joined. | |

W.R. Buller
Lt.Colonel.
Commanding 4/5th Battn. The Black Watch.

Army Form C. 2118.

# WAR DIARY
## INTELLIGENCE SUMMARY.
*(Erase heading not required.)*

Instructions regarding War Diaries and Intelligence Summaries are contained in F. S. Regs., Part II. and the Staff Manual respectively. Title pages will be prepared in manuscript.

| Place | Date | Hour | Summary of Events and Information | Remarks and references to Appendices |
|---|---|---|---|---|
| | | | | |

CONFIDENTIAL

**WAR DIARY**
or
**INTELLIGENCE SUMMARY.**

Army Form C. 2118.

Vol 41

34 H.
Usher

Secret and Confidential

4/5th Bn. The Black Watch.

WAR DIARY.

DECEMBER 1918.

Volume No. 421.

Army Form C. 2118.

# WAR DIARY
## or
## INTELLIGENCE SUMMARY.
*(Erase heading not required.)*

Instructions regarding War Diaries and Intelligence Summaries are contained in F. S. Regs., Part II. and the Staff Manual respectively. Title pages will be prepared in manuscript.

| Place | Date | Hour | Summary of Events and Information | Remarks and references to Appendices |
|---|---|---|---|---|
| Chievres. | Decr. 1. | | Battalion attended Divine Service. Inspection of Billets by Brig. Gen. commdg. 44th. Inf. Brigade. Draft 9 Other Ranks. | |
| " | " 2. | | Coys. at disposal of Coy.Commanders for fitting of Equipment and rifle inspection. Battalion at Baths. 5 N.C.Os. to U.K. for Exchange. 44th. Inf. Brigade "Gymkhana". | |
| " | " 3. | | Major Rogers, D.S.O. R.A.M.C. left Battalion for demobilization. Lt. C. Mitchell, M.O.R.C., U.S.A. taken on strength. Black Watch v Seaforths.-- A win for Seaforths. 1-0. | |
| " | " 4. | | Parades under Coy. arrangements. Draft of 4 Other Ranks. Concert in evening by 5th. Gordon Highlanders. | |
| " | " 5. | | Parades under Coy. arrangements. Battalion at Baths. Lecture by Capt. & Adjt. J.I. Buchan, D.S.O. - Subject - "A Soldier's Life in India." Divisional Cinema. | |
| " | " 6. | | Party for Special Parade for H.M. The King's visit left for Tourpes. Battalion Sports. Draft of 5 Other Ranks. | |
| " | " 7. | | Kit Inspection. Capt. A.N. Duke, 2Lt. A. Scott, M.C., Lt. D. Kinnoch and 7 Other Ranks taken on strength. Black Watch v Gordons. 2 - 2. | |
| " | " 8. | | Battalion attended Divine Service. | |
| " | " 9. | | Battalion Ceremonial Parade. Capt. R.F.D. Bruce takes over duties of Demobilization Officer. Lt. H.S. Muir, M.C. assumes command of C. Coy. | |

Army Form C. 2118.

# WAR DIARY
## or
## INTELLIGENCE SUMMARY.
*(Erase heading not required.)*

Instructions regarding War Diaries and Intelligence Summaries are contained in F. S. Regs., Part II. and the Staff Manual respectively. Title pages will be prepared in manuscript.

| Place | Date | Hour | Summary of Events and Information | Remarks and references to Appendices |
|---|---|---|---|---|
| Chievres. | Decr. 10. | | Battalion Route March. | |
| " | " 11. | | Adjutant's Parade. Party of 26 Miners Demobilized. | |
| " | " 12. | | Adjutant's Parade. Party of 36 Other Ranks demobilized (Miners). | |
| " | " 13. | | Parades under Coy. arrangements. Draft of 7 Other Ranks. | |
| " | " 14. | | Ceremonial Parade. Draft of 5 Other Ranks. | |
| " | " 15. | | Battalion attended Divine Service. Advance party for billeting in new Area leave for Ronquieres. | |
| " | " 16. | | Parades under Coy. arrangements. | |
| " | " 17. | | Battalion moved to Ronquieres, spending night at Soignies. | |
| Soignies. | " 18. | | Battalion reached Ronquieres arriving at Mid-day. | |
| Ronquieres. | " 19. | | Cleaning up, rifle and foot inspections. Honours :- Bar to Military Medal :- 268692. Pte. (L/C) W.F. Hill, M.M. "C" Coy. Military Medal ;- 240228., Pte. (L/C) W. Dalgetty. "C" Coy. 201262. Pte. T. Rankine. "B" Coy. 4271. Pte. C. Scott. "D" Coy. | |
| " | " 20. | | Parades under Coy. arrangements.. Lt. C.H.B.C. Penney takes over duties of Adjt. Capt J.I. Buchan, D.S.O. going on Paris Leave. | |

Army Form C. 2118.

# WAR DIARY
## or
## INTELLIGENCE SUMMARY.
*(Erase heading not required.)*

Instructions regarding War Diaries and Intelligence Summaries are contained in F. S. Regs., Part II. and the Staff Manual respectively. Title pages will be prepared in manuscript.

| Place | Date | Hour | Summary of Events and Information | Remarks and references to Appendices |
|---|---|---|---|---|
| Ronquires | Decr. 21. | | Parades under Coy. arrangements. | |
| " | " 22. | | Battalion moved to Nivelles. | |
| Nivelles. | " 23. | | Cleaning Billets. | |
| " | " 24. | | Cleaning Billets. Draft of 3 Other Ranks. | |
| " | " 25. | | Cleaning Billets. No Parades. | |
| " | " 26. | | Parades under Coy. arrangements. Classes resumed. Party of 15 Other Ranks demobilized (Miners). | |
| " | " 27. | | Parades under Coy. arrangements. Party of 7 Other Ranks demobilized (Miners). | |
| " | " 28. | | Parades under Coy. arrangements. Party of 40 Other Ranks demobilized (Miners). | |
| " | " 29. | | Battalion attended Divine Service. Party of 17 Other Ranks demobilized (Miners). | |
| " | " 30. | | Parades under Coy. arrangements, as per programme. Party of 2 Other Ranks demobilized (Miners). | |
| " | " 31. | | Battalion Route March. Lecture on Venereal Diseases. | |

Abraham Carroll Lt. Col.
Comdg. 4/5th Bn. The Black Watch

Army Form C. 2118.

# WAR DIARY
## INTELLIGENCE SUMMARY.
*(Erase heading not required.)*

Instructions regarding War Diaries and Intelligence Summaries are contained in F. S. Regs., Part II. and the Staff Manual respectively. Title pages will be prepared in manuscript.

| Place | Date | Hour | Summary of Events and Information | Remarks and references to Appendices |
|---|---|---|---|---|

4/5th Bn. The Black Watch.

WAR DIARY

for

period ending 31-1-19.

VOLUME No. .............

Army Form C. 2118.

# WAR DIARY
# INTELLIGENCE SUMMARY.
*(Erase heading not required.)*

Instructions regarding War Diaries and Intelligence Summaries are contained in F. S. Regs., Part II. and the Staff Manual respectively. Title pages will be prepared in manuscript.

| Place | Date | Hour | Summary of Events and Information | Remarks and references to Appendices |
|---|---|---|---|---|
| NIVELLES BELGIUM | 1919 Jany 1 | | New Year Dinner to men which was a great success. | |
| | 2 | | Parades under Company arrangements. "A" & "B" Coys. at Baths. Battalion Concert. | |
| | 3 | | do "C" & "D" Coys. at Baths. do | |
| | 4 | | Ceremonial Parade with Colours. | |
| | 5 | | Battalion paraded for Divine Service. | |
| | 6 | | Parades under Company arrangements. | |
| | 7 | | Battalion Route March. | |
| | 8 | | Adjutant's Parade. Divisional Concert Party for four evenings. | |
| | 9 | | Parades as per Training Programme. | |
| | 10 | | Company Route Marches. | |
| | 11 | | Ceremonial Parade with Colours. | |
| | 12 | | Battalion paraded for Divine Service. | |
| | 13 | | Kit Inspection by all Companies. | |
| | 14 | | Parades as per Training Programme. | |
| | 15 | | Physical Training & Specialist Parades. | |
| | 16 | | Parades under Company arrangements. Lecture on Journalism by Capt. McMurray, Royal Scots. Divisional Concert Party. | |

Army Form C. 2118.

## WAR DIARY (Continued)

### INTELLIGENCE SUMMARY.

*(Erase heading not required.)*

Instructions regarding War Diaries and Intelligence Summaries are contained in F. S. Regs., Part II. and the Staff Manual respectively. Title pages will be prepared in manuscript.

| Place | Date | Hour | Summary of Events and Information | Remarks and references to Appendices |
|---|---|---|---|---|
| | 17 | | Parades as per Training Programme. 5th Gordons' Concert Party give concert. | |
| | 18 | | Parades under Company arrangements. Adjytant's Inspection of Billets. | |
| | 19 | | Battalion paraded for Divine Service. | |
| | 20 | | Parades as per Training Programme. Lecture by Capt. E.A. Aldridge. | |
| | 21 | | Battalion Route March with Cookers to WATERLOO. Very interesting day and enjoyed by all ranks. | |
| | 22 | | "B" & "D" Companies attend Baths. Other parades as per Training Programme. | |
| | 23 | | "A" & "C" Companies attend Baths. -do- 2/Lieut. M.G. Kinloch joined Battalion from 7th Black Watch. | |
| | 24 | | Company Route Marches. Lt.Col. R.A. Bulloch, D.S.O. resumes Command of the Battalion. | |
| | 25 | | Parades under Company arrangements. | |
| | 26 | | Battalion paraded for Divine Service. | |
| | 27 | | Kit & Lewis Gun Inspections & Specialist Training. 44th Brigade Concert Party perform. | |
| | 28 | | Parades under Company arrangements. Lt.Col. R.A. Bulloch, D.S.O. assumes command of 44th Infy. Bde. | |
| | 29 | | Battalion Route March. | |
| | 30 | | Parades as per Training Programme. | |
| | 31 | | Battalion Route March. | |

31st Jany. 1919.

W. Bulloch
Lieut. Colonel,
Commdg., 4/5th Bn. The Black Watch.

// 43

4/5th Bn. The BLACK WATCH.

WAR DIARY

for

FEBRUARY 1919

CONFIDENTIAL.

Army Form C. 2118.

# WAR DIARY
## INTELLIGENCE SUMMARY.
*(Erase heading not required.)*

Instructions regarding War Diaries and Intelligence Summaries are contained in F. S. Regs., Part II. and the Staff Manual respectively. Title pages will be prepared in manuscript.

| Place | Date | Hour | Summary of Events and Information | Remarks and references to Appendices |
|---|---|---|---|---|
| NIVELLES. | Feby. 1st | — | C.Os. Inspection of Billets. 1 O.R. Rejoined from Hospital. 6 O.R. to U.K. for Demobn. | |
| do | 2nd | — | Bn. attended Divine Services. Lieut. J. Wallace & 7 O.R. to U.K. for Demobilization. | |
| do | 3rd | — | 2 Coys. attended Baths; 2 Coys. parades under Coy. arrangements. 3 O.R. to U.K. for Demobn. 1 O.R. Evacuated. | |
| do | 4th | — | 2 Coys. attended Baths; 2 Coys. parades under Coy. arrangements. 2 O.R. Rejoined from Hospl. | |
| do | 5th | — | Bn. Route March. 1 O.R. Evacuated. | |
| do | 6th | — | Lecture by C.O. on Demobilization and Re-enlistment. 2 O.R. Evacuated. 1 O.R. Rejoined from Hospital. | |
| do | 7th | — | Parades under Coy. arrangements for Cross Country Running and P.T. | |
| do | 8th | — | C.Os. Inspection of Billets. 1 O.R. Rejoined from Hospital. Lt. G.G. Weir to U.K. on leave. | |
| do | 9th | — | Bn. attended Divine Service. 3 O.R. to U.K. for Demobilization. | |
| do | 10th | — | Kit Inspection under Coy. arrangements. 2 O.R. to U.K. for Demobilization. Band of 2nd Grenadier Regt.(Belgian) gave performance in Town Hall. | |
| do | 11th | — | Bn. Route March. Capt. D. Cameron, C.F. to U.K. on leave. Capt. H.S. Muir, M.C. to C.C.S. (Sick). | |
| do | 12th | — | 2 Coys. attended Baths; 2 Coys. parades under Coy. arrangements. 1 O.R. Rejoined from Hospl. | |
| do | 13th | — | 2 Coys. attended Baths; 2 Coys. parades under Coy. arrangements. 19 O.R. to U.K. for Demobn. | |
| do | 14th | — | Coy. parades for Training. Lt. G.A. Butler to U.K. on leave. 29 O.R. to U.K. for Demobn. 1 O.R. Evacuated. | |

Army Form C. 2118.

# WAR DIARY
## INTELLIGENCE SUMMARY
*(Erase heading not required.)*

Instructions regarding War Diaries and Intelligence Summaries are contained in F. S. Regs., Part II. and the Staff Manual respectively. Title pages will be prepared in manuscript.

| Place | Date | Hour | Summary of Events and Information | Remarks and references to Appendices |
|---|---|---|---|---|
| NIVELLES | 15th | — | Lecture by Adjt. on Re-enlistment. 21 O.R. to U.K. for Demobilization. 1 O.R. Evacuated. | |
| do | 16th | — | Bn. attended Divine Services. 2 O.R. Rejoined from Hospital. 3 O.R. Evacuated. 26 O.R. to U.K. for Demobilization. | |
| do | 17th | — | Parades for Training under Coy. arrangements. 1 O.R. Evacuated. 18 O.R. to U.K. for Demobn. The "JOCKS" (Divn. Concert Party) performed in Bde. Hall. | |
| do | 18th | — | Coys. employed on general fatigues, clearing snow, etc. "JOCKS" performed in evening. | |
| do | 19th | — | Coys. employed on general fatigues. | |
| do | 20th | — | 2 Coys. attended Baths. 2 O.R. to U.K. for Demobilization. | |
| do | 21st | — | 2 Coys. attended Baths. Advance Party left for BRAINE LE COMTE. 15 O.R. to U.K. for Demobn. 1 O.R. Evacuated. | |
| do | 22nd | — | Bn. parade for reorganisation into 2 Coys. to take effect on arrival in BRAINE LE COMTE. Lt. J. Keir to C.C.S. (Sick). 18 O.R. to U.K. for Demobilization. | |
| do | 23rd | — | Bn. attended Divine Services. 2 O.R. Evacuated. 10 O.R. to U.K. for Demobilization. 2/Lieuts. H.B. Harley and M.G. Kinloch to U.K., Draft Conducting. | |
| do | 24th | — | Bn. moved by march route to BRAINE LE COMTE, leaving NIVELLES at noon and arriving at BRAINE LE COMTE at 1530, with one half for tea en route. On arrival Bn. reformed into 2 Coys.- "B" Coy. - Officers and O.R. for Armies of Occupation; "A" Coy. - Remainder of Bn. Bn. was billetted in private houses. 2/Lt. C.K. Collins to U.K., Draft Conducting. 36 O.R. to U.K. for Demobilization. 1 O.R. Rejoined from Hospital. | |
| BRAINE LE COMTE. | 25th | — | No parades. | |
| do | 26th | — | Coys. scrubbing equipment. C.Os. Inspection of Billets. | |

Army Form C. 2118.

# WAR DIARY
## or
## ~~INTELLIGENCE SUMMARY.~~

(Erase heading not required.)

| Place | Date | Hour | Summary of Events and Information | Remarks and references to Appendices |
|---|---|---|---|---|
| BRAINE LE COMTE. | 27th | — | Parades under Coy. arrangements. | |
| do | 28th | — | Bn. Parade for Inspection by C.O. Lt. D. Kinnoch to U.K. Draft Conducting. 4 O.R. to U.K. for Demobilization. | |

J.S. Buchan. Capt & Adj
for. Lieut. Colonel,
Commanding 4/5th Bn. The Black Watch.

Army Form C. 2118.

# WAR DIARY
## *or*
## INTELLIGENCE SUMMARY.

*(Erase heading not required.)*

Instructions regarding War Diaries and Intelligence Summaries are contained in F. S. Regs., Part II. and the Staff Manual respectively. Title pages will be prepared in manuscript.

| Place | Date | Hour | Summary of Events and Information | Remarks and references to Appendices |
|---|---|---|---|---|
| | | | | |

Army Form C. 2118.

WAR DIARY
or
INTELLIGENCE SUMMARY.
(Erase heading not required.)

4/5th Bn. The Black Watch.

WAR DIARY

for

MARCH 1919.

Serial N°

Army Form C. 2118.

# WAR DIARY

## INTELLIGENCE SUMMARY

*(Erase heading not required.)*

Instructions regarding War Diaries and Intelligence Summaries are contained in F. S. Regs., Part II. and the Staff Manual respectively. Title pages will be prepared in manuscript.

| Place | Date | Hour | Summary of Events and Information | Remarks and references to Appendices |
|---|---|---|---|---|
| BRAINE LE COMTE. | 1st to 30th. | | During the month 10 Officers and 18 Other Ranks were despatched to U.K. for Demobilization. 1 O.R. Evacuated; and 1 O.R. sent to U.K. on furlough on re-enlistment. 1 Officer (2/Lt. R. Hughes) joined 6th Bn. with Rhine Army; thus reducing Battalion to Cadre Strength of 4 Officers and 47 Other Ranks. <br><br> (Officers demobilized :— Capt. D. Cameron, C.F. (Attached) ; Lieut. J.G. Laing; Lieut. B. Hunter; 2/Lt. J. Davidson; Capt. S. Norie-Miller, M.C. Capt. R.E. Badenoch, M.C. 2/Lt. D.A. Neill; Lieut. A. Scott, M.C. 2/Lt. W.A. Shand; Lieut. J. Keir; Lieut. A.G. Baker.) <br><br> 7-5-19. <br><br> M.W.Bruce <br> Lieut. Colonel, <br> Commanding 1/5th Bn. The Black Watch. | |

WAR DIARY
INTELLIGENCE SUMMARY

4/5th Bn. The BLACK WATCH.

WAR DIARY

for

APRIL 1919.

Army Form C. 2118.

# WAR DIARY
## *or*
## INTELLIGENCE SUMMARY.

*(Erase heading not required.)*

Instructions regarding War Diaries and Intelligence Summaries are contained in F. S. Regs., Part II. and the Staff Manual respectively. Title pages will be prepared in manuscript.

| Place | Date | Hour | Summary of Events and Information | Remarks and references to Appendices |
|---|---|---|---|---|
| | | | | |

A7050. Wt. W2285/M1292. 750,000. 1/17. D. D. & L., Ltd. Forms/C2118/1.

**CONFIDENTIAL.**

Instructions regarding War Diaries and Intelligence Summaries are contained in F.S. Regs., Part II. and the Staff Manual respectively. Title pages will be prepared in manuscript.

# WAR DIARY

## or

## INTELLIGENCE SUMMARY

(Erase heading not required.)

Army Form C. 2118.

| Place | Date | Hour | Summary of Events and Information | Remarks and references to Appendices |
|---|---|---|---|---|
| BRAINE-<br>-LE-<br>-COMTE.<br>BELGIUM. | 1919<br>Mch.<br>1st<br>to<br>31st. | | DEMOBILIZATION was practically completed during the month.<br><br>1 Officer (Lt. J. Davidson) and 57 O.R. were demobilized.<br><br>2 Officers (2/Lts. N.D. Stevenson and M.G. Kinloch) and 26 O.R. proceeded to U.K. to join Regular Forces.<br><br>10 Officers :- Capt. G.A. Butler,      Lt. W.G. Robertson,      Lt. G.G. Weir,<br>                Lt. H. Harrison,      Lt. A. Leitch,           2/Lt. C.K. Collins,<br>                2/Lt. J. Herald,      2/Lt. H.B. Harley,<br>                Lt. D. Kinnoch,      2/Lt. J. McGladdery.<br><br>and 167 O.Rs. were transferred to the Army of Occupation :- the Officers to the 6th Bn. The Black Watch and the O.Rs. to the 8th Bn. The Black Watch. The Officers with the exception of the two last named (who were on leave) and 127 O.Rs. proceeded from Braine-le-Comte on 23-3-19.<br><br>The strength of the Bn. thus was reduced to - 16 Offs. 60 O.Rs. - Effective Strength;<br>                                                                          6 Offs. 48 O.Rs. - Actually with Bn. as at 31-3-19.<br><br>3-4-19.<br><br>                                                                          Captain,<br>                        Commanding 4/5th Bn. The Black Watch. | |

Army Form C. 2118.

# WAR DIARY
## *or*
## INTELLIGENCE SUMMARY.

*(Erase heading not required.)*

Instructions regarding War Diaries and Intelligence
Summaries are contained in F. S. Regs., Part II.
and the Staff Manual respectively. Title pages
will be prepared in manuscript.

| Place | Date | Hour | Summary of Events and Information | Remarks and references to Appendices |
|---|---|---|---|---|
| | | | | |

(A10266) W1 W3304/1713 750,000 3/16 Sch. 82 Forms/C2118/16 D. D. & L., London, E.C.

www.ingramcontent.com/pod-product-compliance
Lightning Source LLC
Chambersburg PA
CBHW080812010526
44111CB00015B/2544